Macmillan English

Teacher's Guide

1

Mary Bowen

Printha Ellis

Louis Fidge

Liz Hocking

Wendy Wren

MACMILLAN

Macmillan Education
Between Towns Road, Oxford OX4 3PP
A division of Macmillan Publishers Limited
Companies and representatives throughout the world

ISBN 978-1-4050-1373-4

Acknowledgements for Macmillan English Language Teacher's Book 1
The publishers gratefully acknowledge the following for permission to
reproduce copyright material:
Happy Birthday Words and Music by Patty S Hill and Mildred Hill copyright ©
Summy Birch-Birchard Music A Division of Summy-Birchard Inc., USA/EMI
Music Publishing, London, WC2H 0QY 1935 renewed 1962, reprinted by
permission of WarnerChappell Music Ltd.

Design: Thomas Nicolaou, based on an original design by Big Top.
Project instruction pages illustrated by Dimitri Kamenos.
Cover design by Oliver Design.
Cover illustration by Pencil and Pepper

Printed in Malaysia

2017   2016   2015   2014   2013
10   9   8   7   6   5   4

Contents

Introduction
The Macmillan English author team...4
Course components...5
Methodology...8
Features of teachers' notes pages...11

Scope and sequence...12

Teachers' notes
KG revision...14
Unit 1...16
Unit 2...28
Unit 3...40
Revision 1...52
Unit 4...54
Unit 5...66
Unit 6...78
Revision 2...90
Unit 7...92
Unit 8...104
Unit 9...116
Revision 3...128
Unit 10...130
Unit 11...142
Unit 12...154
Revision 4...166
Unit 13...168
Unit 14...180
Unit 15...192
Revision 5...204
Unit 16...206
Unit 17...218
Unit 18...230
Revision 6...242

Project instructions...244
Games list...248

Language Book 1 answer key...249
Practice Book 1 answer key...252

Introduction

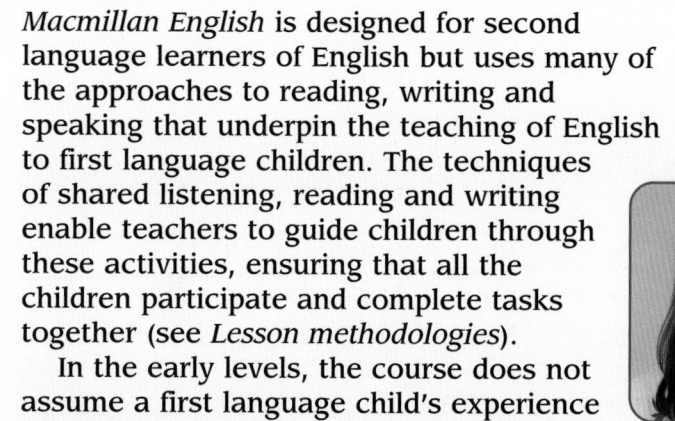

Macmillan English is designed for second language learners of English but uses many of the approaches to reading, writing and speaking that underpin the teaching of English to first language children. The techniques of shared listening, reading and writing enable teachers to guide children through these activities, ensuring that all the children participate and complete tasks together (see *Lesson methodologies*).

In the early levels, the course does not assume a first language child's experience of spoken English or culture. Language structures are introduced and practised to give a firm grounding in grammar, but from the start, the exposure to new language is more extensive than in traditional second language courses. As children move up through the course, they experience more first language teaching methods. At the upper levels children cover the same aspects of English as do first language learners, though the needs of second language learners are always taken into account.

Each level of the course is delivered through eighteen units. Each unit has six lessons requiring a minimum of seven teaching sessions.

The *Macmillan English* author team

Mary Bowen BA (Hons), PGCE (TEFL), has taught English as a second language in the UK, France, Spain, and in the former Yugoslavia. She is a hugely successful author, specialising in books aimed at young learners. In addition to writing, she also works as a producer of educational audio material for children.

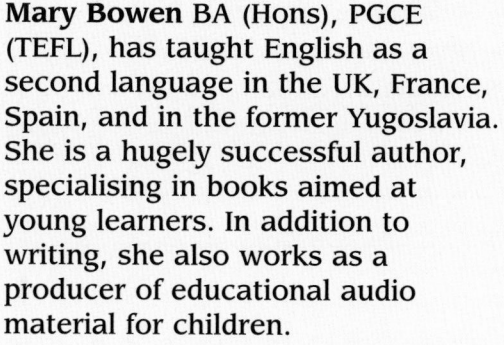

Printha Ellis BA (Hons), MA, taught English as a second language for many years throughout the world, including Thailand, Libya and France. She was also a teacher trainer in Europe. In 1992–1993, she was the British Council Summer School writer in residence at Durham University. An innovative and versatile author, she wrote a number of best-selling course and skills books.

Wendy Wren BA, MA is a successful and highly respected author of best-selling courses for UK schools. She has taught in secondary schools in the UK and primary schools in Zimbabwe. Her teacher training and lecturing has taken her to many parts of the world.

Louis Fidge BA, MA, Cert TEFLA, is passionate about the importance of quality primary education and has over thirty-five years' experience in urban, rural and international schools where he has worked as head teacher, adviser and educational consultant. He is a widely published author of children's educational textbooks in the UK and internationally. Louis has been involved in curriculum development and in-service training in Europe, Asia, Africa and the Caribbean.

Liz Hocking BA, Cert TEFL, is a qualified English teacher and has taught at secondary level in the UK. She has edited teaching materials for primary level in the UK and is an experienced ELT editor. She has previously written supplementary materials for Macmillan.

Fluency Book, Fluency Audio CD and posters

Fluency Book

Lesson 1: Fluency The Fluency Book helps children to develop natural intonation in speaking English. It tells an exciting 18-episode adventure story featuring four child characters and uses some narrative, but mainly dialogue. The book is highly illustrated to engage young learners and provide stimulus for speaking.

Posters

Eighteen large posters for teacher-led listening to each episode accompany the Fluency Book and the Fluency CD.

Fluency CD

All episodes of the story are on the CD with introductory and closing songs. Each dialogue section is reproduced with pauses for children to practise accurate repetition.

Language Book, Language Audio CD and flashcards

Language Book

Lesson 2: Reading Children read two pages written and illustrated in the style of an authentic children's book. This might be a story, a poem or a non-fiction text.

Lesson 3: Comprehension and sentence building Children complete comprehension activities on the Lesson 2 text. They practise key vocabulary from Lessons 1 and 2. They learn and practise written English skills including punctuation and recognition of parts of speech.

Lesson 4: Grammar and listening Key language from Lesson 1 is practised orally and in writing. Listening activities include listening for specific information, for gist and songs.

Lesson 5: Phonics Children learn how words are broken down into separate sounds, then how the sounds are joined to make words; they practise reading, writing and saying them.

Lesson 6: Class writing Children are presented with pictures and words that prompt the key language and vocabulary. The teacher helps the class to select their best ideas and writes these as an accurate model for children to read together before writing.

Revision There are two Revision pages after every three Language Book units. These pages practise the key vocabulary and structures, and give reading, listening and speaking practice. Ideas are also given in the Teacher's Guide for additional classroom activities and there are suggestions for small projects to accompany the story in the Fluency Book.

Language Audio CD

This contains all the Lesson 2 reading texts, Lesson 4 listening activities and songs, and Lesson 5 phonic rhymes.

Flashcards

At level 1, 172 flashcards support the teaching of new language in the Fluency Book and Language Book. The pack includes the Fluency Book characters for use in dialogue practice in Lesson 1 of each unit.

Practice Book and Teacher's Guide

Practice Book

This contains practice exercises for the Language Book activities. It is intended for children to complete for homework or for quiet class time. Practice Book pages should be done when the corresponding page in the Language Book has been finished. If there is time at the end of the Language Book lesson, teachers may like to go through some or all of the exercises orally before children work independently.

The Practice Book has two pages of writing exercises which follow on from *Class writing* in the Language Book. Suggestions for preparing the class for this work are given in the Teacher's Guide. Teachers may prefer children to complete these pages in class if they have extra lesson time available.

After every three Practice Book units there is a two-page *Check-up* on grammar, punctuation and phonics, followed by two pages of general revision.

Teacher's Guide

Every lesson has two pages of resources to assist the teacher. The first page shows:
- the pupils' material in facsimile
- brief notes on each step of the lesson related by pointers to the facsimile.

This allows teachers to conduct the lesson with the stimulus material and main teaching points together. Additional notes available on the second page are indicated by ⬇.

The second page contains:
- the lesson summary, including the aim, specific targets, key words and language, materials needed and advance preparation required
- a chart showing the proportion of time recommended for each lesson section
- a Warm-up to begin the lesson
- detailed notes for aspects of each lesson which teachers may wish to use, for example, questions and methods of presenting parts of the pupils' material
- audioscripts for listening activities
- extension activities.

Teaching methodology

Participation It is frequently recommended that after individuals read or speak, the whole class reads again or repeats. This ensures that all children get practice and are keeping up with the lesson. Teaching sessions are tightly structured and the emphasis is on the active involvement of the whole class to keep children focussed and motivated.

Exposure to language Reading texts often contain expressions and vocabulary which are not for detailed study. They enrich the text and are for understanding only, as listed in the lesson summary. They should be explained as necessary to make sense of the text as a whole. A precise grammatical understanding of every word of the reading text is not required. Like first language learners, children benefit from exposure to language, so long as they are well supported in learning the key words and structures which are the focus.

Games and class activities These reinforce lesson work, revise vocabulary and structures and maintain number and alphabetical order skills. Teachers can repeat those they find most useful and omit others if they wish.

Lesson methodologies

Lesson 1: Fluency

Before listening
- Children look at the large poster picture first and the teacher asks questions. Suggestions are given in the lesson notes but others may be asked as appropriate. Children say as much as possible about the poster before they work on it.
- New key vocabulary for the unit is taught using the poster and flashcards.

Shared listening
1 Children listen to the recorded episode and follow events illustrated on the poster. The teacher directs attention to different parts of the poster and to the characters as they speak. This ensures that children connect what they are seeing and hearing and that all children have followed the sequence of events correctly.

2 The teacher asks questions to check children's understanding of the story line.
3 The teacher asks questions to check understanding of the dialogue. Suggested questions are given in the lesson notes.
4 Children listen to the story a second time guided by the teacher.

Dialogue practice
1 Children look in their books and find characters and key vocabulary named by the teacher. This enables them to look more closely at the pictures.
2 Children name characters/objects from flashcard prompts.
3 Children close books and look at the teacher. The teacher plays the CD and shows the flashcard of each character as he or she speaks. Children repeat the character's words in the pause with the same expression and intonation.
4 The class is divided so there is one group for each character. Each group has a character flashcard. The group says the lines for that character with the original expression and intonation. If time allows, groups can change cards and practise another character's lines.
5 Confident children can hold a flashcard each and act out the scene as individual characters. As children become used to the dialogue practice, all children should be able to speak individually.
6 Children listen to the story a final time, looking in their books. They may point to the pictures and characters as they listen or follow the text. However, the focus of these lessons is accuracy of speaking, not reading, the dialogue.

After listening
Follow-up activities are suggested to practise or reinforce the key language or vocabulary.

Lesson 2: Reading

Before reading
1 New words are taught using flashcard pictures. Show a flashcard and name the object. Class repeats. Do the same with other flashcards. Show them again in any order. Class names the objects.
2 Children look in their books at the illustrations and the teacher asks questions about the pictures. A suggested list is given in the lesson notes.

Shared reading

1 The teacher plays the CD. Children listen to the text and follow the words in their books.

2 The teacher reads the text to the class a line or a section at a time, in the style of the recorded version. Children follow the words again. The teacher asks questions about each line or section as he/she reads. This step ensures that children are following the correct part of the text; the questions reinforce understanding of the text. The teacher can take parts of the text more slowly or go over anything that has not been understood.

3 The complete text is read by the teacher with the whole class joining in. The class should be encouraged to imitate the expression of the recorded reading. This step allows the teacher to check that children have been following the text accurately, and to pick out any words or phrases that children are finding difficult.

Reading practice

1 Teachers can choose all or some of these methods of giving reading practice.
   - Children read again as a whole class.
   - Groups read different sentences or sections.
   - Individuals read different parts.
2 The class listens to the recording and follows the text a final time.

This reading practice gives teachers the opportunity to monitor reading skills of the class generally and the progress of individuals. It also ensures that children are well-prepared for comprehension work in the next lesson.

After reading

Suggestions are given for activities which practise reading in a more active way. These may be team, group or whole class games.

Lesson 3: Comprehension and sentence building (2 teaching sessions)

First session: Reading and understanding

- The reading text is always re-read at the start of the lesson. This gives children another opportunity to take in the piece as a whole before comprehension work.
- Comprehension activities always end with *Get active!* This activity reinforces the language and gives children the chance to work in groups or teams and to practise language actively. The game element is designed to motivate and interest children so that they use language for enjoyment as well as to learn.

Second session: Working with words; Sentence building

- Children do a variety of vocabulary work on key words in the unit.
- In *Sentence building*, written English skills are presented in clear terms with examples. It is important that children master each rule as they move through the book. These rules are the foundation of accurate writing and apply at even the most basic level. Detailed guidance is given to help teachers present the information simply and involve children in promoting understanding of it.
- Children complete one or two activities which put the rule into practice.

Lesson 4: Grammar and listening

- Example structures are presented using characters from the Fluency Book story so that children are reminded of the context for the language. The presentation on the Grammar page gives children a clear model to refer back to.
- The structure is practised orally and in written exercises, allowing the teacher to check children's ability to use it correctly.
- The listening activities reinforce the structures and vocabulary for the unit and help children to develop their aural skills.

Lesson 5: Phonics

- The target phonemes (units of sound) are always presented through a short illustrated rhyme which makes the meanings of new words clear. Children listen to then read the rhyme which strongly features words with the target sounds.
- The teacher uses phoneme cards to present and practise the component parts of each word so that children see and hear the phonic structure of it before they read and say the whole word. The component sounds are presented and practised.

Teachers may wish to follow this method: children stand in a line and hold the phoneme cards for, e.g. *cat*. Point to them in turn. Say each sound separately: *c – a – t*. Move the children closer and say the sounds again, leaving less time between them. Do this a few times until the children are holding the cards close together and the whole word is said at once. Repeat the procedure with the class joining in saying the sounds. Children read, say and write the whole word.

- Children write target words in the context of a sentence.
- Children practise reading and spelling the target group of words.
- All lessons end with one or two games or activities to practise previously taught phonic skills.
- This methodology gives children a strategy for reading, pronouncing and spelling new words.

Lesson 6: Writing

Shared writing

- Using the stimulus material in the Language Book, the teacher guides the class towards producing model language.
- The teacher writes sentences on the board and the class reads each sentence as they produce them so that they practise correct language.
- The class reads the finished piece together so that they all experience what they have created collectively.
- Normally, the work can be erased before children write in their books. However, if they need support in writing, a framework can be left for them to follow.

Teacher's classroom resources

A list of games used in the course and suggestions for making letter, number and colour cards for use in classroom activities are given on pages 244–248 at the back of this book.

pointers connect relevant notes to the pupil material

facsimile of pupil material for the lesson

Before writing
1 Lesson 6 warm-up ▶
2 Read Miss Plum's speech bubble (LB p25).
3 Children name objects.
4 📢 Play LC track 17. ▶
5 Children colour according to the instructions.

Shared writing
1 Read Miss Plum's box (LB p25). Write the sentences on the board. Circle the capital letters and full stops.
2 Ask a child to read the sentences.
3 Elicit the other sentences. Write them on the board.
4 Continue with the other sentences.
5 Children write. ▶

Practice Book
Writing
1 (PB p14) Children read words in box.
2 Children complete sentences.
Your writing
1 Point out Dan (PB p15). Read speech bubble. Ask What is in Dan's room?
2 Activity 1: Children read sentences and colour.
3 Activity 2: Children read the first sentence. They complete the others according to the picture they coloured.

After writing
Children write about something of their own. ▶

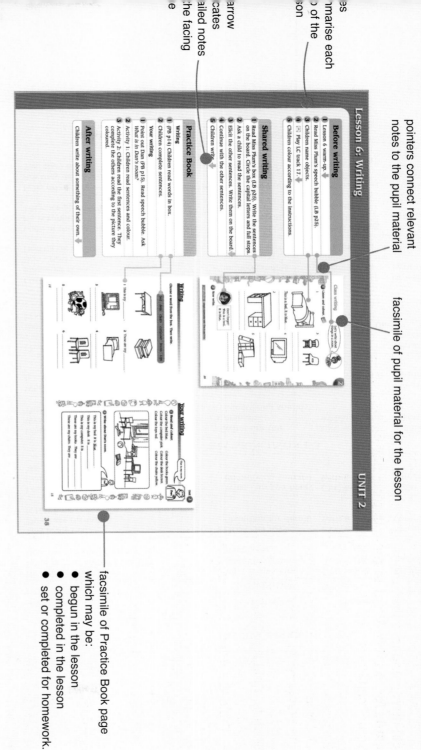

facsimile of Practice Book page which may be:
● begun in the lesson
● completed in the lesson
● set or completed for homework.

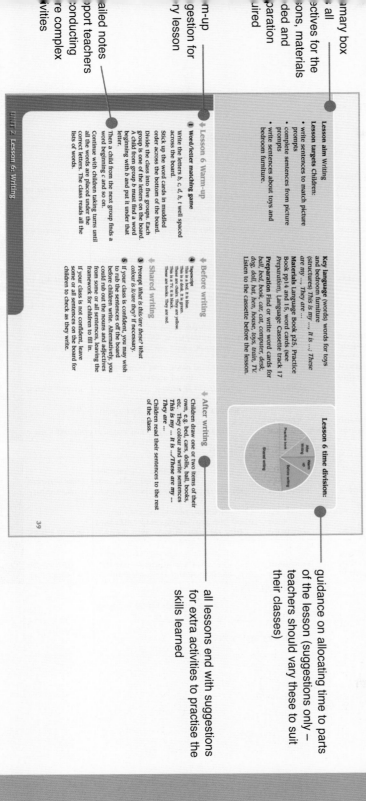

Lesson aim Writing
Lesson targets Children:
• write sentences to match picture prompts
• complete sentences from picture prompts
• write sentences about toys and bedroom furniture.

Key language (words) words for toys and bedroom furniture (structures) This is my ...; It is ...; These are my ...; They are .... These are my ...; It is ...
Materials Language Book p25, Practice Book, pp14 and 15, word cards (see Preparation), Language Cassette track 17
Preparation Find or write word cards for ball, bed, book, car, cat, computer, desk, dog, doll, hat, hen, house, toys, train, TV. Listen to the cassette before the lesson.

Lesson 6 time division:

(pie chart: Warm-up, Before writing, Shared writing, Practice Book, After Writing)

Lesson 6 Warm-up
1 **Word/letter matching game**
Write the letters b, c, d, h, t well spaced across the board.
Stick up the word cards in muddled order across the bottom of the board. Divide the class into five groups. Each group is one of the letters on the board. A child from group b must find a word beginning with b and put it under that letter.
Then a child from the next group finds a word beginning c and so on. Continue with children taking turns until all the words are placed under the correct letters. The class reads all the lists of words.

Before writing
4 **Tapescript**
This is a bed. It is blue.
This is a desk. It is green.
These are chairs. They are yellow.
This is a TV. It is black.
These are books. They are red.

Shared writing
3 Prompt What is this/are these? What colour is it/are they? If necessary.
5 If your class is confident, you may wish to rub the sentences off the board before children write. Alternatively, you could rub out the nouns and adjectives from some or all sentences, leaving the framework for children to fill in. If your class is not confident, leave some or all sentences on the board for children to check as they write.

After writing
Children draw one or two items of their own, e.g. bed, cars, dolls, ball, books, etc. They colour and write sentences This is my ...; It is ...; These are my ...; They are ...
Children read their sentences to the rest of the class.

guidance on allocating time to parts of the lesson (suggestions only – teachers should vary these to suit their classes)

all lessons end with suggestions for extra activities to practise the skills learned

FLUENCY BOOK 1		LANGUAGE BOOK 1			LANGUAGE BOOK 1			
		Reading and understanding	Working with words	Sentence building	Grammar	Listening	Phonics	Class writing
		REVISION			**REVISION**			
Unit 1	*The island of adventure*	reading text: *My family and me* text type: autobiography vocabulary: family	family members	sentences – capital letters and full stops	Hi/Hello. What is your name? I am Tilly. How old are you? I am six.	Who is speaking? (identifying family members)	CVC words with a short **a**	My friends and I (simple sentences)
Unit 2	*Sam's house*	reading text: *A new room for Amy* text type: descriptive text and poem vocabulary: toys and furniture	furniture toys	common nouns	This is my bed. These are my books. Is this your radio? Yes, it is. / No, it isn't.	Draw the toys (listening for detail)	CVC words with a short **e**	My room (simple description)
Unit 3	*The moon and the stars*	reading text: *Can the moon see me?* text type: poem (x2) vocabulary: night sky	the night sky and creatures	*a* and *an*	I can see a plane. I can't hear an owl. Can you see the moon? Yes, I can. / No, I can't.	What can you hear? (identifying sounds)	CVC words with a short **i**	What can we see? (simple sentences)
		REVISION: UNITS 1-3			**REVISION: UNITS 1-3**			
Unit 4	*Sam's garden*	reading text: *My secret garden* text type: information text vocabulary: animals and colours	animals and colours	sentences – questions	What is this? It is a nest. What are these? They are small blue eggs.	What are the animals? (identifying sounds)	CVC words with a short **u**	Animals (questions and answers)
Unit 5	*Sam's island*	reading text: *Where is my house?* text type: puzzle poem vocabulary: numbers; prepositions	numbers	adjectives – colour words	Where is the mouse? It is in / on / under / next to the table.	Complete the picture (listening for location)	CVC words with a short **o**	Where is it? (writing about location)
Unit 6	*On the beach*	reading text: *We love the beach* text type: story with familiar setting vocabulary: seaside words	marine features and creatures	proper nouns – people's names	I have got a starfish. Have you got a starfish? Yes, I have. / No, I haven't. Has he got a rock? Yes, he has. / No, he hasn't.	What has she got? (listening for detail)	words beginning or ending with the **sh** phoneme	What have they got? (describing possessions)
		REVISION: UNITS 4-6			**REVISION: UNITS 4-6**			
Unit 7	*In the jungle*	reading text: *Do or don't?* text type: information text vocabulary: action verbs	action verbs	verbs – imperatives	Listen! Please sit down! Don't run! Don't look behind you!	*Simon Says* (understanding commands)	words beginning or ending with the **ch** phoneme	Crossing the road (writing commands)
Unit 8	*Monkey fun*	reading text: *Where are the animals?* text type: information text vocabulary: animals; colours; actions	animals	sentences – statements and questions	Look at the parrot. It is sitting in the tree. He is running. They are playing football.	What are they doing? (identifying activities)	words ending with the **ll** phoneme	What are they doing? (1) (writing about activities)
Unit 9	*In the cave*	reading text: *Playtime* text type: descriptive text and traditional rhymes vocabulary: action verbs	more action verbs	verbs – is/are with -ing	Is he riding a horse? Yes, he is. / No, he isn't. Are they dancing? Yes, they are. / No, they aren't.	*Two Little Hands* (following a sequence of actions)	words ending with the **ng** phoneme	What are they doing? (2) (questions and answers)
		REVISION: UNITS 7-9			**REVISION: UNITS 7-9**			

	FLUENCY BOOK 1	LANGUAGE BOOK 1			Grammar	Listening	Phonics	Class writing
		Reading and understanding	Working with words	Sentence building				
Unit 10	*In the tree house*	reading text: *Suki's day* text type: story with familiar setting vocabulary: times; feelings	feelings	proper nouns – days of the week	It is Saturday. What is the time? It is nine o'clock. It is half past three.	Harry's week (matching days and activities)	words ending with the **ck** phoneme	Days of the week (writing about days, times and locations)
Unit 11	*Look at that ship!*	reading text: *Here comes the train!* text type: information text vocabulary: action verbs	matching verbs and nouns	pronouns	What is he doing? He is eating an ice cream. What are they doing? They are swimming.	People are getting off the train. (locating items in a picture)	words beginning with blends **br cr dr gr** or **tr**	Activities (writing questions and answers)
Unit 12	*On the ship*	reading text: *We all love the mall* text type: descriptive text vocabulary: shops	shops	prepositions	There is a ball under the chair. There are toys in the box.	Where are they? (identifying locations)	words beginning with blends **bl cl fl** or **pl**	The park (description)
		REVISION: UNITS 10-12			REVISION: UNITS 10-12			
Unit 13	*A hundred steps*	reading text: *Dani can count!* text type: story with patterned language vocabulary: numbers	numbers 1-100	verbs – to have	How many trees are there? There are two trees.	How many are there? (listening for detail)	words beginning or ending with the **th** phoneme	Our classroom (description including numbers)
Unit 14	*The weather man*	reading text: *Splish, splash, splosh!* text type: story with familiar setting vocabulary: weather	weather	adjectives and nouns	What is the weather like? It is raining / snowing / cold / hot / sunny. Is it cold? Yes, it is. / No, it isn't.	What's the weather like? (identifying weather types)	words beginning with blends **st sm sw sp** or **sn**	The weather (completing a weather diary)
Unit 15	*A ride on an elephant*	reading text: *Animal puzzles* text type: puzzle text vocabulary: body parts	parts of the body and physical features	verbs – to be	They have got long ears. We have got little ears. We have not got long ears.	What are the animals? (identifying animals)	words ending with the blends **nd nt** or **nk**	Animals (describing animals)
		REVISION: UNITS 13-15			REVISION: UNITS 13-15			
Unit 16	*A picnic by the river*	reading text: *Let's have a picnic* text type: poem (rap) vocabulary: food	food and drink	nouns – singular and plural with s	I like grapes. He likes sandwiches. She likes cakes.	Mobi likes everything! (identifying preferences)	words with the spelling pattern **a_e** or **i_e**	Favourite food (writing about food preferences)
Unit 17	*Time to go home*	reading text: *At the airport* text type: information text vocabulary: vehicles; clothes; colours	clothing	sentences – word order	Whose hat is this? It is Tilly's. Whose socks are these? They are Sam's.	Whose voice is this? (identifying people)	words with the spelling pattern **ue u_e** or **o_e**	What are they packing? (writing about clothes)
Unit 18	*Fireworks!*	reading text: *Fireworks!* text type: shape poems vocabulary: fierworks; colours	a word game	verbs – to like	The bird is going onto / over / along the roof. The children are going round / towards / into the house.	What's your favourite? (identifying descriptions)	words ending with the blends **ld lk lp** or **lt**	At the fun fair (description)
		REVISION: UNITS 16-18			REVISION: UNITS 16-18			

Hello

Language Book pp6-7

1 Activity 1: Use the alphabet frieze to revise the names and sounds of the letters. Play the *Alphabet song* (LCD1 track 1). Children join in.

2 Activity 2: Children look at the picture. Prompt them to name anything they can. Help them to find the bikes, ball, dog, rainbow, frog, mouse, cat, trees, flower, sun. Ask *What colour is ...?* Play LCD1 track 2. Children listen and point.

3 Activity 3: Children tell each other their names.

4 Activity 4: Play LCD1 track 3. Children listen to the sounds and point to the animals on the page.

5 Activity 5: Play the *Rainbow song* (LCD1 track 4). Children listen and sing.

6 Activity 6: Children work in pairs. They point and make statements about things on the pages.

Language Book pp8-9

1 Children look at the classroom picture. Ask them to say what is in it.

2 Activity 1: Play LCD1 track 5. Children listen to the dialogue and point to Miss Plum and Nina as they speak.

3 Activity 2: Practise the dialogue with individuals around the class. Children repeat the activity in pairs.

4 Activity 3: Play the *Numbers song* (LCD1 track 6). Children listen then join in.

5 Activity 4: Play LCD1 track 7. Children listen and follow the commands.

6 Activity 5: Play LCD1 track 8. Children listen and point to the objects in the classroom posters. They answer the questions.

7 Activity 6: Play LCD1 track 9. Children point to the objects when Tilly says where they are.

8 Activity 7: Read Miss Plum's questions. Ask children these and similar questions about items in the picture.

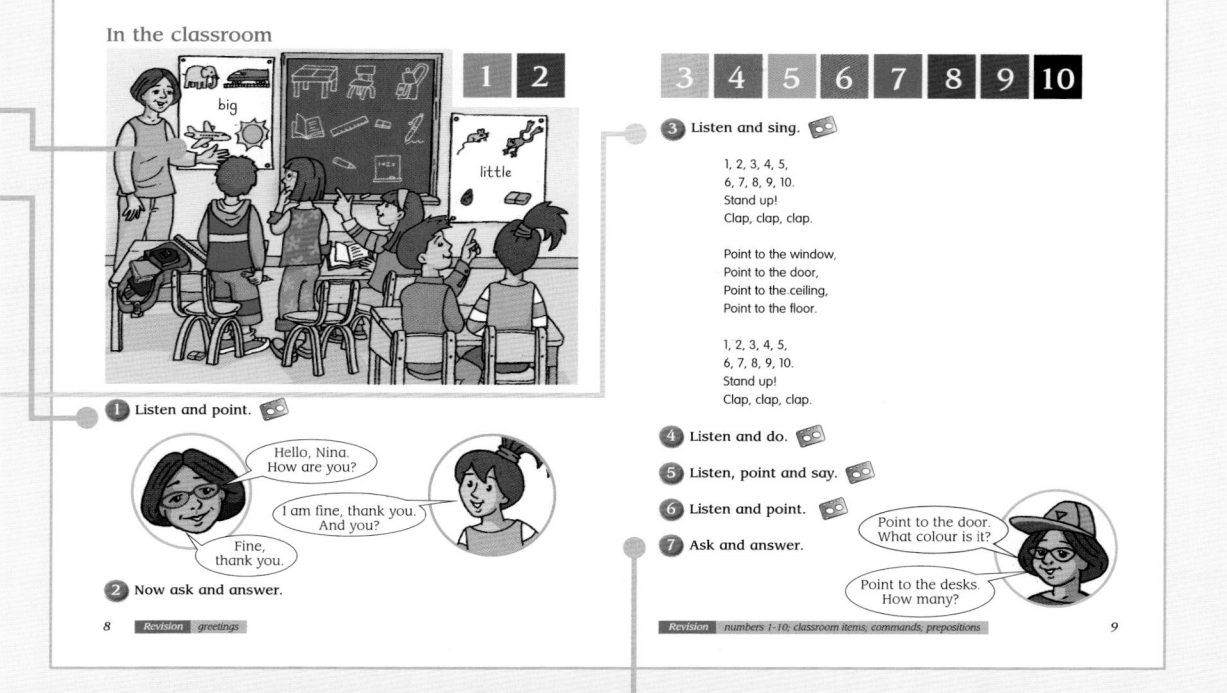

⬇ Language Book pages 6–7 audioscripts

1 Presenter   **Hello. 1 Listen and sing the alphabet song.**
Children   abc, defg, hijklm, nopq, rstu, vwxyz

2 Presenter   **2 Listen and point.**
Tilly   Hi, I am Tilly. Look at my bike. It is blue. Look at my ball. It is red and yellow.
Ben   Hello, I am Ben. Look at my bike. It is green. Look at my dog. It is brown and white.

4 Presenter   **4 Listen, point and say.**
Voice   Listen. *[bird]* It is a bird. Listen. *[cat]* It is a cat. Listen. *[parrot]* It is a parrot. Listen. *[dog]* It is a dog. Listen. *[frog]* It is a frog.

⬇ Language Book pages 8–9 audioscripts

5 Presenter   **4 Listen and do.**
Miss Plum   Stand up! Sit down! Point to the floor. Point to a desk. Point to a pencil.

6 Presenter   **5 Listen, point and say.**
Voice   Point to the train. Big or little?
Point to the frog. Big or little?
Point to the rubber. Big or little?
Point to the elephant. Big or little?
Point to the mouse. Big or little?

7 Presenter   **6 Listen and point.**
Ben   Where is my rubber?
Tilly   It is under your chair.
Ben   Oh, and where is my ruler?
Tilly   It is on your desk.
Ben   Thanks. Where is my book?
Tilly   It is in your bag.
Ben   Where is my pencil?
Tilly   It is in your hand.

Fluency Book introductory pages 4–7

1 Let children look at these four pages for a few minutes at the end of a Language Book revision lesson.

2 Children look at the characters (FB p4). Prompt them to name anything they can, e.g. *parrot, girls, boys.*

3 Children look at the map (FB p5). Read the title. Prompt children to name anything they can, e.g. *monkey, elephant, zebra.*

4 Children look at the picture (FB pp6–7). Prompt them to name, e.g. bag, box. Ask *How many bags?/boxes?*

5   Play FCD track 1. Children listen.

6 Explain that the children in the picture are going to the island on page 5.
Tell the class they will find out what happens on the island in the next lesson.

Fluency Book page 7 audioscript

Miss Plum   Come on, children, it's time to go!

Children   We're going to the island of adventure.
Come with us! Come with us!

We're going to the island of adventure.
Come with us and play!
Our bags are packed. We're ready to go.
Come on, everybody! Don't be slow!

We're going to the island of adventure.
Come with us and play!
The sun is hot. The sky is blue.

The island of adventure is waiting for you.
We're going to the island of adventure.
Come with us and play!

We're going to the island of adventure.
Come with us! Come with us!

We're going to the island of adventure.
Come with us and play!

Before listening

1 Lesson 1 warm-up.

2 Show poster 1. Read the title. Ask questions.

3 Point and name new objects (*helicopter, island*). Children come forward; find objects on the poster.

4 Explain *adventure*, if necessary.

Shared listening

1 Play FCD track 2. Point to characters when they speak.

2 Show flashcards 1–6. Name the characters. Class repeats.

3 Ask questions about characters.

4 Play FCD track 2 and point to characters again.

Dialogue practice

1 Name characters. Children point in books (FB pp8–9). Point on poster for children to check.

2 Show flashcards 1–6. Children name.

3 Children close books. Play FCD track 3 and show flashcards 1–6. Class repeats lines in pauses.

4 Groups say lines by character.

5 (optional) Individuals act dialogue.

6 Play FCD track 2 again. Children follow text or point to main picture.

After listening

1 Practise dialogue with individuals.

2 Practise dialogue with pairs.

3 Ask about Mobi.

1 The island of adventure

helicopter

island

1 The island of adventure

Nina, Ben and Tilly are in a helicopter. Their teacher is in the helicopter too. Her name is Miss Plum.

Look! The island!

Wow!

The helicopter is on the island.

Here we are!

Miss Plum is in the helicopter.

See you later! Have fun!

Goodbye!

What is that in the sky? Is it a bird? Is it a plane?

Look! What's that?

Hello! I'm Mobi!

This is Sam.
Hi, Sam.
Hello.
I'm Ben.
And I'm Nina.
What's your name?
My name's Tilly.
How old are you, Sam?
I'm eight. How old are you?
I'm six.

Nina, Ben and Tilly are on the island with their new friends, Sam and Mobi. It is the start of a big adventure.

8   Hi   Hello   What is your name?   My name is …   How old are you?   I am …

9

Lesson aim Fluency

Lesson targets Children:

- listen for pronunciation and intonation
- repeat dialogue accurately
- act out dialogue with expression
- introduce themselves and give their age.

Key language (words) *helicopter, island; Ben, Nina, Sam, Tilly; Miss Plum* (structures) *What is your name? My name is ... How old are you? I am ...*

Language for understanding *adventure, bird, boy, friends, name, plane, sky, teacher; am, is, are; Look! Wow! Here we are! Hi! Hello! See you later! Have fun! Goodbye!*

Materials Poster 1, Fluency Book pp8–9, Fluency CD tracks 2–3, flashcards 1–6

Preparation Listen to the CD before the lesson.

Detailed teaching procedures See Introduction, p8

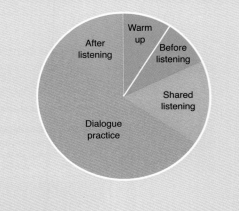

Lesson 1 time division:

⬇ Lesson 1 Warm-up

1 Sing the *Alphabet song* (LB p6, LCD1 track 1).

⬇ Before listening

2 Ask *Can you see girls and boys?*
How many girls?
How many boys?
Can you see the teacher?
What else can you see?

Let children come to the poster, point and name anything they can.

⬇ Shared listening

3 (1st small picture) Ask *Who is in the helicopter?*

(2nd small picture) *Who is on the island?*

Point to child characters in turn. Ask *What is his/her name?*
How old is he/she?

Point to Miss Plum. Ask *What is her name?*
Who is she?

Point to Mobi. Ask *What is his name?*
What is he?

⬇ Dialogue practice

For a detailed explanation of dialogue practice, see Introduction, p8.

⬇ After listening

1 Practise around the class:
What's your name?
My name's ...
How old are you?
I'm ...

2 Repeat the previous activity, but bring two children forward and let one of them ask the questions.

Repeat with other pairs.

3 Ask children where they think Mobi has come from. How do they know? Teach *parachute*, if necessary.

17

Before reading

1 Lesson 2 warm-up.

2 Teach new family member words with flashcards 10–15.

3 Children open books (LB pp10–11). Ask questions. Children point.

Shared reading

1 Play LCD1 track 10. Children follow text in book.

2 Read line by line. Ask questions.

3 Read with the class.

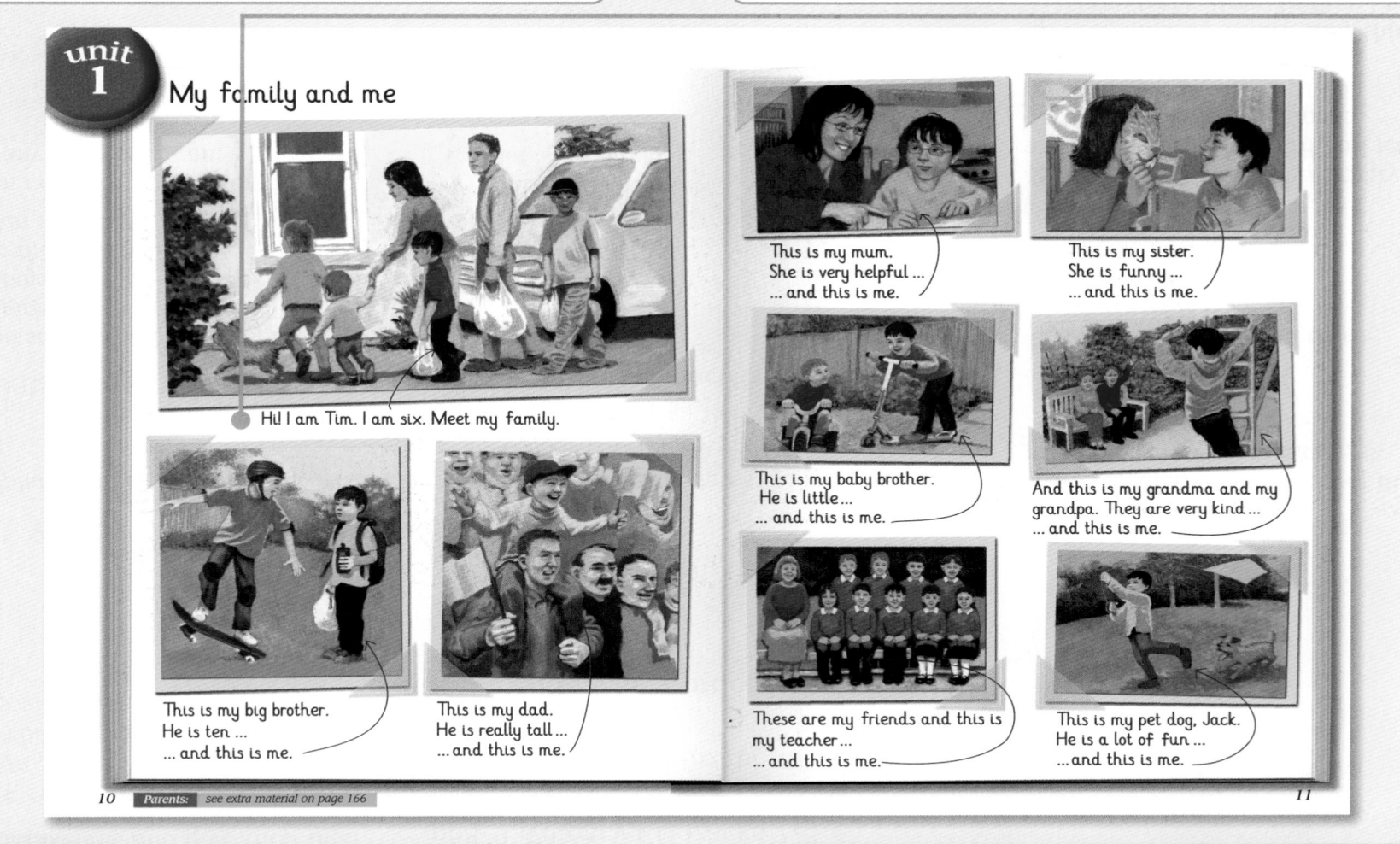

unit 1

My family and me

Hi! I am Tim. I am six. Meet my family.

This is my big brother.
He is ten ...
... and this is me.

This is my dad.
He is really tall ...
... and this is me.

This is my mum.
She is very helpful ...
... and this is me.

This is my sister.
She is funny ...
... and this is me.

This is my baby brother.
He is little ...
... and this is me.

And this is my grandma and my grandpa. They are very kind ...
... and this is me.

These are my friends and this is my teacher ...
... and this is me.

This is my pet dog, Jack.
He is a lot of fun ...
... and this is me.

10 Parents: see extra material on page 166

11

Reading practice

1 Give reading practice. Use some or all of the following:
- Children read again as a class.
- Groups read different sections.
- Individuals read different sections.

2 Class listens again to LCD1 track 10 and follows in LB.

After reading

1 Do the matching words and flashcards activity.

2 Ask Who is this?

Lesson aim Reading

Lesson targets Children:

- follow a text read out to them
- listen for pronunciation and intonation
- read the text aloud with accurate pronunciation and intonation
- learn and understand new vocabulary items
- understand the sense of the text as a whole
- answer simple comprehension questions.

Key language (words) *brother, father, grandmother, grandfather, mother, sister, big, funny, helpful, kind, little, tall*

(structures) *This is ..., He/She is ..., They are ...*

Words for understanding *baby, fun, pet, meet, really, very*

Materials Language Book pp10–11, Language CD1 track 10, flashcards 10–15, word cards

Preparation Listen to the CD before the lesson. Make family word cards for *brother, father, grandmother, grandfather, mother, sister*. Make adjective word cards for *big, funny, helpful, kind, little, tall*

Detailed teaching procedures See Introduction, pp8–9

Lesson 2 time division:

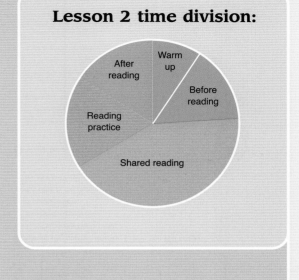

⬇ Lesson 2 Warm-up

1 Sing the *Numbers song* (LB p9, LCD1 track 6).

⬇ Before reading

3 Ask *Can you see mother/a big/little brother, etc? Point to mother/father, etc. Can you see a dog? What colour is the dog?*

⬇ Shared reading

2 Ask *How many in Tim's family?*
Is Tim's brother big? How old is he?
Is Tim's dad tall or short?
Who is helpful?/funny?/little?
Is Grandma kind? Is Grandpa kind?
Can you see Tim's friends?
How many friends can you see?
How many boys/girls?
What is the dog's name?

⬇ After reading

1 Put the six family flashcards on the board. Class names them.

Show family word cards in any order. Class reads. Shuffle and place on your desk.

Children take turns to take a word card and place it under the correct picture.

Ask the rest of the class if it is correct. If it is not, another child has a turn.

Show adjective word cards. Class reads. Shuffle and place on your desk.

In turns, children take a card and place under the correct person. Check with class.

2 (Extension activity) Point to family flashcards. Say *Think about Tim's family.* Ask *Who is helpful?* Elicit **Tim's mother is helpful.** Ask other questions *Who is kind?/ tall?/funny?* etc.

Teacher's note

Mum, dad, grandma and *grandpa* are used by children in everyday conversation to address these family members and to speak about them to other people. *Mother, father, grandmother* and *grandfather* are used in formal situations and often to talk about other children's family members.

Reading and understanding

1 Session 1 warm-up.

2 Re-read *My family and me* (LB pp10–11).

3 Write on board *This is Tim's …*
Hold up flashcards (10–15) at end of phrase. Prompt, e.g. **This is Tim's brother**.

4 Children complete Activity 1 (LB p12).

5 Hold up adjective word cards. Class reads. Ask, e.g. *Who is funny?* Prompt/elicit **Tim's sister is funny**.

6 Children complete Activity 2 (LB p12).

7 Play the *Get active!* game.

8 Prepare children for PB p4. Read the passages with them and check they understand the tasks. Children complete.

Working with words

1 Session 2 warm-up.

2 Stick up word cards/flashcards 10–15. Ask questions. Children match flashcards. Class reads sentences.

3 Children complete Activity 1 (LB p13).

Sentence building

1 Read Mobi's speech bubbles (LB p13). Read sentence.

2 Write sentence. Point and prompt **It's a capital letter/full stop**.

3 Children complete Activity 1 (LB p13).

4 Prepare children for PB p5. Go through the box and check they understand the tasks. Children complete.

Extension activities

1 Do the capital letter/small letter matching activity.

2 Play *Scrambled names*.

Reading and understanding

1 Look and read. Then choose and circle.

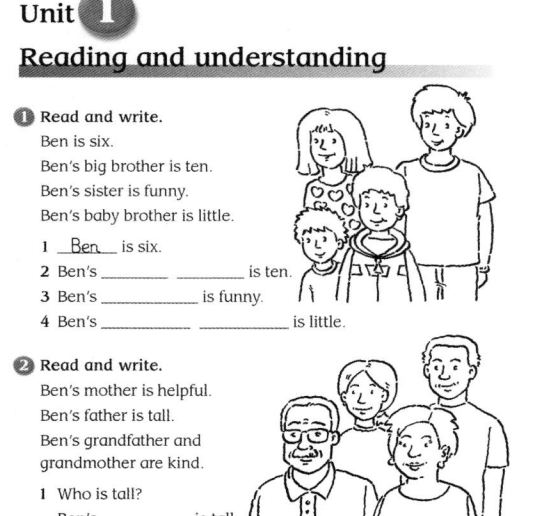

1 This is Tim's — brother. / sister.

2 This is Tim's — mother. / father.

3 This is Tim's — friend. / teacher.

2 Choose the word from the box.

| tall | kind | funny | helpful |

You can also say **very** before these words.

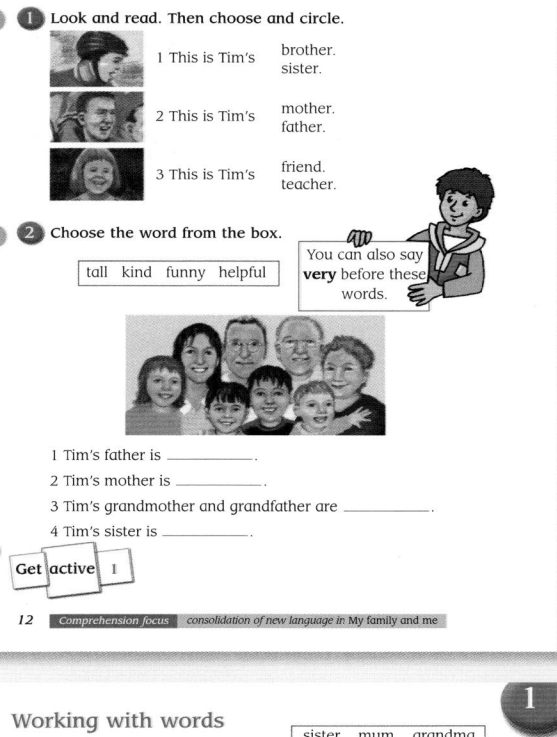

1 Tim's father is _____ .

2 Tim's mother is _____ .

3 Tim's grandmother and grandfather are _____ .

4 Tim's sister is _____ .

Get active 1

12   *Comprehension focus*   *consolidation of new language in My family and me*

Unit 1
Reading and understanding

1 Read and write.
Ben is six.
Ben's big brother is ten.
Ben's sister is funny.
Ben's baby brother is little.

1 __Ben__ is six.

2 Ben's _____ _____ is ten.

3 Ben's _____ is funny.

4 Ben's _____ _____ is little.

2 Read and write.
Ben's mother is helpful.
Ben's father is tall.
Ben's grandfather and grandmother are kind.

1 Who is tall?
Ben's _____ is tall.

2 Who is helpful?
Ben's _____ is helpful.

3 Who is kind?
Ben's _____ and _____ are kind.

4

Working with words

1 Write the words.

| sister | mum | grandma |
| grandpa | dad | brother |

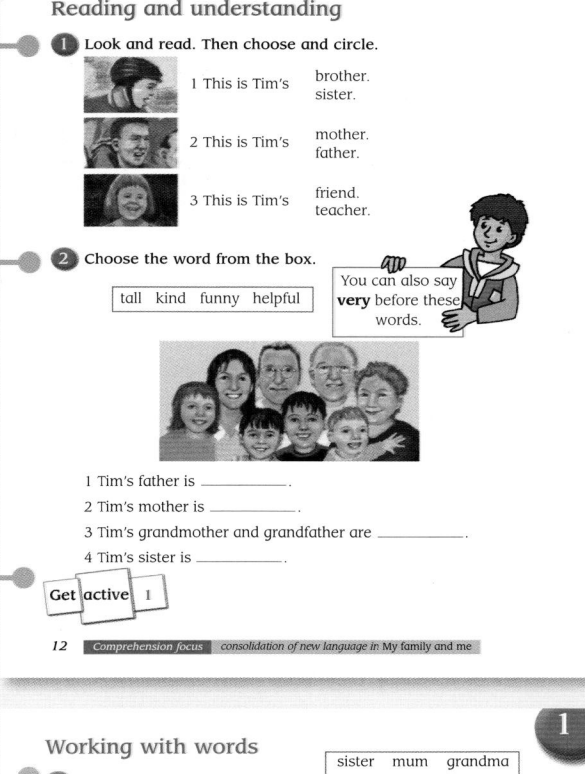

My _____ is big.   My _____ is kind.   My _____ is kind, too.

My _____ is funny.   My _____ is tall.   My _____ is helpful.

Sentence building

A B C D E F G H I J K L M N O P Q R S T U V W X Y Z

A sentence begins with a **capital letter**.

A sentence ends with a **full stop**.

My brother is ten.

1 Read the sentences. Circle the capital letters and full stops.
1 Tim is six.
2 This is my sister.
3 Jack is my pet dog.
4 My mum is helpful.
5 My grandma and grandpa are kind.

Language focus   *family members, capital letters and full stops*   13

Sentence building
Unit 1

capital letter   ⊤his is the island⊙ *full stop*

1 Circle the capital letters. Circle the full stops.
1 T his is my big brother .
2 H ere is my friend .
3 I am seven .
4 T his is my dad .
5 M y sister is six .

2 Write the sentences correctly.

Remember capital letters and full stops.

1 the boy has a dog
__The boy has a dog.__

2 he is nine
_____

3 my brother is three
_____

4 she is my friend
_____

5 this is my mum and dad
_____

5

Lesson aim Comprehension, vocabulary and sentence building

Lesson targets Children:
- read and complete sentences choosing from given words
- read and complete sentences from picture prompts
- answer simple oral comprehension questions
- write answers to simple comprehension questions
- identify capital letters
- use correct punctuation: capital letter and full stop.

Key language
(words) *brother, father, grandma, grandpa, mother, sister, funny, helpful, kind, little, tall*
(structures) *This is ..., He/She is ..., They are ...*

Words for understanding *baby, fun, pet, meet, really, very*

Materials Language Book pp12–13, Practice Book pp4–5, flashcards 10–15, word cards from Lesson 2

Lesson 3 time division:

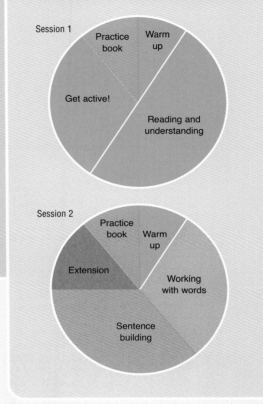

Session 1: Warm up, Reading and understanding, Get active!, Practice book

Session 2: Warm up, Working with words, Sentence building, Extension, Practice book

↓ Lesson 3 Session 1 Warm-up

1 Use flashcards/word cards to revise and read words for family members.

Sing the *Rainbow song* (LB p7, LCD1 track 4).

↓ Reading and understanding

7 Get active!
Tell the class to turn back to LB pp10–11 and look at the people.
Show a child from team 1 a flashcard of a family member. The child mimes the family member doing the activity as shown in Tim's photos, e.g. brother – skateboarding; grandma – sitting in park, etc.
Other children from team 1 guess who it is: *It's Tim's brother.*
Ask team 2 a question about the character, e.g. *How old is he?*
Play again, showing a team 2 child a different character to mime.

↓ Lesson 3 Session 2 Warm-up

Write four or five pairs of capital and small letters scattered on the board. Children draw lines joining the capital and small letter in each pair. Other children circle the capital in each pair.

↓ Working with words

2 Stick adjective word cards on the board, well spaced out. Class reads.

Stick the flashcards and family member word cards underneath. Say, *Think about Tim's family. Who is helpful?* Elicit **Tim's mother is helpful.**

Ask a child find the flashcard for *mother* and place it above the correct adjective. Choose another child to find the correct family word and stick it in front of the adjective. Write *Tim's* and *is* to complete the sentence. Class reads. Repeat with the other adjectives.

Class reads all the sentences in any order. Rub them off the board.

↓ Extension activities

1 Write a column of capital letters on the left of the board. Stick small letters in scrambled order on the right. Children take turns to match correct small letter next to the capital.

2 Scrambled names
Write the letters of a book character's name in scrambled order on the board, e.g. *eBn.* Children volunteer to write the name correctly. Continue with other names.

21

Grammar

1. Lesson 4 warm-up. ⬇
2. Read speech bubbles (LB p14). Children follow.
3. 📖 Class reads speech bubbles. ⬇
4. Activity 1: Children speak in pairs. ⬇
5. Activity 2: Children read and complete.
6. Prepare children for PB p6 by checking they understand the tasks. Children complete.

Listening

1. Read Nina's speech bubble (LB p15).
2. Ask *Who can you see?* ⬇
3. 🎧 Activity 1: Play LCD1 track 11. Children listen. Play it again. Children tick. ⬇
4. 🎧 Activity 2: Play LCD1 track 12 twice. Children listen and sing. ⬇

After listening

1. 🎧 📖 Play LCD1 track 12. Sing the song with flashcards. ⬇

Lesson aim Grammar and listening

Lesson targets Children:

- practise talking about children's ages in pairs
- write their own age and ages of other children
- listen to dialogue and identify family members
- sing and learn a short song.

Key language (words) numbers/words *1–10, mum, dad, sister, brother, grandma, grandpa* (structures) *This is ..., He/She is ..., They are ...*

Materials Language Book pp14–15, Practice Book p6, Language CD1 tracks 11–12, character flashcards 2, 3, 5, age balloons, family member flashcards 10–15 for song

Preparation Play the CD before the lesson. Make age balloons for 6, 7, 8 (see Grammar box, LB p14)

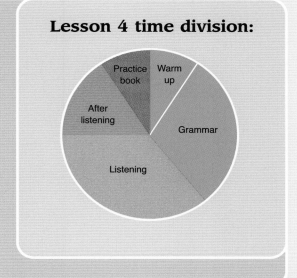

Lesson 4 time division:

Practice book / Warm up / Grammar / Listening / After listening

Lesson 4 Warm-up

1 Practise dialogue with individuals:

What's your name? How old are you?

Ask the whole class: *What is his/her name? How old is he/she?*

Grammar

3 Bring three children forward. Give each a character flashcard and age balloon.

Individuals read out Tilly's statements. Children hold up their flashcards and balloons when their character's name and age is mentioned.

Class reads. Children show cards/balloons.

4 Practise first with the class. Ask *How old is the baby?* Elicit **He is one**. Ask *How old is the big/small girl/boy?* etc. Elicit **She is ten**, etc.

Children then make statements in pairs.

Listening

2 Ask *Can you see Nina's mother? Point to Nina's mother*, etc.

3 Tell children to listen and decide which person in the family is speaking.

Audioscript

Presenter	1
Nina	Hi, Dad.
Dad	Hello, Nina.
Presenter	2
Sister	[singing]
Nina	Hi, Sis!
Sister	Hi!
Presenter	3
[doorbell rings; door opens]	
Grandpa	Hello, Nina.
Nina	Hello, Grandpa.
Presenter	4
Nina	Hello, Danny.
Baby	[gurgles]
Presenter	5
[telephone]	
Grandma	Hello?
Nina	Hello, Grandma.
Presenter	6
[glass breaking]	
Mum	Oh, Nina ...
Nina	Sorry, Mum.

4 The first time children listen and follow the words. Next time they join in.

After listening

Four children hold the family member flashcards. Class sings the song. Children hold up their card when their family member is named.

Write up the song. Put the class in four groups. Give each group a flashcard. Point to the words of the song. Each group says their family member. All say the last line.

Activity 1

1. Lesson 5 warm-up.
2. (LB p16) Point out pictures and words with *a*.
3. 🎧 Play rhyme twice (LCD1 track 13). Children follow in books.
4. Read rhyme.
5. Read line by line and ask questions. ⬇
6. Read with the class.

Activity 2

1. ⬇ Children hold sounds cards. Say the sounds.
2. Close up gradually.
3. Say the word.
4. Children look, say and write.

Activity 3

1. Children look at the picture and read the words. Ask/Help a child to say the whole sentence. Class repeats.
2. Children write the word.
3. Do the same with the second sentence.

Activity 4

1. Write up words. Class/individuals read.
2. Children read in pairs. Listen to pairs.
3. Children check words and tick.

Practice Book

Children complete PB p7. ⬇

Phonics games and activities

1. Play the *Letter-changing game*. ⬇
2. Play *Match the rhyming words*. ⬇

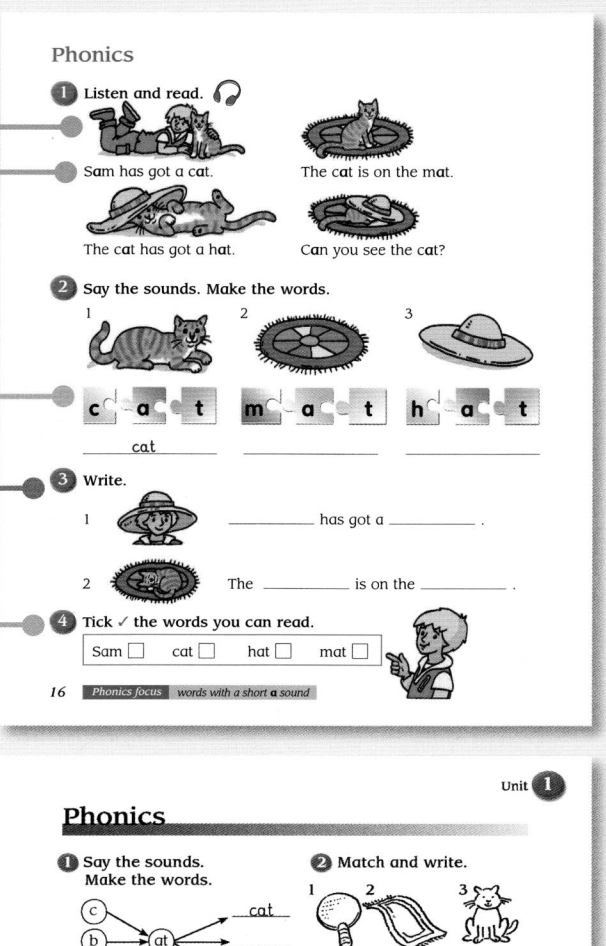

Phonics

1. Listen and read. 🎧

   Sam has got a cat.

   The cat is on the mat.

   The cat has got a hat.

   Can you see the cat?

2. Say the sounds. Make the words.

   1 c a t   cat
   2 m a t
   3 h a t

3. Write.

   1 _____ has got a _____ .

   2 The _____ is on the _____ .

4. Tick ✓ the words you can read.

   Sam ☐   cat ☐   hat ☐   mat ☐

16   Phonics focus   words with a short **a** sound

Unit 1

Phonics

1. Say the sounds. Make the words.

   c
   b → at
   m

   cat _____

2. Match and write.

3. Say the sounds. Make the words.

   1 c a p
   2 m a p
   3 t a p

4. Write.

   1 The _____ has a _____ .
   2 The _____ has a _____ .
   3 The _____ and the _____ are on the _____ .
   4 The _____ and the _____ are on the _____ .

5. Read and colour.
   Colour the *at* words red.   Colour the *ap* words green.

   cat   mat   tap   map   hat

7

24

Lesson aim Phonic recognition

Lesson targets Children:

- read, pronounce and spell cvc (consonant–vowel–consonant) words with short *a*
- recognise and say the individual sounds that make up the cvc words
- write the words from picture prompts.

Target words *Sam, cat, hat, mat, cap, map, tap*

Materials Language Book p16, Practice Book p7, Language CD1 track 13, cards for sounds

Preparation Listen to the CD before the lesson. Make large cards for the sounds/phonemes for *cat, mat, hat* (see p12). Make word cards for *cat, hat, tap, van* for the rhyming words game.

Detailed teaching procedures See Introduction, p10

Lesson 5 time division:

⬇ Lesson 5 Warm-up

1 Play the song from Lesson 4 (LB p15, LCD1 track 12) two or three times. Children join in. After the first time, encourage them to sing the first line without looking in their books.

⬇ Activity 1

5 Ask *Who has got a cat?*
What colour is the mat?
Where is the cat?
What has the cat got?
What colour is the hat?
Where is the cat now?

Make sure all the words in the text are understood.

⬇ Activity 2

Follow the procedure for introducing the phonemes and sounding out each word which is given in detail in the Introduction (p10).

⬇ Activity 4

1 Write the four words on the board. Point in random order. Individuals and/or the class reads them.

2 Children can practise reading the words in pairs.

3 When you are satisfied that children can read the words, they may tick them.

⬇ Practice Book

Cap, map and *tap* are introduced here, so sound these out with the children and point to the pictures in the book.

Children complete the five exercises.

Check they can sound out all the target words before they move on to Exercise 5.

⬇ Phonics games and activities

1 **Letter-changing game**

Write up a known word, e.g. *mat*. Class reads.

Replace the first letter with, e.g. *c*. Class reads the new word.

Then replace *c* with *b*, etc.

When appropriate initial letters have been tried, change final letters e.g. *mat – map, cat – can*, etc.

2 **Match the rhyming words**

Write on the board *mat, bat, map, can*.

Put the word cards you made on your desk.

Children take a word card and stick it next to the word it rhymes with on the board.

Class reads the pairs of rhyming words.

Before writing

1. Lesson 6 warm-up. ⬇
2. Ask who is speaking: **Miss Plum**. Read the speech bubble (LB p17).
3. Ask who is in the picture.
4. Individuals read the sentences.
5. Class reads the sentences.

Shared writing

1. Children look at picture 1 (LB p17). Prompt and write sentence. ⬇
2. Children look at picture 2. Count. Prompt and write sentence. ⬇
3. Children look at Sam (picture 3). Ask *Who ...?* ⬇ Prompt and write sentence.
4. Continue with last picture. ⬇
5. Class reads and writes sentences. ⬇

Practice Book

Writing

1. Read the boy's speech bubble to the class (PB p8). ⬇
2. Class reads numbers in the box.
3. Ask about Emma. Child reads. Class repeats. ⬇
4. Prompt complete sentences about Tom. ⬇
5. Children write remaining sentences.

Your writing

1. Children draw/write about themselves (PB p9). ⬇
2. Children draw/write about a friend. ⬇

After writing

Children read their work to the class.

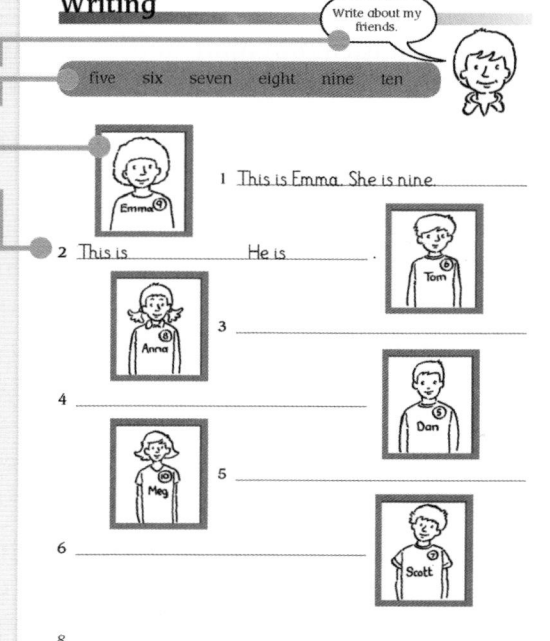

Lesson aim Writing

Lesson targets Children:

- write sentences to match picture prompts
- complete sentences from picture prompts
- write two sentences about themselves and a friend.

Key language (words) *friend*, words for numbers
(structures) *Sam is my friend. He/She is six.*

Materials Language Book p17, Practice Book pp8 and 9

Lesson 6 time division:

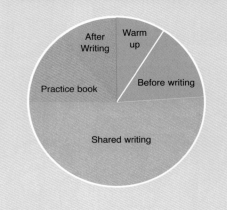

Lesson 6 Warm-up

1. Say the rhyme about Sam and his cat from LB p16.

   Say the numbers chant below:
   One, two three! *(clap, clap clap)*
   Four, five, six! *(clap, clap, clap)*
   Seven, eight, nine! *(clap, clap, clap)*
   Ten! *(clap)* Ten! *(clap)*
   Ten! *(clap, clap, clap)*

Shared writing

1. Ask who is in the picture. Elicit **It is Nina.**

   Point to the empty bubble. Ask *What is she saying?* Prompt/Elicit **I am Nina**. Write it on the board.

2. Prompt the class to count the candles: **Seven**. Point to the empty bubble. Ask *What is she saying?* Prompt/Elicit **I am seven**. Write it on the board.

3. Ask who the other person is: **Sam**. Ask what Nina is saying. If necessary, ask *Is Sam Nina's friend?* Prompt/Elicit **Sam is my friend**. Write it on the board.

4. Elicit **He is eight** for the fourth picture.

5. Class reads the sentences on the board. Leave them on the board, if you wish. Children write the correct sentence in each bubble.

Practice Book

Writing

3. Children look at the picture of Emma. Ask *Who is this? How old is she?*

4. Ask/Help another child to complete the sentences about Tom. Write them on the board. Class reads.

Your writing

1. Children draw and write two sentences about themselves.

2. Remind them of the sentences they wrote on page 8.

Before listening

1. Lesson 1 warm-up.
2. Show poster 1. Ask questions.
3. Show poster 2. Read the title. Ask questions.
4. Point and name new objects. Children come forward; find objects in main picture.
5. Show flashcards 20–25 and name new objects. Class repeats.

Shared listening

1. Play FCD track 4. Point to characters when they speak.
2. Ask questions about Polly.
3. Ask questions about objects and characters.
4. Play FCD track 4 and point to characters again.

Dialogue practice

1. Say new object words. Children point in books (FB pp10–11). Point on poster for children to check.
2. Show flashcards 20–25. Children name.
3. Children close books. Play FCD track 5 and show flashcards 6 and 9. Class repeats lines in pauses.
4. Groups say lines by character.
5. (optional) Individuals act dialogue.
6. Play FCD track 4 again. Children follow text or point to main picture.

After listening

1. Practise dialogue for introductions.
2. Teach the chant.

2 Sam's house

table

TV

bed

chair

books   toys

---

2 Sam's house

Tilly, Ben, Nina and Sam are in the tree house.

Look at this little house!
It is in a tree.
Can you see Sam?
It is his house.

table

bed

TV

chair

books

toys

Welcome to my tree house!

This is my tree house!
Wow!
It's fantastic!

These are my toys.
Oh!
Is this your bed?
Yes.
It's great!

Hello! Hello! Hello!
Oh!
This is my parrot. Her name's Polly.
Hello, Polly!
Hello! Hello! Hello!
She's funny!

Look at me! Hee hee!

Be careful, Mobi!

10   This is ...   These are ...   Is this your ...?   my   his   her

11

28

Lesson aim Fluency

Lesson targets Children:

- listen for pronunciation and intonation
- repeat dialogue accurately
- act out dialogue with expression
- talk about things in a house.

Key language (words) *bed, books, chair, table, toys, TV*
(structures) *This is ..., These are ..., Is this your ...?, my, his, her*

Words for understanding *fantastic, great, house, mobile phone, parrot, tree*

Materials Posters 1 and 2, Fluency Book pp10–11, Fluency CD1 tracks 4–5, character flashcards 6 and 9, object flashcards 20–25

Preparation Listen to the CD before the lesson.

Detailed teaching procedures See Introduction, p8

Lesson 1 time division:

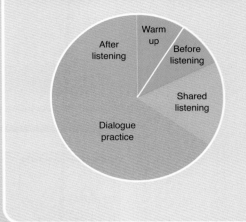

⬇ Lesson 1 Warm-up

① Sing the *Family song* (LB p15, LCD1 track 12).
Practise dialogue:
What's your name? **My name's ...**
How old are you? **I'm ...**

⬇ Before listening

② (poster 1) Ask *Who is this?* (point to each character, children name them) or

Ask *Can you see (name of character)?* Children come forward and point.

Ask *Who lives on the island?*

③ (poster 2, small picture) *Can you see a tree? Where is Sam's house?*

(main picture) *Can you see (name of character)?* Children point on poster.

⬇ Shared listening

② Ask *Can you see Sam's parrot?*
What is her name?
What colours is Polly?
What can she say?

③ Ask *What can Ben see?*
Can Nina see Ben's toys?
How many toys are there?
What colour is the ball?
Who is funny?

⬇ After listening

① Five children stand in a line facing the class. Demonstrate, if necessary, by introducing the first child yourself.

Child A:	*This is my friend. His/Her name's Dan/Leila.*
Child B:	*Hello.*

Class:	*Hello, Dan/Leila.*
Child B:	*This is my friend. His/Her name's ...*
Child C:	*Hello.*
Class:	*Hello.*

Repeat with another group of five children.

② Write the words of the chant below on the board. Say it to the class. Repeat and prompt the class to join in. If you wish, show the class a welcoming gesture with one hand and then the other for lines 3 and 4.

I am Sam! (clap, clap)
Yes, I am! (clap, clap)
Welcome to my island,
Welcome to my home.

Teacher's note
Sam's bed is a hammock, a bed consisting of a long piece of strong cloth tied between two posts or trees.
In the past, sailors slept in them on ships. Nowadays they are used in the garden for relaxing.

29

Before reading

1. 📖 Lesson 2 warm-up. ⬇
2. 📖 Teach new key words with flashcards 24–29.
3. Children open books (LB pp18–19). Ask questions. ⬇

Shared reading

1. 🎧 Play LCD1 track 14. Children follow text in book.
2. Read line by line. Ask questions about each object. Children find the object in the main picture. ⬇
3. Read with the class.

Reading practice

1. Give reading practice. Use some or all of the following:
   - Children read again as a class.
   - Groups read different sections.
   - Individuals read different sections.
2. 🎧 Class listens again to LCD1 track 14 and follows in LB.

After reading

Teach the *Toys* rhyme (LB p19). ⬇

Lesson aim Reading

Lesson targets Children:

- follow a text read out to them
- listen for pronunciation and intonation
- read the text aloud with accurate pronunciation and intonation
- learn and understand new vocabulary items
- understand the sense of the text as a whole
- answer simple comprehension questions.

Key language (words) *ball, computer, desk, doll, elephant, lamp, plane, radio, train*
(structures) *This is ..., He/She is ..., They are ...*

Words for understanding *bedroom, room, love*

Materials Language Book pp18–19, Language CD1 track 14, flashcards 18–22 and 24–29

Preparation Make word cards for all objects on flashcards for this lesson. Listen to the CD before the lesson.

Detailed teaching procedures
See Introduction, pp8–9

Lesson 2 time division:

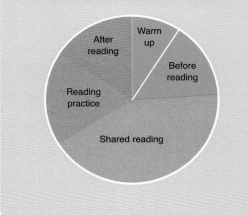

⬇ Lesson 2 Warm-up

1 Practise *This is .../These are ...* with flashcards.
Hold up flashcards 18–22 in turn. Class names the object.
Hold up flashcards 18–22 in turn. Say *This is a .../These are ....*
Prompt class to say the noun. Stick the card on the board.
When all cards are on the board, point to each in turn and prompt/elicit, e.g. **This is a table. These are toys.**

⬇ Before reading

3 Ask *Can you see books? How many?*
What colour is the lamp/radio?
Look at the box. What is in the box?
Point to the bed. How many elephants are on the bed?
Where is the computer?

⬇ Shared reading

2 Ask *Is the bed new or old?*
What colour is the little table?
Is the desk big or small?
What colour is the chair/computer?
Does Amy like story books?
Has Amy got a radio?
How many toys are in the toy box?
What colours are the elephants?
Who loves elephants?
Has she got an elephant lamp?
(rhyme) *What toys are in the toy box?*

⬇ After reading

Write the *Toys* rhyme on the board. Class reads.

Rub off *train* and *ball*. Replace the missing words with the flashcards. Class reads rhyme and supplies the missing words.

Rub off *doll* and *plane*. Replace the missing words with the flashcards. Class reads rhyme and fills in the words.

Rub off the last words of the last two lines. Class reads and fills in the words.

Rub off another significant word from each of the last two lines.

Class says the rhyme again each time you remove two more words.

If your class finds this activity easy, take off one or more flashcards as well. Class supplies the missing words.

Continue to remove words and pictures. If possible, continue until the class can say the whole rhyme from memory.

Reading and understanding

1. Session 1 warm-up.
2. Re-read *A new room for Amy* (LB pp18–19).
3. Activity 1 (LB p20): Individuals read sentence aloud. Class reads sentence aloud. Children circle picture that matches it.
4. Read *Remember!* box to the class. Write up one or two more example sentences.
5. Activity 2: Children read/number lines in order. Class reads poem.
6. Play the *Get active!* game.
7. Prepare children for PB p10 by checking they understand the tasks. Children complete.

Working with words

1. Session 2 warm-up.
2. Hold up flashcards (20, 21, 26–29) for Activity 1 (LB p21). Class names them.
3. Activity 1: Children circle words for the objects.
4. Show flashcards for Activity 1 objects. Ask *Is this in the toy box?/the bedroom?*
5. Activity 2: Children write the words in the correct place.

Sentence building

1. (LB p21) Read the sentence in the box. Class reads. Read the words in the box. Class reads.
2. Demonstrate Activity 1 on the board.
3. Class completes Activity 1.
4. Children complete PB p11.

Extension activities

1. Class makes sentences with *This is/These are*.

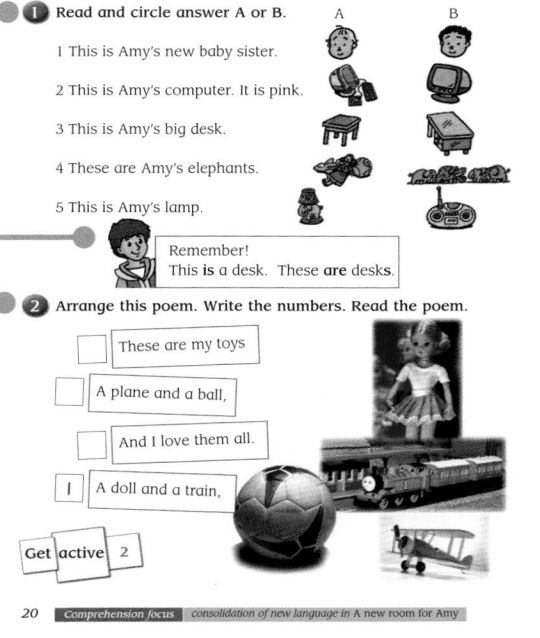

Reading and understanding

1. Read and circle answer A or B.　A　B
   1. This is Amy's new baby sister.
   2. This is Amy's computer. It is pink.
   3. This is Amy's big desk.
   4. These are Amy's elephants.
   5. This is Amy's lamp.

   Remember!
   This **is** a desk.　These **are** desks.

2. Arrange this poem. Write the numbers. Read the poem.
   ☐ These are my toys
   ☐ A plane and a ball,
   ☐ And I love them all.
   1 A doll and a train,

   Get active 2

   20　Comprehension focus　consolidation of new language in A new room for Amy

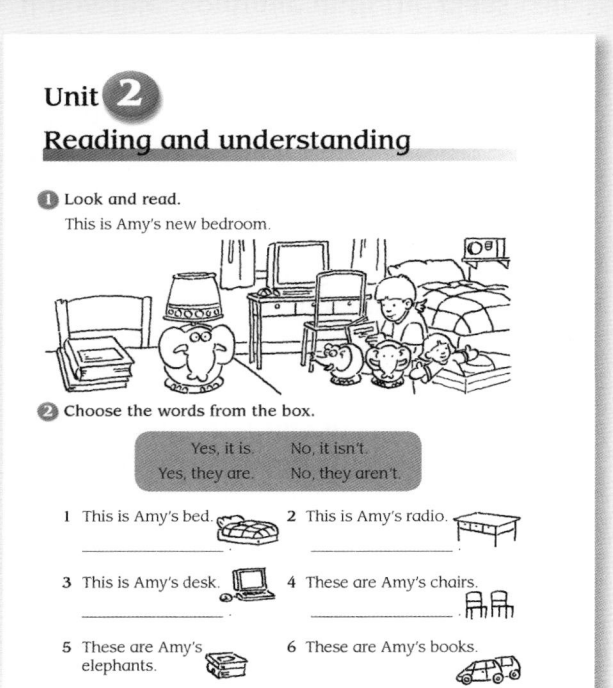

Unit 2
Reading and understanding

1. Look and read.
   This is Amy's new bedroom.

2. Choose the words from the box.

   Yes, it is.　　No, it isn't.
   Yes, they are.　No, they aren't.

   1　This is Amy's bed. _____　2　This is Amy's radio. _____
   3　This is Amy's desk. _____　4　These are Amy's chairs. _____
   5　These are Amy's elephants. _____　6　These are Amy's books. _____

   10

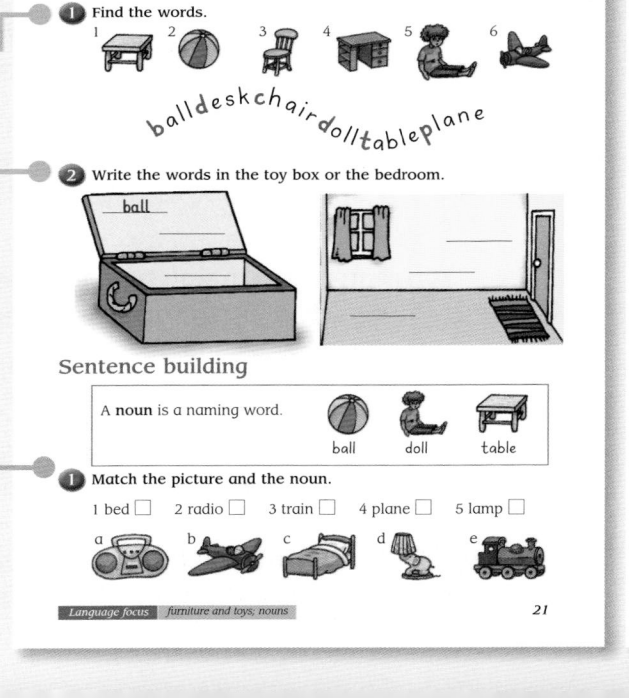

2

Working with words

1. Find the words.
   1　2　3　4　5　6

   balldeskchairdolltableplane

2. Write the words in the toy box or the bedroom.
   ball

Sentence building

   A **noun** is a naming word.
   ball　doll　table

1. Match the picture and the noun.
   1 bed ☐　2 radio ☐　3 train ☐　4 plane ☐　5 lamp ☐
   a　b　c　d　e

   Language focus　furniture and toys; nouns　21

Unit 2
Sentence building

   This is a (parrot.
   noun

1. Find the noun. Circle the noun.
   1　This is my plane.　2　Here is the house.
   3　This is a bed.　4　The boy is nine.
   5　Here is my mum.　6　This is my radio.

2. Finish the sentences. Use the nouns in the box.

   chair　ball　book　tree　doll　box

   1　This is a _____ .　2　This is a _____ .
   3　This is a _____ .　4　This is a _____ .
   5　This is a _____ .　6　This is a _____ .

   11

Lesson aim Comprehension, vocabulary and sentence building

Lesson targets Children:
- match pictures to sentences
- order lines of a known rhyme
- match words to objects
- identify and categorise words
- identify nouns in a sentence.

Key language (words) *table, chair, bed, lamp, desk, computer, radio, doll, ball, plane, train*
(structures) *This is ..., These are ...*

Materials Language Book pp20–21, Practice Book pp10–11, flashcards 20–29, word cards for toys/furniture, *This is .../These are.*

Preparation: Make word cards for flashcards 20–29 and *This is .../These are ...*

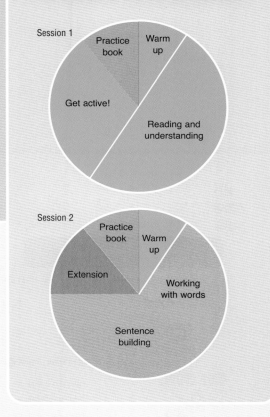

Lesson 3 time division:

Session 1
- Practice book
- Warm up
- Get active!
- Reading and understanding

Session 2
- Practice book
- Warm up
- Extension
- Working with words
- Sentence building

⬇ Lesson 3 Session 1 Warm-up

1 Say the *Toys* rhyme (LB p19). Prompt with flashcards for toys, if you wish.

⬇ Reading and understanding

6 Get active!
Stick flashcards 20–29 on the board; stick all word cards at one side.
A team 1 child names an object, e.g. **This is a bed.**

Another child from team 1 finds the word *bed* and sticks it under the flashcard. Class says **This is a bed.**

If the incorrect word is said or chosen, it is team 2's turn to name an object.

The team that names and labels the most objects correctly wins.

When all the pictures are labelled, point and ask, e.g. *Is this a TV? Are these toys?* Elicit *Yes, it is. No, it isn't. Yes, they are. No, they aren't.*

⬇ Lesson 3 Session 2 Warm-up

Class sings the *Family song* from LB p15, LCD1 track 12. Use family flashcards to prompt, if you wish. Children look at LB p18. Say *Point to Amy's/mother/father/sister.*

⬇ Sentence building

2 Show the ball flashcard. Ask *What is the name of this?* Elicit **ball**. Repeat with *doll* and *table.*

Write *ball* on the board. Stick the *ball* flashcard next to it. Point to the word *ball.* Say *This is the name of this ...*(point to the picture). Repeat with *doll* and *table.*

Point to each word. Say *It is a noun.*

Mix up the pictures. Say: *Match the picture and the noun.*

Children come forward and put the pictures by the correct words.

4 Practice Book, page 11. Demonstrate Activity 1 with a few sentences on the board before the class writes.

⬇ Extension activities

1 Stick up word cards *This is* and *These are.* Stick singular/plural flashcard objects on board.

Volunteers come forward and hold up a flashcard by the correct phrase and say sentence, e.g. **This is a plane. These are books.**

2 Repeat the matching activity from *Sentence building* with other words/flashcards.

33

Grammar

1 Lesson 4 warm-up. ⬇

2 Read speech bubbles (LB p22). Children follow.

3 Activity 1: Individuals/class reads words in the box. Ask individuals to complete sentences orally. Class repeats. Class writes.

4 Activity 2: Children complete the sentences.

5 Activity 3: Individuals say sentences. Class repeats. Children practise in pairs. Listen to some.

6 Prepare children for PB p12 by checking they understand the tasks. Children complete.

Listening

1 Read Nina's speech bubble (LB p23). Explain that class will hear characters talking about their toys.

2 🎵 Activity 1: Play LCD1 track 14a. Children listen. ⬇ Play it again. Children match.

3 Activity 2: Children point and talk about the characters in pairs.

4 🎵 Activity 3: Play LCD1 track 15. Children listen. ⬇

After listening

1 Groups say lines of the rhyme. ⬇

2 Do the matching rhyming words activity. ⬇

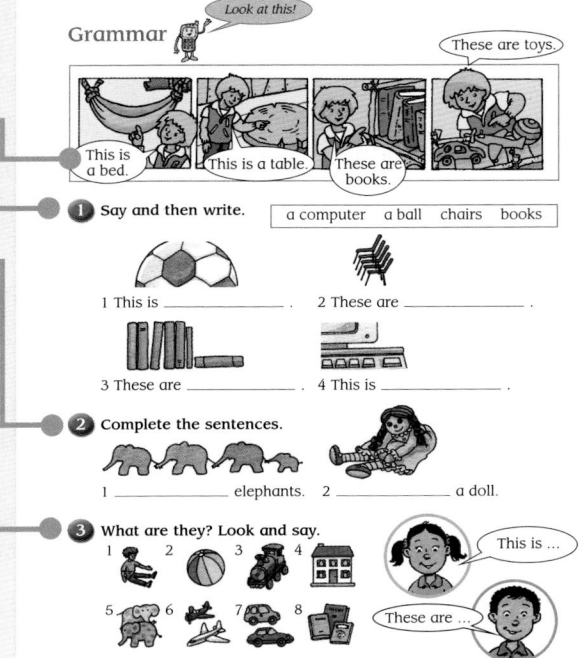

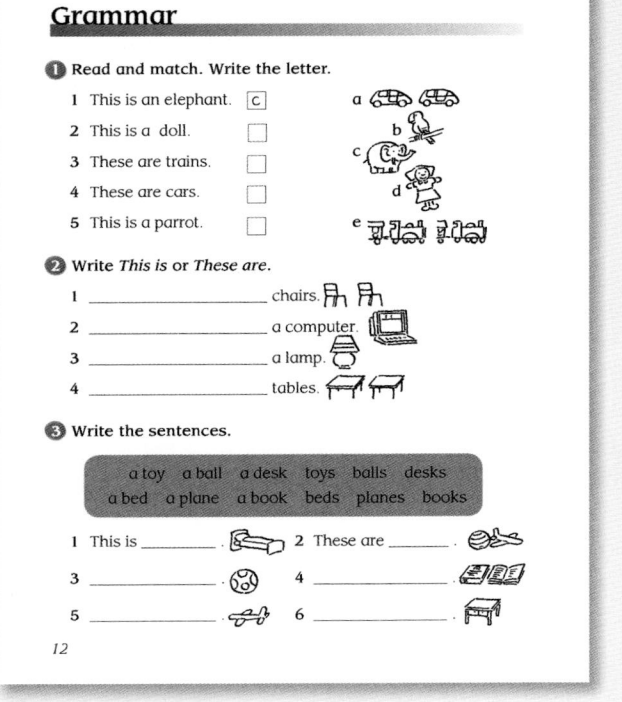

Lesson aim Grammar and listening

Lesson targets Children

- identify objects using correct singular/plural demonstrative pronouns + verb
- talk about other children and their toys/pets
- listen to children talking about their toys; identify the toys
- say and learn a short rhyme.

Key language (words) *ball, cars, computer, dolls, plane, train, cat, dog, frog, hat*
(structures) *This is ..., These are ..., This is my/his/her ... These are my/his/her ...*

Materials Language Book pp22–23, Practice Book p12, Language CD1 tracks 14a–15, flashcards 20–30 for *Warm-up*, word cards for *dog, tall, bat, tap, boy*

Preparation Listen to the CD before the lesson. Make/find word cards for matching rhyming words activity (see *After listening, 2*)

Lesson 4 time division:

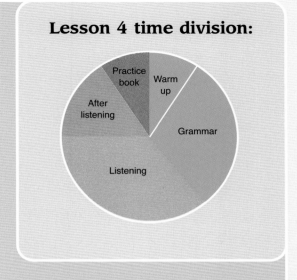

⬇ Lesson 4 Warm-up

1 Flashcard/letter matching game

Write up letters *b, d, l, r, t*.

Stick up flashcards 20–30.

A child chooses a flashcard and names it, e.g. **This is a doll.** Child places it under letter *d*. Class repeats **This is a doll.** Continue with the other cards.

⬇ Listening

2 Audioscript

1	
Sam	Hi. I am Sam. Look! These are my cars.
2	
Tilly	Hello. I am Tilly. These are my dolls.
Dolls	Hi. I am Sue. Hi. I am Kiki.
3	
Nina	Hi. I am Nina. Look at my computer. It is great!
4	
Ben	Hi. I am Ben. These are my planes.
5	
Sally	Hello. I am Sally. Look! This is my ball.
6	
Max	Hi. I am Max. This is my toy train.

4 Ask children to name the characters and animals in the pictures. Tell them to listen to the rhyme and point to the correct picture.

Play the CD twice. Encourage the children to read along with the CD the second time.

⬇ After listening

1 Divide the class into four. Let each group read a sentence of the rhyme from p23. The whole class says **and that's that!**
Choose a child from each group to stand at the front and hold the flashcard of their animal and the hat. They hold up their flashcards when their animal/object is mentioned.

2 Do a matching rhyming words activity: write *frog, ball, mat, cap, toy* on the board. Stick *dog, tall, bat, tap, boy* word cards in muddled order on the board. Volunteers match the rhyming words. Check with the class. Class reads the rhyming pairs.

35

Activity 1

1. Session 1 warm-up. ⬇
2. (LB p24) Point out pictures and words with *e*.
3. 🎧 Play rhyme twice (LCD1 track 16). Children follow in books.
4. Read rhyme.
5. Read and ask questions. ⬇
6. Read with the class.

Activity 2

1. ⬇ Children hold sounds cards. Read the sounds.
2. Close up gradually.
3. Read the word.
4. Children look, say and write.

Activity 3

1. Children say the sentences. Children write. ⬇
2. Children read the sentences and check. ⬇

Activity 4

1. Write up words. Class/individuals read. ⬇
2. Children read in pairs. Listen to pairs.
3. Children check words and tick.

Practice Book

Children complete PB p13. ⬇

Phonics games and activities

1. Play *Start the word*. ⬇
2. Play *Odd one out*. ⬇

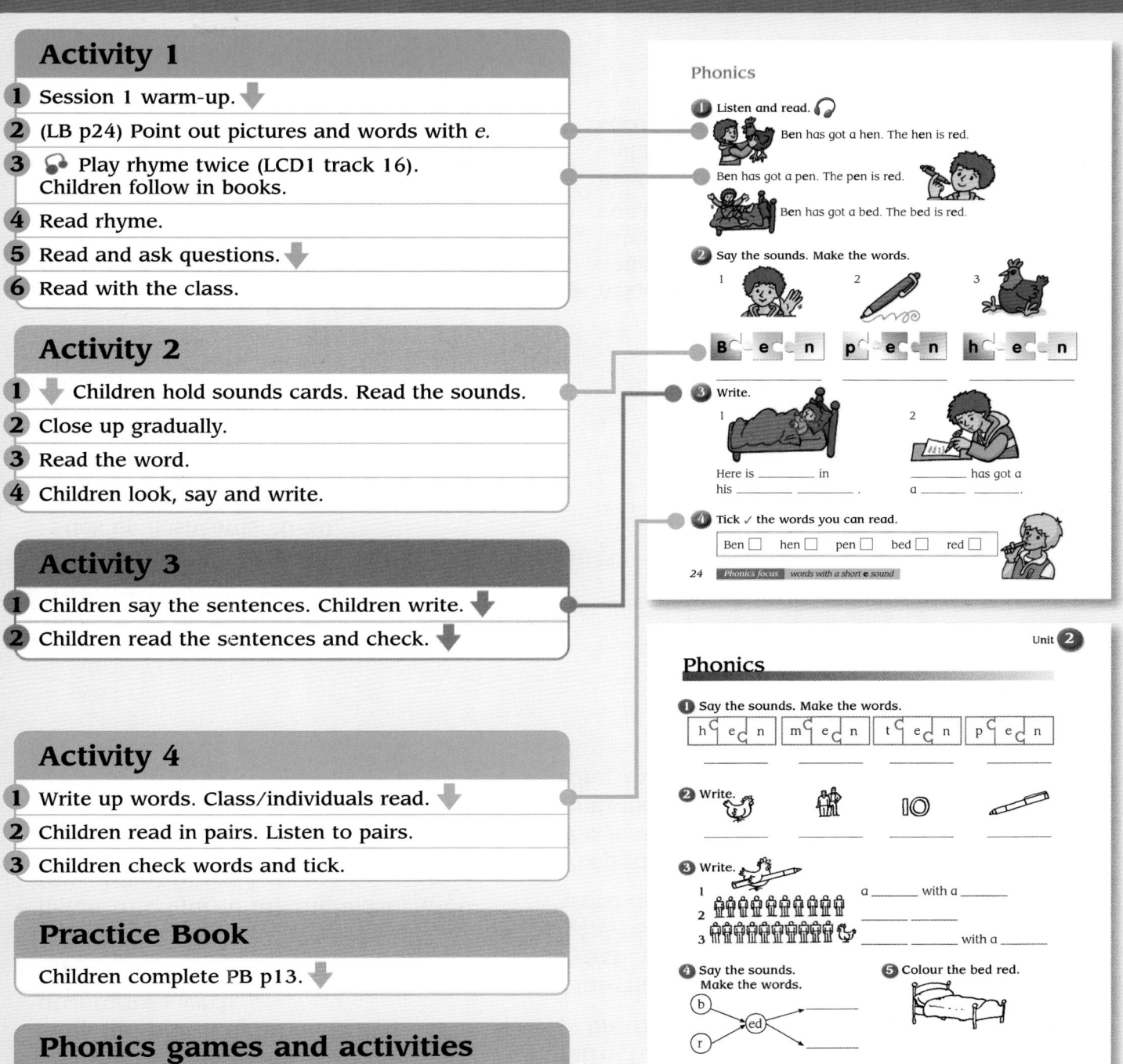

Lesson aim Phonic recognition

Lesson targets Children:

- read, pronounce and spell cvc words with *e*
- recognise and say the individual sounds that make up the cvc words
- write the words from picture prompts.

Target words *bed, Ben, hen, pen, red, men, ten*

Materials Language Book p24, Practice Book p13, Language CD1 track 16, cards for sounds, flashcards 27–28 for *Warm-up*

Preparation Listen to the CD before the lesson. Make large cards for the sounds/phonemes for *Ben, pen, hen, bed, red.* Make word cards for *hen, pen, bed, ten.* Make or find letters on cards: *h, m, p, t* (see *Phonics games, 1*).

Detailed teaching procedures
See Introduction, p10

Lesson 5 time division:

⬇ Lesson 5 Warm-up

1 Say the *Toys* rhyme from Lesson 2 (LB p19). Prompt with flashcards of toys.

⬇ Activity 1

5 Ask *What has Ben got?*
What colour is it?
Who has got a pen?
Is the pen blue?
Has Ben got a ball?
Is the bed red?

Make sure all the words in the text are understood.

⬇ Activity 2

Follow the procedure for introducing the phonemes and sounding out each word which is given in detail in the Introduction (p10).

⬇ Activity 3

1 Children look at the first picture.

Ask *Who is in the bed?* **Ben.** *What colour is the bed?* **Red.** Children look at the sentence with the gaps.

Ask/Help a child to say the whole sentence. Class repeats. Children write the words.

Do the same with the second sentence.

2 Ask children to read sentences. Write them on the board. Children check.

⬇ Activity 4

1 Write the five words on the board. Point in random order. Individuals and/or the class reads them.

⬇ Practice Book

Children complete the exercises.

Check they can sound out all the target words before they move onto Exercise 6.

⬇ Phonics games and activities

1 **Start the word**

Write up a word ending, e.g. *-en*. Stick letters *h, m, p, t* on the board.
Children put up letters to make words, e.g. *pen, hen, ten, men.*

2 **Odd one out**

Put up three words with the same ending and one different, e.g. *hen, pen, bed, ten.* Children say which is the odd one out.
Repeat this with words from Unit 1, e.g. *tap, cat, map, cap* or *mat, hat, tap, bat.*

Before writing

1. Lesson 6 warm-up.
2. Read Miss Plum's speech bubble (LB p25).
3. Children name objects.
4. Play LCD1 track 17.
5. Children colour according to the instructions.

Shared writing

1. Read Miss Plum's box (LB p25). Write the sentences on the board. Circle the capital letters and full stops.
2. Ask a child to read the sentences.
3. Elicit the other sentences. Write them on the board.
4. Continue with the other sentences.
5. Children write.

Practice Book

Writing

1. (PB p14) Children read words in box.
2. Children complete sentences.

Your writing

1. Point out Dan (PB p15). Read speech bubble. Ask *What is in Dan's room?*
2. Activity 1: Children read sentences and colour.
3. Activity 2: Children read the first sentence. They complete the others according to the picture they coloured.

After writing

Children write about something of their own.

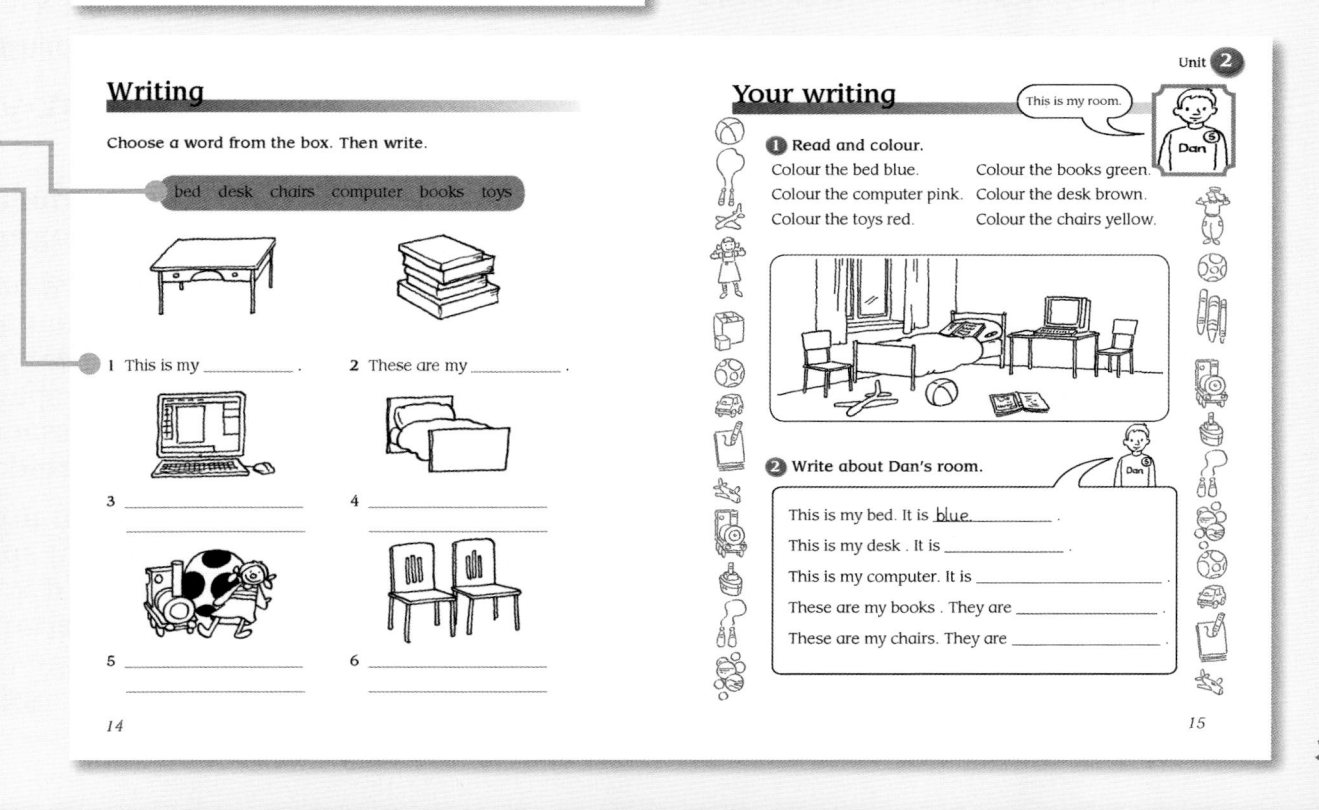

Class writing

Let's write about things in a room.

1 Listen and colour.

This is a bed. It is blue.

Don't forget!
This is a bed.
It is blue.

2 Now write.

Writing focus   simple statements with This is and It is   25

Writing

Choose a word from the box. Then write.

bed   desk   chairs   computer   books   toys

1 This is my _____ .   2 These are my _____ .

3 _____   4 _____

5 _____   6 _____

14

Your writing

This is my room.

Unit 2

1 Read and colour.
Colour the bed blue.   Colour the books green.
Colour the computer pink. Colour the desk brown.
Colour the toys red.   Colour the chairs yellow.

2 Write about Dan's room.

This is my bed. It is blue.
This is my desk . It is _____ .
This is my computer. It is _____ .
These are my books . They are _____ .
These are my chairs. They are _____ .

15

Lesson aim Writing

Lesson targets Children:

- write sentences to match picture prompts
- complete sentences from picture prompts
- write sentences about toys and bedroom furniture.

Key language (words) words for toys and bedroom furniture
(structures) *This is my ..., It is ..., These are my ..., They are ...*

Materials Language Book p25, Practice Book pp14 and 15, word cards (see *Preparation*), Language CD1 track 17

Preparation Find or write word cards for *ball, bed, book, car, cat, computer, desk, dog, doll, hat, hen, house, toys, train, TV.* Listen to the CD before the lesson.

Lesson 6 time division:

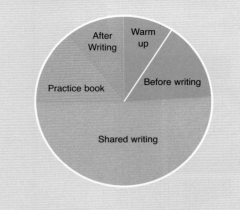

⬇ Lesson 6 Warm-up

1 Word/letter matching game

Write the letters *b, c, d, h, t* well spaced across the board.

Stick up the word cards in muddled order across the bottom of the board.

Divide the class into five groups. Each group is one of the letters on the board. A child from group *b* must find a word beginning with *b* and put it under that letter.

Then a child from the next group finds a word beginning *c* and so on.

Continue with children taking turns until all the words are placed under the correct letters. The class reads all the lists of words.

⬇ Before writing

4 Audioscript
This is a bed. It is blue.
This is a desk. It is green.
These are chairs. They are yellow.
This is a TV. It is black.
These are books. They are red.

⬇ Shared writing

3 Prompt *What is this/are these? What colour is it/are they?* if necessary.

5 If your class is confident, you may wish to rub the sentences off the board before children write. Alternatively, you could rub out the nouns and adjectives from some or all sentences, leaving the framework for children to fill in.

If your class is not confident, leave some or all sentences on the board for children to check as they write.

⬇ After writing

Children draw one or two items of their own, e.g. bed, cars, dolls, ball, books, etc. They colour and write sentences *This is my ... It is .../These are my ... They are ...*

Children read their sentences to the rest of the class.

Before listening

1. Lesson 1 warm-up.

2. Show poster 2. Ask questions. Explain the platform and telescope.

3. Show poster 3. Ask questions.

4. Point and name new objects. Children come forward; find objects in main picture; (optional) *chair*, *telescope*.

5. Show flashcards 31–35 and name new objects. Class repeats.

Shared listening

1. Play FCD track 6. Point to characters when they speak.

2. Ask about the hole and the gold stars.

3. Ask *Who? What?* questions.

4. Play the CD and point to characters again.

Dialogue practice

1. Say new object words. Children point in books (FB pp12–13). Point on poster for children to check.

2. Show flashcards 31–35. Children name.

3. Children close books. Play FCD track 7 and show character flashcards. Class repeats lines in pauses.

4. Groups say lines by character.

5. (optional) Individuals act dialogue.

6. Play FCD track 6 again. Children follow text or point to main picture.

After listening

1. Show flashcards. Ask questions.

2. Teach the *Star chant*.

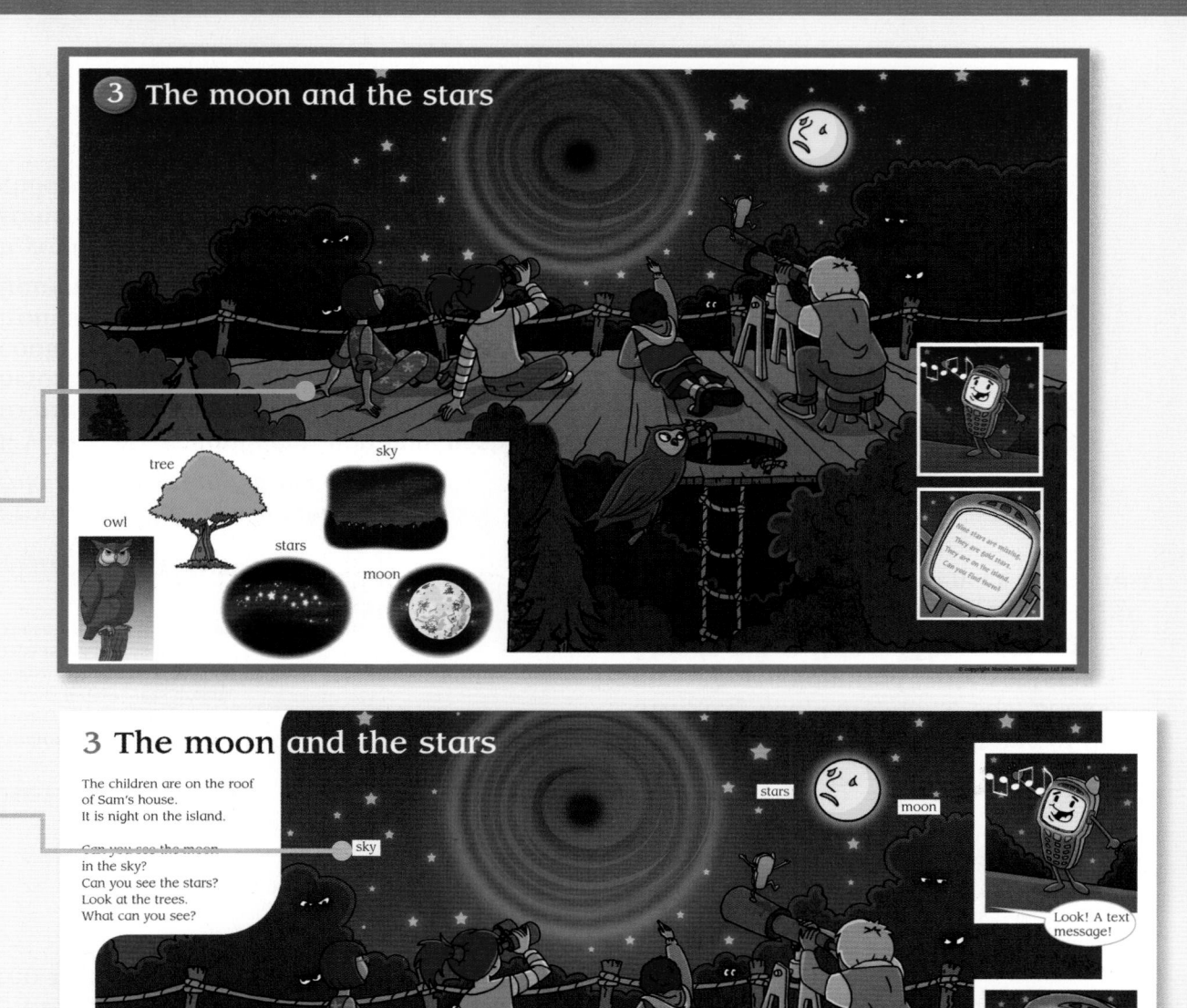

3 The moon and the stars

tree

sky

owl

stars

moon

3 The moon and the stars

The children are on the roof of Sam's house. It is night on the island.

Can you see the moon in the sky? Can you see the stars? Look at the trees. What can you see?

stars

moon

sky

Look! A text message!

Nine stars are missing. They are gold stars. They are on the island. Can you find them?

Look at the sky!
Look at the stars!
Can you see the moon, Nina?
Yes, I can.

Listen!
Tu-whoo! Tu-whoo!
I can hear an owl.
Can you see it?
No, I can't.

I can hear the wind.
What can you see, Sam?
I can see ... a big hole in the sky!
What? A hole in the sky? Where?
Up there! Look!
Oh! Where are the stars?

owl

tree

Star light, star bright,
Nine stars are missing tonight.

12 I can see ...   Can you see ... ?   Yes, I can.   No, I can't.

13

40

Lesson aim Fluency

Lesson targets Children:

- listen for pronunciation and intonation
- repeat dialogue accurately
- act out dialogue with expression
- talk about things they can see and hear at night.

Key language (words) *moon, owl, sky, stars, tree*
(structures) *I can see ..., Can you see ...? Yes, I can. No, I can't.*

Words for understanding *children, night, trees, hole, telescope, wind; see, hear, find; missing, gold; tonight, above*

Materials Posters 2 and 3, Fluency Book pp12–13, Fluency CD tracks 6–7, flashcards 2–6, 31–35

Preparation Listen to the CD before the lesson.

Detailed teaching procedures
See Introduction, p8

Lesson 1 time division:

⬇ Lesson 1 Warm-up

1 Say the *I am Sam!* chant from Unit 2, Lesson 1 (TG p29).

⬇ Before listening

2 Poster 2: Ask *Whose house is this? Who is this?* (point to characters)

(optional) Revise/point to different objects: *Is this/Are these Sam's ...?*

Point to house in small picture: *Is this Sam's house?*
Point to platform above: *This is above Sam's house.*
Point to telescope: *This is Sam's telescope.*

3 Poster 3: Ask *Are the children in Sam's house?*
Are they above Sam's house?
Is this Sam's telescope?
Are these trees?
Is it day? Is it night?

⬇ Shared listening

2 Ask *Can you see the hole?* (child points on poster)
Where is it? **It is in the sky.**
Are the gold stars in the sky? **No, they aren't.**
Where are the gold stars? **They are on the island.**
How many gold stars are missing? **Nine.**

3 Ask *Who can see the moon?*
What can Tilly hear?
What can Nina hear?
Can Tilly see the owl?
Who can see the hole?

⬇ After listening

1 Show cards to elicit affirmative and negative replies:

Can you see a tree? Can you hear an owl?
Yes, I can./No, I can't.
What can you see? **I can see a ...**
What can you hear? **I can hear a ...**

41

Before reading

1 Lesson 2 warm-up. ⬇

2 📖 Revise words with flashcards 31–35.

3 Children open books (LB pp26–27). Ask questions. ⬇

Shared reading

1 🎧 Play LCD1 track 18. Children follow text in book.

2 Read a verse at a time. Ask questions. ⬇

3 Read with the class.

unit 3

Can the moon see me?

I can see the moon
Shining in the sea.
I can see the moon
But can the moon see me?

Oh, shining moon
In shining sea,
Oh, Mr Moon,
Please look at me!

I can hear an owl
Tu-whooing in a tree.
I can hear an owl
But can the owl hear me?

Tu-whit, tu-whoo,
Tu-whoo, tu-whee.
I hear the owl.
Can it hear me?

Star light, Star bright,
First star I see tonight.
I wish I may, I wish I might
Have the wish I wish tonight.

26 Parents: see extra material on page 166

27

Reading practice

1 Give reading practice. Use some or all of the following:

• Children read again as a class.

• Groups read different sections.

• Individuals read different sections.

2 🎧 Class listens again to LCD1 track 18 and follows in LB.

After reading

1 📖 Do the *What can you see/hear?* activity. ⬇

2 Teach the rhyme (LB p27).

Lesson aim Reading

Lesson targets Children:

- follow a text read out to them
- listen for pronunciation and intonation
- read the text aloud with accurate pronunciation and intonation
- understand the sense of the text as a whole
- answer simple comprehension questions.

Key language (words) *moon, owl, sea, star*
(structures) *I can see ..., I can hear ...*

Words for understanding *shining, tu-whooing, tu-whit, tu-whoo, tu-whee, wish, bright, first, light, may, might*

Materials Language Book pp26–27, Language CD1 track 18, flashcards 31–35, flashcards for *After reading*, word cards for *TV, sky, chair, owl, bed, computer, parrot, table, book, helicopter, island, phone*, number cards 1–10 for *Warm-up*.

Preparation Listen to the CD before the lesson. Make word cards as necessary.

Detailed teaching procedures
See Introduction, pp8-9

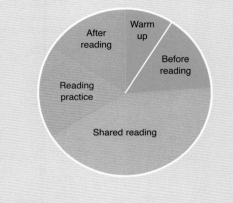

Lesson 2 time division:

After reading · Warm up · Before reading · Reading practice · Shared reading

↓ Lesson 2 Warm-up

① Line-up numbers game

Bring five children forward. Give out number cards 1–5 in any order. Class counts to five. Children must line up in order. Repeat with 6–10.

↓ Before reading

③ Ask *Is it day or night? What can you see? Where is the moon? How many stars? What colour are they?*

↓ Shared reading

② Ask (verse 1) *What can the boy see? Can the moon see the boy?*
(verse 2) *Can the moon look at the boy?*
(verse 3) *What can the boy hear? Can the owl hear the boy?* (verse 4) *What does the owl say?*

(star rhyme) *What can he see? What does he want?*
Teach *I don't know* as necessary.

↓ After reading

① What can you see/hear?

On one side of the board stick up flashcards 31–35.

Stick word cards in muddled order under all the pictures.

Children take turns to read word cards and match flashcards. Class reads all the word cards.

On the other side of the board write up two headings *We can see ... We can hear ...*

Point to e.g. table. Ask a child *Can you see a table?* Elicit **Yes, I can.** Ask *Can you hear a table?* Elicit **No, I can't.** Put the word card for table under the *We can see*

... heading. Say *We can see a table.* Class repeats.

Say *We can't hear a table.* Class repeats. Continue with other objects asking *Can you see ...?/hear ...?* Place them under the correct heading.

When all the word cards are placed use the sentence beginnings and word cards to help the class read sentences, e.g. **We can see a chair. We can hear a TV.** Ask *Can you see a TV?* **Yes, we can.** *Can you hear a book?* **No, we can't.**

If you wish, ask *What can you see/hear?* Let children make statements. Ask questions as necessary.

Reading and understanding

1. Session 1 warm-up.
2. Re-read *I can see the moon* (LB p26).
3. Activity 1 (LB p28): Children look at the pictures. Read the questions. Elicit answers.
4. Activity 2: Children find and circle rhyming words.
5. Activity 3: Children look and talk in pairs. Hear some of them.
6. 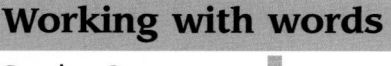 Play the *Get active!* game. Use object flashcards of your choice.
7. Prepare children for PB p16 by checking they understand the tasks. Children complete.

Working with words

1. Session 2 warm-up.
2. Activity 1 (LB p29): Children trace words. Ask *Can you hear/see ...?*

Sentence building

1. Read sentence. Show flashcards 32, 57, 97. Name objects. Class repeats. Children read in their books (LB p29).
2. Repeat with second sentence. Show flashcards 33, 34, 35.
3. Activity 1: Children answer orally.
4. Activity 2: Children write.
5. Prepare children for PB p17 by checking they understand the tasks. Children complete.

Extension activities

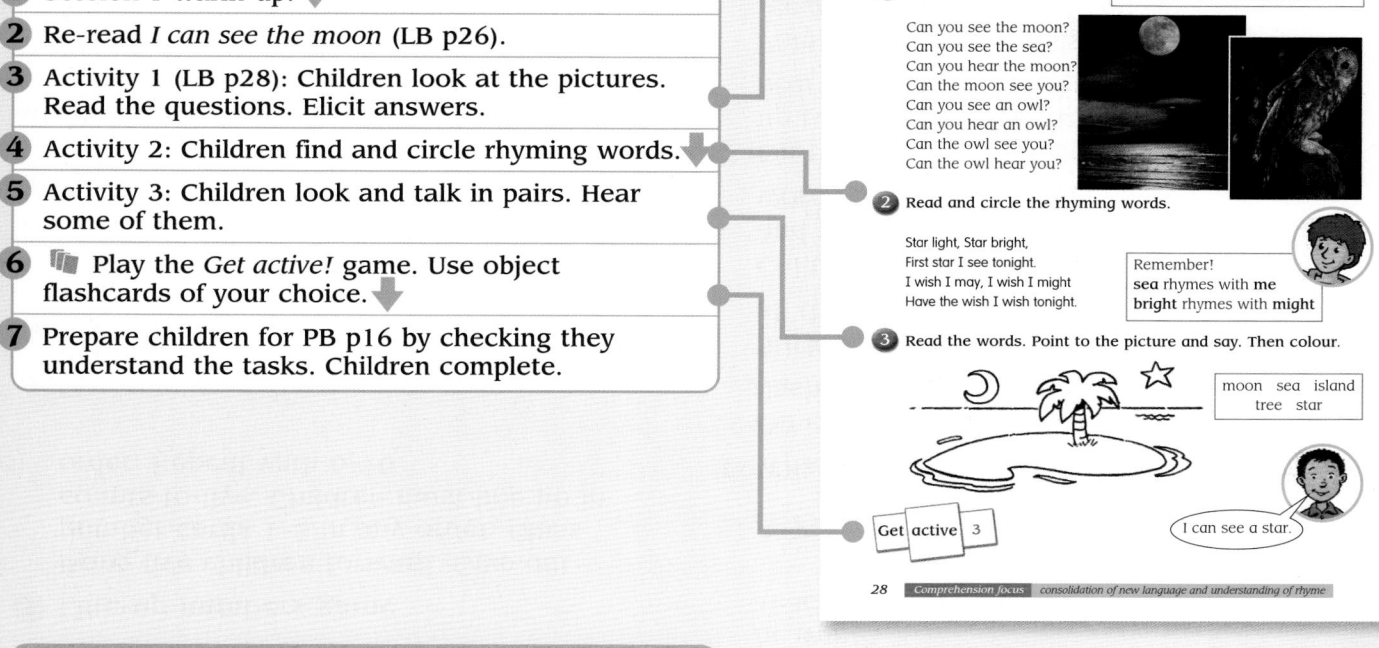

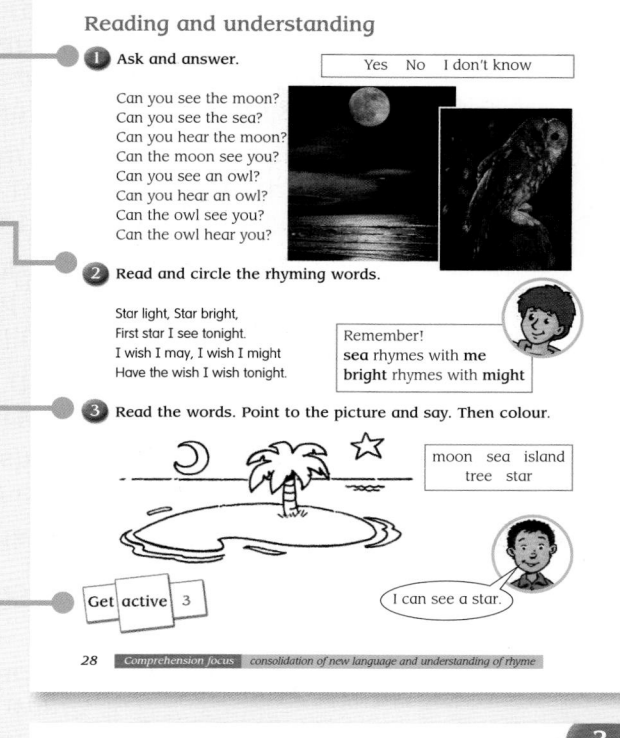

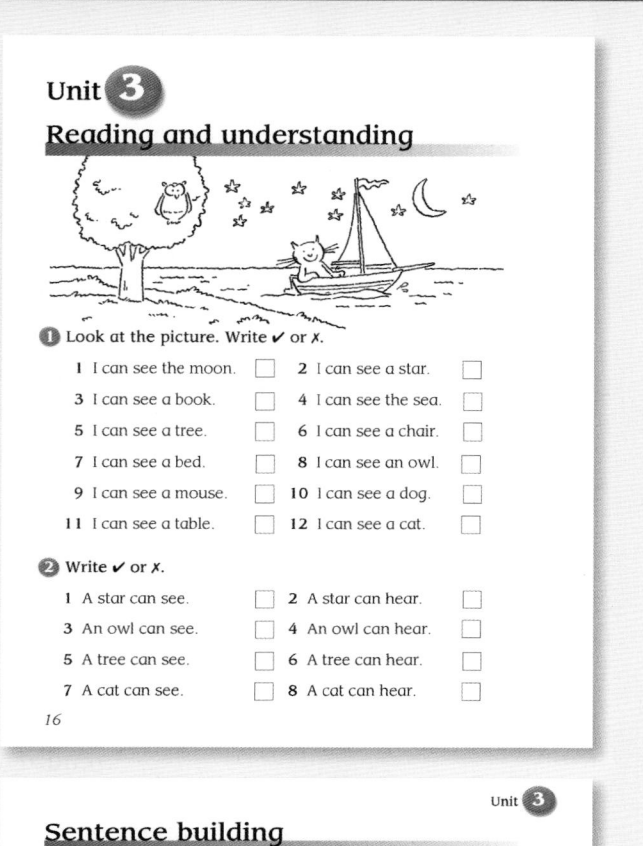

Lesson aim Comprehension, vocabulary and sentence building

Lesson targets Children:
- answer simple comprehension questions
- identify rhyming words
- talk about things they can see
- practise writing key words
- use correct indefinite article for nouns with initial vowels.

Key language (words) *moon, star, tree, owl, sky*
(structures) *Can you see a/an ...? Can you hear a/an ...?*

Words for understanding *apple, egg, ice cream, orange, umbrella*

Materials Language Book pp28–29, Practice Book pp16–17, flashcards for *Warm-up, Sentence building, Get active!* and *Extension activity*, letter cards for *Warm-up*. Bring in an orange and an apple or draw simple pictures of each on A4 paper for *Sentence building*.

Preparation Make letter cards (*a, a, B, b, d, e, e, h, m, n, S, t*) for *Warm-up*.

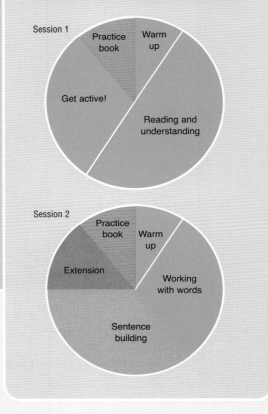

Lesson 3 time division:

Session 1

Session 2

Lesson 3 Session 1 Warm-up

1 Write the *Star light* rhyme (LBp27) on the board. With the class read and say the words. Repeat two or three times until class says it confidently alone.

Reading and understanding

4 Activity 2: Write up the rhyme. Class reads. Children come forward and circle words. Check with class.

Class reads all the rhyming words. Children circle in their books.

Teach the rhyme if you have not already done so.

6 Get active!
Class in two or more teams.
Put six flashcards on the board. Class looks at them. Ask *What can you see?* to practise *I can see a ...*

Take the flashcards down. Shuffle them face down. Remove one. Put the rest back up.
Ask *What can't you see?* The child who first notices what is missing says *I can't see a...* and wins a point.
To make it more difficult, put up more cards and remove more than one.

Lesson 3 Session 2 Warm-up

Play a *Muddled letters* game. Put up flashcards 22, 35, 159. Put letter cards in groups on the board.

Child 1 names an object/character. Child 2 finds the first letter of the word and puts it under the flashcard. Child 3 finds the second, etc. Class reads the word. Repeat with other words.

Sentence building

1 Read the first sentence in the box to the class. Hold up flashcards or objects (see *Materials*). Say *an apple, an egg*, etc. Class repeats.
Children look in books and read the words. Hold up flashcards; ask *What can you see?*

Extension activities

It's a/an ...
Class in two or more teams. Show object flashcards of your choice. The first child to say a correct sentence *It's a/an ...* wins a point.

45

Grammar

1. Lesson 4 warm-up.

2. Show poster 3. Ask questions.

3. Children look at the picture (LB p30). Ask questions. Read the speech bubbles. Children follow. Pairs of children read.

4. Activity 1: Children speak in pairs. Hear some of them.

5. Activity 2: Children complete sentences orally. Class repeats. Children write.

6. Activity 3: Children write answers.

7. Prepare children for PB p18 by checking they understand the tasks. Children complete.

Listening

1. Read Nina's speech bubble (LB p31).

2. Activity 1: Play LCD1 track 19. Children listen.

3. Activity 2: Play LCD1 track 20. Children listen and circle the things they hear.

4. Activity 3: Play LCD1 track 21. Children speak in pauses.

5. Activity 4: Play LCD1 track 22. Children listen and sing.

After listening

Teach the song.

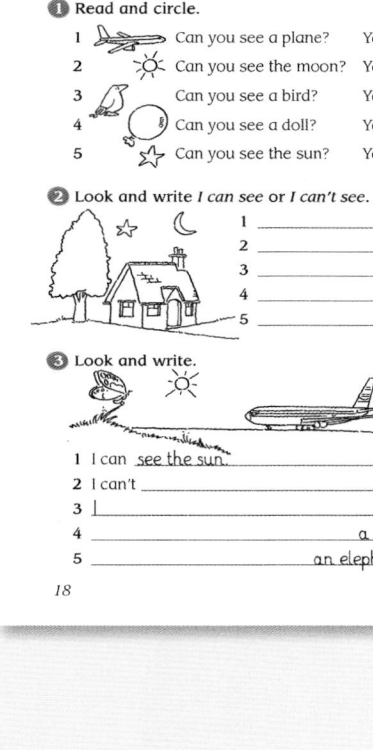

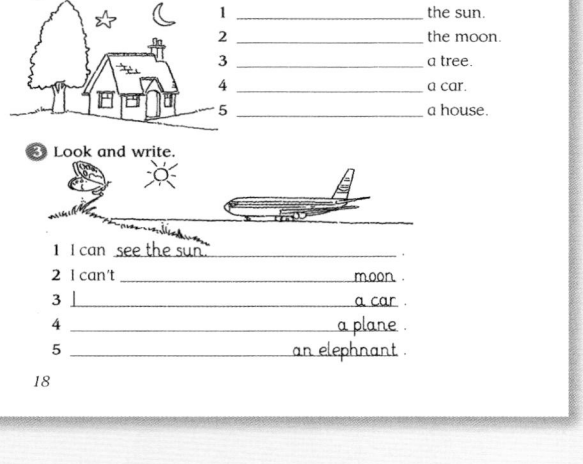

Lesson aim Grammar and listening

Lesson targets Children:

- talk in pairs about what they can and can't see
- practise reading and writing what they can and can't see
- listen to sounds and identify what they can and can't hear
- sing and learn a short song.

Key language (words) words from Lessons 1 and 2
(structures) *Can you see a/an ..., I can/can't see a/an ...*

Materials Language Book pp30–31, Practice Book p18, Language CD1 tracks 19–22, poster 3

Preparation Listen to the CD before the lesson.

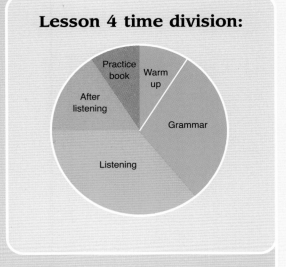

Lesson 4 time division:

⬇ Lesson 4 Warm-up

Say the *Star chant*. Add lines from the rhyme in Lesson 2.

Star chant

Star light, star bright,
Nine stars are missing tonight.
I wish I may, I wish I might
Find the nine stars missing tonight.

⬇ Grammar

2 Ask *Is it day or night?*
Can you see the moon?
Can you see the sun?
Can you see an owl?
Can you see a kite?

3 Ask *Is it day or night?*
Can you see Sam?
Can you see Nina?
Who can you see?

⬇ Listening

3 **Audioscript**
Voice:　　Listen! What can you hear?
　　　　　[owl]
　　　　　[train]
　　　　　[cat]
　　　　　[dog]
　　　　　[boy – whistling for dog: 'Come here, Fido!']
　　　　　[car – drives up, stops, door slams]

4 If you wish, stop the tape and ask individuals *What can you hear?* after each sound.

5 Play track 22 twice. The first time children listen and follow. The second time they join in.

⬇ After listening

Teach the song. Write the words on the board. Class sings.

Rub out a significant word from each line. Class sings and fills in the missing words.

Continue until all the words are rubbed out. Children sing the whole song from memory.

47

Activity 1

1. Lesson 5 warm-up.
2. (LB p32) Point out pictures and words with *i*.
3. Play rhyme twice (LCD1 track 23). Children follow in books.
4. Read rhyme.
5. Read each line and ask questions.
6. Read with the class.

Activity 2

1. Children hold sounds cards. Read the sounds.
2. Close up gradually.
3. Read the word.
4. Children look, say and write.

Activity 3

Children say the word and sentence. Children write.

Activity 4

1. Write up words. Class/individuals read.
2. Children read in pairs. Listen to pairs.
3. Children check words and tick.

Practice Book

Children complete PB p19.

Phonics games and activities

1. Children match rhyming words.
2. Play *Alphabetical order*.

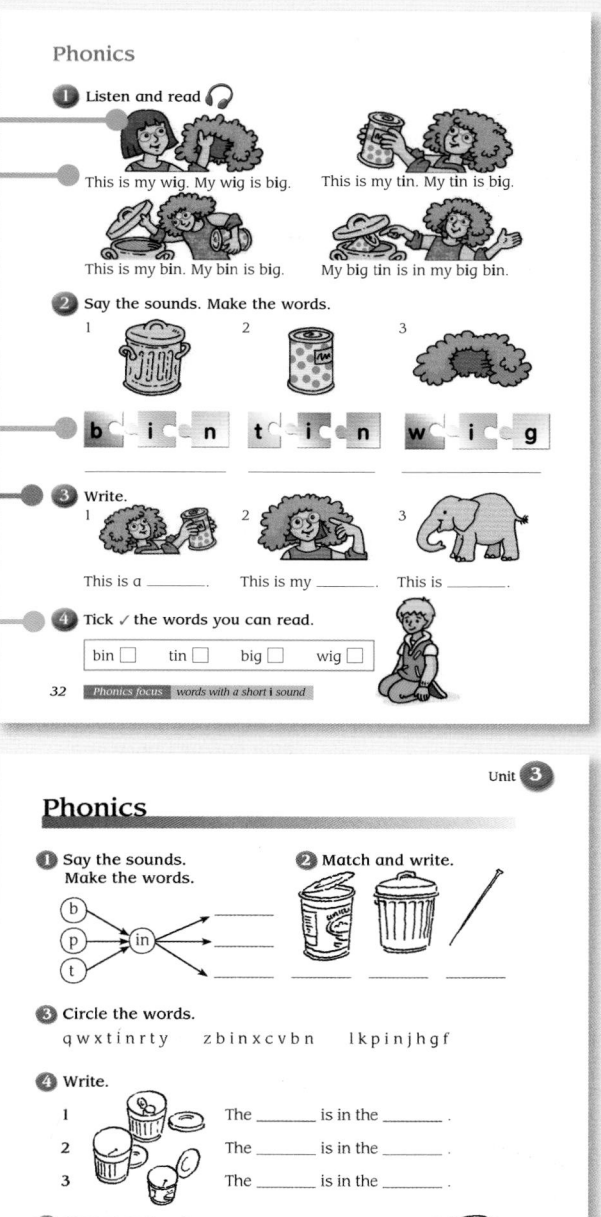

Lesson aim Phonic recognition

Lesson targets Children:

- read, pronounce and spell cvc words with the short *i*
- recognise and say the individual sounds that make up the cvc words
- write the words from picture prompts
- read and write sentences using the key words.

Target words *big, dig, wig, bin, pin, tin*

Materials Language Book p32, Practice Book p19, Language CD1 track 23, cards for sounds, word cards and letter cards for *Phonics games and activities*.

Preparation Listen to the CD before the lesson. Make large cards for the sounds/phonemes for the target words. Make word cards for the rhyming words game. Find or make letter cards a–f.

Detailed teaching procedures See Introduction, p10

Lesson 5 time division:

⬇ Lesson 5 Warm-up

1 Class sings *Twinkle, twinkle little star* (LB p31) all together once.

Make four groups. Give each group one of the first four lines. Children sing the last two lines together.

⬇ Activity 1

5 Ask *Where is Tilly's wig?*
Is it small?
Is the tin big?
Is Tilly in the bin? Where is she?
Where is her tin?

Make sure all the words in the text are understood.

⬇ Activity 2

Follow the procedure for introducing the phonemes and sounding out each word which is given in detail in the Introduction (TG p10).

⬇ Activity 3

Children look at the picture and read the words. Ask/Help a child to say the whole sentence. Class repeats.

Children write the word.

Do the same with the other sentences.

⬇ Activity 4

1 Write the six words on the board. Point in random order. Individuals and/or the class reads them.

⬇ Practice Book

Children complete the six exercises.

Check children can sound out all six target words before they move on to Exercise 6.

⬇ Phonics games and activities

1 Children match rhyming words. Choose six rhyming pairs from phonics Units 1–3. Put six word cards on the board (one from each pair). Put the rhyming words in any order below. Children pair them up. Class reads the rhyming pairs.

2 **Alphabetical order**

Give out letter cards a–f. Class says the letters in order. Children with cards get into alphabetical order.

49

Before writing

1. Lesson 6 warm-up.
2. Read Miss Plum's speech bubble (LB p33).
3. Activity 1: Children read the words, find the objects in the large picture and colour them.

Shared writing

1. Activity 2: Ask individuals to tell you what they can see in any order. Elicit, *e.g.* **I can see a dog.**
2. Write sentences on the board. Class reads each sentence. If your class is confident, rub sentences off.
3. Children write what they can see. Sentences can be in any order.

Practice Book

Writing

(PB p20) Children read, join dots and write words. Ask questions.

Your writing

Children look at the picture (PB p21) and write sentences.

After writing

Do the *I can see ...* chain game.

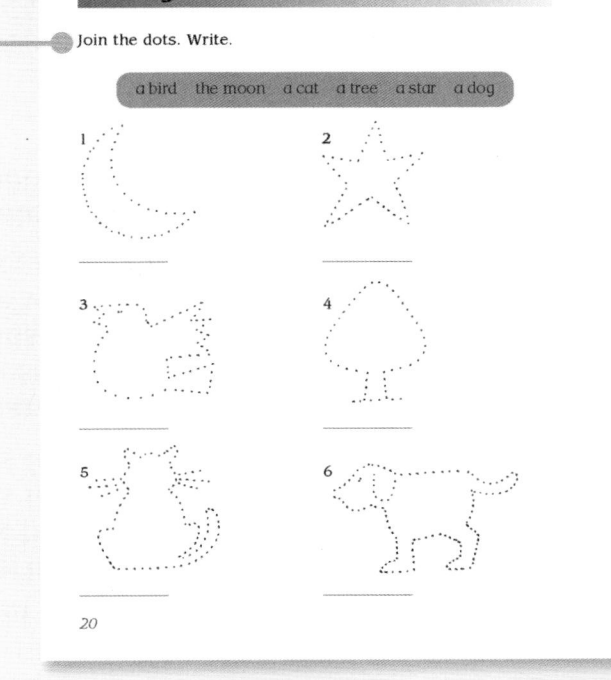

Lesson aim Writing

Lesson targets Children:

- write sentences about what they can see in a picture
- match words to pictures
- complete and write sentences about a picture.

Key language (words) nouns from Units 1–3
(structures) *I can see a ...*

Materials Language Book p33, Practice Book pp20–21

Lesson 6 time division:

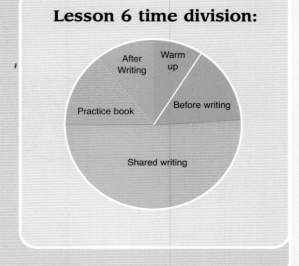

⬇ Lesson 6 Warm-up

1 Play *I can see a/an ...* as a flashcard game in two teams (see Extension, p45).

⬇ Before writing

3 Ask individuals to read the words below the small pictures.

Class reads the words.

Tell children to find the same objects in the picture below and colour them.

As they work, go round and ask children what they can see.

⬇ Practice Book

Writing

Individuals read words in the box. Class reads all the words in the box.

Children join dots.

Ask about each picture: *Look at number 1. What can you see?* Elicit answers. Children label each picture.

Your writing

Children look at the picture. Ask *What can you see?* Elicit statements.

Ask a child to read the first sentence below the picture. Class reads.

Ask a child to read and complete the second sentence. Write it on the board. Class reads.

Continue with the next two sentences. Ask individuals to suggest complete sentences for the final two. Write them on the board. Class reads. Rub off the sentences before children write.

⬇ After writing

I can see ...

Play this chaining activity round the class. Child 1 says, e.g. *I can see a tree.*

Child 2 repeats the sentence and adds another object, e.g. *I can see a tree and a ball.*

Child 3 says the first two items and adds a third, e.g. *I can see a tree, a ball and a computer.*

Children continue to repeat and add items until somebody forgets what the items are or cannot think of one to add. Start again.

If children find it hard to think of items, put flashcards up on the board in any order to give them ideas.

51

Revision 1

You can do it!

1. Look at the pictures. What can you see?

2. Listen and read.

3. Read and say.
Look at picture 1:
What can Sam hear?
Can he see it?

Look at picture 2:
Where is Sam's mobile?
Can Nina see it?
Can she hear it?

Look at pictures 3 and 4:
Can you see Sam's mobile?
What can you see?

Look at picture 5:
Is this Sam's mobile?

1 The children are in Sam's tree house.

2 Ben can hear the mobile. It is in a big box.

4. Listen, point and say which picture.

5. Finish the story.
Look at picture 6.
His name is Mobi.
What is her name?

6. Act out the story.

7. Listen and say the chant.

This is a cat.
This is a hat.
This is a fat cat in a hat.
Miaow.

This is a hen.
This is a nest.
This is a red hen in a nest.
Cluck, cluck.

Lesson aim Revision

Lesson targets Children:

- practise fluency and listening activities, including phonemes *a*, *e* and *i*
- practise language and structures from Units 1–3 through a story, games and writing.

Key language *Hello. What's your name? My name's ... How old are you? I'm ...*

This is ... These are ... Is this your ...? I can see/hear ... Can you see/hear ...? Yes, I can. No, I can't.

Words for understanding *camera, mobile, sunglasses*

Materials Language Book pp34–35, Language Book CD1 tracks 24–26, Practice Book pp22–25, ten flashcards of singular/plural items, number cards

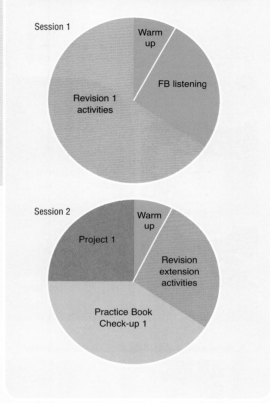

Revision 1 time division:

Session 1 — Warm up, FB listening, Revision 1 activities

Session 2 — Warm up, Revision extension activities, Practice Book Check-up 1, Project 1

Sessions 1 and 2 Warm-ups

Sing favourite songs from Units 1–3.

Listening revision

7 Play Units 1–3 of the Fluency Book (FCD tracks 2–7). Children look in their books and listen. Children close books and repeat in the pauses in the dialogue section.

Revision 1

1 (LB p34) Activity 1: Children say who and what they can see.

2 Activity 2: Play LCD1 track 24. Children listen and follow.

3 Activity 3: Read or let children read out the questions. Elicit answers. Re-read each frame if necessary.

4 (LB p35) Activity 4: Play LCD1 track 25 twice. Children listen and point then name the picture: *It's picture 3.*

Audioscript

Voice	Listen, point and say which picture.
Sam	No. This is my camera.
Tilly	Yes, I can hear it.
Sam	It's my mobile.

Ben	Is this your mobile?
Sam	No. These are my sunglasses.
Tilly	Listen. What is it?
Sam	Listen. It's in this box.

5 Activity 5: Children recall the dialogue and fill gaps.

6 Activity 6: Individuals, groups or the class read narrative and bubbles. Individuals act the story.

7 Activity 7: Play the chant twice (LCD1 track 26). Children listen then join in.

Revision extension activities

1 Number/flashcard match
Put flashcards on the board. Number them.
Put number cards face down on your desk.
Team 1 child picks a number card, shows it only to team 1 who say the number.
Team 2 child points to the correct flashcard and says *This is .../These are ...* If correct, Team 2 repeats.
Change several cards every few turns.

2 Can you see/hear? Show a card, and ask the question. Class answers *Yes/No, we can/can't.*

3 Use the phonic rhyme for reading practice. Teach it, if you wish.

Practice Book

1 Children complete *Check-up 1* (PB pp22–23) as preparation for a test or for homework.

2 Children complete *Move on with Mobi 1* (PB pp24–25). These pages give further revision for homework or class work.

Project 1: Mobi puppet
(See pages 244.)

Before listening

1. Lesson 1 warm-up.
2. Show poster 4. Read the title. Ask questions.
3. Point and name new objects. Children come forward; find in main poster.
4. Show flashcards 16, 38–41 and name new objects. Class repeats.
5. Ask about Sam's and the children's own or school gardens.

Shared listening

1. Play FCD track 8. Point to characters when they speak.
2. Ask about the first gold star.
3. Ask *Who? What?* questions.
4. Play FCD track 8 again and point to characters.

Dialogue practice

1. Say new words. Children point in books (FB pp14–15). Point on poster for children to check.
2. Show flashcards 16, 38–41. Children name.
3. Children close books. Play FCD track 9 and show character flashcards. Class repeats lines in pauses.
4. Groups say lines by character.
5. Individuals act dialogue.
6. Play FCD track 8 again. Children follow text and point to main picture.

After listening

1. Show flashcards 16, 38–41. Ask questions.
2. Make a star poster.
3. Children put the first sticker star in the correct place on FB pp46–47.

4 Sam's garden

snake · butterfly · monkey · flower · bird

4 Sam's garden

It is morning. This is the garden around Sam's tree house.
What can you see in the garden?
Can you see flowers and trees?
Can you see animals and birds?
The children are in the garden.
Can they find the gold stars there?

monkey · snake · bird · flowers · butterfly

What's this?
It's a flower. Be careful!
A star! Look, a gold star!
Hooray!

Look! This is my garden!
Ooooooooo! What's this?
It's a bird.
Wow! What's this, Sam? An elephant?
No! It's a tree, silly!
Oh! What are these, Sam?
They're flowers.

Look! What are these?
Careful! They're snakes!
Help!
Hey! What's that?
It's me!
Oh! It's Mobi!

Star light, star bright,
Eight stars are missing tonight.

The children are very happy.
They have got one gold star.
Can they find eight more stars?
Where are the stars?

14 ▮ What is this? It is a … What are these? They are …

15

54

Lesson aim Fluency

Lesson targets Children

- listen for pronunciation and intonation
- repeat dialogue accurately
- act out dialogue with expression
- talk about things in a garden.

Key language (words) *bird, butterfly, flowers, monkey, snake, tree* (structures) *What is this? It is a ..., What are these? They are ...*

Words for understanding *animals, elephant, happy, morning, Help! Hey! Hooray!*

Materials Poster 4, Fluency Book pp14–15, Fluency CD tracks 8–9, flashcards 2–6, 16, 38–41, flashcards of your choice for *Warm-up*

Preparation Listen to the CD before the lesson. Make a star poster.

Lesson 1 time division:

⬇ Lesson 1 Warm-up

1 Choose ten or more flashcards. Show a card. Practise question and answer with individuals around the class:

Teacher:	*What can you see, Dina?*
Dina:	**I can see a chair.**
Teacher:	*Can you see a chair, Karim?*
Karim:	**Yes, I can.**
Teacher:	*Can you see a table, Sara?*
Sara:	**No, I can't.**

⬇ Before listening

2 Ask *Can you see ...(name of character)?*
Child comes forward and points.
Ask the class *Who is this?* **It is ... (name of character).**
Can you see trees? How many trees? Count with the class.

5 Ask *What is in Sam's garden?*
Have you got a garden?
What is in your garden?
What is in the school garden?

⬇ Shared listening

2 Ask *Is the gold star in the garden?*
Is it in a tree?
Is it in a flower?
Who has got the gold star?

3 Ask *Can Nina see a bird?*
Who can see a tree?
What can Tilly see?
What can Sam hear?
Where is Mobi?
Are the children happy?

⬇ Dialogue practice

5 Children should now be used to dialogue practice. Encourage individuals to act out the dialogue. Each child holds the flashcard of their character. If you wish, they can say the lines from their places. Encourage them to speak with good expression, as they heard on the tape.

⬇ After listening

1 Ask *What is this? What are these? In Sam's/your garden, can you see ...?/hear ...?*

2 Star poster

Before the class, put up a large sheet of dark blue or black paper. Make a large star of yellow or gold paper. Stick it on the poster. Put number 1 in the middle of it, or beside it. Make (e.g.) a pink flower to remind children where the first star came from.

During the class, stick the flower beside the star. Do the same every time the characters find a star. Decide with the class what to put with each star to show where it was found.

This poster project can be expanded to one poster for each star, e.g. for Unit 3, children make flowers, birds, etc. for the poster and add labels or sentences, e.g. *These are flowers.* For Unit 6, children make a rock pool with shells, fish, etc.

55

Before reading

1. Lesson 2 warm-up. ⬇
2. 📖 Teach new words with flashcards 38–39, 41–42, 44, 159.
3. Children open books (LB pp36–37). Ask questions. ⬇
4. Read the title. Explain *secret*.

Shared reading

1. 🎧 Play LCD1 track 27. Children follow text in book.
2. Read line by line. Ask questions. ⬇
3. Read with the class. ●

unit 4

My secret garden

This is my garden.
Here is the key.
Open the door,
And what can we see?

purple flowers on the wall

red apples on a tree

a nest with three small blue eggs

a beautiful yellow butterfly

an orange goldfish in a pond

a long brown snake in the tall grass

a green frog on a rock

a big black beetle

36   Parents: see extra material on page 166

37

Reading practice

1. Give reading practice. Use some or all of the following:
   - Children read again as a class.
   - Groups read different sections.
   - Individuals read different sections.
2. 🎧 Class listens again to LCD1 track 27 and follows in LB.

After reading

1. Play *Guess the object*. ⬇

Lesson aim Reading

Lesson targets Children:

- follow a text read out to them
- listen for pronunciation and intonation
- read the text aloud with accurate pronunciation and intonation
- learn and understand new vocabulary items
- understand the sense of the text as a whole
- answer simple comprehension questions.

Key language (words) *beetle, egg, fish, frog, grass, mouse, pond, rock, wall, beautiful, small, long*
(structures) *What is this? It's a ..., What are these? They're ...*

Words for understanding *bee, spider, worm, secret*

Materials Language Book pp36–37, Language CD1 track 27, flashcards 38–39, 41–42, 44, 159, flashcards for *Guess the object*

Preparation Listen to the CD before the lesson.

Lesson 2 Time division:

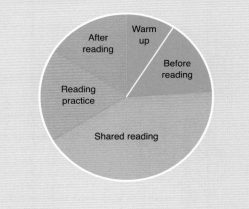

⬇ Lesson 2 Warm-up

1 Sing *Twinkle, twinkle, little star* (LB p31, LCD1 track 22).

⬇ Before reading

3 Ask *Is it day or night?*
Can you see a garden?
Who is looking into the garden?
Is the boy big or little?
Can you see a door?
What colour is it?
What can you see in the garden?

Elicit five or six answers to the final question, e.g. **I can see a tree/flowers/a snake**, etc. Do not ask them to name everything at this stage.

⬇ Shared reading

2 Ask *Is the beetle big or small?*
How many eggs are in the nest?
What colour is the butterfly?
Where is the goldfish?
What colour are the apples?
Where is the frog?
What is on the wall?
Is the snake tall or long?

⬇ After reading

Guess the object

Put the class in two teams.
Put 6–8 object flashcards on the board.
Give a team 1 child a clue about an object, e.g. *They are red. They are on the tree in the garden.*
The child must choose the correct picture. He/She shows it to the rest of the team and asks **What are they?** Team answers **They are apples.**
Then it is the other team's turn.
If the correct picture is not chosen or is not named correctly, the other team can try before their own turn.

Reading and understanding

1. Session 1 warm-up.
2. Re-read *My secret garden* (LB pp36–37).
3. Activity 1 (LB p38): Children colour the pictures and match the phrases.
4. Activity 2: Individuals read the words in the box. Class reads. Help/Ask individuals to read and complete sentences. Class repeats. Children write.
5. Play the *Get active!* game.
6. Prepare children for PB p26 by checking they understand the tasks. Children complete.

Working with words

1. Session 2 warm-up.
2. Activity 1 (LB p39): Children read words. They categorise and write.
3. Activity 2: Children write an object/animal under each colour.

Sentence building

1. Go through the text in the box (LB p39).
2. Activity 1: Children circle capital letters.
3. Activity 2: Children circle question marks. Children read sentences aloud.
4. Prepare children for PB p27. Go through the box and check they understand the tasks. Children complete.

Extension activity

Children ask *What? Where?* questions.

Reading and understanding

1. Read and colour. Match and say.

1 an orange goldfish — on a tree
2 a green frog — on the wall
3 red apples — in the pond
4 a long brown snake — on a rock
5 three small blue eggs — in a nest
6 purple flowers — in the tall grass

Remember! in on

2. Choose the words. Read the sentences.

beautiful small long tall

1 The grass is _____   2 The butterfly is _____
3 The eggs are _____   4 The snake is _____

Get active 4

38 Comprehension focus consolidation of new language in My Secret Garden

---

Unit 4

Reading and understanding

1. Colour.

blue yellow black red green purple brown

2. Colour. Write.

1 This is a blue egg.
   Colour the egg blue.
2 This is _____
   Colour the butterfly yellow.
3 These are _____
   Colour the beetles black.
4 This _____
   Colour the apple red.
5 These _____
   Colour the frogs green.

26

4

Working with words

1. Write the words in the correct box.

brown purple butterfly green goldfish orange flower beetle

colours	animals
brown	

2. Write the name of something from the story under each colour.

blue	red	orange	brown

Sentence building

Look at this sentence. It is a question.

A sentence begins with a **capital letter**.   What is this?   This sentence ends with a **question mark**.

1. Read the sentences. Circle the capital letters.

1 What is this?
2 What are these?
3 Is the frog green?
4 Are the flowers purple?
5 Is the snake in the tall grass?

2. Now circle the question marks.

Language focus colour/creature words; questions

39

Unit 4

Sentence building

What are these flowers?

capital letter   question mark

1. Circle the capital letters. Circle the question mark.

1 What can you see?
2 Can you see the snake?
3 What is your name?
4 How old are you?
5 Are these your toys?

2. Write some question marks.

? ___ ___ ___

3. Write these questions correctly.

Remember capital letters and question marks.

1 is this your house
   _____
2 is this an elephant
   _____
3 can you see the frog
   _____

27

Lesson aim Comprehension, vocabulary and sentence building

Lesson targets Children:
- match two parts of a phrase
- complete sentences choosing from given words
- describe an object or animal
- categorise colours and animals
- identify capital letters
- practise capital letters and using question marks.

Key language; Words for understanding *from Lessons 1 and 2*

Materials Language Book pp38–39, Practice Book pp26–27, flashcards 38–39, 41–42, 44, 159 word cards for *What?* and *Where?* for extension activity

Preparation Make *What? Where?* cards

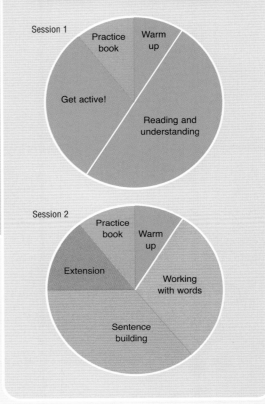

Lesson 3 time division:

Session 1
- Warm up
- Reading and understanding
- Get active!
- Practice book

Session 2
- Warm up
- Working with words
- Sentence building
- Extension
- Practice book

⬇ Lesson 3 Session 1 Warm-up

1 Put flashcards for key words around the classroom. Do the *I can see ...* chain activity (TG p51).

⬇ Reading and understanding

3 Children look back at LB pp36–37. Ask, e.g. *Where is the orange goldfish/green frog?* **It's in the pond/on a rock.** (LB p38) Read the *Remember!* box. Children read the first part of each phrase and colour. Go around while they work. Ask individuals *Where is/are the ...?* If necessary, repeat *Where is/are the ...?* with the whole class after they colour the pictures.

They read the second part of the phrase and write the number of the first matching part in the box.

To check, children read complete phrases.

5 Get active!
Put flashcards on your desk face down. A team 1 child takes a card and looks at the picture but does not show the class. The child must say something about the picture to describe it, e.g. **They are small.** Class guesses. If they cannot answer, or give the wrong answer, the child adds another clue, e.g. **They are blue.**

This could be played as a team game with one side describing objects for the other side to guess.

⬇ Lesson 3 Session 2 Warm-up

Sing the *Rainbow song* from LB p7, LCD1 track 4. Point to objects in the classroom. Ask *What colour is this/are these?*

⬇ Sentence building

1 Read the two sentences at the top. Read *What is this?* Write it up. Read bubbles. Emphasise the capital letter/question mark in *What is this?*

⬇ Extension activity

A child from team 1 takes a flashcard. Show team 1 *What?* or *Where?* Child shows the class the card. Team 1 must ask the correct question **What is this/are these?** or **Where is this/are these?** If they ask correctly they get a point.

Team 2 answers, e.g. **They are flowers./It is in the pond.** If the answer is correct, team 2 gets a point and it is team 2 child's turn to choose a card.

The winning team has the most points.

59

Grammar

1 Lesson 4 warm-up.

2 Show poster 4. Ask questions.

3 Read the speech bubbles (LB p40). Children follow. Class reads speech bubbles.

4 Activity 1: Children ask about singular items.

5 Activity 2: Do the same with plural items.

6 Activity 3: Children complete questions and write answers.

7 Prepare children for PB p28 by checking they understand the tasks. Children complete.

Listening

1 Read Nina's speech bubble (LB p41).

2 Activity 1: Play LCD1 track 28. Children listen and identify animals. Play the track again. Children tick the animal they heard.

3 Activity 2: Play track 29. Children check answers.

4 Activity 3: Play LCD1 track 30. Children listen and say.

After listening

1 Teach the rhyme.

2 Children mime and guess.

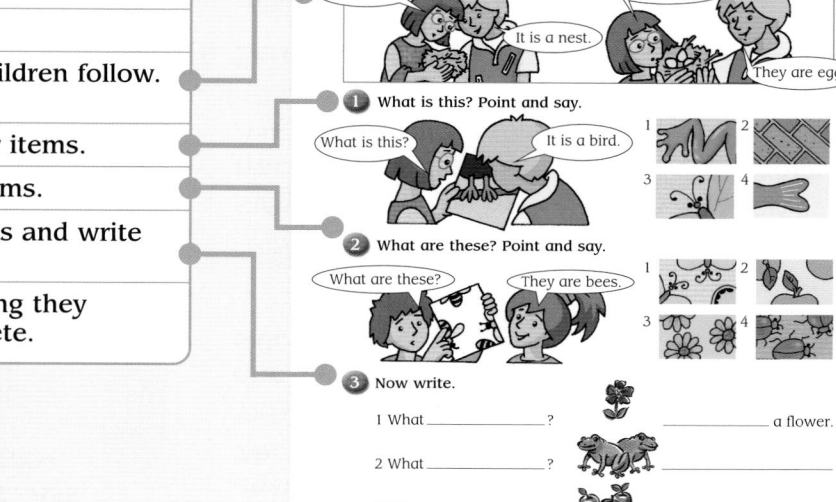

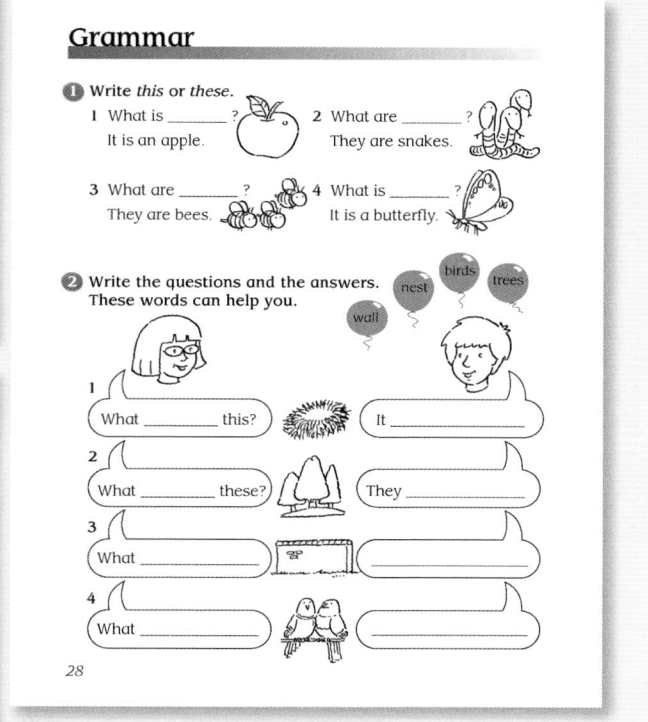

Lesson aim Grammar and listening

Lesson targets Children:

- practise asking questions to identify objects
- practise saying and writing statements to identify objects
- identify animals from the sounds they make
- say and learn a short rhyme.

Key language
(words) words from Lessons 1–3
(structures) *What is this/are these? It is .../They are ...*

Materials poster 4, Language Book pp40–41, Practice Book p28, Language CD1 tracks 28–30, flashcards 35, 38–41, 44, 46 for *After listening*

Preparation
Listen to the CD before the lesson.

Lesson 4 time division:

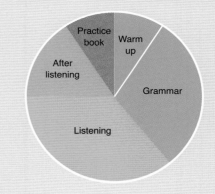

⬇ Lesson 4 Warm-up

1 Write the alphabet in capitals on the board. Leave out several letters. Children fill the blanks.

⬇ Grammar

2 (poster 4) Point to singular and plural items. Ask *What is this/are these?* e.g. **bird, snakes, flowers, tree, butterfly, monkey.**

4 Read speech bubbles or ask children to read them. Class repeats.
Ask about the small pictures. Elicit answers.
Children repeat the activity in pairs.

6 Elicit complete sentences from the class.
Write them on the board. Class reads. Rub them off. Children write.

⬇ Listening

2 **Audioscript**

Voice	1	What is this?	[elephant]
		An elephant or a bird?	[elephant]
Voice	2	What are these?	[monkeys]
		Monkeys or dogs?	[monkeys]
Voice	3	What are these?	[cats]
		Snakes or cats?	[cats]
Voice	4	What is this?	[frog]
		A frog or a mouse?	[frog]

4 Play the rhyme twice. Encourage the children to join in.

⬇ After listening

1 Write the words on the board. Teach the rhyme by rubbing out significant words in each line. Children fill in the words. Continue gradually rubbing out more words each time until all the words are removed.

2 Put flashcards/pictures of animals the children know on your desk. A volunteer chooses one. The volunteer mimes the animal. Children guess which animal it is.

61

Activity 1

1. Lesson 5 warm-up.
2. (LB p42) Point out pictures and words with *u*.
3. 🎧 Play rhyme twice (LCD1 track 31). Children follow in books.
4. Read rhyme.
5. Read and ask questions. ⬇
6. Read with the class.

Activity 2

1. ⬇ Children hold sounds cards. Read the sounds.
2. Close up gradually.
3. Read the word.
4. Children look, say and write.

Activity 3

Children say the word and sentence. ⬇

Activity 4

1. Write up words. Class/individuals read. ⬇
2. Children read in pairs. Listen to pairs.
3. Children check words and tick.

Practice book

Children complete PB p29. ⬇

Phonics games and activities

1. Play *Alphabetical order*. ⬇
2. Play *Letter-changing*. ⬇

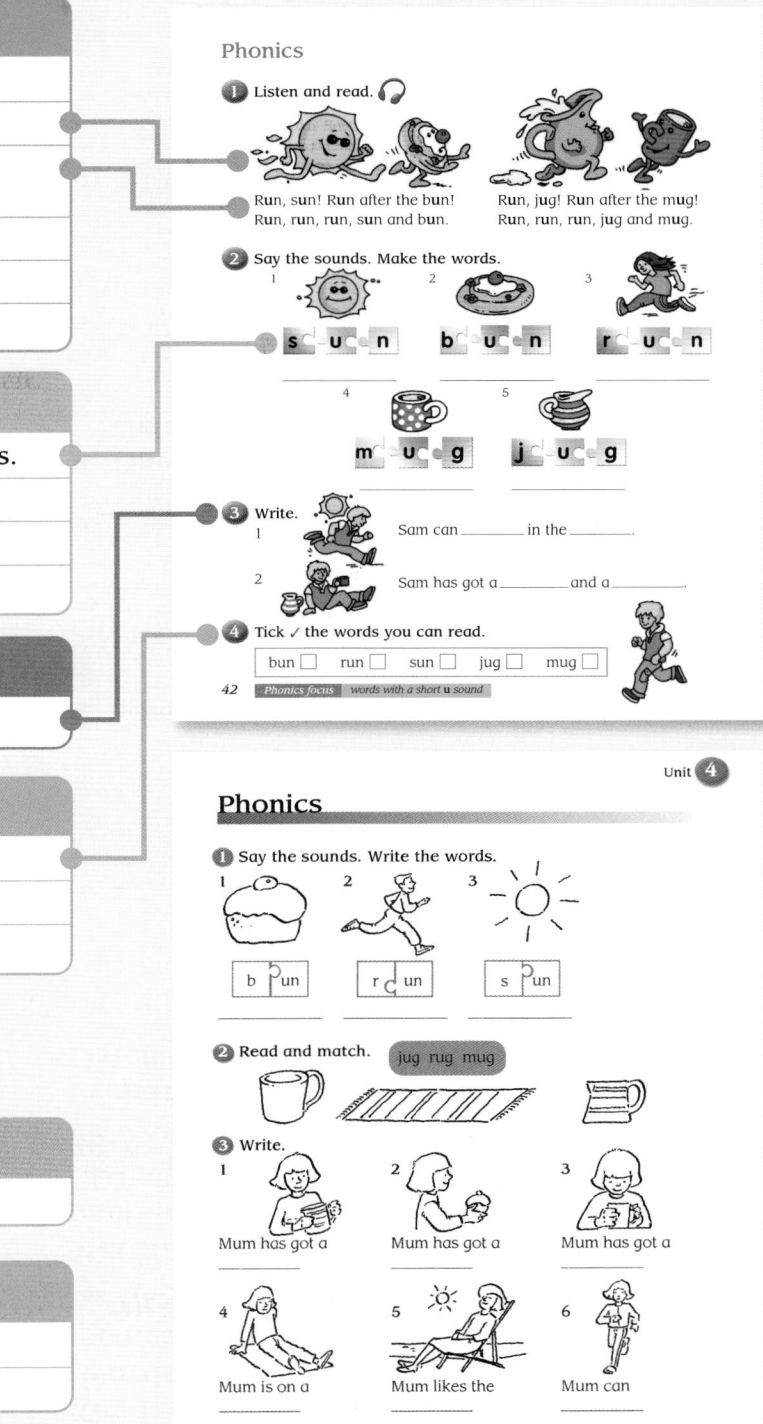

62

Lesson aim Phonic recognition

Lesson targets Children:

- read, pronounce and spell cvc words with the short *u*
- recognise and say the individual sounds that make up the cvc words
- write the words from picture prompts.

Target words *bun, run, sun, jug, mug, rug*

Materials Language Book p42, Practice Book p29, Language CD1 track 31, cards for sounds, alphabet letter cards

Preparation Listen to the CD before the lesson. Make large cards for the sounds/phonemes for the target words.

Lesson 5 time division:

Lesson 5 Warm-up

1 Say the rhyme *Hi! I am Ben* from LB page 23.

Activity 1

5 Ask *Can the bun run?*
What is behind the bun?
What can run after the mug?
Is the jug next to the mug?

Make sure all the words in the text are understood.

Activity 2

Follow the procedure for introducing the phonemes and sounding out each word which is given in detail in the Introduction (p10).

Activity 3

Children look at the picture and read the words. Ask/Help a child to say the whole sentence. Class repeats.

Children write the word.

Do the same with the second sentence.

Activity 4

1 Write the six words on the board. Point in random order. Individuals and/or the class reads them.

Practice Book

Check children can sound out all six target words before they move on to Exercise 3.

Phonics games and activities

1 **Alphabetical order**

Play *Alphabetical order* in two teams: Put letters *a–m* on the board. Team 1 says the whole alphabet. A team 2 child finds the first letter, the next child finds the second, etc. until the letters are in order on the board. If they do this before the other team reaches the end of the alphabet, they get a point.

Put up letters *n–z*. Team 2 says the alphabet, team 1 orders the letters.

2 **Letter-changing**

Write up *rug*. Class reads. Change *r* to *m*. Ask *What is it now?* Class reads. Do the same with *j*.

Do the same with *_un* and initial letters *b*, *s*, *r*. Class reads all the words.

63

Before writing

1 Lesson 6 warm-up.

2 Read Miss Plum's speech bubble (LB p43).

3 Individuals read the names of the animals.

4 Class reads the names.

5 Activity 1: Children do the dot-to-dot puzzles.

Shared writing

1 Children read questions. Class reads questions.

2 Elicit answers. Write them on the board. Class reads.

3 Rub off. Children write. Point out the *Don't forget!* box.

Practice Book

Writing

(PB p30) Children read, draw, then complete and write sentences.

Your writing

1 (PB p31) Class read the instructions and draw the objects.

2 Children read the questions and complete the answers.

After writing

1 Ask and answer in pairs.

2 Play *Muddled letters.*

Let's write about animals.

Class writing

cat   elephant   mouse   frog   monkey   bird

1 Draw the animals.

1 What is this?   2 What are these?

It is an   They are

3 What is this?   4 What are these?

5 What is this?   6 What are these?

2 Write the answers.

Don't forget!
What is … ?   What are … ?
It is a …   They are …

Writing focus | It is … / They are … statements

43

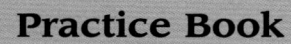

Writing

Draw and write.

fish   flower   butterfly   eggs   apples   snakes

1

This is a _____

2

These are _____

3

4

5

6

30

Your writing

Draw and write.

1 Draw two snakes.   2 Draw a flower.

What are these?   What is this?
They are _____   It is a _____

3 Draw a fish.   4 Draw three eggs.

What is this?   What are these?

5 Draw five apples.   6 Draw a butterfly.

What are these?   What is this?

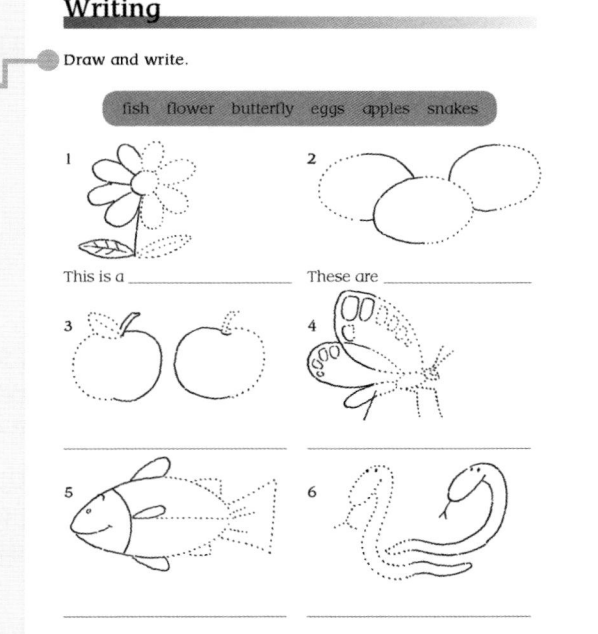

31

Lesson aim Writing

Lesson targets Children:

- read and follow instructions for drawing
- write statements about pictures using prompt words
- read questions and complete/write answers using prompt words.

Key language (words) words from Lessons 1 and 2
(structures) *What is this/are these? It is a/an ...*, *These are ...*

Materials Language Book p43, Practice Book pp30 and 31, flashcards 16, 40, 43, letter cards to spell these words

Preparation Make or find letters as needed for *Muddled letters*.

Lesson 6 time division:

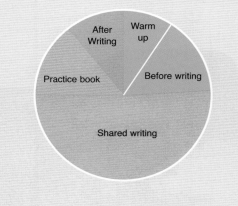

Lesson 6 Warm-up

1. Say *The elephant goes* from Lesson 4 (LB p41, LCD1 track 30).

Before writing

5. Explain that each of the animals in the row is in one of the pictures below. They must find the animal and finish it.

Shared writing

1. Ask a child to read the first question. Class reads the first question.

   Elicit the complete answer. Write it on the board. Class reads. Continue with the other questions, sentences and pictures. Class reads all sentences.

2. Rub all or part of them off before children write. Point out Miss Plum's *Don't forget!* box.

Practice Book

Writing

Individuals/class reads the words in the box. Children complete the pictures.

If your class needs guidance, elicit complete sentences and write them on the board. Class reads. Rub off all or part of sentences before children write.

Your writing

2. Children read the questions, complete the first two sentences and write the next four.

   Check that children understand they write about the object they draw, not anything already in the picture.

After writing

1. Children work in pairs. They take turns to point in each other's books and read the questions. Partners read the answers.

2. **Muddled letters**
   Write the letters of one of these words on the board: *fish, frog, egg, bird, nest.* The letters should be in muddled order. Show the flashcard. Children volunteer to write the word correctly. Continue with another word.

Before listening

1. Lesson 1 warm-up.
2. Show poster 5. Read the title. Ask questions.
3. Point and name new objects. Children come forward; find objects in main picture.
4. Show flashcards (48–50, 54, 60) and name objects. Class repeats.

Shared listening

1. Play FCD track 10. Point to pictures and characters when they speak.
2. Ask about the small picture on the left.
3. Ask questions about the main picture.
4. Play the CD (track 10) and point again.

Dialogue practice

1. Say new words. Children point in books (FB pp16–17). Point on poster for children to check.
2. Show flashcards 48–50, 54, 60. Children name.
3. Children close books. Play FCD track 11 and show character flashcards. Class repeats lines in pauses.
4. Groups say lines by character.
5. Individuals act dialogue.
6. Play track 10 again. Children follow text or point to main picture.

After listening

1. Show flashcards 48–50, 54, 60. Ask questions.
2. Children guess where the stars are.

5 Sam's island

| river | mountain | beach | jungle | sea | island |

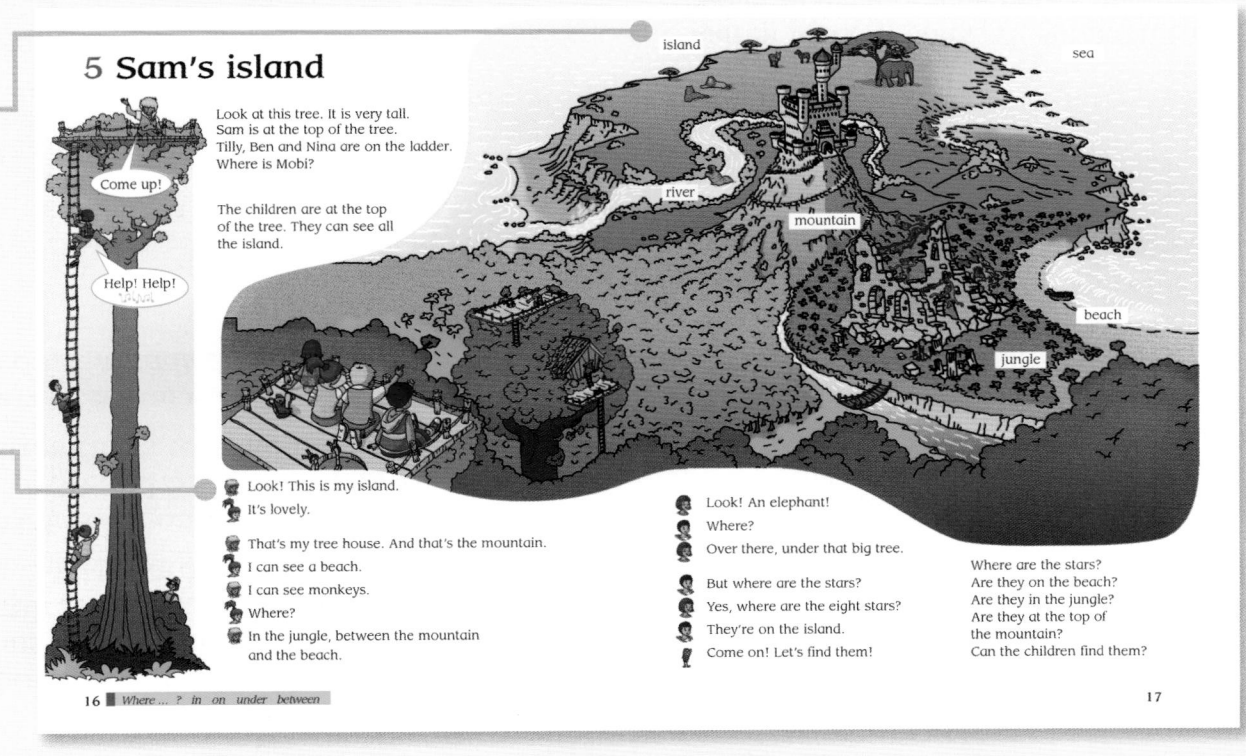

5 Sam's island

Look at this tree. It is very tall. Sam is at the top of the tree. Tilly, Ben and Nina are on the ladder. Where is Mobi?

The children are at the top of the tree. They can see all the island.

Come up!

Help! Help!

- Look! This is my island.
- It's lovely.
- That's my tree house. And that's the mountain.
- I can see a beach.
- I can see monkeys.
- Where?
- In the jungle, between the mountain and the beach.

- Look! An elephant!
- Where?
- Over there, under that big tree.
- But where are the stars?
- Yes, where are the eight stars?
- They're on the island.
- Come on! Let's find them!

Where are the stars?
Are they on the beach?
Are they in the jungle?
Are they at the top of the mountain?
Can the children find them?

16 Where ... ? in on under between

17

66

Lesson aim Fluency

Lesson targets Children:

- listen for pronunciation and intonation
- repeat dialogue accurately
- act out dialogue with expression
- talk about what is on the island.

Key language (words) *beach, island, jungle, mountain, river, sea* (structures) *Where ...? in, on, under, between*

Words for understanding *castle, ladder, monkeys, top, lovely, tall*

Materials Poster 5, Fluency Book pp16–17, Fluency CD tracks 10–11, character flashcards 2–6, object flashcards 48–50, 54, 60, object flashcards of your choice for *Warm-up*

Preparation Listen to the CD before the lesson.

Lesson 1 time division:

⬇ Lesson 1 Warm-up

1 Guess the object
Put object flashcards on the board. Make statements, e.g. *It's small. It's brown.* Children guess, e.g. **It's the mouse.**

⬇ Before listening

2 Ask *Who lives on the island?*
Can you see Sam's house?
Can you see Sam's telescope?
Can you see animals?
How many animals can you see?

⬇ Shared listening

2 Ask *Who is at the top of the tree?*
Who is on the ladder?
Where is Mobi?
Can you see Miss Plum?

3 Ask *What can Sam see? Where are they?*
What can Tilly see? Where is it?
Who can see a beach?
Can you see a big house on the mountain?
(Explain this is called a *castle*).
Can you see zebras on the island?
How many zebras can you see?

⬇ After listening

1 Ask *Where is the jungle?*
Where is the beach?
Where is the castle?
What colour is the sea?
How many rivers can you see?

2 Ask children to guess where the stars are, e.g. **They are under the mountain/in the big house/in the river/in the jungle/on the beach.**

Before reading

1 Lesson 2 warm-up. Play *Team numbers*. ⬇

2 Teach new words. ⬇

3 Children open books (LB pp44–45). Ask questions. ⬇

Shared reading

1 🎧 Play LCD1 track 32. Children follow text in book.

2 Read line by line. Ask questions. ⬇

3 Read with the class.

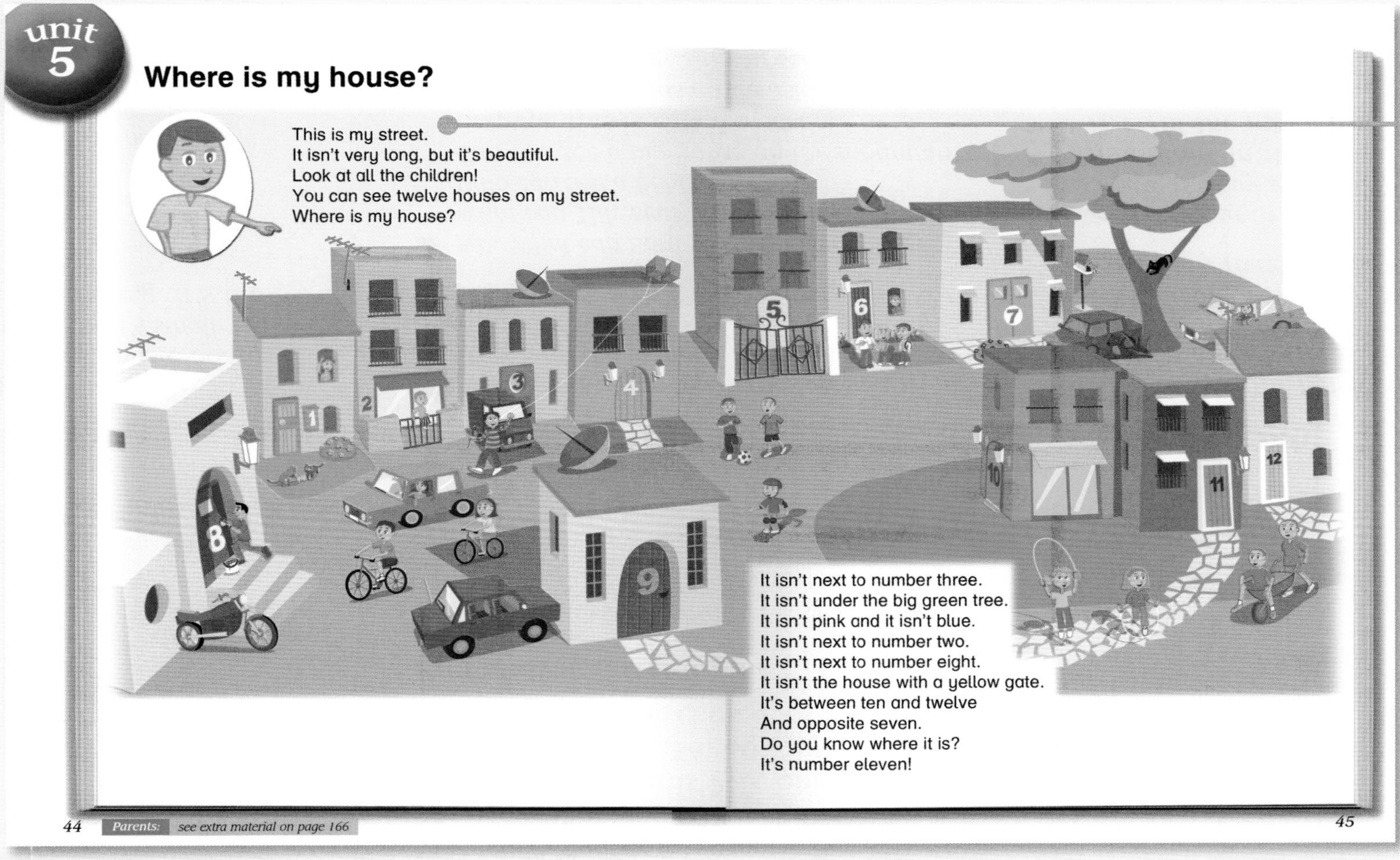

unit 5

Where is my house?

This is my street.
It isn't very long, but it's beautiful.
Look at all the children!
You can see twelve houses on my street.
Where is my house?

It isn't next to number three.
It isn't under the big green tree.
It isn't pink and it isn't blue.
It isn't next to number two.
It isn't next to number eight.
It isn't the house with a yellow gate.
It's between ten and twelve
And opposite seven.
Do you know where it is?
It's number eleven!

44   Parents: see extra material on page 166   45

Reading practice

1 Give reading practice. Use some or all of the following:

- Children read again as a class.
- Groups read different sections.
- Individuals read different sections.

2 🎧 Class listens again to LCD1 track 32 and follows in LB.

After reading

Do the observation activity. ⬇

Lesson aim Reading

Lesson targets Children:

- follow a text read out to them
- listen for pronunciation and intonation
- read the text aloud with accurate pronunciation and intonation
- learn and understand new vocabulary items
- understand the sense of the text as a whole
- answer simple comprehension questions.

Key language (words) *between, next to, opposite, under, eleven, twelve* (structures) *Where is ...? It's opposite ... , It isn't next to ...*

Words for understanding *fun, pet, meet, baby, really, very*

Materials Language Book pp44–45, Language CD1 track 32, number cards for *Warm-up*

Preparation Listen to the CD before the lesson.

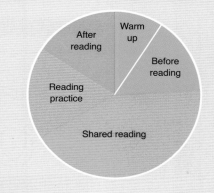

Lesson 2 time division:

Warm up · Before reading · After reading · Reading practice · Shared reading

⬇ Lesson 2 Warm-up

Teach *eleven* and *twelve*, if necessary.

Team numbers
Class in four or six teams: give each team three or four random numbers. Call out numbers in any order. When a team's number is called they put their hands up. Give points to teams who all do it together and quickly. After several turns teams change numbers. Children listen for new numbers.

⬇ Before reading

2 Use children and word cards to teach *between, next to* and *opposite*. Arrange three children in a line; the middle child holds the *between* word card. Say, e.g. *Dina is between Sara and Ali.* Change the order and give the card to the new middle child:

Ali is between Dina and Sara.
Do the same with *next to.*
Bring out a fourth child and place children opposite one another. Say, e.g. *Sara is opposite Ali. Ahmed is opposite Dina.*

3 Ask the class what they can see. Prompt/Elicit answers. Ask *What colour is/are ...? How many ...?*

⬇ Shared reading

2 Ask *Which house is next to number 3? Is it a small tree? Which house is blue/pink? Which house is next to number two? Find number 8. What colour is the door? Which house has a yellow gate? What number comes after ten? Which house is opposite number 7?*

⬇ After reading

Divide the class into two or more teams: give a clue about an object or person in the LB picture. Children try to guess after the first clue. If they cannot, give another, e.g. *It is brown and white ... It is under a car.* **The dog.** *It is very small ... It is grey. It is between the cats.* **The mouse.**

The first team to identify the object correctly wins a point.

Reading and understanding
SESSION 1

1. Session 1 warm-up. ⬇

2. Re-read *Where is my house?* (LB pp44–45).

3. Activity 1 (LB p46): Individuals read sentences. Class repeats. Children look and write the numbers.

4. Activity 2: Children read and circle the correct words. Do the first one together on the board, if necessary.

5. Play the *Get active!* game. ⬇

6. Prepare children for PB p32 by checking they understand the task. Children complete.

Working with words
SESSION 2

1. Session 2 warm-up. ⬇

2. Practise matching numbers and number words. ⬇

3. Activity 1 (LB p47): Children trace and match.

4. Activity 2: Children write number words.

Sentence building

1. Read the sentences in the box (LB p47).

2. Read Mobi's speech bubble. Write up examples. ⬇

3. Individuals read the phrases below the pictures. Class repeats.

4. Activities 1 and 2: Write the phrases on the board. Practise finding the adjective and the noun. ⬇

5. Prepare children for PB p33. Go through the box and check they understand the tasks. Children complete.

Extension activities

Do the colour adjective activities. ⬇

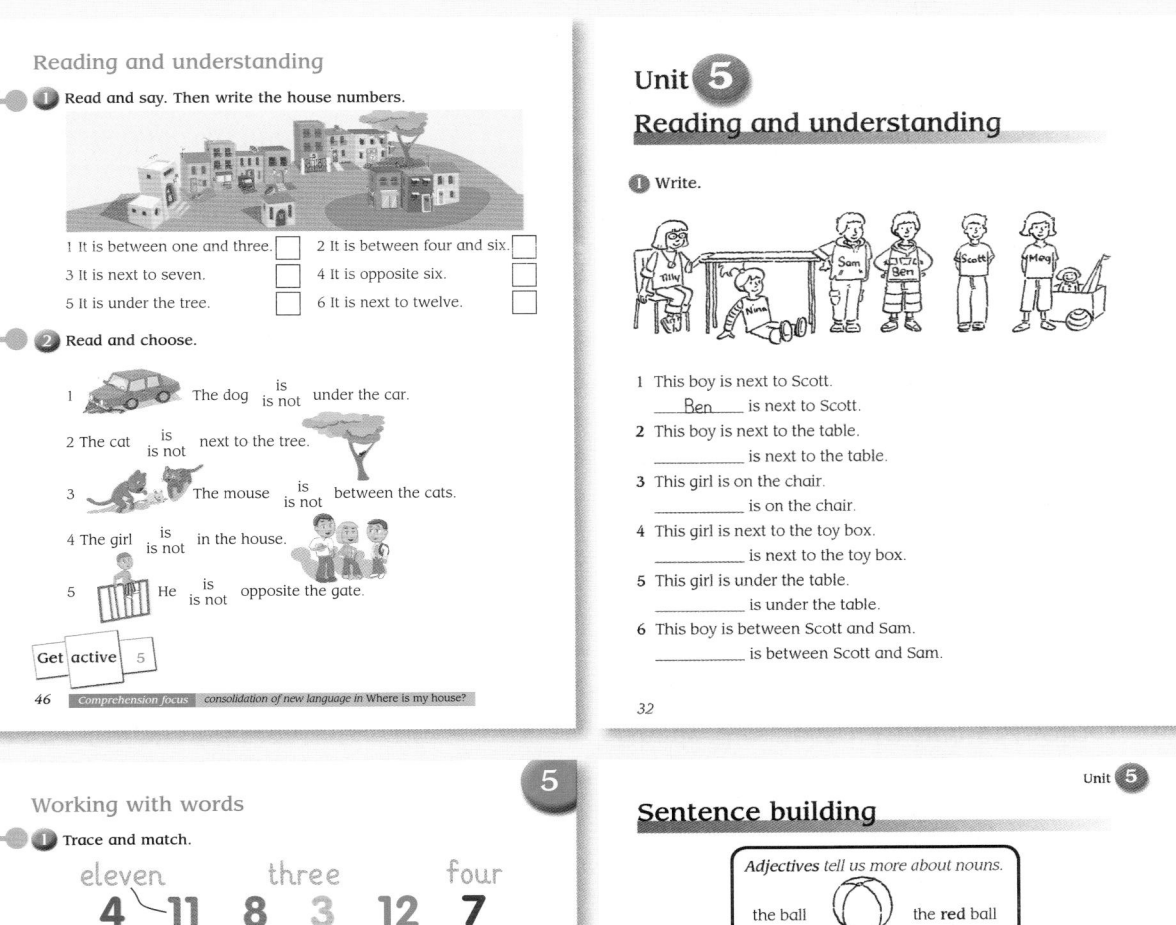

Lesson aim Comprehension, vocabulary and sentence building

Lesson targets Children:
- identify an object from a description of its position
- choose between affirmative and negative sentences to match pictures
- practise writing number words and figures
- identify an adjective and a noun in a sentence.

Key language Words from Lessons 1 and 2

Materials Language Book pp46–47, Practice Book pp32–33, number word cards *one* to *twelve*, number cards 1–12, animal/object flashcards and colour cards for *Extension activities*

Preparation Make colour cards as necessary (p246). Make word and number cards as necessary.

Lesson 3 time division:

Session 1

Session 2

Lesson 3 Session 1 Warm-up

1 Do a short number chain: ask a row or group of children to stand up. They number round from **One**. Repeat with other groups.

Reading and understanding

5 Get active!
Arrange four children in a line. Ask the class, e.g. *Who is between Leila and Karim? Who is next to Sami?*

Bring out four more children. Give them instructions: *Omar, stand opposite Leila, Ali stand next to Omar*, etc. until they are in a line facing the first group. Ask the rest of the class questions: *Who is opposite Karim?/next to Ali?/between Ali and Dina?* etc.

Lesson 3 Session 2 Warm-up

1 Sing the *Rainbow song* from LB p7 (LCD1 track 4).

Working with words

2 Stick all the number words on the board.

Stick the number cards underneath in scrambled order. Children take turns to match numbers and words. If you wish, leave them on the board while children complete Activities 1 and 2.
Check for correct formation of letters while children trace and write.

Sentence building

2 Children name all the colours they can. Write them on the board. Say *These words are adjectives. They can tell us about a noun.*

Hold up e.g. the frog flashcard. Ask *What's this? A frog*. Write up *frog*. Ask *What colour is it? Green*. Write it on the board (add the indefinite article). Class reads: *a green frog*. Point to *green*, say *adjective*; point to *frog*, say *noun*. Repeat with another suitable flashcard, e.g. beetle.

4 Children say which is the adjective and which is the noun in the phrases on the board. Circle adjectives. Underline nouns.

Write additional phrases, e.g. *a green frog*, and ask volunteers to circle and underline.

If you wish, go through Activity 1 and 2 orally before children write.

Extension activities

Show flashcards and objects, e.g. grey elephant, blue book. Ask *What's this?* Elicit *It's a grey elephant*, etc.

Variation: Put up noun word cards. Children choose a colour card. They put it next to a noun card and say, e.g. *a yellow snake* or *It's a yellow snake*. These activities can be done in teams. Award points for accurate sentences and phrases.

71

Grammar

1 Lesson 4 warm-up.

2 Show poster 2. Revise furniture in Sam's house.

3 Children look at the picture (LB p48).
Ask questions.

4 Activity 1: Individuals read sentences. Class repeats.
Children write answers.

5 Activity 2: Children speak in pairs.

6 Activity 3: Individuals read questions. Class repeats.
Elicit answers orally. Children write.

7 Prepare children for PB p34 by checking they
understand the tasks. Children complete.

Listening

1 🎧 Activity 1: Children name the pictures. Play LCD1
track 33. Children listen. Play it again. Children
draw.

2 Activity 2: Children speak in pairs.

3 🎧 Activity 3: Play LCD1 track 34. Children listen.
Demonstrate the actions. Play the song again.
Children do the actions.

After listening

1 Children colour drawings from Activity 1.

2 Teach the song in the usual way.

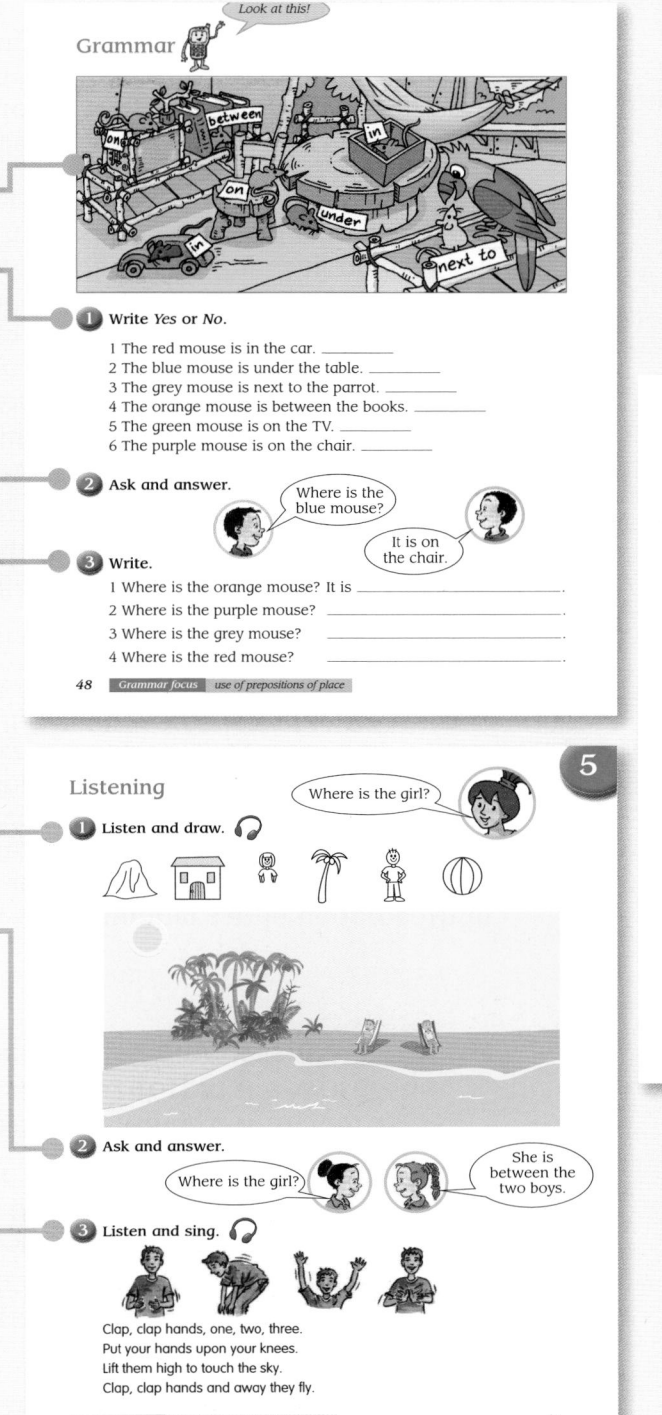

Lesson aim Grammar and listening

Lesson targets Children:

- compare statements about positions of objects to their positions in a picture
- ask where objects and people are
- reply and write answers
- draw items in a picture according to spoken instructions
- sing and learn a short song.

Key language (words) *in, on, under, next to, between*
(structures) *Where is/are the ...?*
He/She/It is ..., They are ...

Materials Language Book pp48–49, Practice Book p34, Language CD1 tracks 33–34, poster 2, objects for *Warm-up*

Preparation Listen to the CD before the lesson. Find suitable objects to demonstrate prepositions (see *Warm-up*)

Lesson 4 time division:

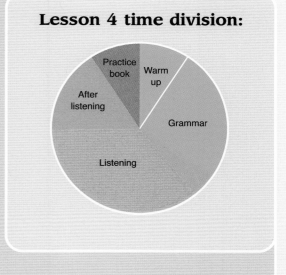

⬇ Lesson 4 Warm-up

1 Place objects on your desk to practise *in, on, under, next to, between*, e.g. a box, a large ball, a doll, a book, a hat.

⬇ Grammar

3 Ask e.g. *Can you see a mouse?* **Yes, I can.** *What colour is it?* **It is purple.** *Where is the purple mouse?* **It is under the table.** Help children to answer *Where is ...?* if necessary.

⬇ Listening

1 Copy the drawings onto the board. Ask *What is this?* for each one. Children name them.

Audioscript
The mountain is next to the jungle.
The house is on the mountain.
The girl is in the sea.
The tree is on the beach.
The man is under the tree.
The ball is between the two boys.

⬇ After listening

1 Children colour the pictures from Activity 1, using whatever colours they choose.

Ask individuals *What can you see?* Elicit, e.g. **I can see a brown mountain, green tree, blue house,** etc.

Activity 1

1. Lesson 5 warm-up.
2. (LB p50) Point out pictures and words with *o*.
3. Play rhyme twice (LCD1 track 35). Children follow in books.
4. Read rhyme.
5. Read and ask questions.
6. Read with the class.

Activity 2

1. Children hold sounds cards. Read the sounds.
2. Close up gradually.
3. Read the word.
4. Children look, say and write.

Activity 3

Children say the word and sentence. Children write.

Activity 4

1. Write up words. Class/individuals read.
2. Children read in pairs. Listen to pairs.
3. Children check words and tick.

Practice Book

Children complete PB p35.

Phonics games and activities

1. Play *What's the word?*
2. Play *Look, write, check.*

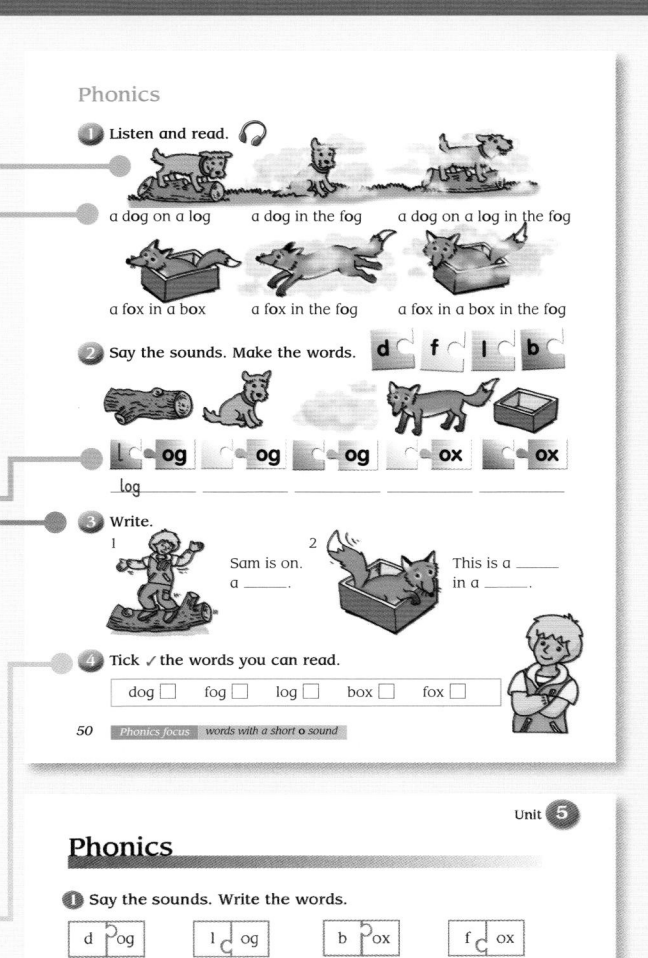

Lesson aim Phonic recognition

Lesson targets Children:

- read, pronounce and spell cvc words with the short *o*
- recognise and say the individual sounds that make up the cvc words
- write the words from picture prompts.

Target words *dog, fog, log, box, fox, hot, not*

Materials Language Book p50, Practice Book p35, Language CD1 track 35, cards for sounds, word cards and letters for *Warm-up*

Preparation Listen to the CD before the lesson. Make large cards for the sounds/phonemes for *log, dog, fog, box, fox*

Lesson 5 Time division:

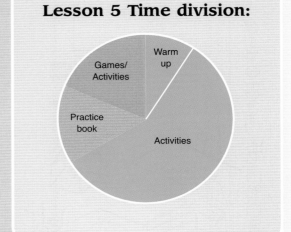

Lesson 5 Warm-up

1 Play *Word/letter match* (p248). Children match words to initial letters.

Activity 1

5 Ask *Where is the dog?*
What colour is the dog?
Can you see in the fog?
What is in the box?
What colour is the fox?
Is the fox on the box?

Make sure all the words in the text are understood.

Activity 2

Follow the procedure for introducing the phonemes and sounding out each word which is given in detail in the Introduction (TG p10).

Activity 3

Children look at the picture and read the words. Ask/Help a child to say the whole sentence. Class repeats. Children write the word.

Do the same with the second sentence.

Activity 4

1 Write the five words on the board. Point in random order. Individuals and/or the class reads them.

Practice Book

Not and *hot* are introduced here, so sound these out with the children. Children complete the five exercises. Check they can sound out all target words before they attempt Exercises 4 and 5.

Phonics games and activities

1 **What's the word?**

Say the phonic sounds of a cvc word. Class tells you what the word is, e.g. say *c-a-t*. Class says ***cat***.

2 **Look, write, check**

Write up a cvc word. Children look. Cover it. Children write. Uncover the word. Children check.

Before writing

1 Lesson 6 warm-up.

2 Read Miss Plum's speech bubble (LB p51).

3 Children look at the picture.

4 Child reads the second speech bubble. Children find house number 1.

5 Ask about the other houses.

Shared writing

1 Children match pictures with the large picture (LB p51).

2 Children suggest sentences.

3 Write them on the board.

4 Children read the sentences. Children write.

Practice Book

Writing

1 Read the question (PB p36).

2 Child reads prepositions. Class repeats.

3 Children look and complete the phrases.

4 Children read out phrases.

Your writing

1 Children look at the picture (PB p37).

2 Children write sentences.

After writing

1 Children colour (PB p37) and describe positions.

2 Do the flashcards positions activity.

Class writing

Let's write about where things are.

1 Talk about the picture. Point and say.

Number one is in the jungle.

in   on   under   next to   opposite   between

2 Now write about these houses.

Number one is _____

Writing focus   *a short composition, using prepositions of place*   51

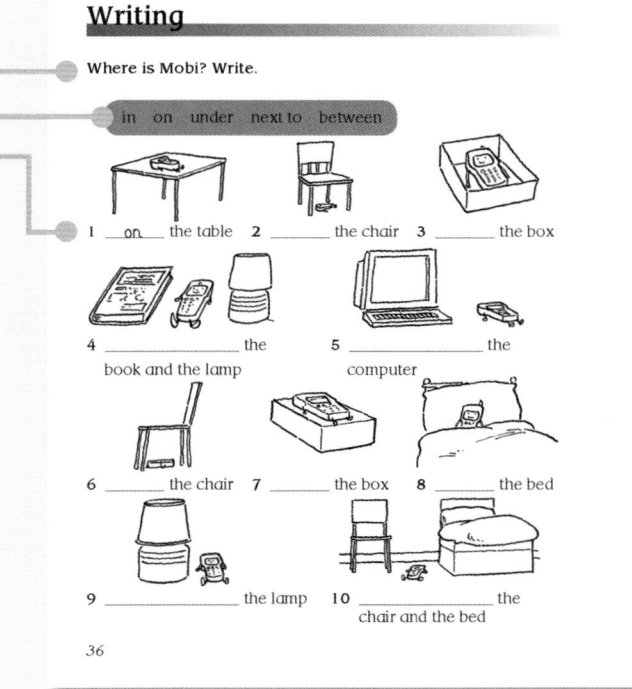

Writing

Where is Mobi? Write.

in   on   under   next to   between

1 __on__ the table   2 _____ the chair   3 _____ the box

4 _____ the book and the lamp   5 _____ the computer

6 _____ the chair   7 _____ the box   8 _____ the bed

9 _____ the lamp   10 _____ the chair and the bed

36

Unit 5

Your writing

Where are the balls? Write.

A ball is on the bed.
A ball is _____

37

Lesson aim Writing

Lesson targets Children:

- write sentences about the positions of houses
- complete phrases with the correct preposition according to pictures
- describe the position of objects in a room.

Key language (words) *in, on, under, between, next to*
(structures) *It's in/on/under/next to/between ...*

Materials Language Book p51, Practice Book pp36–37, flashcards of your choice for *After writing 2*

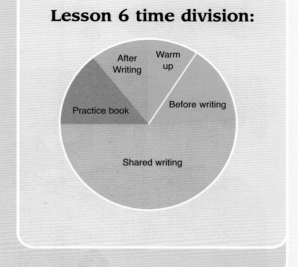

Lesson 6 time division:

After Writing / Warm up / Before writing / Shared writing / Practice book

Lesson 6 Warm-up

1 Sing *Clap, clap hands* from Lesson 4 (LB p49, LCD1 track 34) with the actions.

Before writing

5 Ask *Can you see house number 2? Where is it?*
Repeat with numbers 3 to 6.

Note: Houses 4 and 6 can be described in more than one way: 4 is opposite 3 and next to 5; 6 is next to 5 and under a tree.

Shared writing

2 Children suggest sentences, e.g. **Number 1 is in the jungle.** Where appropriate, ask questions to elicit details, e.g. *What colour is the jungle? Green*. Elicit the complete sentence: **Number 1 is in the green jungle.**

Continue with the other houses.

4 Children read all the sentences. If you wish, rub off all or part of the sentences before children write.

After writing

1 Children colour the balls on PB p37 different colours.

When they have finished, ask *Have you got a red ball? Put your hand up.*
Ask children with hands up *Where is your red ball?* Elicit, e.g. **My red ball is on the bed**. Expect different answers for every colour. Children should show their books for you to check.

2 Put 8 or 10 flashcards on the board in two equal rows.

Describe the positions of objects, e.g. *It's next to the ball. It's opposite the frog. It's between the fish and the table.* Children name the object in that position.

This game can be played in teams. Give a point to the first team to identify the correct object.

After a few turns change the objects in the game and/or their positions.

Before listening

1 Lesson 1 warm-up.

2 Show poster 6. Read the title. Ask questions.

3 Point and name new objects. Children come forward; find objects in the main picture.

4 Show flashcards (51–57) and name new objects. Class repeats.

Shared listening

1 Play FCD track 12. Point to characters when they speak.

2 Ask *Who? What? Where?* questions.

3 Ask about the second gold star.

4 Play the FCD track 12 and point to characters again.

Dialogue practice

1 Say new words. Children point in books (FB pp18–19). Point on poster for children to check.

2 Show object flashcards (51–57). Children name.

3 Children close books. Play FCD track 13 and show character flashcards. Class repeats lines in pauses.

4 Groups say lines by character.

5 Individuals act dialogue.

6 Play FCD track 12 again. Children follow text or point to main picture.

After listening

1 Show object flashcards 51–57. Children name the objects. Ask questions.

2 Teach the *Star chant*.

3 Children put the second sticker star in the correct place on FB pp46–47.

Lesson aim Fluency

Lesson targets Children:

- listen for pronunciation and intonation
- repeat dialogue accurately
- act out dialogue with expression
- talk about things on a beach.

Key language (words) *crab, fish, rock, sand, sea, shell, umbrella* (structures) *I have got ..., He/She has got ..., Have you got ...? Has he/she got ...?*

Words for understanding *water, get, Ouch!, Come here!, Let's go!*

Materials Poster 6, Fluency Book pp18–19, Fluency CD tracks 12–13, character flashcards 2–6, object flashcards 51–57

Preparation Listen to the CD before the lesson.

Lesson 1 time division:

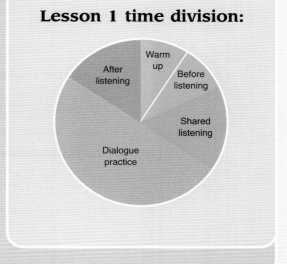

⬇ Lesson 1 Warm-up

1 Play *I can see* from Unit 3 (p51). Start the chain off adding a colour: *I can see a red ball. I can see a red ball and a blue train ...*

⬇ Before listening

2 Ask the class these questions. Choose individuals to come forward, point to characters and answer.

Can you see Sam?
Is Tilly on the beach?
Where is Nina?
Can you find Mobi?
Where is Ben?

⬇ Shared listening

2 Ask *What has Nina got?*
What can she hear?
Where is Mobi?
Who has got a crab?
Where is the fish?
What can Tilly see?

3 Ask *Is star number 2 in the sea?*
Is it on the sand?
Is it in the water?
Who's got star number 2?

⬇ After listening

1 Ask *How many shells can you see?*
How many fish? How many crabs?
What colour is the sand?/the sea?
Who is under the umbrella?
What colour is it?
What colour is the rock? Who can you see?

2 Ask the class how many stars are missing. **Seven.**

Write the star chant on the board and add the extra lines as in the rhyme in Unit 3:

Star light, star bright,
Seven stars are missing tonight.
I wish I may, I wish I might,
Find the seven stars missing tonight.

Teach the rhyme in the usual way.

Before reading

1 Lesson 2 warm-up. ⬇

2 📖 Teach new words with flashcards 52–53, 55–56, 97.

3 Children open books (LB pp52–53). Ask questions. ⬇

Shared reading

1 🔊 Play LCD1 track 36. Children follow text in book.

2 Read line by line. Ask questions. ⬇

3 Read with the class.

unit 6

We love the beach

It is a beautiful day on the beach. The sky is blue and the sea is green.

Mikey is in the water. 'Wow,' he says. 'I have got a crab!' It is a big red crab.

'Come here,' says his sister, Pat. 'Here is a rock pool. I can see a starfish. It is a baby starfish!'

Grandma has got some shells. 'Listen,' she says. 'You can hear the sea.'

'And I have got some rocks,' says Grandpa. 'Look at all the colours.'

'The pink one is very nice,' says Grandma.

'Yes, it is,' says Grandpa.

Mum and Dad are in their beach chairs. Dad has got a funny hat. Mum has got an umbrella. It is very hot.

'Oh, good! I have got the picnic basket,' says Dad.

'And look!' says Grandpa. 'That man has got ice creams.'

52 *Parents:* *see extra material on page 166*

53

Reading practice

1 Give reading practice. Use some or all of the following:
- Children read again as a class.
- Groups read different sections.
- Individuals read different sections.

2 🔊 Class listens again to LCD1 track 36 and follows in LB.

After reading

Do the matching people and objects activity. ⬇

Lesson aim Reading

Lesson targets Children:

- follow a text read out to them
- listen for pronunciation and intonation
- read the text aloud with accurate pronunciation and intonation
- learn and understand new vocabulary items
- understand the sense of the text as a whole
- answer simple comprehension questions.

Key language (words) *ice cream, basket, bucket, rock pool, starfish*
(structures) *I have got ..., He/She has got ..., Have you got ...? Has he/she got ...?*

Words for understanding *hot, nice, picnic, some*

Materials Language Book pp52–53, Language CD1 track 36, flashcards 16, 38–39, 51–57, 165, word cards for *fish, crab, shell, sea, sand, rock, umbrella, starfish, hat, ice cream, bird, flower, butterfly, chair,* word cards for *No, he hasn't. No, she hasn't.*

Preparation Listen to the CD before the lesson. Make word cards.

Lesson 2 time division:

⬇ Lesson 2 Warm-up

1 Do a picture/word matching activity. Put flashcards 52–58 and 19, 37, 38, 41 on your desk. Put the word cards on the board.

A team 1 child chooses a flashcard. Ask *What have you got?* Child answers e.g. **I have got a fish** and sticks it on the board. Team 2 child finds correct word card.

⬇ Before reading

3 Ask *Can you see Mum? Where is she?*
Can you see a dog? What colour is it?
Who has got a basket?
Who has got some rocks? Where are they?
Is the boy next to the rock pool? Where is he?
Is the girl in the sea? Where is she?
Has she got a bucket?

⬇ Shared reading

2 Ask *Where is the family?*
What has Dad/Mum got?
Is the crab little?
Is the starfish big or little?
What has Grandma got in her basket?
Who has got a pink rock?
Has Mum got a picnic? Where is the picnic?
What has the man got?

⬇ After reading

List the family names + *man* in the middle of the board. Place word cards and flashcards in muddled order at the bottom: *crab, starfish, umbrella, shell, rock, hat, ice cream.* Put signs: *No, he hasn't. No, she hasn't.* on your desk.

Ask, e.g. *Who has got an umbrella?* **Mum.** A child places the umbrella flashcard next to *Mum;* another places the word card.

Continue *Who has got a funny hat?/a crab?/a shell?/a rock?/an ice cream? Who can see a starfish?*

When all pictures and words are placed, ask, e.g. *Has Mikey got a starfish?* Elicit **No, he hasn't.** A child comes forward and holds up the correct sign. Class reads.

Ask *What has Mikey got?* Individual/class answers **He has got a crab.**

Continue with other questions to prompt **No, he/she hasn't,** e.g. *Has Dad got an umbrella? Has Mum got a hat? Has Pat got a crab?* etc.

81

Reading and understanding

1. Session 1 warm-up.
2. Ask questions about the picture on LB p54. *Who can you see? What can you see?*
3. Re-read *We love the beach* (LB pp52–53).
4. Activity 1 (LB p54): Children read sentences. Ask questions. Elicit correct answers.
5. Activity 2: Children read sentences and circle answers.
6. 📖 Play *Get active!*
7. Prepare children for PB p38. Read the sentences with them and check they understand the tasks. Children complete.

Working with words

1. Session 2 warm-up.
2. Activity 1 (LB p55): Children name the objects.
3. Activity 2: Children write the words.

Sentence building

1. Go through the summary box (LB p55).
2. Activity 1: Children write names.
3. Prepare children for PB p39. Go through the box with them and check they understand the tasks. Children complete.

Extension activities

1. Children make their own speech bubbles like Mobi's.
2. They write *My name is …*
3. Check for capital letters and full stops.
4. Children read their bubbles to the rest of the class.

Reading and understanding

1. These sentences from the story are not true. Say them correctly.

   1 The sea is blue.
   2 Mum and Dad have got hats.
   3 It is not very hot.
   4 Mikey's crab is brown.
   5 Mikey is next to a rock pool.
   6 The starfish is big.
   7 Grandpa has got some shells.
   8 Pat has got a starfish.

2. Read and circle *Yes* or *No*.

   1 Has he got an ice cream?   Yes.   No.
   2 Has he got a fish?   Yes.   No.
   3 Has she got a book?   Yes.   No.
   4 Has she got a basket?   Yes.   No.
   5 Has he got a cap?   Yes.   No.

Get active 6

54   *Comprehension focus*   consolidation of new language in We love the beach

---

Unit 6
Reading and understanding

1. Look and read.

It is a beautiful day on the beach. The sky is blue and the sea is green.
Mum and Dad are in their beach chairs. Dad has got a hat. Mum has got an umbrella.
Mikey is in the water. He says, 'I've got a big red crab.'
Pat says, 'I can see a starfish in the rock pool.'

2. Cross out the wrong answers.

1 It is a beautiful day on the	~~moon~~.	beach.
2 The sky is	green.	blue.
3 Mum and Dad are sitting in their	tables.	chairs.
4 Dad has got a	hat.	cat.
5 Mum has got an	owl.	umbrella.
6 Mikey is in the	tree.	water.
7 The crab is	red.	black.
8 Pat can see a	goldfish.	starfish.

38

Working with words

1. Find the words.

   1 bcra   2 ishf   3 lehls   4 rcok

2. Colour and write the words under the pictures.

   1   2   3   4

   a ____

Sentence building

A noun is a naming word.
The name of a person is a **proper noun**.

My name is Mobi.

A **proper noun** begins with a capital letter.

1. Write the proper nouns.

   1   2   3

   Remember the capital letters.

   4   5   6

Language focus   seaside objects; proper nouns   55

Unit 6
Sentence building

My brother is Ben. — *proper noun*

1. Find the proper noun. Circle the proper noun.

   1 Has Ben got a hat?
   2 Is Mobi on the beach?
   3 Sam has got a ball.
   4 Nina is under the tree.
   5 Tilly is in the sea.

2. Write the names.

Tilly   Sam   Ben   Nina   Mobi

   1 ____   2 ____   3 ____

   4 ____   5 ____

3. Write your name. ____

39

Lesson aim Comprehension, vocabulary and sentence building

Lesson targets Children:
- correct incorrect statements
- identify correct statement from picture prompts
- describe objects
- order letters to write words
- practise capital letters for proper nouns.

Key language (words) nouns from Lessons 1 and 2
(structures) *Has he/she got a ...?, What have you got?, Have you got a/an ...?*

Materials Language Book pp54–55, Practice Book pp38–39, flashcards 16, 38, 51–53, 56, 159 word cards for *fish, shell, rock, crab, bird, flower, apple, frog*

Preparation Make word cards.

Lesson 3 time division:

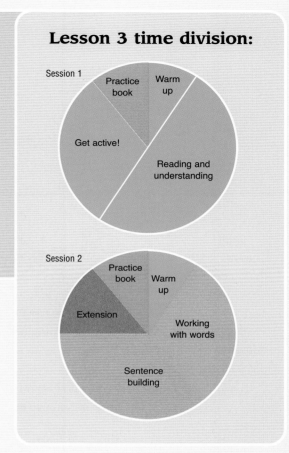

⬇ Lesson 3 Session 1 Warm-up

1 Sing *The elephant goes* (LB p41, LCD1 track 30). Children do the actions.

⬇ Reading and understanding

4 Activity 1: Explain that the sentences are about the story. They are all wrong. Class must say them correctly.

A child reads first sentence, then the class reads. Ask *Is the sea blue?* Elicit **No, it isn't.** Ask *What colour is it?* Elicit **It is green.**

5 Activity 2: Individuals read sentences. Class repeats each time.
Elicit answers orally before children work in their books.

6 **Get active!**
Flashcards 16, 38, 51–53, 56, 159, face down on desk:
Team 1 child takes card and says e.g. *It is big. It is red.*
Team 2 guesses *Have you got a crab?*

⬇ Lesson 3 Session 2 Warm-up

1 Play *Alphabetical order* (p248).

⬇ Working with words

2 Put the flashcards on the board for *fish, shell, rock, crab, bird, flower, apple, frog*, word cards below in muddled order. Ask children *Number 1, what is it?* Elicit **It's a crab.** Child comes forward and finds the correct word, places it beside flashcard.

Class reads all the words.

3 Remove the words before children do Activity 2. Remind them to look in the shapes to find the letters for each word.

⬇ Sentence building

1 Read the first sentence in the box. Put some noun word cards in a list on the board. Remind the class: *These are all nouns.* Write *noun* at the top of the list. Say *They are the names of things.*

2 Read the second sentence. Write *proper noun* on the board at the top. Read Mobi's bubble. Children repeat. Write *Mobi* under proper noun on the board. Read the last sentence. Point out the capital *M*. Ask children for the names of characters in the Fluency Book. Write them on the board under *Mobi*. Point out the capital letters. Add a few names of children in the class. Say *These are all proper nouns.* Ask children to tell you some more proper nouns. Write them on the board. Point out the capitals.

83

Grammar

1 Lesson 4 warm-up.

2 Show poster 6. Ask questions.

3 Read speech bubbles (LB p56). Class/groups repeat.

4 Activity 1: Children make statements. This can be repeated in pairs.

5 Activity 2: Children ask questions and answer.

6 Activity 3: Ask a child to complete each sentence. Class repeats. Children write.

7 Prepare children for PB p40 by checking they understand the tasks. Children complete.

Listening

1 Read Nina's speech bubble (LB p57).

2 Activity 1: Play LCD1 track 37. Children tick the objects.

3 Activity 2: Children talk about the girl.

4 Activity 3: Play the song (track 38). Children listen and sing.

After listening

1 Teach the song in the usual way.

2 Teach actions to the song.

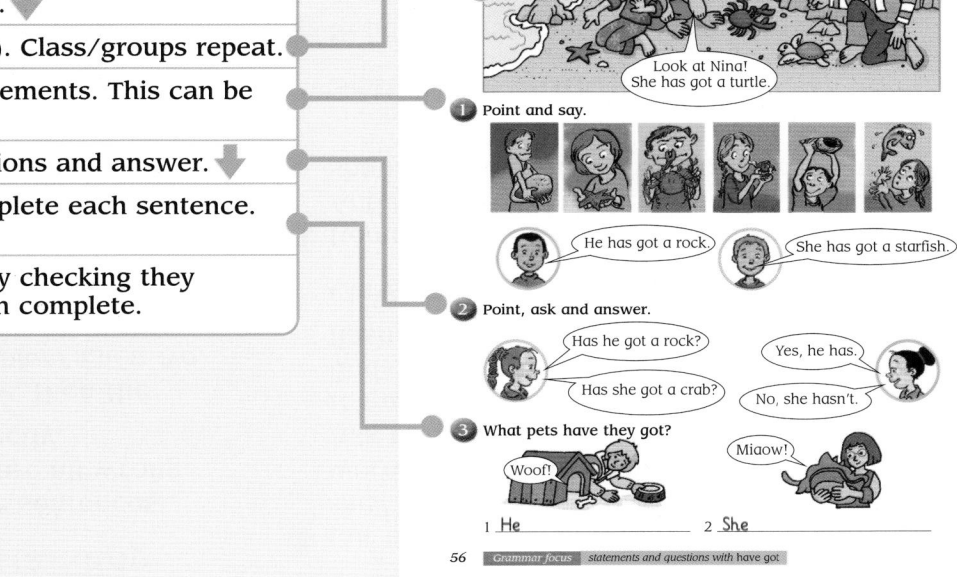

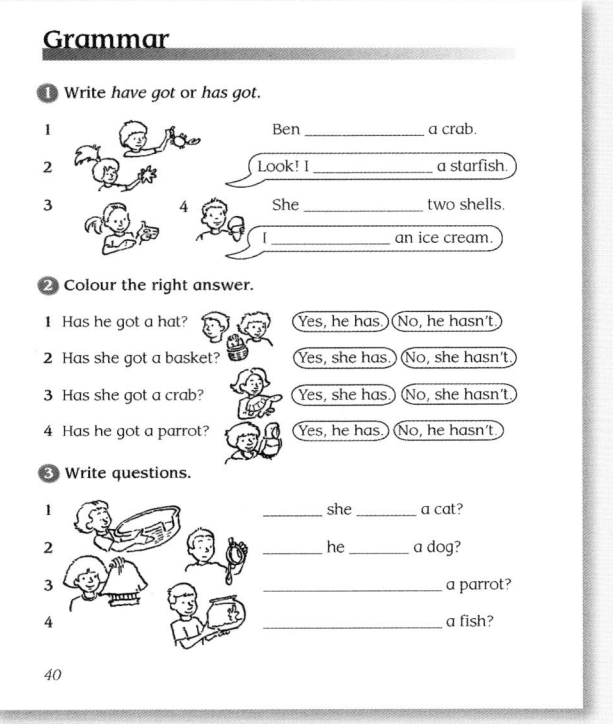

Lesson aim Grammar and listening

Lesson targets Children:

- make statements and ask questions about what children have got
- write sentences about what children have got
- listen for specific information
- sing and learn a short song.

Key language (words) nouns from Lessons 1 and 2
(structures) *I have got a ..., He/She has got a ..., Has he/she got a ...?, Yes/No, he/she has/hasn't.*

Materials Language Book pp56–57, Practice Book p40, Language CD1 tracks 37–38, colour cards for *Warm-up*, flashcards 42, 44, 51–53 (see *Grammar*), poster 6

Preparation
Listen to the CD before the lesson.

Lesson 4 time division:

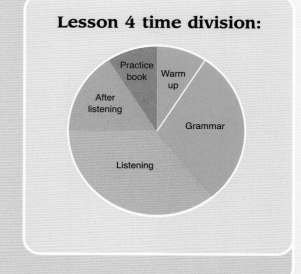

⬇ Lesson 4 Warm-up

1 Stand-up colours (p248)

Each team has a colour card. Team stands up when you say their colour. Change colours after a few turns.

⬇ Grammar

2 (main picture) Ask *What has Ben got?/Mobi got?/Nina got?*
(small picture) *What has Ben got now?*

5 Practise with the whole class: use poster 6. Ask questions, e.g. *Has Nina got a shell? Has Sam got a crab? Has Tilly got a flower?* Elicit **Yes, he/she has. No, he/she hasn't.** If you wish, let individuals come forward and ask the class questions about poster 6: show a flashcard, e.g. *umbrella, shell, ice cream.* Children ask questions about the characters.

Continue this activity in pairs: children ask questions about the pictures in Activity 1.

⬇ Listening

2 Ask *Where is the girl? What has she got? What else can you name in the picture?*

Ask what the photographs show, e.g. *a pink shell, a white shell,* etc.

Tell the class to listen to the girl on the beach. Play the CD. Children listen only. Play the CD again. Children tick the objects she mentions.

Audioscript

Girl   Look in my bucket. I have got a little green crab ... and ... a shiny black rock. *[splashing]* I have got a blue fish ... and ... a silver fish. I have got a little pink shell. And look! Here's a baby starfish!

3 Ask children what things the girl has and hasn't got. This activity can be repeated in pairs.

⬇ After listening

2 Line 1: right hand making waves
Line 2: right hand shades eyes.
Line 3: left hand shades eyes.
Line 4: point to floor.

85

Activity 1

1. Lesson 5 warm-up.
2. (LB p58) Point out pictures and words with *sh*.
3. 🎧 Play sentences twice (LCD1 track 39). Children follow in books.
4. Read sentences.
5. Read and ask questions.
6. Read with the class.

Activity 2

1. Children hold sounds cards. Read the sounds.
2. Close up gradually.
3. Read the word.
4. Children look, say and write.

Activity 3

Children say the word and sentence.
Children write.

Activity 4

1. Write up words. Class/individuals read.
2. Children read in pairs. Listen to pairs.
3. Children check words and tick.

Practice Book

Children complete PB p41.

Phonics games and activities

1. Children make words with phoneme cards.
2. Play *Start the word*.

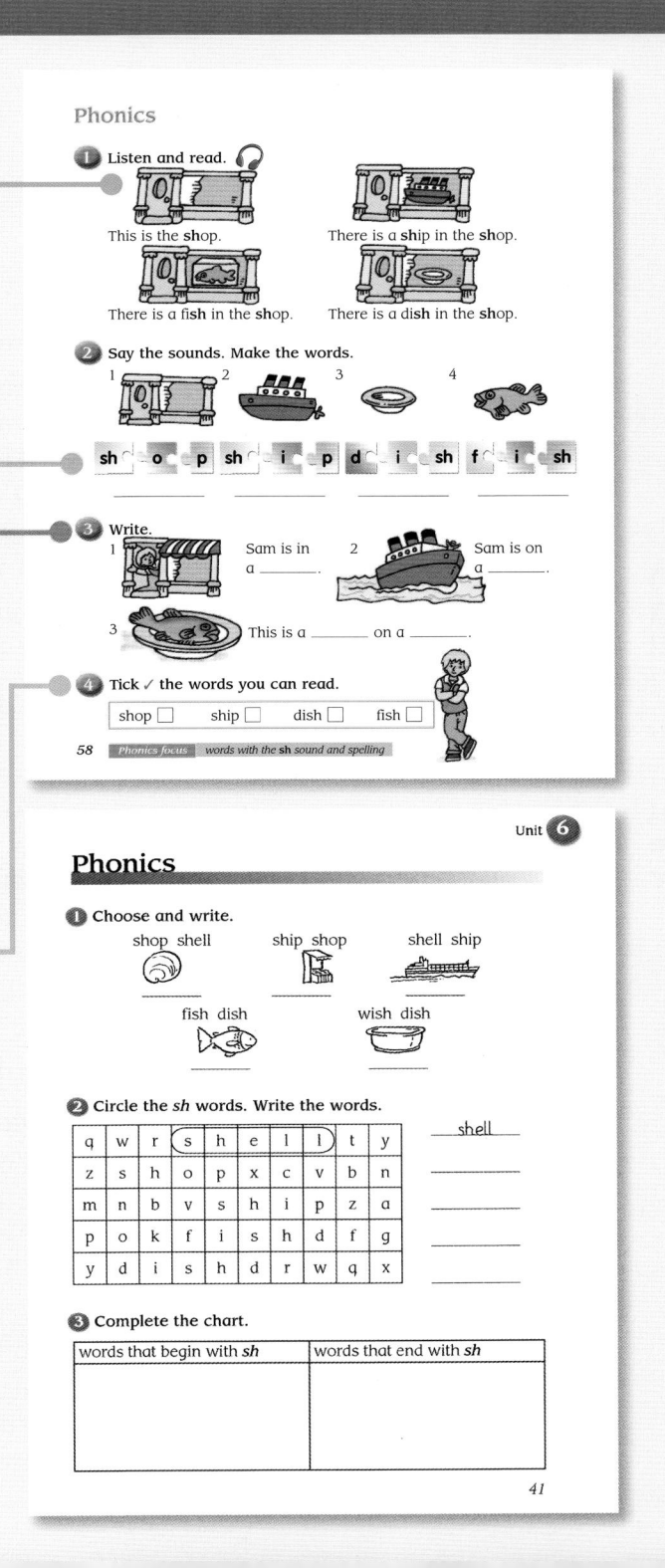

Lesson aim Phonic recognition

Lesson targets Children:

- read, pronounce and spell words with phoneme *sh*
- recognise and say the individual sounds that make up the words
- write the words from picture prompts.

Target words *shell, shop, ship, dish, fish*

Materials Language Book p58, Practice Book p41, Language CD1 track 39, cards for sounds

Preparation Listen to the CD before the lesson. Make large cards for the sounds/phonemes for *shop, ship, dish, fish*. Make small phoneme cards for group work for new key words and *cat, dog, frog, tin, bin, red, hen, ten.*

Lesson 5 time division:

⬇ Lesson 5 Warm-up

① Sing *Clap, clap hands* from Lesson 4 (LB p49, LCD1 track 34).

⬇ Activity 1

⑤ Ask *What can you see?*
What is in the shop?
Is the ship big or small?
Is there a fish in the shop? What colour is it?
Is the dish beautiful?
Make sure all the words in the text are understood.

⬇ Activity 2

Follow the procedure for introducing the phonemes and sounding out each word which is given in detail in the Introduction (p10). Ensure children understand that the letters *sh* make one sound.

⬇ Activity 3

Children look at the picture and read the words. Ask/Help a child to say the whole sentence. Class repeats. Children write the word.

Do the same with the other sentences.

⬇ Activity 4

① Write the four words on the board. Point in random order. Individuals and/or the class reads them.

⬇ Practice Book

Children complete the three exercises.

Check they can sound out all the target words before they move on to Exercise 3.

⬇ Phonics games and activities

① Give sets of phoneme cards to groups. Children order them to spell words. Groups change sets.

② **Start the word**
Write up a word ending, e.g. *_an*. Put letter cards below, e.g. *c, m, v, w, b, f, d*. Children take turns to find initial letters to make words. Class reads. Do the same with other endings, e.g. *_ig, _ish*.

Before writing

1. Lesson 6 warm-up. ⬇
2. Read Miss Plum's speech bubble (LB p59).
3. Ask about the pictures. ⬇
4. Children draw and colour the pictures.
5. Children say what each character has got. ⬇

Shared writing

1. (LB p59) Children suggest sentences for each of the other three pictures. Write them on the board. ⬇
2. Children complete the second sentence according to the colour they have used. ⬇

Practice Book

Writing

1. (PB p42) Individuals/Class read the words in the box.
2. Children write under the correct pictures.

Your writing

1. (PB p43) Individuals/Class read the instructions.
2. Children colour accordingly.
3. Children write sentences. ⬇

After writing

Ask questions to practise adjective + noun. ⬇

Lesson aim Writing

Lesson targets Children:

- write sentences to match picture prompts
- write sentences from picture prompts
- follow instructions to colour pictures correctly.

Key language (words) *book*, words from Lessons 1 and 2
(structures) *She has got a fish. It is blue.*

Materials Language Book p59, Practice Book pp42–43, colour flashcards, word cards for colours (see *Warm-up*)

Lesson 6 time division:

⬇ Lesson 6 Warm-up

1 Stick up colour cards and colour words in scrambled order. Children match.

Write up sentences, e.g. *Ben has a red ball.* Children come forward and underline nouns, circle adjectives and put a box around proper nouns.

⬇ Before writing

3 Ask *Who is in picture 1/2/3/4? Have they all got a bucket?*

5 Child reads the bubble. Class repeats.

Ask as many children as possible what other characters have got. Children answer according to the colours they have used.

⬇ Shared writing

1 Ask *What has Ben got?* Elicit **He has got a crab.** Write it on the board.

2 Ask a child what colour it is. Child replies according to his/her own drawing. Make sure children realise they must write the colour they have used. Write up, e.g. *It is green.*

Point out the *Remember!* box before children write. Rub off all or part of sentences before children write.

⬇ Practice Book

3 **Your writing**
If you wish, ask e.g. *What has Nina got? What colour is it?* to prepare children before they write.

⬇ After writing

(questions for Practice Book page 43)
Ask *Has Nina got a white shell?
Has Ben got a yellow ice cream?
Has Meg got a blue starfish?
What has she got?
Has Scott got a green hat?
What has he got?
What has Tilly got?
What has Nina got?*

Revision 2

You can do it!

1 Look at the pictures. What can you see?

2 Listen and read.

3 Read and say.
Look at picture 1:
Who has got a birthday?
How many cards and presents are there?

Look at picture 2:
What is Tilly and Nina's present?
What has it got?
Does Sam like it?

Look at picture 3:
What is Ben's present?
What colour is it?
How many has Sam got?

Look at picture 4:
What can you see on the table?
What can you see under the table?

Look at pictures 5 and 6:
Who can you see?
What is in the box?
What is the present?
Can you sing it?

1 Today is Sam's birthday. Sam has got cards and presents from his friends.

What are these?

They are cards.

And these are your presents.

3 Sam has got a new ball from Ben.

What's this? Oh! It's a ball.

Have you got a ball?

Yes, I have but it's very old. This is great. Thanks.

5 What's in the box? Can you guess?

Oh! It's a box.

2 Sam has got a lovely book from Nina and Tilly.

What's this? Oh! It's a book. Thank you.

Yes, it's a story book.

Has it got pictures?

Yes, it has.

4 The birthday cake is on the table. One more present is under the table. Who is it from?

Where is the cake?

It's on the table.

6 Mobi is in the box!

Surprise! My present is a song!

Happy birthday to you.
Happy birthday to you.
Happy birthday, dear Sam.
Happy birthday to you.

4 Listen and say. What comes next?

5 Act out Sam's birthday.

6 Write about this picture.

7 Listen and say the chant.

What's in the shop?
A big black box.
What's in the box?
A big green bucket.
What's in the bucket?
A big blue shell.
What's in the shell?
Look! A little red fish.

Lesson aim Revision

Lesson targets Children:
- practise fluency and listening activities, including phonemes *a*, *e*, *i*, *o*, *u* and *sh*
- practise language and structures from Units 4–6 through a story, games and writing.

Key language *What is this? It is a ..., What are these? They are ..., Where is .../are ...?, I have got ..., He/She has got ..., Have you got ...?, Has he/she got ...?*

Words for understanding *birthday, cake, card, pictures, present, surprise*

Materials Language Book pp60–61, Language CD1 tracks 40–42, Practice Book pp44–47

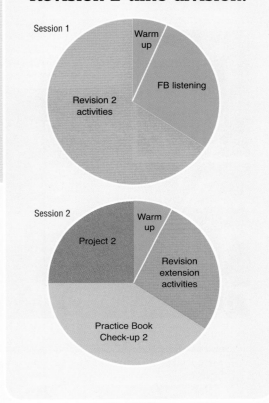

Revision 2 time division:

Session 1
- Warm up
- FB listening
- Revision 2 activities

Session 2
- Warm up
- Revision extension activities
- Practice Book Check-up 2
- Project 2

Sessions 1 and 2 Warm-ups

Sing a favourite song from Units 4–6.

Listening revision

Play Units 4–6 of the Fluency Book (FCD tracks 8–13). Children look in their books and listen. Children close books and repeat in the pauses in the dialogue section.

Revision 2

1. (LB p60) Activity 1: Children say as much as they can from observation: who and what they can see.
2. Activity 2: Play LCD1 track 40. Children listen and follow.
3. Activity 3: Read or let children read out the questions. Elicit answers. Re-read each frame if necessary.
4. (LB p61) Activity 4: Play LCD1 track 41. Children listen and say the next sentence. They look in their books if necessary.

Audioscript

Voice	Listen and say. What comes next?
Sam	What are these?
Sam	Has it got pictures?
Ben	Have you got a ball?
Ben	Where is the cake?
Narrator	One more present is under the table.
Narrator	What's in the box?

5. Activity 5: Individuals, groups or the whole class read narration and speech from their places. Individuals come forward to read and act the story.
6. Activity 6: Ask, e.g. *Whose birthday is it? What has Mobi got?* Write up example sentences. Rub off all or part before children write.
7. Activity 7: Play the chant twice (LCD1 track 42). Children listen then join in.

Revision extension activities

1. Play flashcard games introduced in Units 4–6, e.g. *What is it?*
2. Use the phonic rhyme for reading practice. Teach it, if you wish.

⬇ Practice Book

Children complete *Check-up 2* (PB pp44–45) as a test, as preparation for a test or for homework.

Children complete *Move on with Mobi 2* (PB pp46–47). These pages give further revision for homework or class work.

Project 2

Carry out projects in groups or whole class: 1 Island of adventure model; 2 Garden and/or beach frieze. See page 245 for instructions.

Before listening

1. Lesson 1 warm-up.

2. Show poster 7. Read the title. Ask questions.

3. Show flashcards 58–61. Say the verbs. Class repeats.

4. Show flashcards (see *Preparation*, p93). Say negative imperative. Children find the matching symbol at the bottom of the poster.

5. Read the notice board line by line.

Shared listening

1. Play FCD track 14. Point to characters when they speak.

2. Ask *Who? What? Where?* questions.

3. Ask questions about the small picture.

4. Play FCD track 14 and point to characters again.

Dialogue practice

1. Say negative imperatives. Children point in books (FB pp20–21). Point on poster for children to check.

2. Show positive and negative imperative flashcards (64–67). Children respond.

3. Children close books. Play FCD track 15 and show character flashcards. Class repeats lines in pauses.

4. Groups say lines by character.

5. Individuals act dialogue.

6. Play CD track 14 again. Children follow text or point to main picture.

After listening

1. Show flashcards 58–61. Ask questions.

2. Play the *Instruction team game.*

92

Lesson aim Fluency

Lesson targets Children:

- listen for pronunciation and intonation
- repeat dialogue accurately
- act out dialogue with expression
- follow positive/negative imperatives.

Key language (words) *Don't ...!, climb, fall, jump, run*
(structures) *Run!, Don't run!, Jump!, Don't jump!*

Language for understanding *help, dark, scared, Quick!, Oh, no!, OK*

Materials Poster 7, Fluency Book pp20–21, Fluency CD tracks 14–15, character flashcards 2–6, flashcards 58–61

Preparation Listen to the CD before the lesson. Use or make a clear plastic sleeve for each flashcard. Glue onto the front a coloured paper cross (X). Slip the flashcards into the sleeves to teach the negative command.

Lesson 1 time division:

Warm up, Before listening, Shared listening, Dialogue practice, After listening

Lesson 1 Warm-up

1 Sing the *Rainbow song* from LB p7, LCD1 track 4.

Before listening

2 Ask *Can you see animals?* Child comes forward and points: *I can see a ... Can you see the children?* Child comes forward and points: *I can see (name of character).*
Can you see flowers?/trees?/a ladder?

Shared listening

2 Ask *Who is scared?*
What can Nina hear?
Who is under the tree?
Where is Ben?

3 Ask *Who is on the tree?*
Is Ben on the tree?
Can you see Ben?

After listening

1 Ask *Can Nina run?*
Can Sam climb?
What can Sam climb?
Can Tilly jump?

2 Instruction team game
Show the class how to mime each action, e.g. run on the spot; jump on the spot; climb: lifting arms and legs; fall: raising arms and leaning sideways.

Divide the class into four teams. Number them 1–4. Say, e.g. *Team 1* and show a flashcard, e.g. *climb*. Team 1 mimes climbing. Say *Team 1, don't climb*. Team 1 must all stop immediately.

Continue with other teams and other instructions. Give all teams a turn at the different instructions.
When the class is used to these instructions, try variations.

Variation 1: Start a team off with their action mime, but do not stop them. Start one or two more teams off. Stop the first team when you choose. Teams lose points if they do not follow instructions quickly and accurately. Children must listen for their team number, look at the flashcard and listen to you.

Variation 2: Instead of stopping a team's action, show them a different flashcard. The team must all change to the new action.

93

Before reading

1 Lesson 2 warm-up. ⬇

2 Use actions to teach new words.

3 Children open books (LB pp62–63). Ask children what places they can see.

Shared reading

1 🎧 Play LCD1 track 43. Children follow text in book.

2 Read line by line. Ask questions. ⬇

3 Read with the class.

Reading practice

1 Give reading practice. Use some or all of the following:
- Children read again as a class.
- Groups read different sections.
- Individuals read different sections.

2 🎧 Class listens again to LCD1 track 43 and follows in LB.

After reading

Play *Simon says.* ⬇

Lesson aim Reading

Lesson targets Children:

- follow a text read out to them
- listen for pronunciation and intonation
- read the text aloud with accurate pronunciation and intonation
- learn and understand new vocabulary items
- understand the sense of the text as a whole
- answer simple comprehension questions.

Key language (words) *get up, open, shut, sit down, stand up* (structures) commands and requests

Words for understanding *biscuit, higher, shooting star, swimming pool, outdoors, indoors, Come on!, Stop!*

Materials Language Book pages 62–63, Language CD1 track 43

Preparation Listen to the CD before the lesson.

Lesson 2 time division:

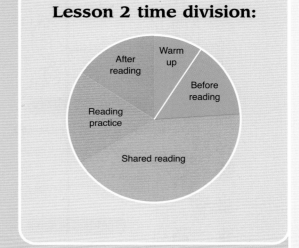

Lesson 2 Warm-up

1 Sing the *Actions song* (LB page 9, LCD1 track 6).

Shared reading

2 Ask *Where is the boy? Is it morning or night?*
Do you stand up on the bus?
Is the boy next to the door?
Where is the paper?
Can the girl run?
Where is the girl?
What can the boy do? Is he indoors or outdoors?
Is Mum happy? Is the boy outdoors? Where is he?
What has Grandma got?
Where is the chair?
What can the girl see?
Who says goodnight?

After reading

Simon says

Teach *Simon says* if your class does not already know this game. Children only follow commands preceded by *Simon says ...* If you say *Simon says stand up*, children obey. If you say *Stand up*, children must not do the action. If they do, they are out of the game. Practise a few commands with and without *Simon says* without getting any children out. When children have understood what they have to do, begin the game. Instructions children should now understand: *Stand up. Jump. Don't jump. Sit down. Open your book. Close your book. Look (at the window/floor/ceiling). Run (on the spot). Clap hands.*

Reading and understanding SESSION 1

1. Session 1 warm-up.
2. Re-read *Do or don't?* (LB pp62–63).
3. Activity 1 (LB p64): Individuals read phrases. Class repeats. Children match.
4. Activity 2: Read Ben's *Remember!* box. Make sure children understand. Children circle. Children read out answers.
5. Play *Get active!*
6. Prepare children for PB p48 by checking they understand the task. Children complete.

Working with words   SESSION 2

1. Session 2 warm-up.
2. Revise the key words with flashcards 58–61.
3. Activity 1 (LB p65): Children find the words.
4. Activity 2: They write them under the correct picture.

Sentence building

1. Explain the information in the box (LB p65).
2. Activity 1: Children find and circle the verbs.
3. Prepare children for PB p49 by checking they understand the tasks. Children complete.

Extension activities

Practise identifying verbs, nouns, adjectives.

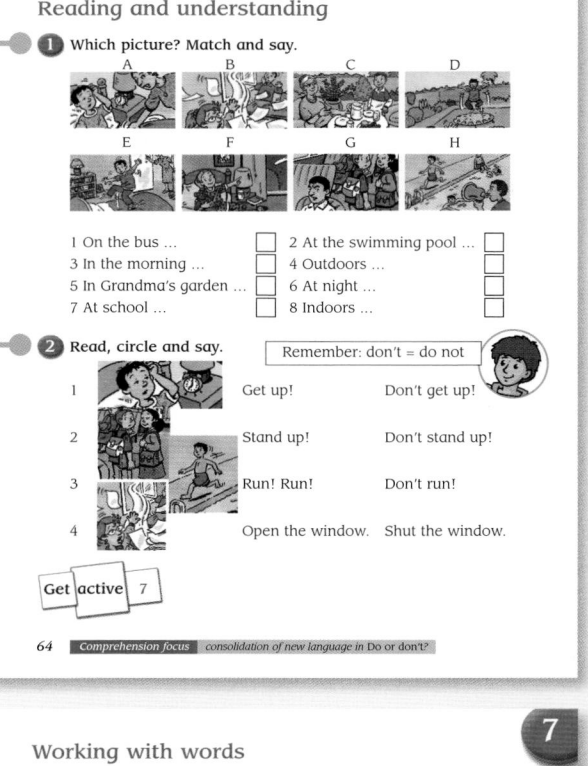

Reading and understanding

1. Which picture? Match and say.

A B C D
E F G H

1 On the bus ... 2 At the swimming pool ...
3 In the morning ... 4 Outdoors ...
5 In Grandma's garden ... 6 At night ...
7 At school ... 8 Indoors ...

2. Read, circle and say.

Remember: don't = do not

1 Get up! Don't get up!
2 Stand up! Don't stand up!
3 Run! Run! Don't run!
4 Open the window. Shut the window.

Get active 7

64 Comprehension focus consolidation of new language in Do or don't?

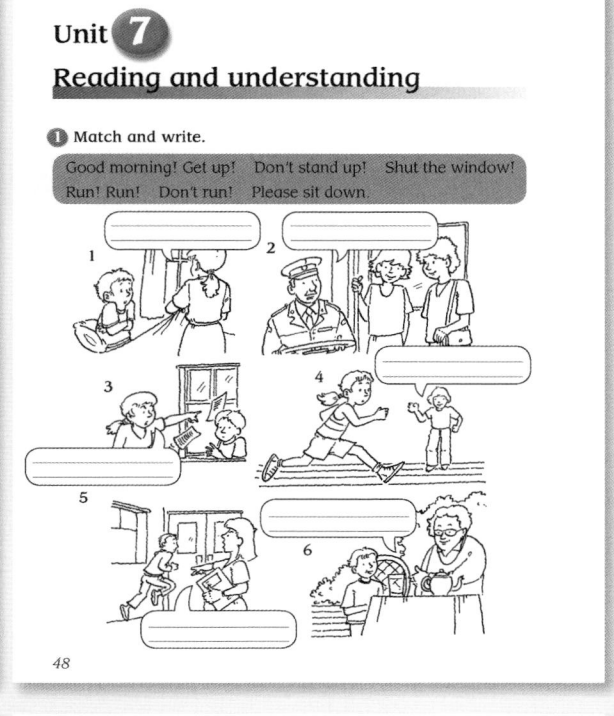

Unit 7
Reading and understanding

1. Match and write.

Good morning! Get up! Don't stand up! Shut the window!
Run! Run! Don't run! Please sit down.

48

Working with words   7

1. Find the words.

climblookjumpopenrunsit

2. Write the words under the pictures.

1 2 3
4 5 6

Sentence building

A **verb** is a doing word.

jump draw run

1. Read the sentences. Circle the verbs.

1 Ben, open the window.
2 Tilly, climb the ladder.
3 Nina, look at the ball.
4 Sam, jump over the wall.

Language focus action verbs 65

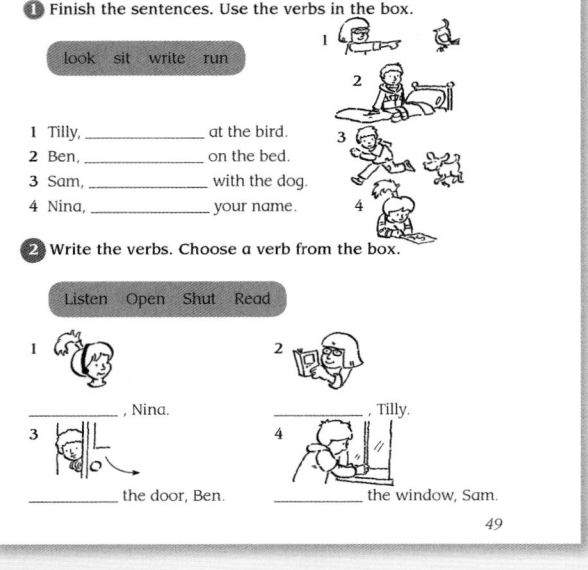

Sentence building   Unit 7

Verbs *are doing words.*   run   jump

1. Finish the sentences. Use the verbs in the box.

look sit write run

1 Tilly, _____ at the bird.
2 Ben, _____ on the bed.
3 Sam, _____ with the dog.
4 Nina, _____ your name.

2. Write the verbs. Choose a verb from the box.

Listen Open Shut Read

1 _____, Nina.
2 _____, Tilly.
3 _____ the door, Ben.
4 _____ the window, Sam.

49

Lesson aim Comprehension, vocabulary and sentence building

Lesson targets Children:
- match phrases to pictures
- match affirmative and negative commands to pictures
- find words in a word snake, match and write under pictures
- identify the verb in a sentence.

Key language (words) words, phrases and commands from Lessons 1 and 2 (structures) verbs from Lessons 1 and 2

Materials Language Book pp64–65, Practice Book pp48–49, word cards for *Get up, Don't stand up, Don't run, Jump, Don't jump, Sit down, Don't get up, Close the window* (no punctuation at the end), flashcards 58–61

Preparation Make the word cards.

Lesson 3 time division:

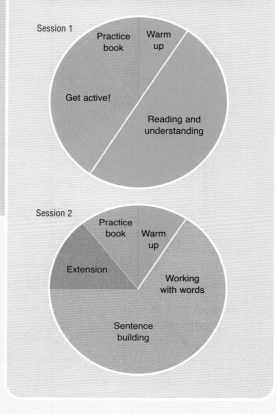

Session 1

Practice book · Warm up · Get active! · Reading and understanding

Session 2

Practice book · Warm up · Extension · Working with words · Sentence building

⬇ Lesson 3 Session 1 Warm-up

1 Sing *A sailor went to sea* (LB p57, LCD1 track 38).

⬇ Reading and understanding

5 **Get active!**
Write the phrases from Activity 1 on the board with a small letter for the first word and a full stop at the end.
Put the commands word cards in scrambled order below.

Children match instructions word cards with the phrases, e.g. *Don't stand up on the bus.* Stick up the card in front of the phrase. Class reads the sentences.

Children mime one of the people in the story. Others guess where they are.

⬇ Lesson 3 Session 2 Warm-up

1 Play the *Alphabetical order* game (p248).

⬇ Working with words

2 Show the class the flashcards for *climb, jump* and *run.* Class names and mimes them.

Give instructions: *Please sit down. Open your books. Look at page 65.*

⬇ Sentence building

1 Read the sentence. Say *The verb tells us what somebody is doing.* Ask children to read the words below the picture. Ask the class to stand up. Say *Jump.* Class jumps. Say *We jump.* Do the same with the other words (mime *drawing*). Add in some other verbs. Do the actions/ mimes. Prompt class to do the same. Say, e.g. *We look/climb/sit.*

⬇ Extension activities

Write up sentences, e.g. *Draw a big shell. Look at the red ball. Climb the tall tree.* Ask children to underline the verb, circle the noun and draw a box round the adjective in each sentence.

Grammar

1. Lesson 4 warm-up. ⬇

2. Use poster 7 to revise negative commands.

3. Individuals read the speech bubbles in the box (LB p66).

4. Activity 1: Children match commands to pictures. ⬇

5. Activity 2: Children complete the sentences. ⬇

6. Prepare children for PB p50 by checking they understand the tasks. Children complete.

Listening

1. Children look at the pictures (LB p67). Ask *What is the game?*

2. Read or ask a child to read Nina's speech bubble.

3. 🎧 Activity 1: Play LCD1 track 44. Children listen and follow. ⬇

4. Activity 2: Class plays the game.

5. 🎧 Activity 3: Play the song (LCD1 track 45). ⬇

After listening

Teach the song. ⬇

Lesson aim Grammar and listening

Lesson targets Children:

- match commands to pictures
- complete commands for pictured situations
- follow a game and play it
- sing and learn a short song with actions.

Key language (structures) commands from Lessons 1 and 2

Materials Language Book pp66–67, Practice Book p50, Language CD1 tracks 44–45, word cards for *run, jump, climb, fall, look, sit, stand, open, close, write, draw* for *Warm-up*, poster 7

Preparation Listen to the CD before the lesson. Make word cards as necessary.

Lesson 4 time division:

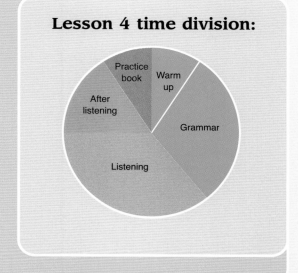

Lesson 4 Warm-up

1 **Action mime**
Play *Action mime* in teams: show a verb word card to team 1. Children mime/do actions. Team 2 guesses.

Grammar

4 Individuals read sentences. Class repeats each sentence. Children match. To check answers, ask individuals to read the sentence and say the letter in the box.

5 Individuals read the words in the box. Class repeats.

Children look at the pictures. Help/Ask individual to say first complete sentence. Class repeats. Class writes answer.

Continue with the other pictures.

Listening

3 If you wish, let children read the speech bubbles for each picture, before they listen and follow again.

Audioscript

Miss Plum	Simon says: Stand up.
Miss Plum	Simon says: Walk.
Miss Plum	Simon says: Look at your friends.
Miss Plum	Simon says: Run.
Miss Plum	Stop!
Children	Oh no!
Miss Plum	Simon says: Sit down.

5 Children listen and follow. Children look at the pictures. Go through the actions with the class.

Children listen and do the actions. (If they do not have space to turn round, they can wave a circle in the air with one hand.)

After listening

This song is very easy to learn just by listening and doing the actions. Lead the class with the actions. Play the CD again and encourage children to sing as well as do.

99

Activity 1

1. Lesson 5 warm-up.
2. (LB p68) Point out pictures and words with *ch*.
3. 🎧 Play rhyme twice (LCD1 track 46). Children follow in books.
4. Read rhyme.
5. Read and ask questions.
6. Read with the class.

Activity 2

1. Children hold sounds cards. Read the sounds.
2. Close up gradually.
3. Read the word.
4. Children look, say and write.

Activity 3

1. Children look and read. Children match.
2. Children write. Children circle.

Activity 4

1. Write up words. Class/individuals read.
2. Children read in pairs. Listen to pairs.
3. Children check words and tick.

Practice Book

Children complete PB p51.

Phonics games and activities

1. Children sort *sh* and *ch* words.
2. *Look, write and check.*

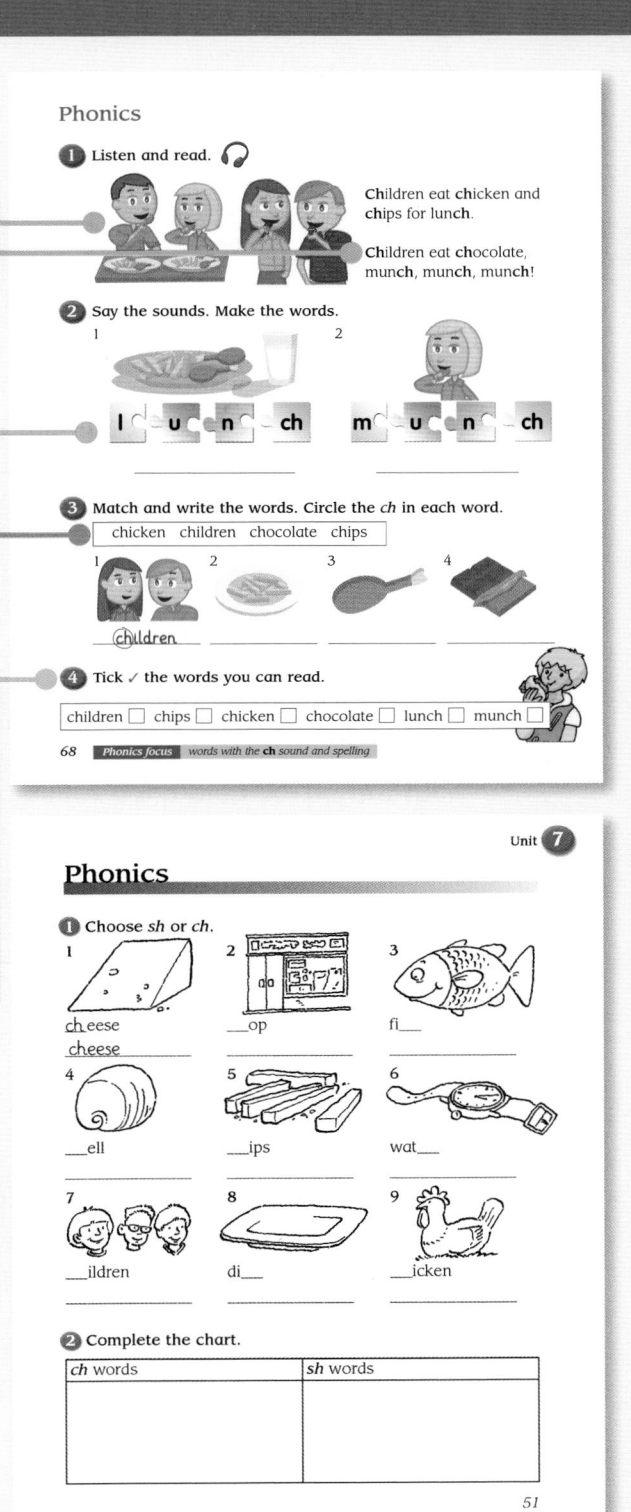

Phonics

1. Listen and read. 🎧

Children eat chicken and chips for lunch.

Children eat chocolate, munch, munch, munch!

2. Say the sounds. Make the words.

1   l — u — n — ch   2   m — u — n — ch

3. Match and write the words. Circle the *ch* in each word.

chicken   children   chocolate   chips

1 children   2 _____   3 _____   4 _____

4. Tick ✓ the words you can read.

children ☐   chips ☐   chicken ☐   chocolate ☐   lunch ☐   munch ☐

68   **Phonics focus**   *words with the **ch** sound and spelling*

Unit 7

Phonics

1. Choose *sh* or *ch*.

1 ch.eese
   cheese

2 ___op

3 fi___

4 ___ell

5 ___ips

6 wat___

7 ___ildren

8 di___

9 ___icken

2. Complete the chart.

ch words	*sh* words

51

Lesson aim Phonic recognition

Lesson targets Children:

- read, pronounce and spell words with the phoneme *ch*
- recognise and say the individual sounds that make up *lunch, munch*
- match the words with *ch* to pictures.

Target words *cheese, children, chips, chicken, chocolate, dish, fish, lunch, munch, shell, shop, watch*

Materials Language Book p68, Practice Book p51, Language CD1 track 46, cards for sounds

Preparation Listen to the CD before the lesson. Make large cards for the sounds/phonemes for *lunch, munch*. Make word cards for *ch* target words and for *fish, dish, shell, ship, shop*. Draw a large chair shape, big enough to stick *ch* word cards onto. Draw a large fish shape, big enough to stick *sh* words onto.

Lesson 5 time division:

Lesson 5 Warm-up

1 Play the *Stand up!, Sit down!* song from Lesson 4 (LB p67, LCD1 track 45). Children join in.

Activity 1

5 Ask *What have they got for lunch? What have the children got? What do the children do?*

Make sure all the words in the text are understood.

Activity 2

Follow the procedure for introducing the phonemes and sounding out each word which is given in detail in the Introduction (p10). Ensure the children understand that the letters *ch* make one sound.

Activity 3

1 Children look at the pictures and read the words. Class reads. Children match the words and pictures.

2 Children write the words. Children circle the *ch* in each word.

Activity 4

1 Write the six words on the board. Point in random order. Individuals and/or the class reads them.

Practice Book

Children complete the two exercises.

Ask children to read the words in the chart. Ensure children can hear the *ch* or *sh* in each word.

Phonics games and activities

1 Put up the chair and fish shapes. Put the word cards on the board. Children put the words in the correct shape. If possible, keep these up in the classroom.

2 **Look, write and check**
Write a word on the board. Children look at it.

Cover the word. Children write it. Uncover the word. Children check. If you wish, revise cvc words from previous units.

101

Before writing

1. Lesson 6 warm-up. ↓
2. Read Miss Plum's speech bubble (LB p69).
3. Read the sentence. Explain crossing the road. ↓
4. Children look at the pictures. Ask questions. ↓
5. Individuals read the sentences in the box.
6. Class reads the sentences.

Shared writing

1. Children look at the pictures (LB p69). Help them to suggest the correct sentences. Write them up. ↓
2. Class reads all the sentences. Rub them off. Class writes.

Practice Book

Writing

1. (PB p52) Individuals/Class read the sentences in the box.
2. Children look at pictures and write sentences under the correct picture.

Your writing

(PB p53) Children write sentences next to each picture.

After writing

Say the road safety chant. ↓

7

Class writing

1 Match and write.

Cross the road safely!

Listen! Stop! Look all around!
Walk! Don't run! Look and listen! Wait!

1 Stop!
2
3
4
5
6

Remember: Walk! ✔ Don't run! ✘

Writing focus command forms

69

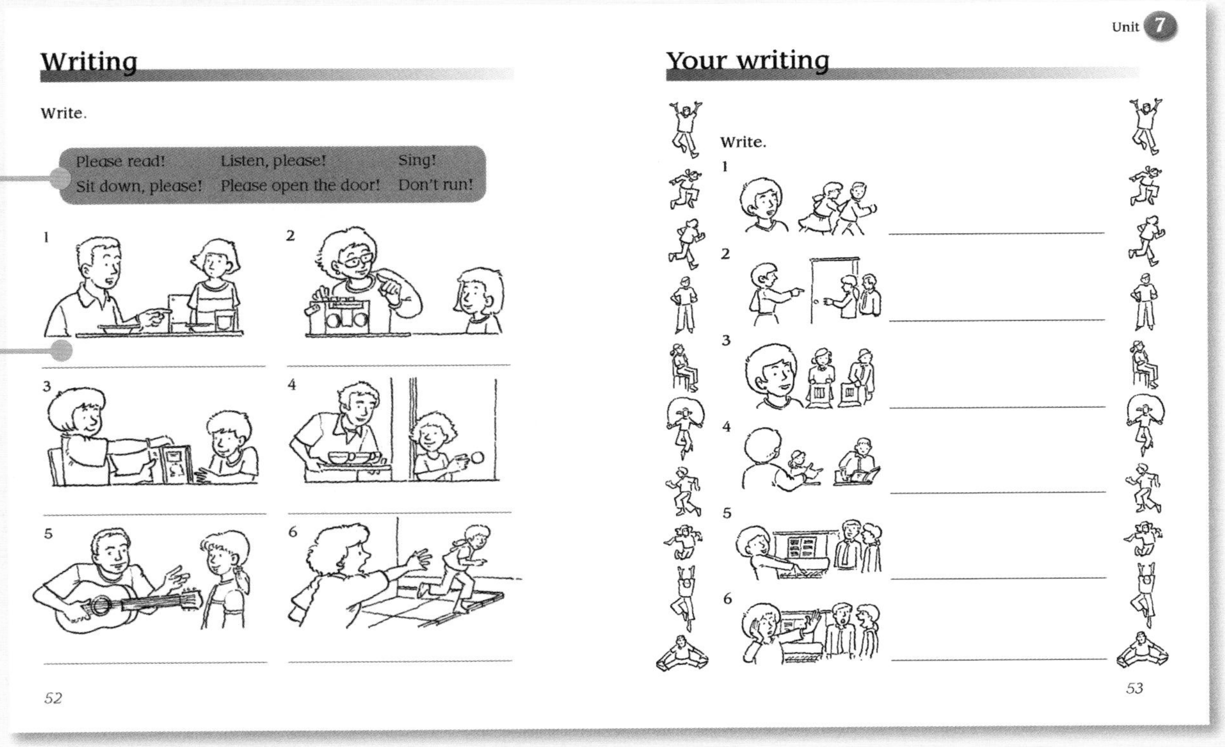
Writing

Write.

Please read! Listen, please! Sing!
Sit down, please! Please open the door! Don't run!

1
2
3
4
5
6

52

Unit 7

Your writing

Write.

1
2
3
4
5
6

53

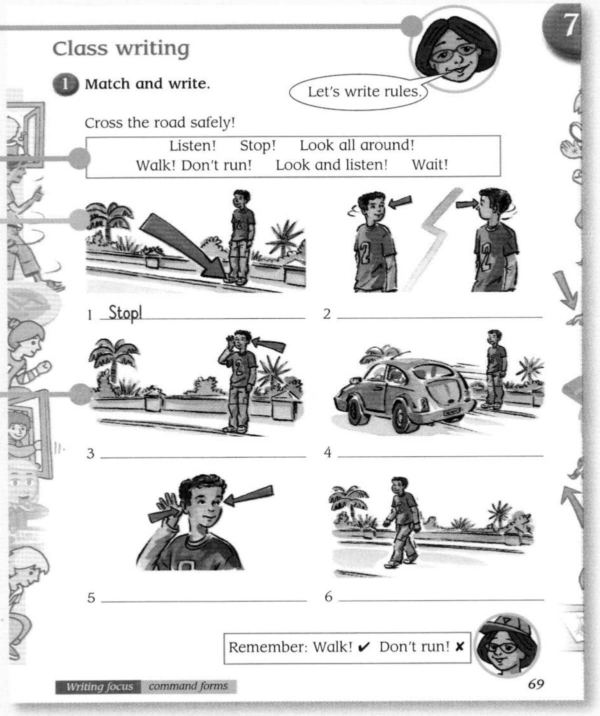

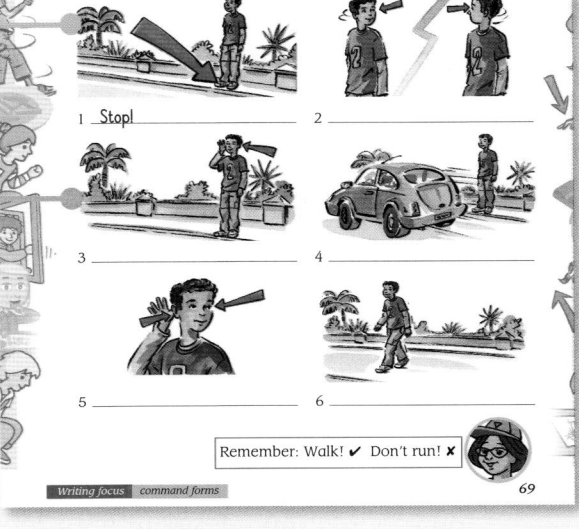

Lesson aim Writing

Lesson targets Children:

- write commands to match picture prompts
- write requests to match picture prompts
- learn a chant about road safety.

Key language (words) affirmative commands with *please*, negative commands
(structures) imperative verbs with *please*

Materials Language Book p69, Practice Book pp52 and 53

Lesson 6 time division:

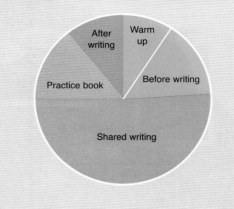

Lesson 6 Warm-up

1 Play *Alphabetical order* (p248) with capital letters.

Before writing

3 Point out the road in the first picture. Draw a road on the board. Ask *What can you see in the road?* Elicit **cars, buses, vans**. Draw some simple vehicle shapes on the road. Draw a stick person on one side of the road.

Say *Look! Cars, buses and vans. Be careful when you cross the road.* Draw a dotted line from the person to the other side of the road.

4 Ask *Where is the boy/girl?* Elicit **He/She is next to the road.** Say *Be careful!* Ask *Do you run across the road?* Elicit **No.**

Shared writing

1 Children look at the pictures. Point out the arrows.

Ask a child to read the command under the first picture.

Tell the class to look at the second picture. Remind them where the arrow is.

Ask a child to suggest the correct sentence for the second picture. Write it on the board. Do the same with the other pictures.

After writing

Road safety chant

Stop! *(clap clap)*
Look all around!
Listen! *(clap clap)*
Wait for the cars!
Look and listen! *(clap clap)*
Then walk! *(clap clap)*
Don't run. *(clap clap,clap)*
Don't run!

Before listening

1 Lesson 1 warm-up. ⬇

2 Show poster 8. Read the title. Ask questions. ⬇

3 Point and say the verbs. Children come forward; find verbs in main picture.

4 🂠 Show flashcards (58–59, 67–69, 74–75) and name verbs. Class repeats.

5 Point out the small picture, left. Ask questions. ⬇

Shared listening

1 🎧 Play FCD track 16. Point to characters when they speak.

2 Ask questions about the gold star. ⬇

3 Ask *Who? What? Where?* questions. ⬇

4 🎧 Play FCD track 16 and point to characters again.

Dialogue practice

1 Say new verbs. Children point in books (FB pp22–23). Point on poster for children to check.

2 🂠 Show flashcards 74–75. Children name.

3 🎧 🂠 Children close books. Play FCD track 17 and show character flashcards. Class repeats lines in pauses.

4 🂠 Groups say lines by character.

5 🂠 Individuals act dialogue.

6 🎧 Play FCD track 16 again. Children follow text or point to main picture.

After listening

1 🂠 Show flashcards 58–59, 67–69, 74–75. Ask questions. ⬇

2 Play *Action mime*. ⬇

3 Children put the next sticker star in the correct place on FB pp46–47.

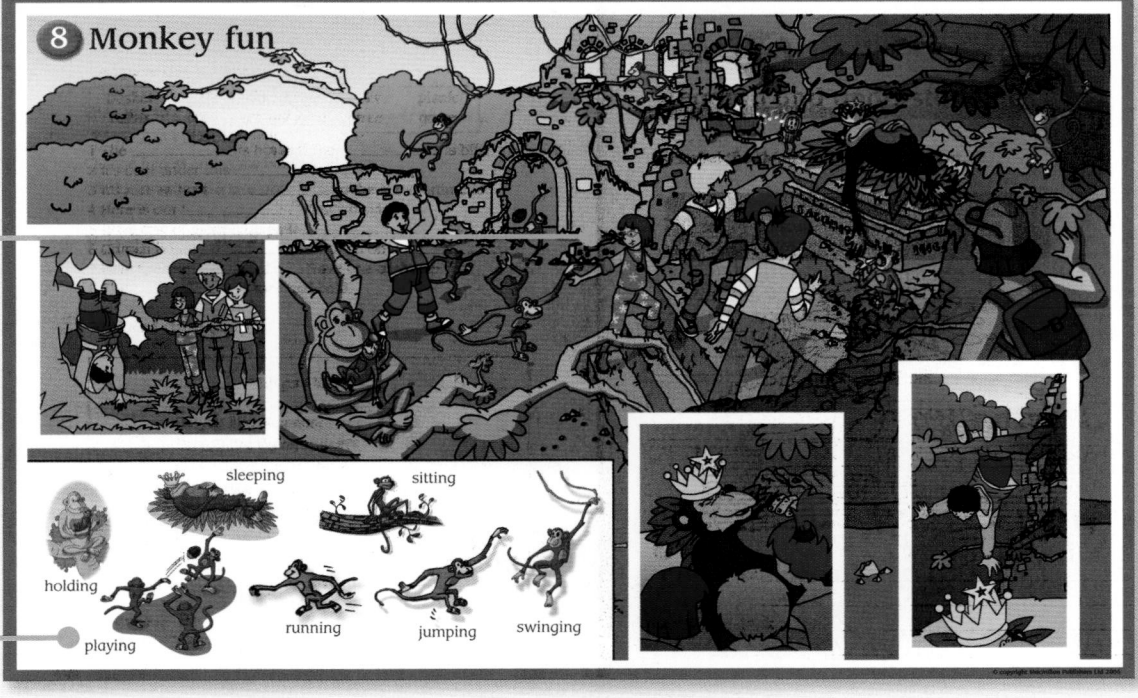

8 Monkey fun

Oh, look at Ben!
He is swinging on the branch of a tree.
Is he OK?

Ben! Are you OK?

Yes, I'm fine.

swinging

sleeping

playing

running

sitting

holding

jumping

I can get it!

Look at the crown on his head!

He's the king of the monkeys.

Oh! I can see a gold star.

A gold star! Hooray!

Can Ben get the gold star? Be careful, Ben!

Oh! Look at the monkeys!

They're running and jumping.

They're swinging in the trees. They're funny.

Look at the big orange monkey! She's holding a baby.

Ah!

The little brown monkeys are playing football.

I can see a big black monkey.

Where?

Under the tree. He's sleeping.

𐓦ꮔꮥ

Shhh! Be quiet, Mobi!

22 ▌ *He/She is sleeping.   They are playing.*

23

Lesson aim Fluency

Lesson targets Children:

- listen for pronunciation and intonation
- repeat dialogue accurately
- act out dialogue with expression
- say what different monkeys are doing.

Key language (words) *holding, jumping, playing, running, sitting, sleeping, swinging*
(structures) *He/She is sleeping. They are playing.*

Language for understanding *baby, crown, football, head, king, big, little, I'm fine. Shh! Be quiet.*

Materials Poster 8, Fluency Book pp22–23, Fluency CD tracks 16–17, character flashcards 2–5, flashcards for verbs 58–59, 67–69, 74–75

Preparation Listen to the CD before the lesson.

Lesson 1 time division:

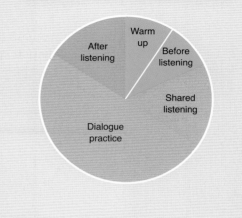

Lesson 1 Warm-up

① Say the *Star chant*.

Sing *Stand up! Sit down!* from Unit 7 Lesson 4 (LB p67, LCD1 track 45).

Before listening

② Ask *Can you see animals?*
What animals can you see?
Can you see the children?
Are the children on the beach?
Where are they?

⑤ Ask *Can Tilly, Sam and Nina see Ben?*
Where is Ben?
Is he swinging on the tree?
Is he OK?

Shared listening

② Ask *Who has a crown?*
What is on the crown?
Is Ben on a tree?
Is he running?/jumping?
What is he doing?

③ Ask *Who can see the big orange monkey?*
What is the big orange monkey holding?
What are the little brown monkeys doing?
Who can see the big black monkey?
Where is the big black monkey?
What is he doing?
What is on the crown?

After listening

① Show all the actions cards (monkeys 39, 68–71 and characters 64–67).

Ask *What is/are he/she/it/they doing?*

② **Action mime**

Divide the class into two teams. A child from team 1 mimes an action. The other team guesses, e.g. **He/She is sleeping.**

Then a child from team 2 mimes and team 1 guesses.

When children are used to this game, ask pairs to mime. The other team guesses **They are ...**

Before reading

1 Lesson 2 warm-up. ⬇

2 📖 Teach new words with flashcards 70–73, 145.

3 Children open books (LB pp70–71). Ask questions. ⬇

Shared reading

1 🎧 Play LCD1 track 47. Children follow text in book.

2 Read about each animal. Ask questions. ⬇

3 Read with the class.

unit 8

Where are the animals?

In the forest …

An owl is sitting in a tree. It is brown and white.
It is very still. Where is it? Can you find it?
The butterflies are yellow and orange and red.
They are beautiful. Can you see them?
What are they doing?

In the jungle …

The tiger is black and yellow. It can run very fast.
But now it is sleeping. Can you see it? Where is it?
A snake is sleeping, too.
It is black and green. Where is it?

By the river …

Be careful! There is a crocodile here.
It is swimming in the river. Can you see it?
What colour is it?
A big grey elephant is walking in the trees.
You can see its long trunk and big ears.
Can you find it?

In the snow …

Some animals live in the cold ice and snow.
They are white. Can you find the white fox?
What is it doing? What is the polar bear doing?
What colour is it?

70 Parents: see extra material on page 166

71

Reading practice

1 Give reading practice. Use some or all of the following:
* Children read again as a class.
* Groups read different sections.
* Individuals read different sections.

2 🎧 Class listens again to LCD1 track 47 and follows in LB.

After reading

Do the flashcards and word cards activity. ⬇

Lesson aim Reading

Lesson targets Children:

- follow a text read out to them
- listen for pronunciation and intonation
- read the text aloud with accurate pronunciation and intonation
- learn and understand new vocabulary items
- understand the sense of the text as a whole
- answer simple comprehension questions.

Key language (words) *bear, crocodile, fox, hippo, tiger*
(structures) *It is sleeping. Is it flying?*

Words for understanding *giraffe, zebra; fast, still*

Materials Language Book pages 70–71, Language CD1 track 47, flashcards 70–73, 145, word cards for *fox, tiger, crocodile, polar bear, hippo, owl, butterfly, snake, elephant*

Preparation Listen to the CD before the lesson. Make word cards as necessary.

Lesson 2 time division:

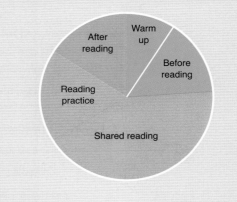

Lesson 2 Warm-up

1 Sing *Clap, clap hands* (LB p49, LCD1 track 34).

Before reading

3
Ask *Can you find the jungle? What can you see in the jungle?*
Can you see a big animal next to the river? What is it?
Look at the forest. What colours are the flowers?
Can you see the white snow? How many animals are in the snow?

Shared reading

2 Ask (picture 1) Owl: *Where is the owl? What colour is it? Is it flying?*
Butterflies: *Where are the butterflies? Are they flying? What colours are they?*
(picture 2) Tiger: *Is it running? Where is it? What colours is it?*
Snake: *Is it going fast? What colours is it?*
(picture 3) Crocodile: *Where is the crocodile? What is it doing?*
Elephant: *Has it got little ears? What colour is it? Is it running fast?*
(picture 4) Fox: *Is it sleeping? Can it run fast?*
Polar bear: *Where does it live? Is the polar bear looking at the fox?*

After reading

Put up the animal flashcards with their word cards in scrambled order below.

Children take turns to read word cards and match to flashcards.

Take down the animal flashcards to leave the word cards. Class reads the words.

107

Reading and understanding

1. Session 1 warm-up.

2. Re-read *Where are the animals?* (LB pp70–71). Point out the hippo. Teach the word.

3. Activity 1 (LB p72): Children look at the picture. Ask questions. Explain the task to the class.

4. Activity 2: Children tick words that match the statements.

5. Activity 3: Children write words to match the statement.

6. Play *Get active!*

7. Prepare children for PB p54. Read the descriptions with them and check they understand the tasks. Children complete.

Working with words

1. Session 2 warm-up

2. Activity 1 (LB p73): Children read sentences. They say the missing word. Check with the class. Children write the sentence number in the box.

Sentence building

1. Go through the information in the box.

2. Activity 1 (LB p73): Children write questions.

3. Prepare children for PB p55. Go through the box and check they understand the tasks. Children complete.

Extension activity

Hold up an animal flashcard.

One team says a statement, e.g. **The elephant is big.** The other team makes it a question. The first team answers the question. Repeat with different flashcards.

Reading and understanding

1. Which sentences are about the picture? Read and ✓ tick.

1. It is sitting in a tree. ☐
2. It is white. ☐
3. It can run very fast. ☐
4. There is ice and snow. ☐
5. It is swimming in the river. ☐
6. It is not running now. ☐

2. Read and ✓ tick.

1 It is cold.	ice ☐	snow ☐	the jungle ☐
2 They can be white.	foxes ☐	bears ☐	crocodiles ☐
3 They can be grey.	tigers ☐	hippos ☐	elephants ☐
4 They have got big ears.	hippos ☐	foxes ☐	elephants ☐

3. What is it? Write the answer.

1. It can be black, brown or white. It rhymes with chair. _____
2. They have got wings but they are not birds. _____
3. It is long and it hasn't got any legs. It rhymes with cake. _____
4. It is green and it can jump. It rhymes with dog. _____

Get active 8

8

Working with words

1. Read and number the animal names.

1. Can you see the ___ ?   polar bear ☐
2. Where is the ___ ?   elephant ☐
3. The ___ is white.   crocodile ☐
4. I can see a ___ .   tiger ☐
5. The ___ is running.   fox ☐

Sentence building

This sentence **tells** us something. It is a **statement**.
Ben is six.
It has got a capital letter and a full stop.

This sentence **asks** us something. It is a **question**.
Is Ben six?
It has got a capital letter and a question mark.

1. Read the sentences. Make these statements into questions.

1. The elephant is red. _____
2. The boys are happy. _____
3. She is nine. _____
4. The dog is black. _____

Unit 8
Reading and understanding

1. Read and write.

This owl is brown and white. It is sitting in a tree. It is very still.	This bear is white. It lives in the cold ice and snow. It is sleeping.
This crocodile is green. It is swimming in the river.	This tiger is black and yellow. It can run very fast.

What is …
a) black and yellow?   The tiger is black and yellow.
b) white? _____
c) green? _____
d) brown and white? _____

2. Label the pictures.

Unit 8

Sentence building

*A **statement** tells us something.*   Tilly is happy.
*A **question** asks us something.*   Is Tilly happy?

1. Finish the sentences with a full stop or a question mark.

1. Ben is holding a ball ___
2. Is Tilly cold ___
3. Is the elephant grey ___
4. Nina is sleeping ___

2. Make these statements into questions.
1. He is swimming. _____
2. They are playing football. _____

3. Make these questions into statements.
1. Are the boys fishing? _____
2. Are they singing? _____

Lesson aim Comprehension, vocabulary and sentence building

Lesson targets Children:
- identify correct statements about a picture
- match definitions to correct subject
- identify animals from clues; match definitions to pictures
- match words to pictures
- recognise the difference between statements and questions.

Key language (words) words from Lessons 1 and 2, *hippo* (structures) *It is/is not running. They have got ...*

Words for understanding *fun, pet, meet, baby, really, very*

Materials Language Book pp72–73, Practice Book pp54–55, animal flashcards of your choice for *Extension activity*

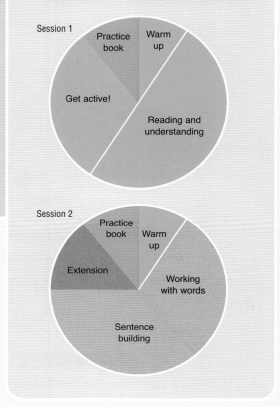

Lesson 3 time division:

Session 1
Practice book / Warm up / Get active! / Reading and understanding

Session 2
Practice book / Warm up / Extension / Working with words / Sentence building

⬇ Lesson 3 Session 1 Warm-up

1 Class sings the elephant song from LB p41, LCD1 track 30.

⬇ Reading and understanding

3 Ask *What is it? What colour is it? Can it run fast? Where does it live?*
Read the first sentence. Ask *Is the fox sitting in a tree?* **No**. Say *The fox is not sitting in a tree. Don't tick the box.*

A child reads the next sentence. Class repeats. Ask *Is the fox white?* **Yes**. Say *The fox is white. Tick the box.*

Continue with the other statements. When the class has answered the question about the picture, ask them if they should tick the box or not.

4 Read sentence 1. Class reads. Read the words. Class reads. Tell children *Tick each thing that is cold.*

Continue with the other sentences. To check answers ask *What is cold?* etc.

5 Ask what is in each picture.
Read sentence 1. Class reads. Ask *What is it?* Children suggest the animal. Write the word on the board for them to check spelling.
Continue with the other sentences.

6 **Get active!**
Guess the animal: Class in two teams. Describe an animal, e.g. *This animal is big. It is white. It lives in the snow.* Teams can guess at any time, but if they are wrong they cannot guess again until the other team has guessed.

⬇ Lesson 3 Session 2 Warm-up

1 Play *What's missing?* with animal flashcards from Lesson 2.

What's missing?

Put up 6–8 flashcards. Children look and remember. Take them down. Remove one. Put the rest up in any order. Children identify what is missing.

⬇ Sentence building

1 Read the first two sentences in the box. Read the example statement and write it on the board.
Ask *What does Mobi say?* If possible, let a child read Mobi's bubble.
Let another child circle the capital letter and full stop on the board.
Do the same for the second two sentences and the example question.

2 Ask a child to read the first statement. Class repeats.
Ask another child to make it a question. Class repeats.
If you wish, write it on the board and class reads again.
Continue with the other sentences. Rub them off the board before children write.

109

Grammar

1 Lesson 4 warm-up. ⬇

2 Individuals/Class read the sentences (LB p74).

3 Activity 1: Children look at the pictures, read and circle. ⬇

4 Activity 2: Children complete the sentences. ⬇

5 Prepare children for PB p56 by checking they understand the tasks. Children complete.

Listening

1 Read Nina's speech bubble (LB p75).

2 🎧 Activity 1: Play LCD1 track 48. Children tick the picture that matches what they hear.

3 🎧 Activity 2: Play track 49. Children say the statement that matches what they hear. ⬇

4 🎧 Activity 3: Play track 50. Children listen. Play again. Children join in.

After listening

Teach the song in the usual way.

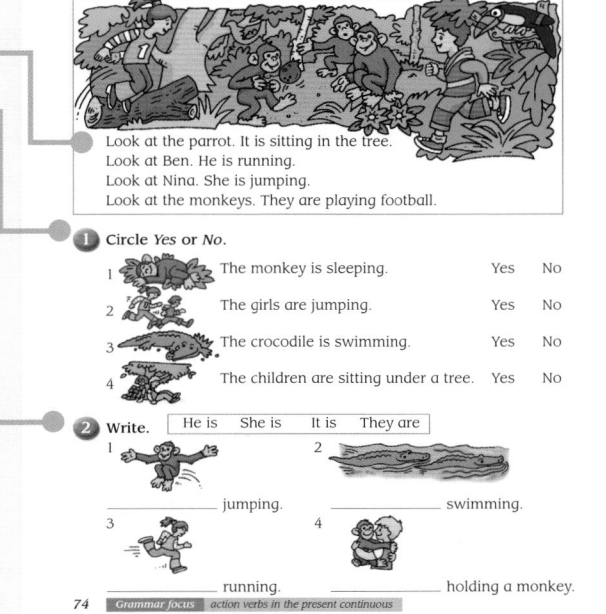

Grammar — *Look at this!*

Look at the parrot. It is sitting in the tree.
Look at Ben. He is running.
Look at Nina. She is jumping.
Look at the monkeys. They are playing football.

1 Circle *Yes* or *No*.

1 The monkey is sleeping. Yes No
2 The girls are jumping. Yes No
3 The crocodile is swimming. Yes No
4 The children are sitting under a tree. Yes No

2 Write. | He is She is It is They are |

1 _____ jumping.
2 _____ swimming.
3 _____ running.
4 _____ holding a monkey.

74 | Grammar focus | action verbs in the present continuous

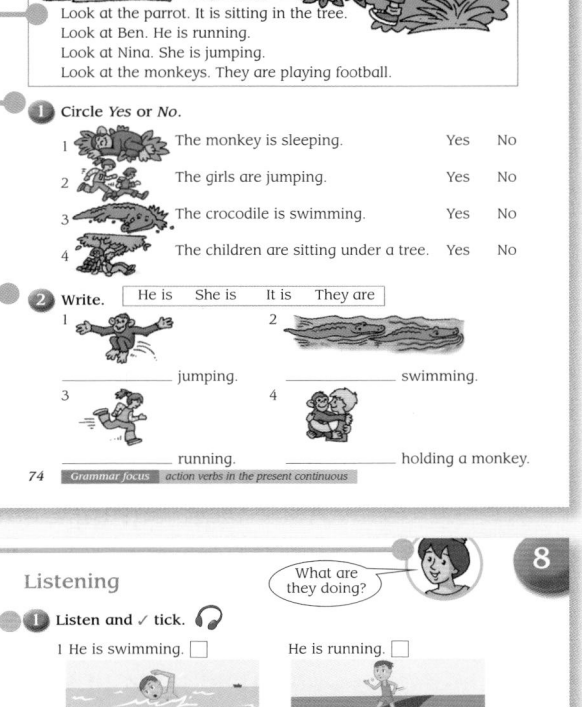

Listening — *What are they doing?*

1 Listen and ✓ tick. 🎧

1 He is swimming. ☐   He is running. ☐

2 They are sitting in the classroom. ☐   They are playing in the playground. ☐

3 She is holding a bird. ☐   She is holding a cat. ☐

4 It is climbing a tree. ☐   It is sleeping. ☐

2 Listen, point and say. 🎧 — *He is swimming.*

3 Listen and sing. 🎧

Two little birds sitting on a wall.
Here is Peter. Here is Paul.
Fly away Peter. Fly away Paul.
Come back Peter. Come back Paul.

| Listening focus | the present continuous   75

Grammar

1 What is Ben saying? Read and match. Write the letters.

1 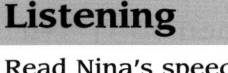 ☐   a (I am swimming.)   b (I am jumping.)
2 ☐
3 ☐   c (I am swinging.)

2 Complete the sentences. Use the words in the box.

| He is She is It is They are |

1 _____ holding an umbrella.
2 _____ playing football.
3 _____ sleeping.
4 _____ sitting under a tree.

3 Write sentences. These words can help you.

| swimming jumping sleeping |

1 _____
2 _____
3 _____
56

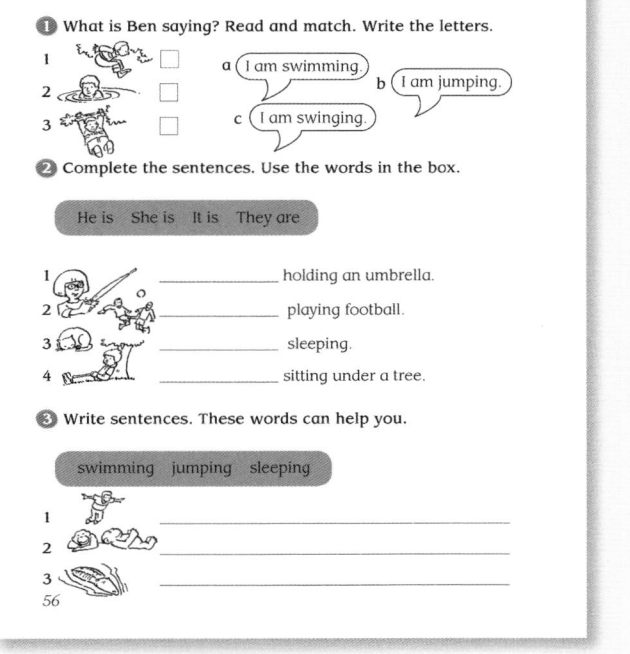

8

Lesson aim Grammar and listening

Lesson targets Children:

- read statements about a picture
- identify correct statements about a picture
- write statements about a picture
- listen to dialogue and identify family members
- sing and learn a short song.

Key language (words) nouns and verbs from Lessons 1 and 2
(structures) *He/She/It is running. They are playing.*

Materials Language Book pp74–75, Practice Book p56, Language CD1 tracks 48–50, flashcards 58–61, 70–73, 145 for *Warm-up*

Preparation Listen to the CD before the lesson.

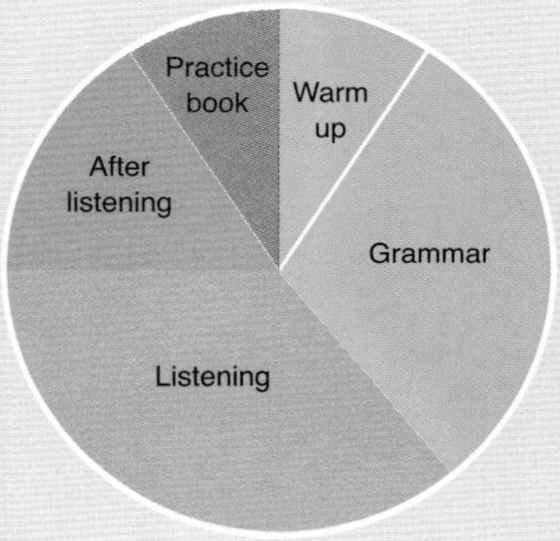

⬇ Lesson 4 Warm-up

1 Show action flashcards. Say *Look at ... What is/are he/she/they doing?* Children make statements, e.g. **He is climbing. She is running,** etc.

⬇ Grammar

3 Ask a child to read the first sentence, a second makes it a question and the third answers it.

Continue with the other sentences.

Children read alone and circle.

4 Individuals/Class read the words in the box.

Ask/Help a child to say a complete sentence. Class repeats.
Children write.

⬇ Listening

3 Individuals/Class read the sentences. Play the CD. Children listen and look at the pictures.

Play a second time. Children listen and tick the sentence that matches the sounds they hear.

Audioscript

Voice	1
	[swimming pool]
Boy	Come on, Dan!
	[dive/splash + swimming/splashing]
Voice	2
	[playground, children playing]
Voice	3
Girl	Hello, Sweetie!
	[singing canary]
Voice	4
	[bear-like snores]

111

Activity 1

1. Lesson 5 warm-up.
2. (LB p76) Point out pictures and words with *ll*.
3. Play rhyme twice (LCD1 track 51). Children follow in books.
4. Read rhyme.
5. Read and ask questions.
6. Read with the class.

Activity 2

1. Children read the words in the box.
2. Children write the words under the correct picture.
3. Children circle the *ll* ending.

Activity 3

Children say the words and sentences. Children write.

Activity 4

1. Write up words. Class/individuals read.
2. Children read in pairs. Listen to pairs.
3. Children check words and tick.

Practice Book

Children complete PB p57.

Phonics games and activities

1. Children find *ll* words.
2. *Look, write, check.*

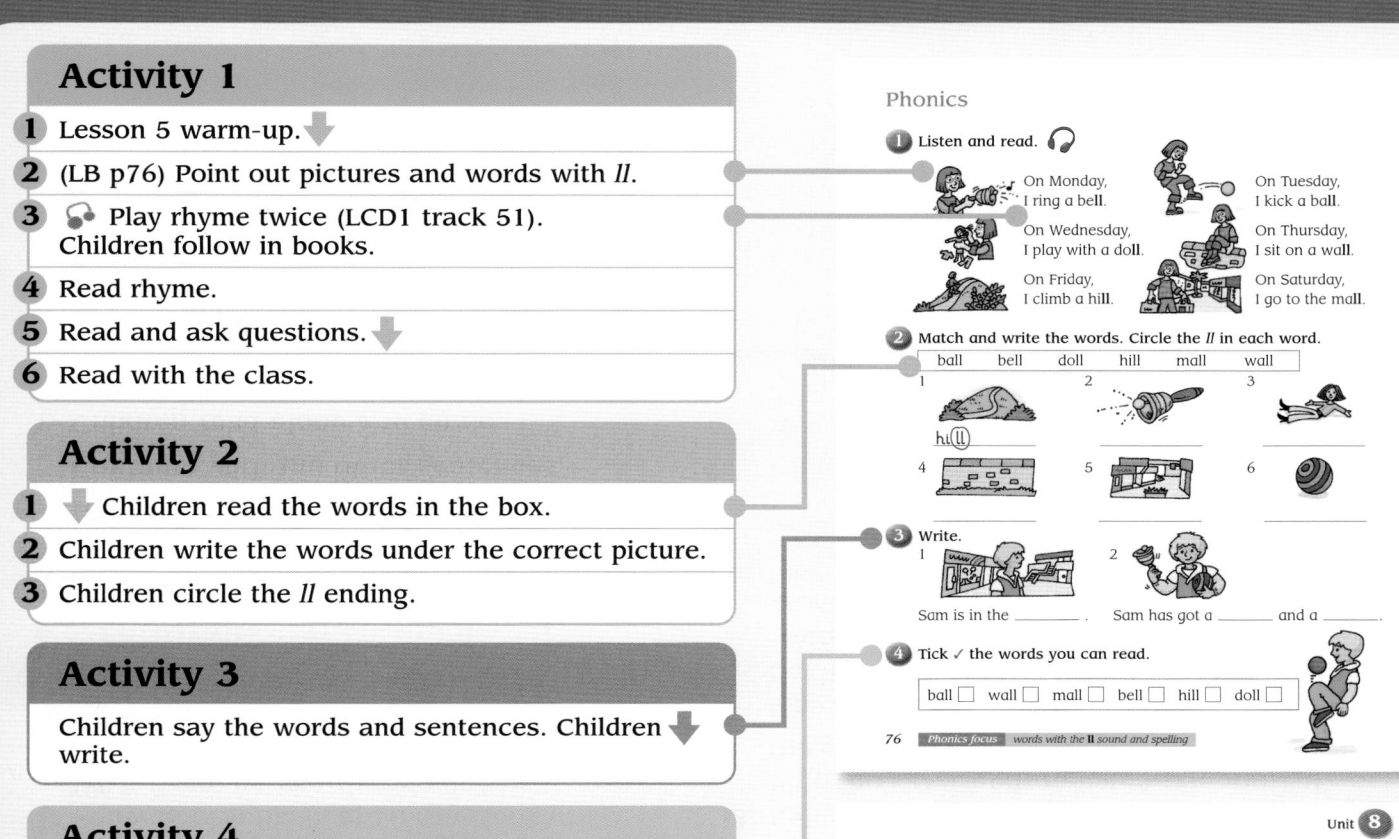

Phonics

1. Listen and read.

On Monday, I ring a bell.
On Tuesday, I kick a ball.
On Wednesday, I play with a doll.
On Thursday, I sit on a wall.
On Friday, I climb a hill.
On Saturday, I go to the mall.

2. Match and write the words. Circle the *ll* in each word.

| ball | bell | doll | hill | mall | wall |

1. hi(ll)
2.
3.
4.
5.
6.

3. Write.

1. Sam is in the _____ .
2. Sam has got a _____ and a _____ .

4. Tick ✓ the words you can read.

ball ☐   wall ☐   mall ☐   bell ☐   hill ☐   doll ☐

76   *Phonics focus*   words with the **ll** sound and spelling

Phonics

Unit 8

1. Say the sounds. Write the words.

1. i ⏀ ll
2. h c i ⏀ ll
3. t c i ⏀ ll
4. f c i ⏀ ll

2. Write.

1. you go up this
2. you see this in a shop → t
3. not well
4. to make full → f i

3. Choose and write.

1. wall mall
2. ball bell
3. doll dull

57

112

Lesson aim Phonic recognition

Lesson targets Children:

- read, pronounce and spell words with *ll* ending
- match the words to pictures
- write the words from picture prompts.

Target words *all, ball, mall, wall, bell, doll, fill, hill, ill, till*

Materials Language Book p76, Practice Book p57, Language CD1 track 51, a large picture of a wall, letter cards for *Warm-up*

Preparation Listen to the CD before the lesson. Write phonemes on separate pieces of paper for each of the target words and *fall, tall* and *shell*; draw a picture of a wall, large enough to stick ten or more words on.

Lesson 5 time division:

Lesson 5 Warm-up

1 Team letters game
Divide class into four to six teams. Give each team two or three letter cards, e.g. team 1: *b, n, w*; team 2: *p, h, e*; team 3: *c, d, a*; team 4: *g, t, i*; Say cvc words, e.g. *bed, pen, bat, hat, cat, tin, wig, dig, big, hen*, etc. If teams think one or more of their letters is in the word, the team must stand up and show their letters. Class checks.

Activity 1

5 Ask e.g. *What does Tilly do on Tuesday? When does Tilly climb a hill?*

Ask questions until each activity has been talked about. Make sure all the words in the text are understood.

Note: The purpose of this rhyme is to teach words with *ll* endings, not the days of the week. These are taught later (Unit 10).

Activity 2

3 Individuals/Class read all the words in the box before matching and writing. Ensure the children understand that the letters *ll* make only one sound. Check answers together.

Activity 3

Children look at the picture and read the words. Ask/Help a child to say the whole sentence. Class repeats. Children write the word.

Do the same with the second sentence.

Activity 4

1 Write the six words on the board. Point in random order. Individuals and/or the class reads them.

Practice Book

Children complete the three exercises. You may wish to do the crossword together orally as a class before children are asked to do it.

Phonics games and activities

1 Draw a wall. Ask the class to tell you words ending *ll*. They should be able to remember words from the lesson, also *tall, fall* and *shell*. Give groups letters for each word the class remembers. The group makes the word. Stick the words on the wall.

2 Do *Look, write, check* (p75) with words from previous units.

113

Before writing

1 Lesson 6 warm-up.

2 Read Miss Plum's speech bubble (LB p77).

3 Individuals read the words.

4 Class reads the words.

Shared writing

1 Individuals/class reads the example sentences under the pictures (LB p77).

2 Children draw and write pairs of sentences.

Practice Book

Writing

(PB p58) Individuals/Class read words. Children write under correct picture.

Your writing

1 (PB p59) Children complete and write sentences 2–4.

2 They write pairs of sentences for the other pictures.

After writing

Children read sentences.

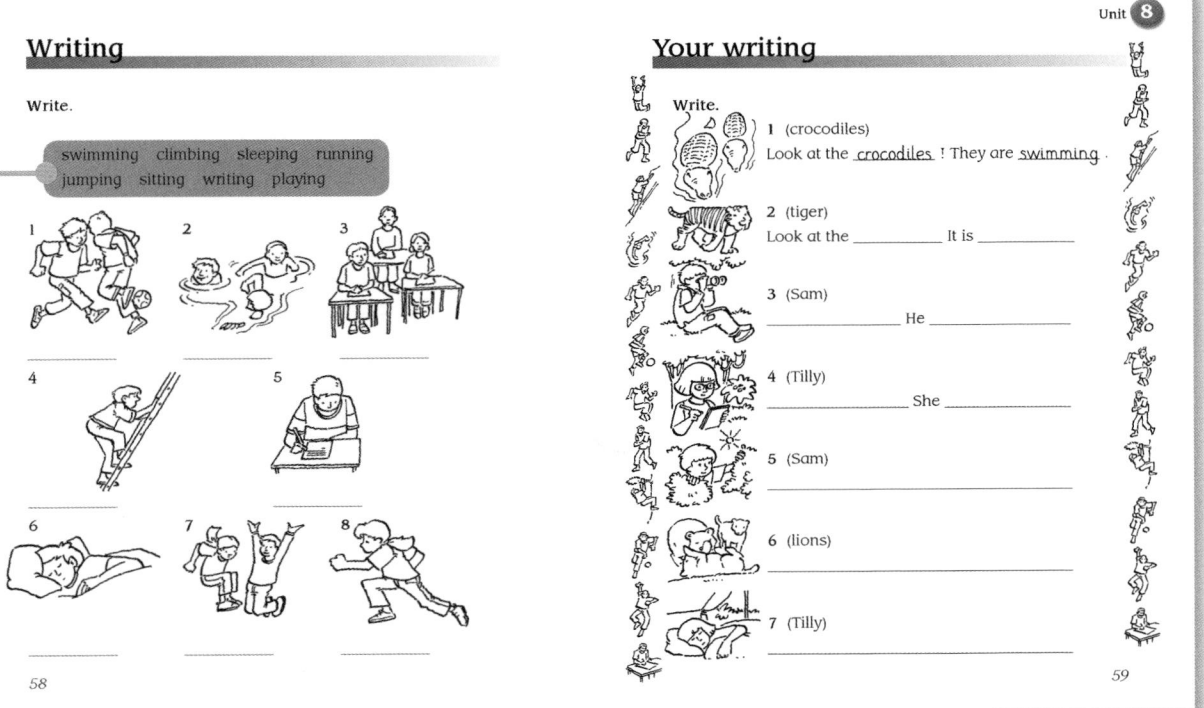

Lesson aim Writing

Lesson targets Children:

- write sentences to match picture prompts
- write pairs of sentences about what people and animals are doing.

Key language (words) verbs from Units 7 and 8
(structures) *Look at the ...*, *He/She/It is ...*, *They are ...*

Materials Language Book p77, Practice Book pp58–59, word cards for four or more of nouns, adjectives and verbs

Lesson 6 time division:

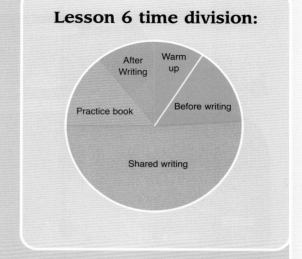

Lesson 6 Warm-up

1 Say *Two little birds* from Lesson 4 (LB p75).

Do a *Find the word* activity.
Write up three headings:
nouns   adjectives   verbs
Put three or four word cards for each part of speech in scrambled order on the board.
Team 1 child names a part of speech. A team 2 child finds a word and puts it under a heading. Team 1 child wins a point by saying if has been done correctly or not. Team 2 wins a point if a child can say a correct sentence with the word in.

Shared writing

Children suggest the verb for the third picture. Ask what picture to draw. Draw, and then ask for sentences. Write them on the board. Do the same with the other three pictures. Rub off the sentences or leave a framework, if you wish.

Point out Miss Plum's *Remember!* box.

Children draw and write in their books.

Practice Book

Writing
If you wish, go through the exercise orally first. Ask *Picture 1. What are they doing?* Elicit answers for all pictures, then children write.

Your writing
1 If you wish, prepare children orally: individuals/class read the first sentence. Ask children to complete the next three sentences.
2 Ask children for two sentences for the next three pictures.

After writing

Individuals read the pairs of sentences. Other children check. If you wish, class repeats the sentences.

115

Before listening

1. Lesson 1 warm-up.
2. Show poster 9. Read the title. Ask questions.
3. Point and name new verbs. Children come forward; find objects in main picture.
4. Show flashcards (76–79) and name new verbs. Class repeats.
5. Ask questions about the first small picture, left.

Shared listening

1. Play FCD track 18. Point to characters when they speak.
2. Ask about the fourth gold star.
3. Ask *Who? What?* questions.
4. Play FCD track 18 and point to characters again.

Dialogue practice

1. Say new words. Children point in books (FB pp24–25). Point on poster for children to check.
2. Show flashcards 76–79. Children name.
3. Children close books. Play FCD track 19 and show character flashcards. Class repeats lines in pauses.
4. Groups say lines by character.
5. Individuals act dialogue.
6. Play FCD track 18 again. Children follow text or point to main picture.

After listening

1. Show flashcards. Ask questions.
2. Say the *Star chant*.
3. Do the questions activity.
4. Children put the next sticker star in the correct place on FB pp46–47.

9 In the cave

dancing

riding

playing

singing

fishing

9 In the cave

Hooray! Ben's got the star!

singing

playing

riding

dancing

fishing

Star light, star bright,
Six stars are missing tonight.

The children can see a cave.
What is inside?

Look! A cave!

Come on! Let's go!

Look at these people!
Are they riding horses?

No. They aren't riding horses.
They're riding elephants.

Look at that man.

He's playing a drum.

Look at this woman.

Is she singing?

Yes, and the little girl is dancing.

Is this boy fishing?

Yes, he is.

Has he got a fish?

No. He's got ... He's got ...

A star! A gold star!

Listen!

Who is it?

Hello! Hello!

I don't know.

I'm scared!

Star light, star bright,
Five stars are missing tonight.

Who is in the cave with the children?
Can you guess?

24 *Is he/she singing?   Are they riding?   He/She is not singing.   They are not riding.*

25

116

Lesson aim Fluency

Lesson targets Children:

- listen for pronunciation and intonation
- repeat dialogue accurately
- act out dialogue with expression
- ask questions about what people are doing and not doing.

Key language (words) *dancing, fishing, riding, singing;* (revision) *playing;* (structures) *Is he/she singing? Are they riding? He/She is not singing. They are not riding.*

Words for understanding *cave, drum, girl, horses, man, people, woman*

Materials Poster 9, Fluency Book pp24–25, Fluency CD tracks 18–19, character flashcards 1–6, flashcards 76–79, flashcards for *Warm-up*

Preparation Listen to the CD before the lesson.

Lesson 1 time division:

⬇ Lesson 1 Warm-up

1 Play *What is it?* (TG p45) in two or more teams. Use flashcards for nouns from Units 1–8.

⬇ Before listening

2 Ask *Are the children on the mountain?/on the beach?/ in a cave?*
Is it dark in the cave?

5 Ask *Who has got a gold star?*
Where is Ben?
What is he doing?
Is he happy?
Is this star number one?/two?/three?
How many stars are missing now?

⬇ Shared listening

2 Ask *Is the gold star in the cave?*
Who can see the gold star?
Who has got the gold star?
What is the boy doing?
How many stars have they got now?

3 Ask *Who can Ben see?*
What is the man doing?
What animals can Tilly see?
Can Tilly see people?
What are the people doing?
Who is singing?/dancing?
Who is in the cave with the children?

⬇ After listening

1 Show the action flashcards. Ask *Is/Are he/she/they playing/riding?* Ask questions that require positive and negative responses. After a negative answer, ask *What is/are he/she/they doing?*

3 Continue Step 1 with the class in two teams. Show team 1 a card, e.g. girls dancing.
A team 1 child asks any question: *Are they dancing/running/singing?* Team 2 answers *Yes, they are/No, they aren't.* After a negative answer, team 1 asks *What are they doing?* A team 2 child answers.

Show a different action card to team 2. A team 2 child asks the question.

117

Before reading

1. Lesson 2 warm-up.
2. Teach new words with flashcards 58, 60, 74, 76.
3. Children open books (LB pp78–79). Ask questions.

Shared reading

1. Play LCD1 track 52. Children follow text in book.
2. Read line by line. Ask questions.
3. Read with the class.

Reading practice

1. Give reading practice. Use some or all of the following:
   - Children read again as a class.
   - Groups read different sections.
   - Individuals read different sections.
2. Class listens again to LCD1 track 52 and follows in LB.

After reading

Do the action mime activity.

Lesson aim Reading

Lesson targets Children:

- follow a text read out to them
- listen for pronunciation and intonation
- read the text aloud with accurate pronunciation and intonation
- learn and understand new vocabulary items
- understand the sense of the text as a whole
- answer simple comprehension questions.

Key language (words) *horse, marching, skipping*
(structures) *What are they doing? Are they riding horses?*

Words for understanding *climbing frame, want, finished, up, down*

Materials Language Book pages 78–79, Language CD1 track 52, flashcards 67–69

Preparation Listen to the CD before the lesson.

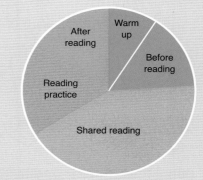

Lesson 2 time division:

(Pie chart labels: Warm up, Before reading, Shared reading, Reading practice, After reading)

⬇ Lesson 2 Warm-up

1 Play *Simon says* (TG p95). Use as many of the new action words as possible: show the class mimes for *Hold the baby, Sleep, Swim.*

⬇ Before reading

3 Ask *Are the children in school?*
Are they having lessons?
Do you have playtime?
What do you do at playtime?

⬇ Shared reading

2 Ask *Where are the children?*
What are they doing?
What are the boys doing?
How many girls are holding hands?
What are the girls riding?
What are the boys playing?
Who is watching the children?
Who is skipping?
What does the bell say?

⬇ After reading

Children take turns to mime one of the activities in the story.

Ask *What is he/she/are they doing?*
Other children guess *He/She is/They are playing a drum.*

Let pairs mime for the plural form.

If you wish, tell children which actions from the story to do: *march up and down; dance in a circle; ride a horse; play football; climb the climbing frame; skip*

119

Reading and understanding

1. Session 1 warm-up.
2. Re-read *Playtime* (LB pp78–79).
3. Activity 1 (LB p80): Individual reads a sentence. Class repeats. Elicit the answer. Do the same with the other sentences. Children write.
4. Activity 2: Individuals read sentences. Class repeats. Children number the pictures.
5. Play the *Get active!* game.
6. Prepare children for PB p60 by checking they understand the task. Children complete.

Working with words

1. Session 2 warm-up.
2. Activity 1 (LB p81): Children read the words. Class repeats. Children categorise the words.

Sentence building

1. Go through the information in the box (LB p81).
2. Activity 1: Children write the correct form of the auxiliary *is/are*.
3. Prepare children for PB p61. Go through the box and check they understand the task. Children complete.

Extension activity

Action flashcards activity.

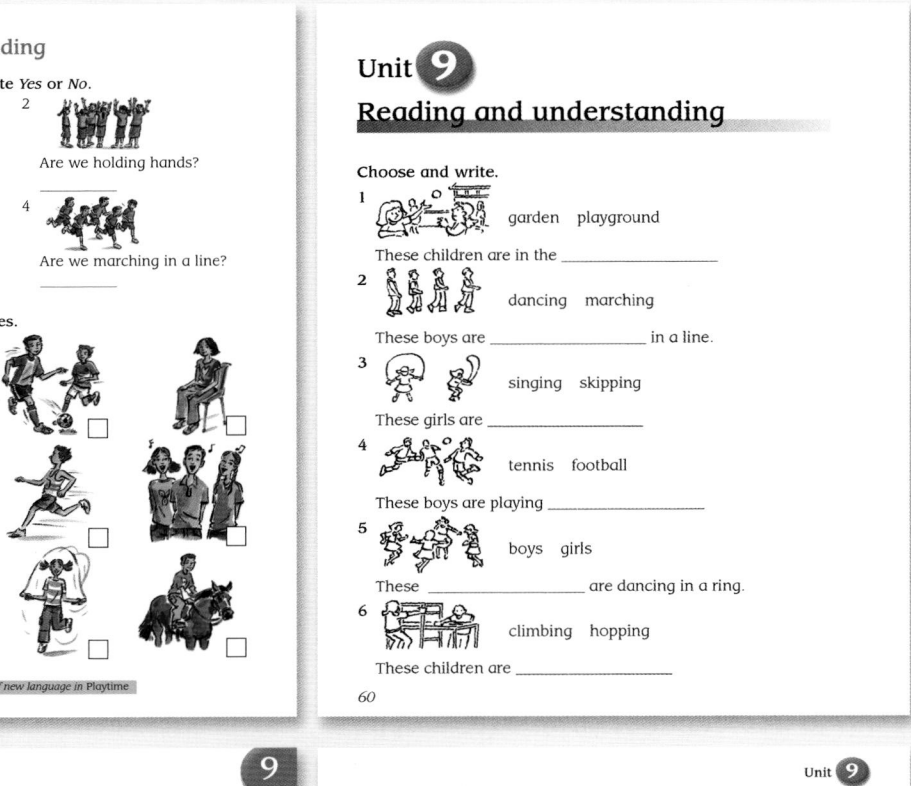

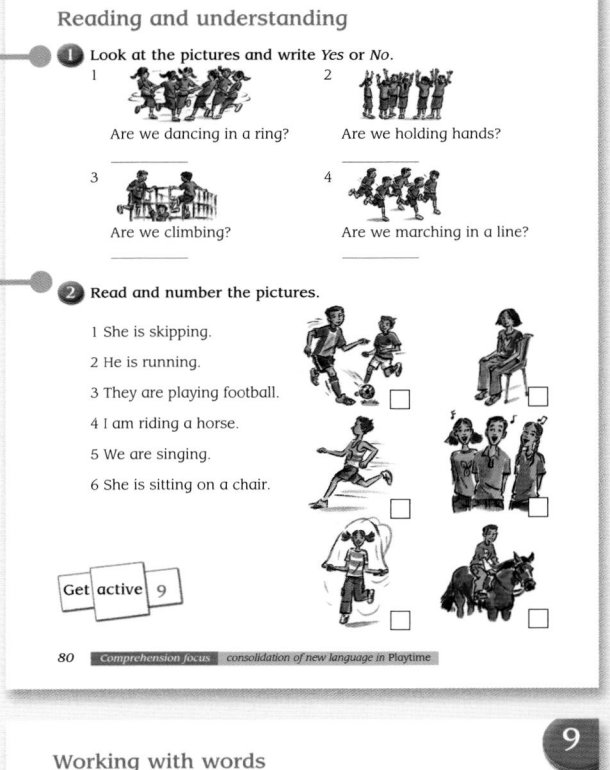

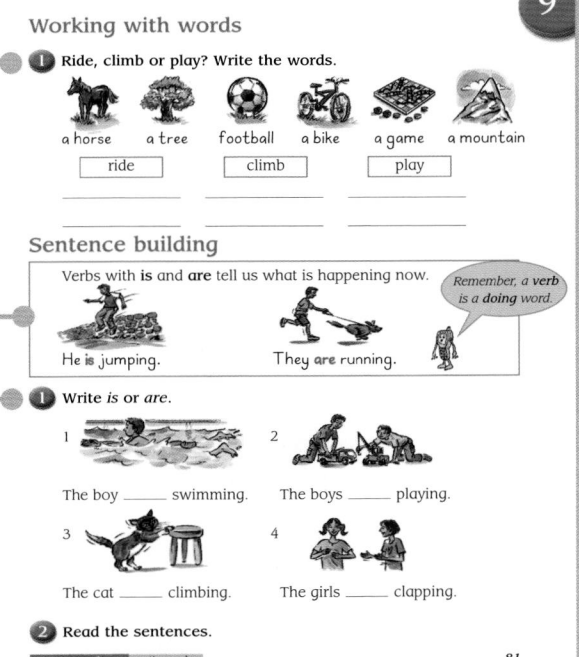

120

Lesson aim Comprehension, vocabulary and sentence building

Lesson targets Children:

- answer questions about pictures
- match statements to pictures
- match nouns to verbs
- read about the function of the present continuous
- write sentences using the present continuous.

Key language (words) verbs from Units 7, 8 and 9
(structures) *Are we (verb) + ing?, They are running.*

Materials Language Book pp80–81, Practice Book pp60–61, instructions on cards or paper for *Get active!*
Flashcards 67–69, 76–79 for *Extension activity.*

Preparation Write the instructions for *Get active!*

Lesson 3 time division:

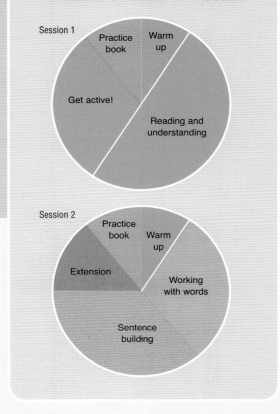

Session 1 — Practice book / Warm up / Get active! / Reading and understanding

Session 2 — Practice book / Warm up / Working with words / Sentence building / Extension

Lesson 3 Session 1 Warm-up

1 Class sings *Two little birds* (LB p75, LCD1 track 50) or another favourite song from Units 1 to 8.

Reading and understanding

5 **Get active!**
Bring a child to the front. Show him/her an instruction. Use the list below, or other actions to suit your class. The child does/mimes the action, e.g. sits on a chair.

Ask the class *Is he/she skipping?* Elicit **No, he/she is not skipping.** *(What is he/she doing?)* **He/She is sitting.**

If you wish, write the sentences on the board. Class reads.

Continue with the other instructions. Each time ask the class a question to prompt a negative answer first. Use the verbs they have learned: *dancing, singing, riding, playing, fishing, skipping.*

Bring two children forward sometimes, to practise the plural form.

Instructions:
sit on a chair; jump up and down; climb a ladder; write on the board; look at the door; hold a book; swim in the pool; clap your hands

Lesson 3 Session 2 Warm-up

1 Play the *Chain game* with adjectives, e.g. **I can see a yellow chair. I can see a yellow chair and a red plane**, etc.

Working with words

2 Tell children to look at the pictures. Ask *What can you ride?* Elicit answers. Ask *What can you climb?/play?* If necessary, do the exercise on the board before children write.

Sentence building

1 Read the sentence at the top of the box. Ask children to read the sentences below the pictures. Ask a child to read Mobi's bubble. Ask a child to write

his/her name on the board. As the child writes, ask *What is he/she doing now?* Elicit **He/She is writing.**

Repeat with two children drawing an object. Ask the question. Class replies **They are drawing.**

Extension activity

1 Show action flashcards from Units 8 and 9. First child to make a sentence, e.g. **He is swinging or They are playing football** wins a point.

121

Grammar

1. Lesson 4 warm-up. ⬇

2. Show poster 8. Ask about the monkeys. ⬇

3. Pairs read speech bubbles (LB p82). Class repeats. ⬇

4. Activity 1: Ask the question or help a child to ask the question. Elicit answers. ⬇

5. Activity 2: Children tick the picture that matches the sentences. ⬇

6. Activity 3: Children complete sentences. ⬇

7. Prepare children for Practice Book p62 by checking they understand the tasks. Children complete. ⬇

Listening

1. Read Nina's speech bubble (LB p83). Explain the activity. ⬇

2. Children look at the pictures for a few moments.

3. 🎧 Activity 1: Play LCD1 track 53. Children listen and point.

4. 🎧 Activity 2: Play LCD1 track 54. Children listen and do the actions.

5. 🎧 Activity 3: Play LCD1 track 55. Children listen and sing.

After listening

Practise the song with the class. ⬇

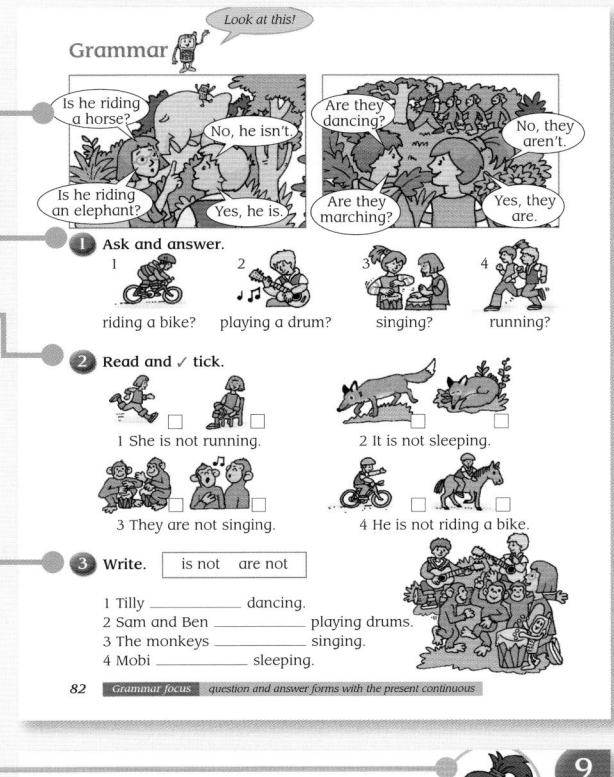

Lesson aim Grammar and listening

Lesson targets Children:

- read questions about people's actions
- practise talking about people's actions
- match statements to pictures and complete statements
- listen to a song and match actions to pictures
- sing and learn the song with actions.

Key language (words) verbs from Units 8 and 9

(structures) *He/She is not verb + ing, They are not verb + ing*

Materials Language Book pp82–83, Practice Book p62, Language CD1 tracks 53–55, poster 8, actions flashcards 67–69, 76–79 for *Warm-up*

Preparation Listen to the CD before the lesson.

Lesson 4 time division:

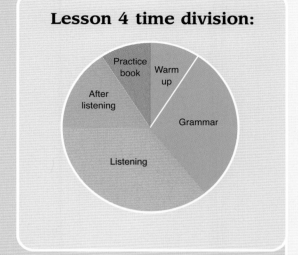

Lesson 4 Warm-up

1 Show actions cards from Units 8 and 9. Ask *Are they riding horses?* **No, they aren't.** *Is she clapping hands?* **No, she isn't,** etc.

Grammar

2 Point to different monkeys on the poster. Ask questions to elicit positive and negative answers, singular and plural, e.g. *Is she holding a book?/a baby monkey? Is he sleeping? Are they dancing? Is it playing football?*

5 Individuals read sentences. Class repeats. Tell children to look at the first sentence and pictures. Ask which picture matches the sentence. If necessary, say *Look at picture 1. Is Tilly running?* **Yes.** *Look at picture 2. Is Tilly running?* **No.** *Say Tick picture 2.* Do the same with the next sentence. Ask the class which picture to tick.

6 Ask individuals to complete sentences. Class repeats. Children write.

Listening

1 Tell the class the song on the page has actions. The pictures show the actions.

3 Help children to identify some of the actions, e.g. *Look at picture 4/10/12. What is she doing?* **She is clapping/pointing/sleeping.**

Audioscript
I've got two little hands
They're hiding away.
Now here comes one
and the other, to play!
Now they are clapping
And shaking and tapping
They are rolling and pushing
And pulling and pointing.
To the right, to the left
To the left, to the right.
And now they are going to bed.
Good night!

After listening

Sing/Say the song slowly with the class a few times. As they learn the actions they will also learn the words.

123

Activity 1

① Lesson 5 warm-up. ⬇

② (LB p84) Point out pictures and words with *ng*.

③ 🎧 Play rhyme twice (LCD1 track 56). Children follow in books.

④ Read rhyme.

⑤ Read and ask questions. ⬇

⑥ Read with the class.

Activity 2

① ⬇ Children hold sounds cards. Read the sounds.

② Close up gradually.

③ Read the word.

④ Children look, say and write.

Activity 3

Children say the word and sentence. ⬇
Children write.

Activity 4

① Write up words. Class/individuals read. ⬇

② Children read in pairs. Listen to pairs.

③ Children check words and tick.

Practice Book

Children complete PB p63. ⬇

Phonics games and activities

① Do the rhyming words activity. ⬇

② Play *What's the word?* ⬇

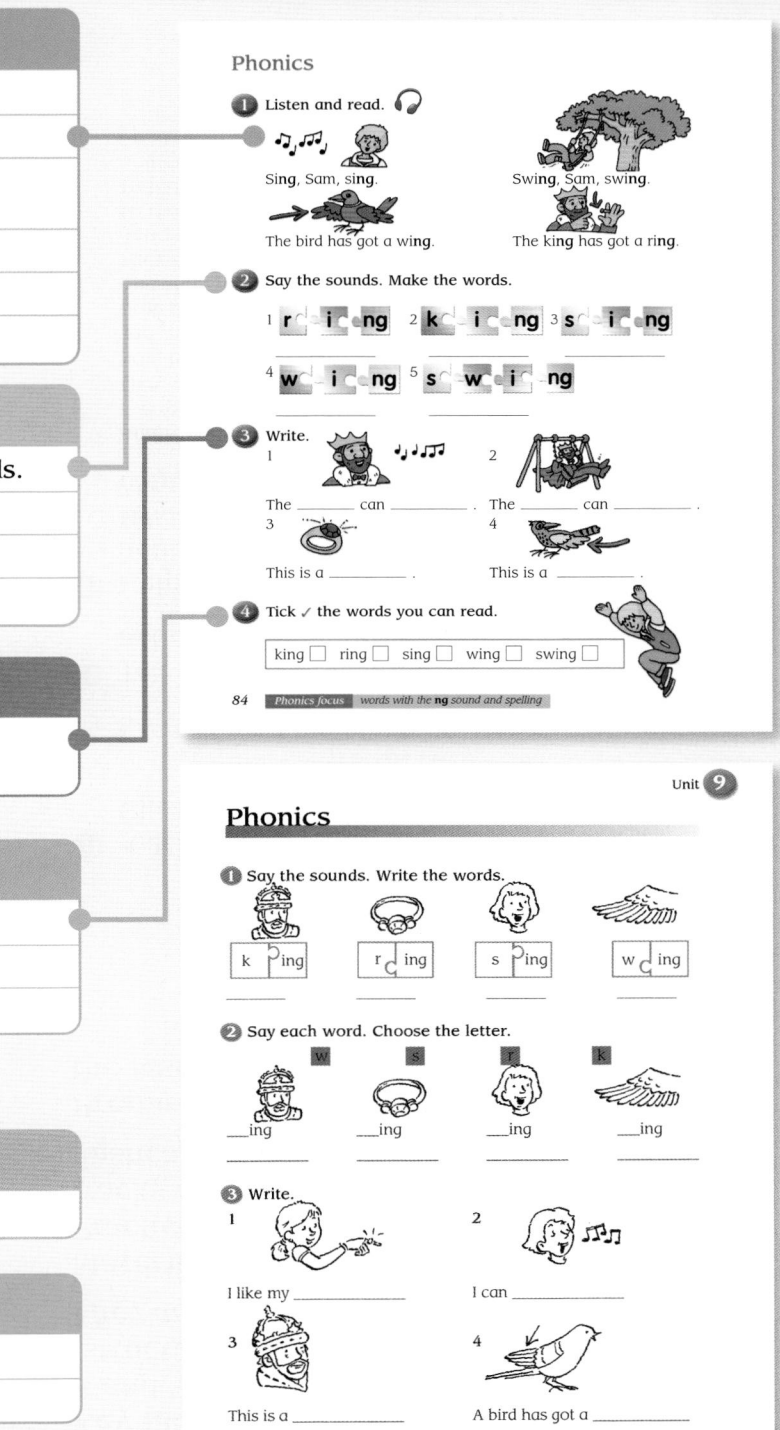

Lesson aim Phonic recognition

Lesson targets Children:

- read, pronounce and spell words with *ng*
- recognise and say the individual sounds that make up the words
- write the words from picture prompts.

Target words *king, ring, sing, swing, wing*

Materials Language Book p84, Practice Book p63, Language CD1 track 56, cards for sounds, word cards for rhyming words (see *Phonics activities*, 1)

Preparation Listen to the CD before the lesson. Make large cards for the sounds/phonemes for the target words in Activity 2.

Lesson 5 time division:

Lesson 5 Warm-up

1 Sing *I've got two little hands* from Lesson 4 (LB p83, LCD1 track 55).

Activity 1

5 Ask *What is Sam doing?*
Is Sam dancing? What is he doing?
What has the bird got?
What colour is the bird?
What has the king got?
What colour is it?

Make sure all the words in the text are understood.

Activity 2

Follow the procedure for introducing the phonemes and sounding out each word which is given in detail in the Introduction (p10). Ensure children understand that the letters *ng* make one sound.

Activity 3

Children look at the picture and read the words. Ask/Help a child to say the whole sentence. Class repeats. Children write the words.
Do the same with the other three sentences.

Activity 4

1 Write the five words on the board. Point in random order. Individuals and/or the class read them.

Practice Book

Children complete the three exercises. Check they can read all the words in Exercise 1 before they move on to Exercise 2.

Phonics games and activities

1 Use words from Units 1–9, e.g. *fog, dog, fox, box, shell, bell, fish, dish, lunch, munch, wall, tall, swing, king.* Children match rhyming pairs. Class reads the rhyming pairs.

2 **What's the word?**
Say phonic sounds. Children tell you the word.

125

Before writing

1. Lesson 6 warm-up.
2. Read Miss Plum's speech bubble (LB p85).
3. Children look at the pictures.
4. Ask what the characters are doing.
5. Children ask questions about each character and answer.

Shared writing

1. Activity 2 (LB p85): Children read sentences.
2. Elicit questions and answers for the other characters. Write them on the board. Children write.

Practice Book

Writing

1. Class reads the words in the box. (PB p64)
2. Ask *What is Nina doing?*
3. Child reads. Class repeats.
4. Do the same with the other characters.
5. Children write positive statements.

Your writing

1. (PB p65) Children look and say what the characters are doing.
2. Children write.

After writing

Do the *Action mime* game with questions.

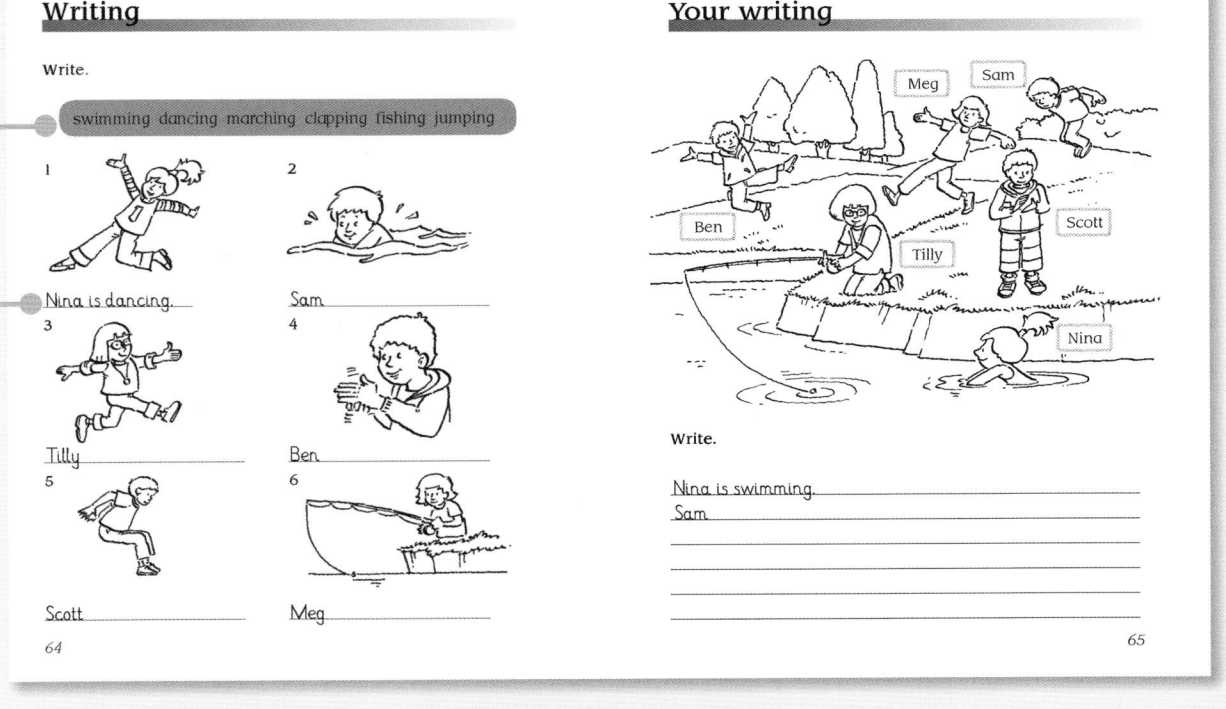

Lesson aim Writing

Lesson targets Children:

- ask and write questions about what people are doing
- say and write short negative answers
- complete sentences about what people are doing
- write what people are doing in a picture.

Key language (words) verbs from Units 8 and 9

(structures) *Is Sam swimming? No, he isn't.*

Materials Language Book p85, Practice Book pp64–65, letters for cvc words for *Warm-up*, verb word cards of your choice for *After writing*

Lesson 6 time division:

Warm up, Before writing, Shared writing, Practice book, After Writing

Lesson 6 Warm-up

1 Play *Team letters* (p248) with cvc words.

Before writing

4 Ask questions about the characters, e.g.
Look at Tilly. Is she swimming?
Ask *Who is dancing?/riding a horse? What is Sam doing?/Mobi doing?*

5 Tell children *Look at number 1.* Ask *Who is this?* **This is Sam.** Two children read the speech bubbles. Class repeats.
Say *Look at number 2. Who is this?* **This is Nina.** Ask a child to form the question.
Is she dancing? Another child answers **Yes, she is.**
Continue with the other characters.

Shared writing

1 Ask two children to read the sentences. Write them on the board. Class reads.

2 Write *dancing?* on the board. Prompt a child to form the whole question. Class repeats. Elicit the answer. Write it up.

Do the same with the other questions, if necessary.
Alternatively, let children ask the whole question without any prompt.

Point out the *Remember!* box before children write.
Rub off some or all of the sentences from the board before children write.

After writing

Action mime
Show a verb word card to a team 1 child, e.g. *climb.* He/She mimes climbing. Show the same or a different word card to team 1. They ask team 2 *Is he/she climbing/jumping?* Team 2 answers *Yes/No, he/she is climbing.*

Continue with the other action verbs.

127

Revision 3

You can do it!

1 Look at the picture. What can you see?

2 Listen and read.

3 Read and say.
Point to Tilly:
Where is she?
What is she doing?
What is Mobi saying?

Point to Ben:
Where is he?
What is he doing?
What is Ben saying?
What is Mobi saying?

Point to Sam:
Where is he?
What is he doing?
What is Mobi saying?

Who is on the elephant?
What is she doing?
What is Mobi saying?

Who is under a tree?
What is she doing?
Who has got balloons?
What colour are they?

4 Listen, point and say who Mobi is talking to.

5 Finish the story. Say who the balloons are for.

6 Act out the story.

7 Listen and say the chant.

Chicken and chips,
Chicken and chips.
We all love chicken and chips.
Ring the bells!
Bang the drums!
It's chicken and chips
for lunch!
HOORAY!

Tilly is on the swing. She is swinging very high.

Miss Plum is sitting under a tree. She is holding four balloons. Who are they for?

Be careful!

Come here, children!

Ben is on the bridge. He is running very fast.

Stop! Don't run!

Look at me!

Where's my balloon?

Sit down, Nina.

Don't fall!

Sam is on the climbing frame.

Nina is riding on an elephant. She is standing up.

Lesson aim Revision

Lesson targets Children:

- practise fluency and listening activities, including phonemes *ch*, *ll* and *ng*
- practise language and structures from Units 7–9 through a story, games and writing.

Key language *Don't run/jump/climb/ fall! He/She is sleeping. They are playing. Is he/she singing? He/She is not singing. Are they riding? They are not riding.*

Words for understanding *balloons*

Materials Language Book pp86–87, Language CD1 tracks 57–59, Practice Book pp66–69

Revision 3 time division:

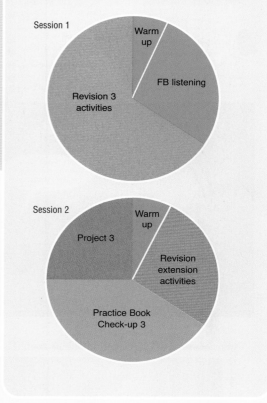

Sessions 1 and 2 Warm-ups

Sing a favourite song from Units 7–9.

Listening revision

Play Units 7–9 of the Fluency Book (FCD tracks 14–19). Children look in their books and listen. Children close books and repeat in the pauses in the dialogue section.

Revision 3

1 (LB p86) Activity 1: Children say as much as they can from observation.

2 🎧 Activity 2: Play LCD1 track 57. Children listen and follow the text.

3 Activity 3: Read or let children read out the questions. Elicit answers.

4 (LB p87) Activity 4: Play LCD1 track 58 twice. Children listen and point then name person.

Audioscript

Voice	Listen, point and say who Mobi is talking to.
Mobi	Stop! Don't run! ... Sit down! ... Where's my balloon? ... Be careful! ... Don't fall!

5 Activity 5: Children match balloons to characters (colour of clothes).

6 Activity 6: Individuals, groups or the whole class read narrative and bubbles. Individuals come forward and act.

7 🎧 Activity 7: Play the chant twice (LCD1 track 59). Children listen, then join in.

Revision extension activities

1 Play flashcard games from Units 7–9.

2 Use the phonic rhyme for reading practice. Teach the rhyme if you wish.

⬇ Practice Book

1 Children complete *Check-up 3* (PB pp66–67) as a test, as preparation for a test or for homework.

2 Children complete *Move on with Mobi 3* (PB pp68–69) for homework or class work.

Project 3: Monkey pictures or frieze

Children make monkeys (see p246). Photocopy one for each child.

1 **Individual:** Children choose an action for their monkey. They arrange arms/legs for that action and stick the monkey on paper. They write sentences, e.g. *This monkey is brown. It is running.*

2 **Group:** Children stick their monkeys on a frieze. They can make a scene, e.g. several monkeys playing football. Children draw or cut out extra items, e.g. a football, a tree. Children write sentences and stick them on the frieze.

Whole class: Children arrange monkeys on a single frieze. Children write sentences as space allows. Talk with the class about the frieze.

129

Before listening

1. Lesson 1 warm-up.
2. Show poster 9. Ask questions.
3. Show poster 10. Ask about the small picture.
4. Read the title on poster 10. Ask about the main picture.
5. Show and name word cards for days of the week. Children come forward; find in main picture.
6. Show word cards and name days of the week again. Class repeats.

Shared listening

1. Play FCD track 20. Point to characters when they speak.
2. Ask *Who? What?* questions.
3. Ask about the stars.
4. Play FCD track 20 and point to characters again.

Dialogue practice

1. Say new words. Children point in books (FB pp26–27). Point on poster for children to check.
2. Show word cards for days of the week. Children name.
3. Children close books. Play FCD track 21 and show character flashcards. Class repeats lines in pauses.
4. Groups say lines by character.
5. Individuals act dialogue.
6. Play FCD track 20 again. Children follow text or point to main picture.

After listening

1. Ask about the pictures on Miss Plum's board.
2. Play *Days of the week*.

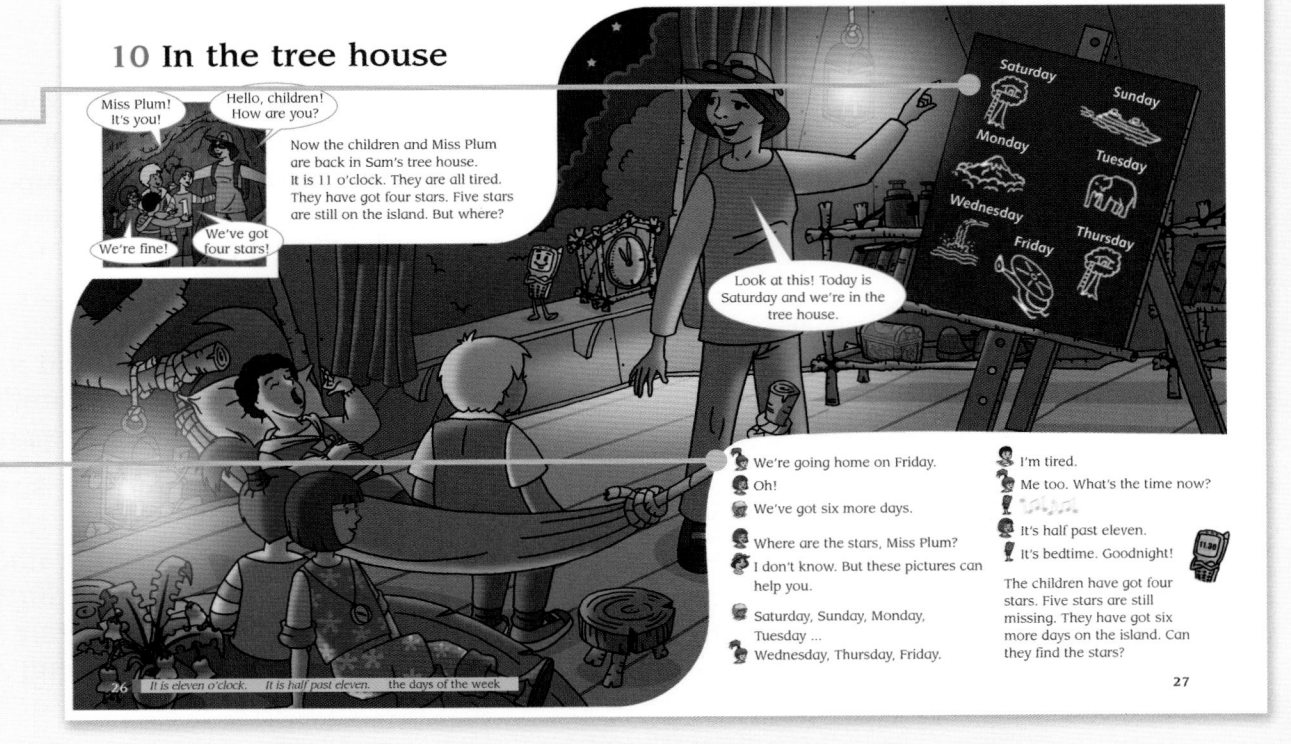

130

Lesson aim Fluency

Lesson targets Children:

- listen for pronunciation and intonation
- repeat dialogue accurately
- act out dialogue with expression
- talk about days of the week.

Key language (words) *Saturday, Sunday, Monday, Tuesday, Wednesday, Thursday, Friday* (structures) *It is eleven o'clock. It is half past eleven. How are you? Me too! What's the time? It's ... o'clock. It's half past ... Good night!*

Words for understanding *bedtime, days, pictures, going, tired, home, now, today*

Materials Posters 9 and 10, Fluency Book pp26–27, Fluency CD tracks 20–21, character flashcards 1–6, word cards for days of the week

Preparation Listen to the CD before the lesson. Make large word cards for days of the week.

Lesson 1 time division:

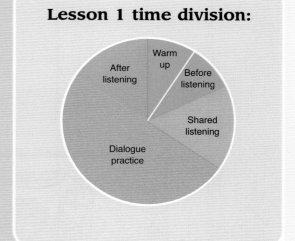

Lesson 1 Warm-up

1 Sing *I've got two little hands* (LB p83, LCD1 track 55).

Before listening

2 Ask *Where are the children? How many stars have the children got? Who is in the cave with the children?*

3 Ask *Is Miss Plum in the cave with the children? Are the children happy?*

4 Ask *Is this Sam's tree house? Is it day? Is it night? Can you see Sam's bed? Can you see Polly? Can you see Mobi?*

Shared listening

2 Ask *What day is it? What time is it? Who is on Sam's bed? Who is tired? Is Nina tired too? Who is sitting next to Nina?*

3 Ask *How many stars have they got? How many stars are missing? When are they going home? How many days do they have on the island?*

After listening

1 *Look at Saturday. What can you see? Can you see an elephant/a helicopter? What day? Can you find a mountain/water? What day? Look at Sunday. Can you see a big ship on the sea?*

2 **Days of the week**
Divide the class into seven groups. Give each one a day of the week card. Ask each group *What day have you got?* Groups reply.

Instruct groups in turn, e.g. *Monday, stand up* (or *hands up*). *Tuesday, stand up. Sunday, stand up. Tuesday, sit down* (or *hands down*). *Sunday, sit down. Thursday, stand up*, etc. Groups must listen for their day and follow the instruction. When the class is used to the game, go faster. Change over the cards after a few turns.

131

Before reading

1 Lesson 2 warm-up.

2 Teach times using the clock flashcard (85).

3 Children open books (LB pp88–89). Ask questions.

Shared reading

1 Play LCD2 track 60. Children follow text in book.

2 Read line by line. Ask questions.

3 Read with the class.

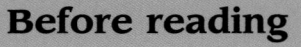

unit 10

Suki's day

It's Saturday.
It's seven o'clock.
Good morning, Suki!
Suki is still sleepy.

It's ten o'clock.
Suki is playing with her friends.
She's very happy!

It's half past twelve.
Say goodbye to your friends!
Suki is a little bit sad.

Time for lunch!

It's three o'clock.
Suki is thirsty.
Milk and a cake. Yummy!

It's half past five.
Suki is hungry.
Hooray! Pizza for dinner!

It's half past seven.
Suki is very, very, very tired.
Goodnight, Suki!

I wake in the morning early
And always, the very first thing,
I poke out my head
And I sit up in bed
And I sing and I sing and I sing.

Rose Fyleman

88   Parents: see extra material on page 166

89

Reading practice

1 Give reading practice. Use some or all of the following:
- Children read again as a class.
- Groups read different sections.
- Individuals read different sections.

2 Class listens again to LCD2 track 60 and follows in LB.

After reading

Practise the new adjectives.

Lesson aim Reading

Lesson targets Children:

- follow a text read out to them
- listen for pronunciation and intonation
- read the text aloud with accurate pronunciation and intonation
- learn and understand new vocabulary items
- understand the sense of the text as a whole
- answer simple comprehension questions.

Key language (words) *hungry, thirsty, happy, sad, tired*, days of the week (structures) *It is eleven o'clock. It is half past eleven.*

Language for understanding *sleepy, milk, cake, pizza, lunch, dinner*, words of rhyme

Materials Language Book pages 88–89, Language CD2 track 60, flashcards 22, 85–88, 90, 96, 162, *After reading*. Cards with happy face and sad face drawn on. Word cards for *After reading*.

Preparation Make word cards for *After reading*. Make cards with happy face and sad face.

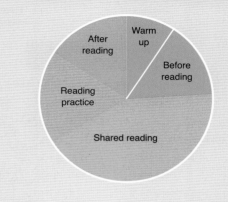

Lesson 2 time division

⬇ Lesson 2 Warm-up

1 Say the numbers chant (p27). Sing the numbers song (LB p9, LCD1 track 6).

Play *Line-up numbers* (TG pp43, 248) with numbers 1–10.

⬇ Before reading

2 Practise saying the numbers on the clock. Move the hands. Show/Say *one o'clock*.

Write it on the board. Move the hour hand to two. Say *two o'clock*. Continue round the clock face.

Do the same for half past.

3 (rhyme picture) Ask Is *it day or night? What time is it? Where is the boy?* (other pictures) *It is ten o'clock. Where is Suki? It's three o'clock. Is Suki playing? It's half past seven. What has Suki got?*

⬇ Shared reading

2 Ask (picture 1) *What day is it? What time is it? Where is Suki?*
(picture 2) *Who is Suki playing with? Is Suki happy?*
(picture 3) *What time is it? Is Suki happy now?*
(picture 4) *What has Suki got?*
(picture 5) *What has Suki got for dinner? Is she hungry?*
(picture 6) *What time is it? Is Suki going to bed?*

⬇ After reading

Children look at the reading pages.

Say *Suki is thirsty. What time is it?* Ask similar questions for *hungry, tired, happy, sad.*

Put word cards on board for *hungry, thirsty, happy, sad, tired* and flashcards for *juice, cakes, bed, sad face, happy face.* Put below.

Say *Suki is hungry. Suki is happy,* etc. Children match pictures to words.

133

Reading and understanding

1 Session 1 warm-up.

2 Re-read *Suki's day* (LB pp88–89).

3 Revise words: see *After reading* on TG p133.

4 Activity 1 (LB p90): Children read and circle. Demonstrate the first sentence on the board.

5 Activity 2: Ask children the time on each clock face. Individuals/Class read the sentences. Children match.

6 Activity 3: Children complete the rhyme with words in the boxes.

7 Play the *Get active!* game.

8 Prepare children for PB p70. Read the text under the pictures with them and check they understand the task. Children complete.

Working with words

1 Session 2 warm-up.

2 Activity 1 (LB p91): Children complete the crossword.

3 Activity 2: Children write sentences.

Sentence building

1 Go through the information in the box.

2 Activity 1: Children write the capital letters.

3 Prepare children for PB p71. Go through the box and check they understand the tasks. Children complete.

Extension activities

1 Children match capital and small letters.

2 Capital name activity.

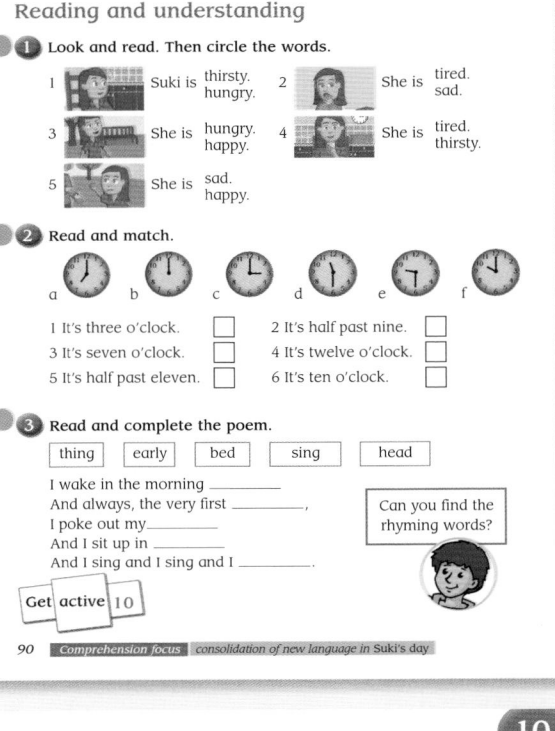

Reading and understanding

1 Look and read. Then circle the words.

1 Suki is thirsty. hungry.
2 She is tired. sad.
3 She is hungry. happy.
4 She is tired. thirsty.
5 She is sad. happy.

2 Read and match.

a   b   c   d   e   f

1 It's three o'clock.   □
2 It's half past nine.   □
3 It's seven o'clock.   □
4 It's twelve o'clock.   □
5 It's half past eleven.   □
6 It's ten o'clock.   □

3 Read and complete the poem.

| thing | early | bed | sing | head |

I wake in the morning _____
And always, the very first _____,
I poke out my_____
And I sit up in _____
And I sing and I sing and I _____.

Can you find the rhyming words?

Get active 10

90 Comprehension focus   consolidation of new language in Suki's day

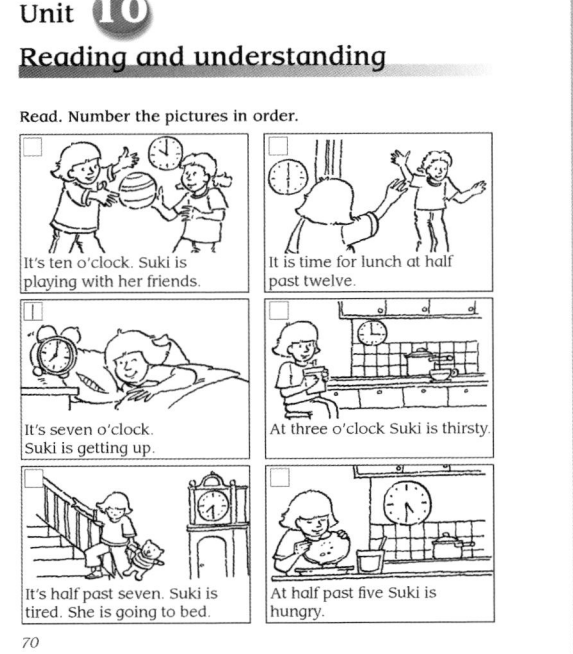

Unit 10

Reading and understanding

Read. Number the pictures in order.

It's ten o'clock. Suki is playing with her friends.

It is time for lunch at half past twelve.

It's seven o'clock. Suki is getting up.

At three o'clock Suki is thirsty.

It's half past seven. Suki is tired. She is going to bed.

At half past five Suki is hungry.

70

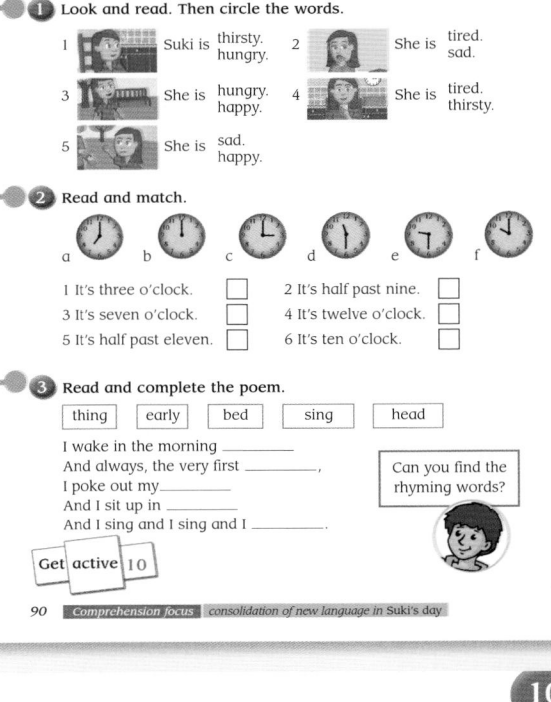

Working with words   10

1 Find and write the words.

2 Write sentences.

He _____

Sentence building

The days of the week are **proper nouns**.

Monday Tuesday Wednesday

Proper nouns begin with a capital letter.

1 Begin each proper noun with the correct capital letter.

| □aturday | □unday | □onday | □uesday |
| □ednesday | □hursday | □riday |

Language focus   days of the week, proper nouns   91

Unit 10

Sentence building

The days of the week are **proper nouns**.
Proper nouns begin with **capital letters**.

1 What day is it? Write.

1 It is S _ t _ _ _ _ _. Ben is running.
2 It is S u _ _ _ _. Ben is fishing.
3 It is M _ _ _ _ _. Ben is riding.
4 It is T _ e _ _ _ _. Ben is drawing.
5 It is W _ _ n _ _ _ _ _. Ben is climbing.
6 It is T _ _ r _ _ _ _. Ben is sleeping.
7 It is F _ _ _ _ _. Ben is singing.

2 Complete the missing words. Use words from the box.

| Saturday Sunday Monday Tuesday |
| Wednesday Thursday Friday |

1 Saturday ⟶ _____ ⟶ Monday
2 Sunday ⟶ _____ ⟶ Tuesday
3 Monday ⟶ _____ ⟶ Wednesday
4 Tuesday ⟶ _____ ⟶ Thursday

71

Lesson aim Comprehension, vocabulary and sentence building

Lesson targets Children:

- match statements to pictures
- match clocks to times
- complete a rhyme from given words
- write words from picture clues
- complete sentences from picture prompts
- practise capital letters for days of the week.

Key language (words) *hungry, thirsty, tired, sad, happy,* days of the week, the time *(o'clock, half past)*
(structures) *She is tired. It is three o'clock. It is Monday.*

Words for understanding words in rhyme

Materials Language Book pp90–91, Practice Book pp70–71, number word cards 1 to 12, clock flashcard 85

Lesson 3 time division:

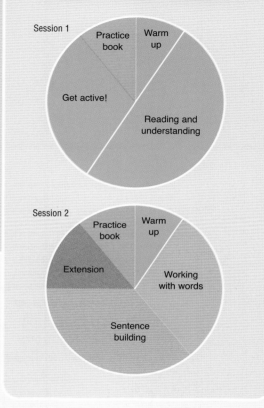

Lesson 3 Session 1 Warm-up

1 Say the rhyme from *Suki's Day*. Unit 10, Lesson 2 (LB p88). Write it on the board. Class reads.

Rub off the last word of each line. Class supplies the missing word.

Reading and understanding

6 Individuals/Class read the words in the boxes. Ask a volunteer to read the first line and fill in the last word. Do the same with the other lines. Children write the words.

Class reads the rhyme.

7 **Get active!**
Show a team 1 child a number word. Team 1 child moves hands on clock and asks *What's the time?* Team 2 reads the time.

Change over: show a team 2 child a number word.

Put the hands at half past. Teams take turns to ask *What's the time?* The other team says the time.

Lesson 3 Session 2 Warm-up

1 Play the *Alphabetical order* game (p248).

Working with words

2 Children look at the pictures. Ask for suggestions for the first picture. Ask a volunteer to write the word on the board.

Continue with the other pictures. Rub off the words before children complete the puzzle.

Sentence building

Read the sentence in the box. Ask a child to read Mobi's bubble. Children read the days of the week. Write them up. Underline the capital letters.

Extension activities

1 Write capital letters at random on the left-hand side of the board and the corresponding lower case letters on the right, also in random order. Children come to the board and draw a line to match.

2 Ask the children to say proper nouns. Write them on the board without the capital letter. Children come and write the capital.

135

Grammar

1. 📖 Lesson 4 warm-up. ⬇

2. Class reads the numbers on the flags (LB p92).

3. Pairs read the speech bubbles. Class repeats.

4. Activity 1: Point out the Remember! box. Children ask the time and answer. ⬇

5. Activity 2: Individuals say the time. Class repeats. Children write.

6. Prepare children for PB p72 by checking they understand the tasks. Children complete.

Listening

1. Read/Ask a child to read Nina's speech bubble (LB p93).

2. 🎧 Activity 1: Play LCD2 track 61. Children listen and match days with pictures. ⬇

3. 🎧 Activity 2: Play LCD2 track 62. Children listen again. Children make statements.

4. 🎧 Activity 3: Play the poem LCD2 track 63. Children listen. Children join in.

After listening

Children make statements with days of the week cards as action cards.

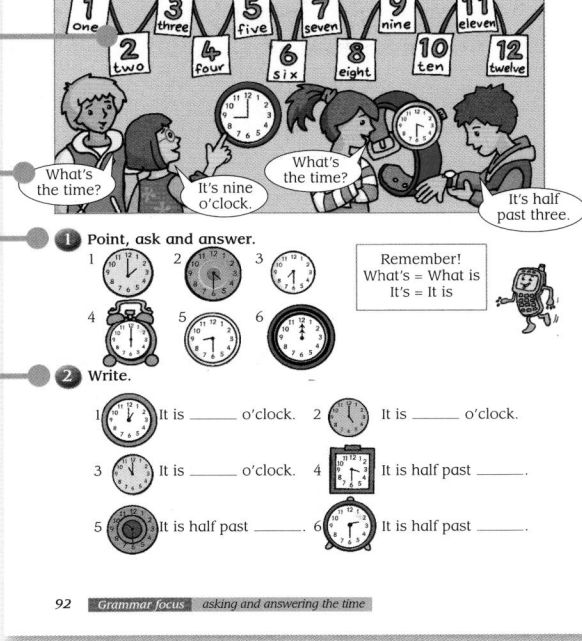

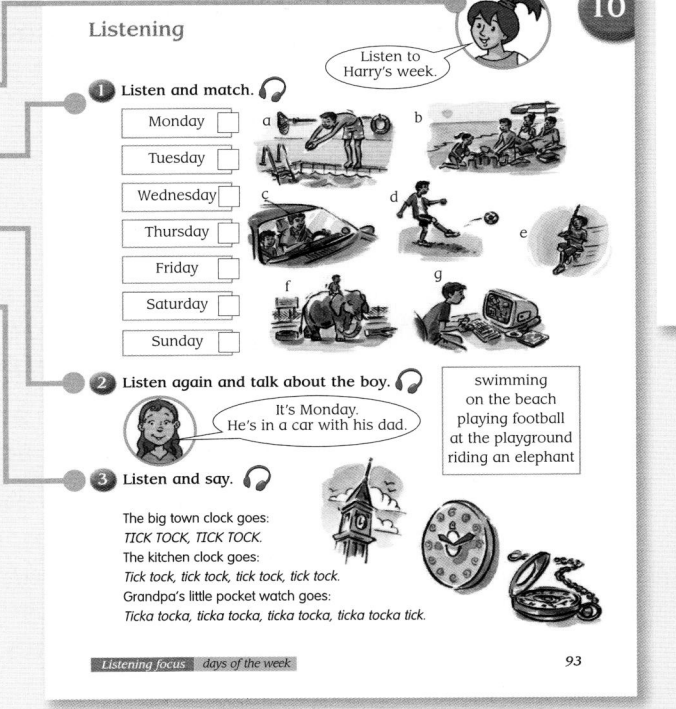

Lesson aim Grammar and listening

Lesson targets Children:

- practise asking and telling the time
- practise writing the time
- listen for specific information
- talk about a boy's activities during a week
- sing and learn a short song.

Key language (words) numbers/days of the week
(structures) *What's the time? It's ... o'clock. It's half past ..., It's Saturday.*

Materials Language Book pp92–93, Practice Book p72, Language CD2 tracks 61–63, flashcard clock (85), actions flashcards of your choice, days of the week word cards

Preparation Listen to the CD before the lesson.

Lesson 4 time division:

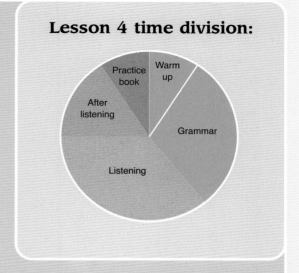

⬇ Lesson 4 Warm-up

1 Play the *Team numbers* game (pp69, 248).
Use the flashcard clock to practise the time.

⬇ Grammar

4 Children look at the first clock. Ask *Number 1. What's the time?* Elicit answers. Class repeats.

Children repeat the activity in pairs. Go around listening to them.

⬇ Listening

2 Individuals/Class read the days of the week. Ask questions. Play the CD once. Children listen and look. Play the CD again. Children match.

Audioscript

Voice	1
	It's Monday. [car driving, tooting]
Harry	Look at all these cars, Dad!
Voice	2
	It's Tuesday.
	[running, panting, kicking ball]
Harry	Goal!!
Voice	3
	It's Wednesday.
	[seaside, gentle waves, gulls calling]
Harry	This beach is fantastic!
Voice	4
	It's Thursday. [elephant trumpeting]
Harry	This elephant's really big!
Voice	5
	It's Friday. [exciting computer game + music]
Harry	Wow! This game's great!
Voice	6
	It's Saturday. [swimming pool]
Boy 2	Come on, Harry!
Harry	OK! [splash]
Voice	7
	It's Sunday. [playground]
Harry	This playground's fantastic! Wahay!

⬇ After listening

Pairs of children come forward. One chooses a day. The other chooses an action. They make statements. *It's Saturday. We are running.*

Activity 1

1 Lesson 5 warm-up. ⬇

2 (LB p94) Point out pictures and words with *ck*.

3 🎧 Play rhyme twice (LCD2 track 64). Children follow in books.

4 Read rhyme.

5 Read and ask questions. ⬇

6 Read with the class.

Activity 2

1 ⬇ Children hold sounds cards. Read the sounds.

2 Close up gradually.

3 Read the word.

4 Children look, say and write.

Activity 3

Children say the word and sentence. ⬇ Children write.

Activity 4

1 Write up words. Class/individuals read. ⬇

2 Children read in pairs. Listen to pairs.

3 Children check words and tick.

Practice Book

Children complete PB p73. ⬇

Phonics games and activities

1 Do the clock rhyme activity. ⬇

2 Play *Look, write, check* (p75).

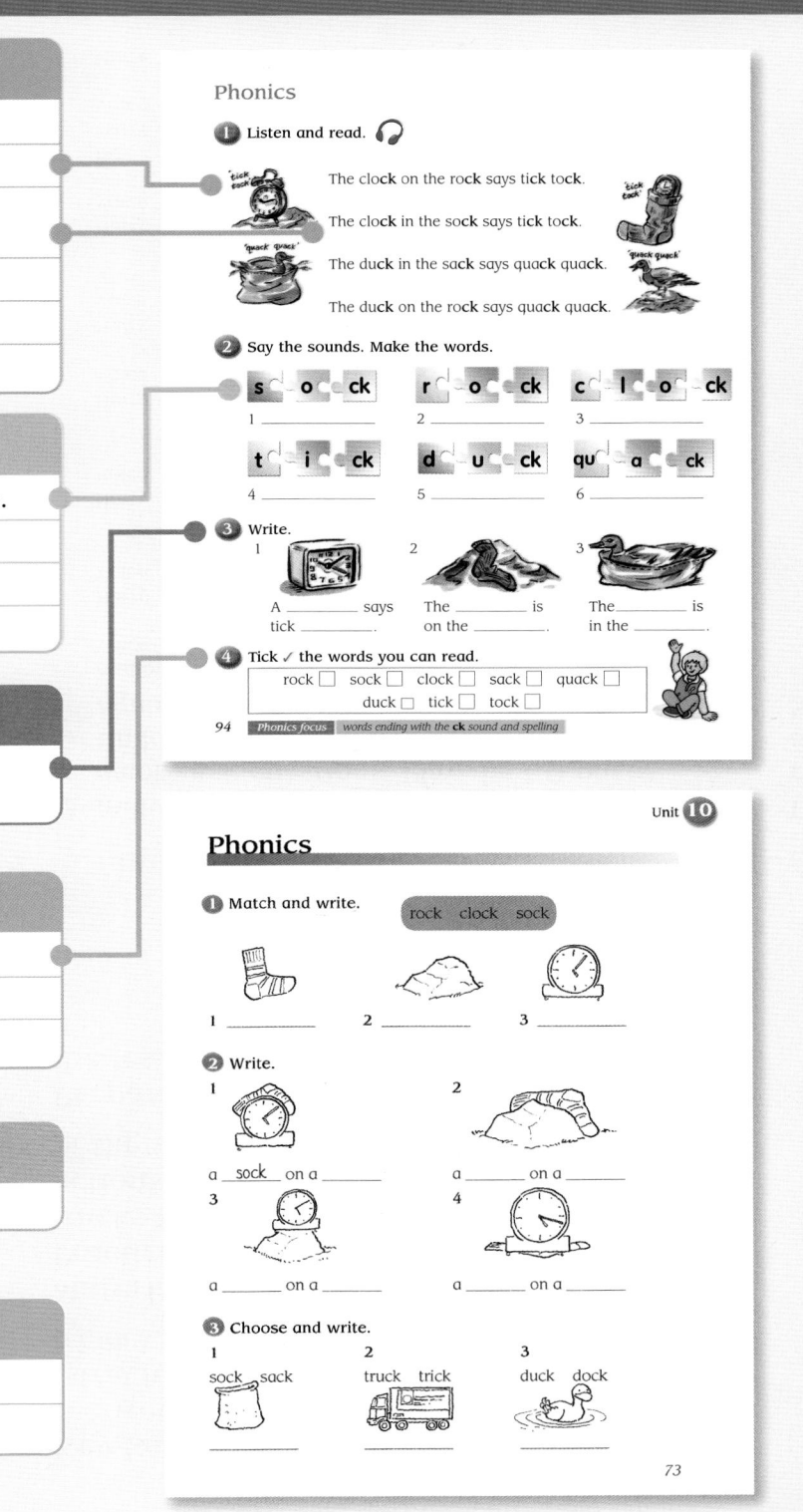

Lesson aim Phonic recognition

Lesson targets Children:

- read, pronounce and spell words ending *ck*
- recognise and say the individual sounds that make up the words
- write the words from picture prompts.

Target words *rock, sock, clock, sack, quack, duck, truck*

Materials Language Book p94, Practice Book p73, Language CD2 track 64, cards for sounds for target words

Preparation Listen to the CD before the lesson. Make large cards for the sounds/phonemes for the target words.

Lesson 5 time division:

Lesson 5 Warm-up

1 Say *The big town clock* from Lesson 4 (LB p93).

Activity 1

5 Ask *Where is the clock? What does it say? What is in the sock? What does it say? What is in the sack? What does it say? Where is the duck? What does it say?*

Make sure all the words in the text are understood.

Activity 2

Follow the procedure for introducing the phonemes and sounding out each word which is given in detail in the Introduction (p10). Ensure the children understand that the letters *ck* make one sound.

Activity 3

Children look at the picture and read the words. Ask/Help a child to say the whole sentence. Class repeats. Children write the word.

Do the same with the other sentences.

Activity 4

1 Write the eight words on the board. Point in random order. Individuals and/or the class reads them.

Practice Book

Children complete the three exercises. Check they can read all the words when they complete the activities.

Phonics games and activities

1 Write up the clock rhyme from Lesson 4 (LB p93), with just the first two words of lines 2, 4 and 6. Children come forward and circle *ck* in each line. Say the lines with the class. Children raise their hands when a word with *ck* is said.

139

Before writing

1. Lesson 6 warm-up.
2. Read Miss Plum's speech bubble (LB p95).
3. Class reads the days of the week.
4. Individuals/Class read times.
5. Individuals read places.
6. Class reads.

Shared writing

1. (LB p95) Elicit sentences. Write them on the board.
2. Activity 1: Children read about Sam.
3. They draw and write about Tilly, then themselves.

Practice Book

Writing

(PB p74) Children read words, write words and complete sentences.

Your writing

1. (PB p75) Children complete the first two sentences.
2. Children write sentences.

After writing

Children read what they wrote about Tilly and themselves to the class.

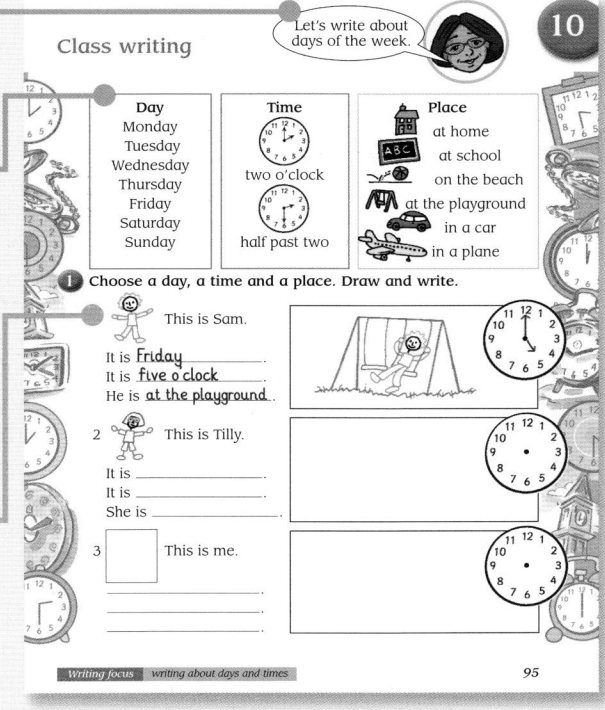

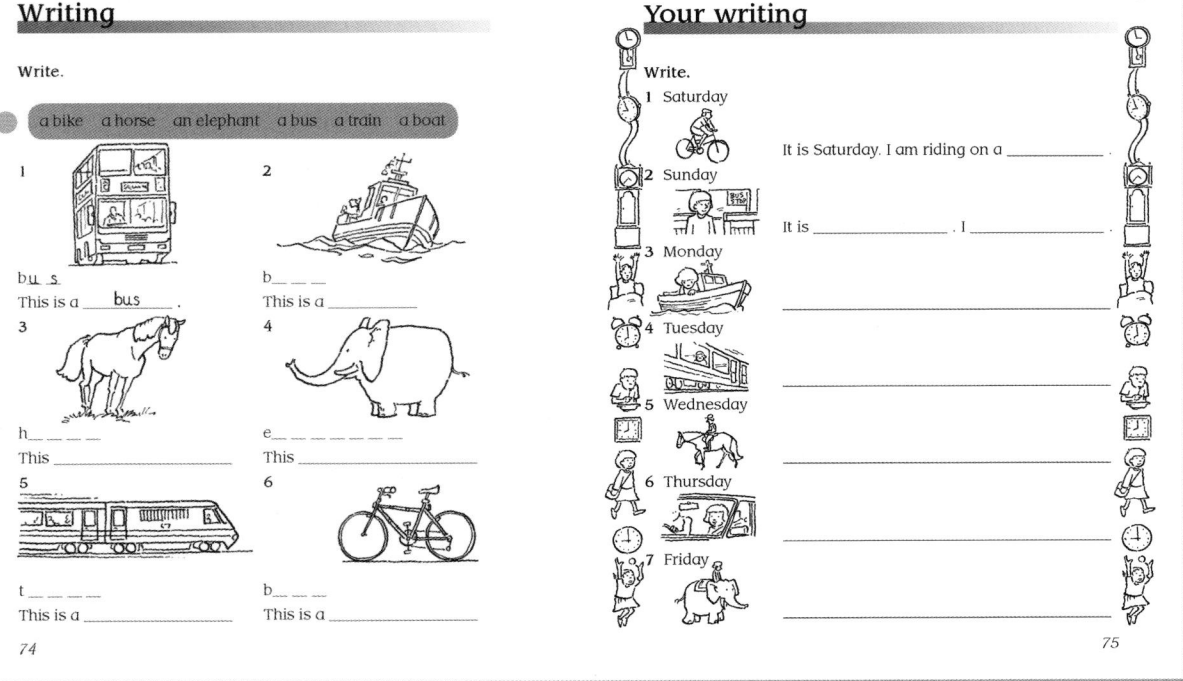

Lesson aim Writing

Lesson targets Children:

- choose times and given places to complete sentences about characters
- complete sentences from picture prompts
- write two sentences about the day and means of travel.

Key language (words) words for transport, times, locations (structures) *It is Monday. Tilly is on the beach.*

Materials Language Book p95, Practice Book pp74 and 75, days of the week word cards, character flashcards 2 and 4, locations flashcards 48-50, 54, clock flashcard 85

Lesson 6 time division:

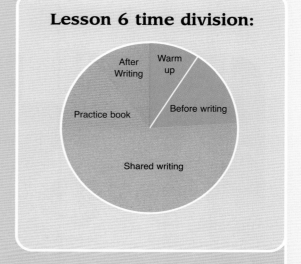

⬇ Lesson 6 Warm-up

1 Do a sentence making activity. Put up days of week word cards, Nina and Ben flashcards, the clock flashcard and the locations flashcards. Children take turns to choose cards, set the clock and say sentences, e.g. *It is Monday. It is three o'clock. Ben is on the beach.* Help with prepositions, but do not focus on them. Elicit sentences about the two characters.

⬇ Shared writing

1 Let a child choose a character. Elicit sentences, e.g. *It is Sunday. It is one o'clock. Nina is at home.* Write the sentences on the board. Class reads.

Elicit sentences about other characters. Write them on the board. Class reads.

2 Activity 1: Class reads about Sam.

Point out the time drawn on the clock and the picture.

3 Ask for suggestions about Tilly. Write one set of sentences about her. Then elicit a second set.

Explain to the class that they can choose the day, time and place to write about Tilly then about themselves.

⬇ Practice Book

Writing
Individuals/Class read words. Child reads the word for picture 1 and the sentence below. Class repeats word and sentence. Children write.

1 Your writing
Check that children correctly identify the activity illustrated for each day. Ask, e.g. *It is Saturday. What does he say?*

⬇ After writing

Children read the three sentences they have written about themselves on page 95. Hear as many of them as possible.

141

Before listening

1. Lesson 1 warm-up.
2. Show poster 11. Read the title. Ask questions.
3. Point and name new verbs. Children come forward; find verbs in main picture.
4. Show flashcards (92–94) and name new verbs. Class repeats.

Shared listening

1. Play FCD track 22. Point to characters when they speak.
2. Ask *What? How?* questions.
3. Ask about the small picture, right.
4. Play FCD track 22 and point to characters again.

Dialogue practice

1. Say the new verbs. Children point in books (FB pp28–29). Point on poster for children to check.
2. Show flashcards (71, 85–88). Children name.
3. Children close books. Play FCD track 23 and show character flashcards. Class repeats lines in pauses.
4. Groups say lines by character.
5. Individuals act dialogue.
6. Play FCD track 22 again. Children follow text or point to main picture.

After listening

1. Show flashcards. Ask questions.
2. Play *Action mime*.

11 **Look at that ship!**

eating swimming sitting drinking walking

11 Look at that ship!

It is Sunday morning. The children are standing on a hill next to the sea. Can they see a ship? Yes! A big white ship is sailing past the island.

walking sitting swimming

eating drinking

Let's go!

Look at that ship!
Wow!
Who is on the ship? Can you see, Sam?
I can see lots of people.

What are they doing?
They're walking around the ship.
They're sitting in the sun.
They're swimming.

I'm thirsty! I'm thirsty!
Be quiet, Mobi!

I can see a boy.
What's he doing?
He's eating an ice cream.

I can see a girl.
What's she doing?
She's drinking. Orange juice, I think.

The children are in a little boat. Are they going to the big ship? Can they find a star there?

28 *What is he/she doing? What are they doing?* 29

Lesson aim Fluency

Lesson targets Children:

- listen for pronunciation and intonation
- repeat dialogue accurately
- act out dialogue with expression
- talk about events in the story.

Key language (words) *drinking, eating, swimming, walking,* (revision) *sitting* (structures) *What is he/she doing? What are they doing?*

Language for understanding *boat, hill, ice cream, orange juice, ship, sun, doing, standing, lots of, past.*

Materials Poster 11, Fluency Book pp28–29, Fluency CD tracks 22–23, character flashcards 2–6, action flashcards 92–94

Preparation Listen to the CD before the lesson.

Lesson 1 time division:

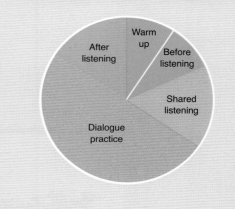

Lesson 1 Warm-up

1 Sing or say the rhyme *A sailor went to sea* from Unit 7 Lesson 4 (LB p57).

Before listening

2 Ask *What is Sam holding?*
What is on the sea?
Is Sam looking at the ship?
Are all the children looking at the ship?

Let children come to the poster, point and name anything they can.

Shared listening

2 Ask *What is the boy/the girl doing?*
What is the man/the woman doing?
How many boys are swimming?
How many children are walking?
What is Polly doing?

3 Ask *Where are the children?*
What are Nina and Tilly doing?
Who is standing?
What is Ben looking at?
Where are they going?

After listening

1 Use the five action cards for this lesson and choose three more from Unit 8. Ask *What is/are he/she/they doing?*

2 **Action mime**
Show a volunteer an action card. Child mimes the action. Other children guess. If you wish, add in some actions learned in earlier units for revision.

143

Before reading

1 Lesson 2 warm-up. ⬇

2 Teach new words using word cards.

3 Children open books (LB pp96–97). Ask questions. Children point. ⬇

Shared reading

1 🎧 Play LCD2 track 65. Children follow text in book.

2 Read line by line. Ask questions. ⬇

3 Read with the class.

Here comes the train!

The train

Here comes the train!
It is going very fast.
Listen! The train is making a noise.
Can you hear it?

Clickety clack

On the train

People are sitting on the train.
What are they doing?
Some people are reading and some are talking.
Some people are listening to music,
and some are looking out of the window.
Some people are also eating and drinking.
You can buy food on a train.

Tickets please!

Here comes a man.
He is checking the tickets.

In the town

Now the train is in the town.
Listen!

We are now arriving at the station.

Here is the station. The train is stopping.
The doors are opening. The people are getting off.
They are walking very fast! Everyone is in a hurry!

96   Parents: *see extra material on page 166*

97

Reading practice

1 Give reading practice. Use some or all of the following:

- Children read again as a class.
- Groups read different sections.
- Individuals read different sections.

2 🎧 Class listens again to LCD2 track 65 and follows in LB.

After reading

Do the phrase building activity. ⬇

Lesson aim Reading

Lesson targets Children:

- follow a text read out to them
- listen for pronunciation and intonation
- read the text aloud with accurate pronunciation and intonation
- learn and understand new vocabulary items
- understand the sense of the text as a whole
- answer simple comprehension questions.

Key language (words) *reading, talking, listening, walking, getting off* (structures) *What are they doing? Some people are verb + ing.*

Words for understanding *checking, hurry, noise, music, food, buy tickets, arriving, town, station, out of*

Materials Language Book pages 96–97, Language CD2 track 65, word cards for *listening, reading, talking, walking, getting off, looking, eating, drinking, buying, checking*

Preparation Listen to the CD before the lesson. Make word cards.

Lesson 2 time division:

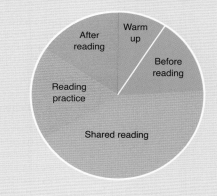

Lesson 2 Warm-up

1 Play the *Chain game* (TG p51) using words beginning with each letter of the alphabet: *In my bag I've got an apple. In my bag I've got an apple and a bat*, etc.

Before reading

3 Ask *What is in the (first) picture?*
What are the people doing on the train?
Do you ride on a train?
Where does the train go?

Shared reading

2 Ask *Is the train slow or fast?*
Is the train quiet or noisy?
What noise does it make?
What are the people doing on the train?
What are people listening to?
What can you buy on the train?
What is the man doing?
Where is the station?
What are the people doing?
Are the people walking slowly?

After reading

Write up these phrases as a list:
a book, to music, to friends, out of the window, an apple, water, food, the tickets.
Arrange word cards for *listening, reading, talking, looking, eating, drinking, buying, checking* in scrambled order below.

Children take turns to match and make phrases. Child reads. Class reads.

145

Reading and understanding SESSION 1

1. Session 1 warm-up.
2. Re-read *Here comes the train!* (LB pp96–97)
3. Activity 1 (LB p98): Children talk about the pictures, read the sentences and match.
4. Activity 2: Children read the questions, look at the pictures and find the matching answers.
5. Play *Get active!*
6. Prepare children for PB p76. Read the passage with them and check they understand the task. Children complete.

Working with words SESSION 2

1. Session 2 warm-up.
2. Activity 1 (LB p99): Read the first three new words to the class.
3. Class repeats.
4. Individuals read next three words. Class repeats.
5. Do the same with the verbs.
6. Children match the words to the correct verb.

Sentence building

1. Go through the information in the box.
2. Activity 1: A child reads the first sentence. Class repeats. Ask/Help a child to complete the following sentence with the correct pronoun. Do the same with the other sentences. Children write.
3. Prepare children for PB p77. Go through the box and check they understand the tasks. Children complete.

Extension activities

Do the mime activity with pronouns.

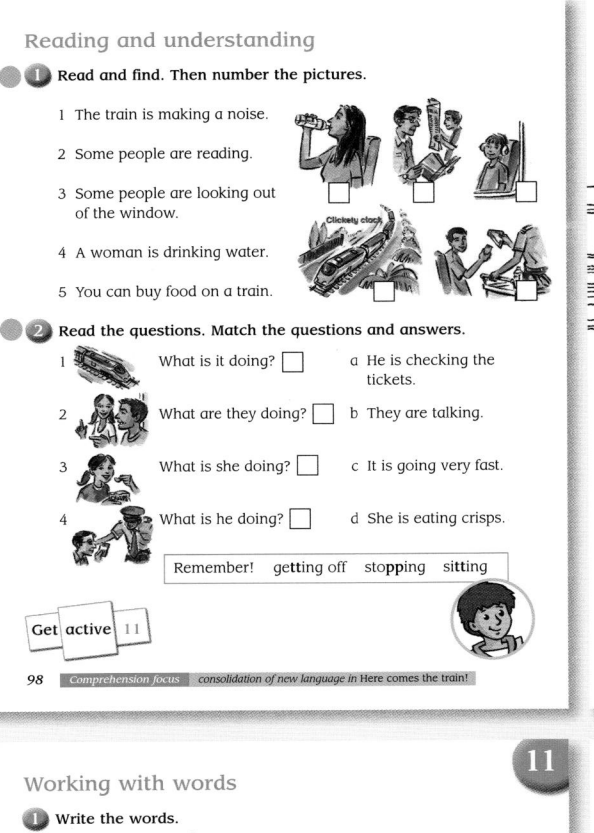

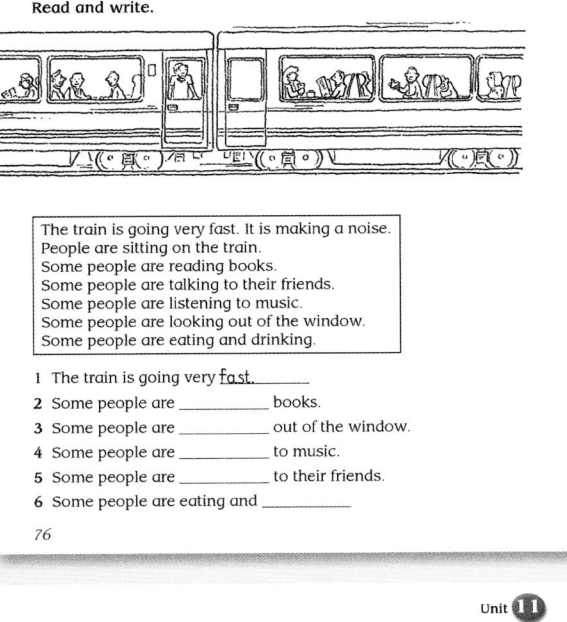

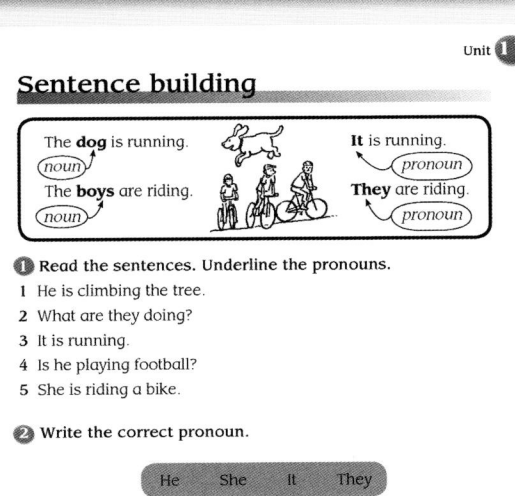

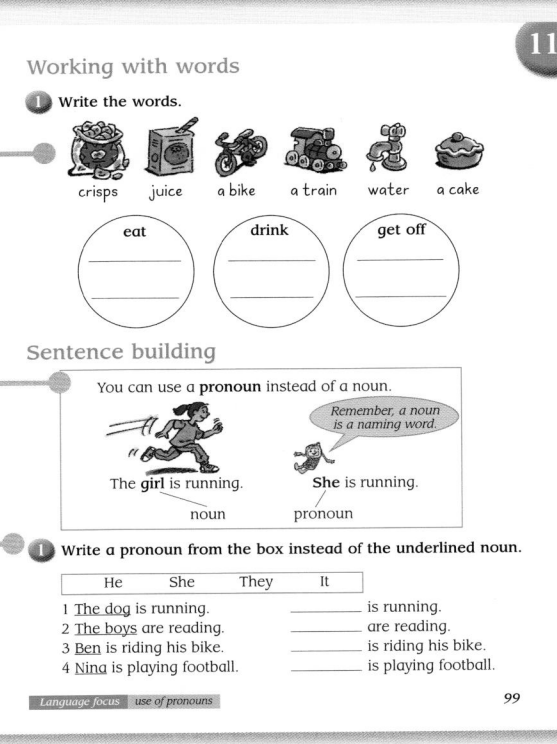

Lesson aim Comprehension, vocabulary and sentence building

Lesson targets Children:
- match statements to pictures
- match answers to questions from picture prompts
- match objects to verbs
- substitute pronouns for nouns.

Key language (words) nouns and verbs from Lessons 1 and 2 (structures) *What is/are he/she/it/they doing?*

Words for understanding *crisps, juice*

Materials Language Book pp98–99, Practice Book pp76–77, action or object flashcards of your choice for Session 2 *Warm-up*, flashcards 58, 60–61, 74, 76, 92, 94–95 for *Get Active!*

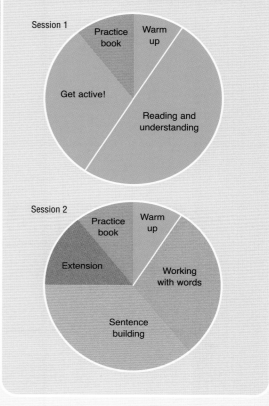

Lesson 3 time division:

Session 1

Session 2

⬇ Lesson 3 Session 1 Warm-up

1 Say *The big town clock* (LB p93).

⬇ Reading and understanding

3 Ask what people are doing in each of the small pictures. Help children form sentences as necessary.

Individuals read sentences. Class repeats. Children match sentences and pictures.

4 Individuals read questions. Class repeats.
A child reads first answer. Class repeats. Ask children which question it matches. Elicit **Number 4**. Children write. Continue with the other sentences.

Ask pairs of children to read the question and matching answer.

Point out the *Remember!* box. Children look at pages 96–97. Read the first sentence under the second picture. Write *sit ... sitting* on the board. Do the same with the last pictures and *stop ... stopping, get off ... getting off.*

5 **Get active!**
Play an *Action mime* game.
Use flashcards for *eating, drinking, walking,* + previous words: *marching, climbing, jumping, falling.*
Show two team 1 children a card. They mime. Team 1 asks *What are they doing?* Team 2 guesses.

⬇ Lesson 3 Session 2 Warm-up

Play *What's missing?* (TG p107) with action flashcards or object flashcards.

⬇ Sentence building

1 Read the sentence in the box to the class. Ask if anyone can say what a noun is. In any case, read Mobi's bubble.

Write up *The girl is running.* Class reads. Ask a child to circle the noun. Write up *She is running.* Circle the pronoun. Name it. Write up one or two more examples. Volunteers circle the noun and the pronoun in the pairs of sentences.

⬇ Extension activities

Individuals/Pairs do actions. Class makes statements, e.g. *Karim is jumping. He is jumping,* etc. *Karim and Dina are running. They are running,* etc.

147

Grammar

1. Lesson 4 warm-up. ⬇

2. Show poster 11. Ask what people are doing.

3. Pairs of children read the questions and answers (LB p100).

4. Point out the *Remember!* box. Children close books. Write up the short forms. Children say full forms.

5. Activity 1: Children write the questions. Elicit answers. ⬇

6. Prepare children for PB p78 by checking they understand the tasks. Children complete.

Listening

1. Children look at the picture and read the speech bubble (LB p101). ⬇

2. 🎧 Activity 1: Play LCD2 track 66. Children listen and look. Play it again. Children tick. ⬇

3. Activity 2: Children talk about the people they have ticked. ⬇

4. 🎧 Activity 3: Play the song LCD2 track 67. Play it again. Children sing along.

After listening

Teach the song in the usual way.

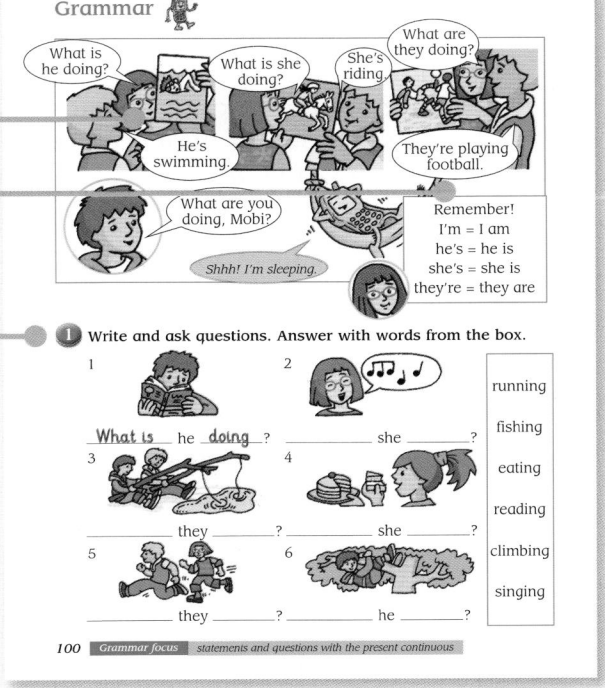

Lesson aim Grammar and listening

Lesson targets Children:

- practise asking questions and talking about what people are doing
- write questions about what children are doing
- listen for specific information
- sing and learn a short song.

Key language (words) verbs from Units 7–11
(structures) *What is/are he/she/it/they doing? He/She/It is ..., They are ...*

Materials Language Book pp100–101, Practice Book p78, Language CD2 tracks 66–67, letter cards for *Warm-up*

Preparation Listen to the CD before the lesson.

Lesson 4 time division:

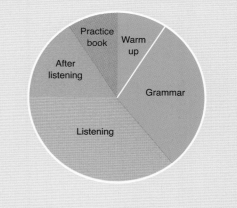

⬇ Lesson 4 Warm-up

1 Play *Alphabetical order* (TG p49, p248).

⬇ Grammar

5 A child reads the first question. Class repeats. Individuals complete the other questions orally. Class repeats. Children write.

Individuals/Class read the words in the box.

Individuals read each question. Elicit answers.

⬇ Listening

1 Ask *What are the people doing?* Children tell you as much as they can. Help them form sentences. If necessary, ask leading questions, e.g. *Can you see a girl/man/people in the café? What is/are he/she/they doing?*

2 Explain to children; they listen and tick the people they hear about on the CD.

3 Children talk in pairs. While they do so, listen to some of them and check the ticks in Activity 1.

Audioscript
This is the train station.
Look at the trains.
And look at all the people.
What are they doing?
You can see people getting off the train.
Some people are walking very fast.
A man is running.
Some people are sitting down. Can you see them?
Some people are in the café. They are eating and drinking.
A little girl is riding on a horse.
Look. One train is going. Can you hear it?

149

Activity 1

1. Lesson 5 warm-up.
2. (LB p102) Point out pictures and words with consonant + *r*.
3. Play sentences twice (LCD2 track 68). Children follow in books.
4. Read sentences.
5. Read and ask questions.
6. Read with the class.

Activity 2

1. Say the sounds.
2. Ask *What is it?* Children say the word.
3. Children circle and write.
4. Write on board. Children check.

Activity 3

Children say the words then the sentence. Children write.

Activity 4

1. Write up words. Class/individuals read.
2. Children read in pairs. Listen to pairs.
3. Children check words and tick.

Practice Book

Children complete PB p79.

Phonics games and activities

1. Play *What's the word?*
2. Play *Start the word.*

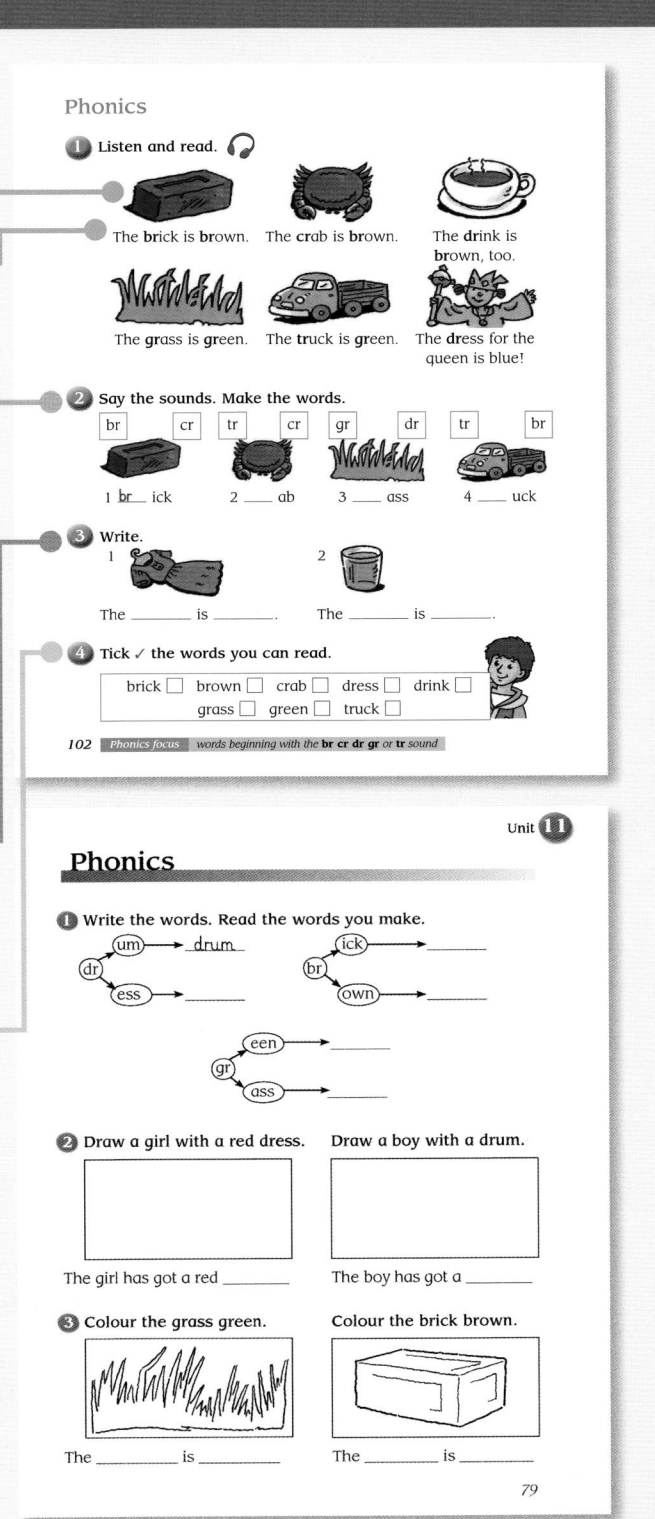

Lesson aim Phonic recognition

Lesson targets Children:

- read, pronounce and spell words with initial consonant blends: consonant + *r*
- recognise and say the consonant blend that starts each target word
- write the words from picture prompts.

Target words *brick, brown, crab, dress, drink, drum, grass, green, truck*

Materials Language Book p102, Practice Book p79, Language CD2 track 68, flashcards and word cards of your choice for *Warm-up*

Preparation Listen to the CD before the lesson.

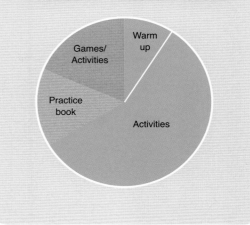

Lesson 5 time division:

⬇ Lesson 5 Warm-up

① Find the pairs

Put up six object flashcards and matching word cards, e.g. *fish, shell, fox, doll, ball, duck*. Stick them face down in scrambled order, well spaced on the board. Pairs of children come forward. One turns a card and shows it, then the other. If they have a matching picture and word, they keep them. Otherwise they replace them. Pairs take turns until the last cards are matched.

⬇ Activity 1

② Ask *Can you see a crab? What colour is it? Can you see grass? What colour is it?*

Write up *crab, brown, grass, green*. Circle the consonant blends and sound them out to the class. Class repeats.

⑤ Ask *Is the brick green? Is the crab blue? What colour is the drink? Is the grass blue?*

What colour is the truck? What is blue? Make sure all the words in the text are understood.

⬇ Activity 2

① Say the two choices of consonant blends for the first word. Class repeats each blend. Ask what the picture shows. Elicit *(a) brick*.
Children circle the correct blend for the beginning of the word. They write the word. Write it on the board. Children check.
Do the same with the other three words.

⬇ Activity 4

① Write the eight words on the board. Point in random order. Individuals and/or the class reads them.

⬇ Practice Book

Children complete the three exercises. Check they can read all the words in Exercise 1 before they move on to Exercise 2.

⬇ Phonics games and activities

① Play *What's the word?* (TG p75). Play the game, saying e.g. *c–r–a–b*.

② Start the word
Write up word endings: *_ess, _ass, _ab, _ ick, _own*. Put up consonant blends *br, gr, cr, dr*. Children place them to make words.

Class reads.

151

Before writing

1. Lesson 6 warm-up.
2. Read Miss Plum's speech bubble (LB p103).
3. Activity 1: Children write activities. Other children act them out.
4. Activity 2: Children say what people/the bird are doing.

Shared writing

1. Activity 3 (LB p103): Children read sentences. Children choose pictures. Elicit questions and answers. Write them on the board. Class reads.
2. Point out the *Remember!* box. Children write three questions. Children exchange books and write answers.

Practice Book

Writing

1. (PB p80) Children look at pictures, read words and circle. Check answers.
2. Children read and complete sentences. Class repeats. Children write.

Your writing

(PB p81) Talk about the picture with the class. Children write sentences.

After writing

Children read out their questions and answers from Activity 3 (LB p103).

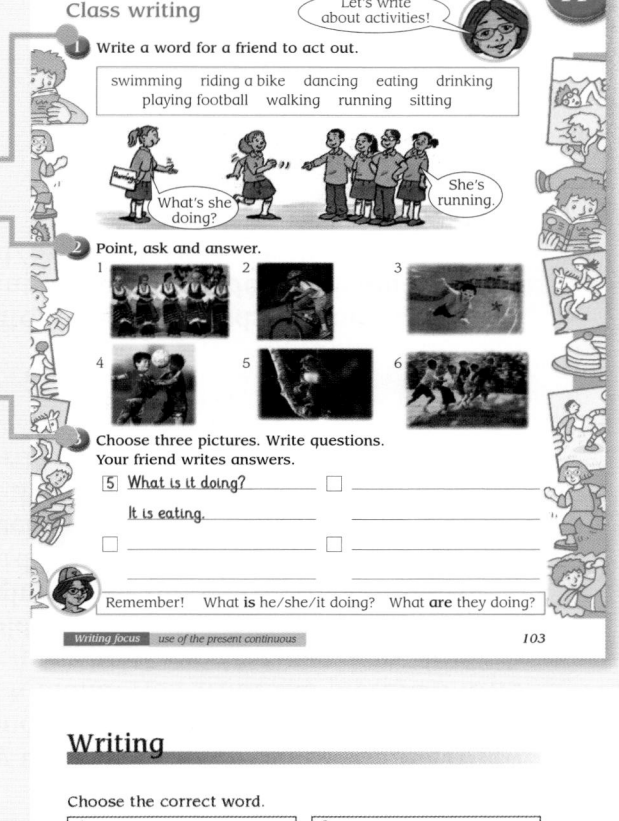

Lesson aim Writing

Lesson targets Children:

- ask and write questions about what people are doing
- complete sentences from picture prompts and choice of two words
- identify people and animals in a picture and write what they are doing.

Key language (words) verbs from Units 7–11

(structures) *I can see ..., He/She/It is verb + ing. They are verb + ing.*

Materials Language Book p103, Practice Book pp80 and 81, flashcards of your choice for *Warm-up*, actions flashcards of your choice for *Shared writing*

Lesson 6 time division:

Lesson 6 Warm-up

1 Show flashcards of people and objects, singular and plural. Ask *He, she, it or they?* Class says the pronoun.

Before writing

3 Individuals read the words. Class repeats.

Children choose a word/phrase and write it on a slip of paper. Children exchange papers.

Children mime/do the action. Class guesses.

Shared writing

1 Two children read the question and answer for picture 5. Class repeats. Ask a child to choose any other picture. Tell the child to say the question. Write it on the board. Class reads.
Elicit the answer from the class. Write it up. Class reads.
Continue with the other pictures.
If you wish, class reads all the sentences again. Rub them off the board.

2 Point out the *Remember!* box. Show two or three flashcards of actions. Ask some full questions, e.g. *What is he doing? What is it doing? What are they doing?*

Rub them off before children choose three pictures and write the question. Children exchange books and write the answers.

Practice Book

Writing
Ask questions about each picture, e.g. *What can you see?* Elicit answer. Class repeats. Ask *What is/are he/she/it/they doing?* Elicit answer. Class repeats.

After writing

Children read their own questions and their friend's answers. Ask them to say if they think the answers are correct. If not, they must say what is wrong and correct it. Otherwise, ask the class if both question and answer are correct.

Go through any necessary corrections. Check understanding of children who try to correct sentences that are already correct.

Before listening

1. Lesson 1 warm-up. ⬇
2. Show poster 12. Read the title. Ask questions. ⬇
3. Point to the small pictures. Name them. Children find the objects in the main picture.
4. 🎴 Show object flashcards (97, 103, 105) and name new objects. Children come forward and find objects in main picture.
5. 🎴 Show flashcards 97, 101–105 and name. Class repeats.

Shared listening

1. 🎧 Play FCD track 24. Point to characters when they speak.
2. Ask about the places on the ship. ⬇
3. Ask about the small pictures, right. ⬇
4. 🎧 Play FCD track 24 and point to characters again.

Dialogue practice

1. Say the new words. Children point in books (FB pp30–31). Point on poster for children to check.
2. 🎴 Show object flashcards (97, 101–105). Children name.
3. 🎧🎴 Children close books. Play FCD track 25 and show character flashcards. Class repeats lines in pauses.
4. 🎴 Groups say lines by character.
5. 🎴 Individuals act dialogue.
6. 🎧 Play FCD track 24 again. Children follow text or point to main picture.

After listening

1. Children look in their books. Ask questions. ⬇
2. Do the matching shops and items activity. ⬇
3. Children put the next sticker star in the correct place on FB pp46–47.

12 On the ship

Swimming pool · Sweet shop · Sweets · Toys · cafe · Toy shop · toy shop · balloons · ice creams

12 On the ship

The children are on the big ship. There is a clown on the ship. His name is Mr Fun.

Hello!
Welcome to my ship! I'm Mr Fun.

balloons · sweet shop · toy shop · swimming pool · cafe · ice creams

Give me the balloon, please!
Pop!
Look A gold star!
Fantastic!

Star light, star bright, Four stars are missing tonight.

The children have got five gold stars. Where are they going now?

- Do you want to see my ship?
- Yes, please!
- There's a big swimming pool.
- Wow!
- And there's a cafe.
- Mmm! Look at the ice creams!
- There are shops too.
- Oh! Look at the toy shop!
- And the sweet shop! Yum!
- Look at the balloons!
- They're funny!
- Can I have a balloon, please?
- Yes. Here you are.
- Thank you.

30 ▮ There is … There are …

31

Lesson aim Fluency

Lesson targets Children:

- listen for pronunciation and intonation
- repeat dialogue accurately
- act out dialogue with expression
- talk about what there is/are on the ship.

Key language (words) *balloons, cafe, ice creams, sweet shop, swimming pool, toy shop*
(structures) *There is ..., There are ...*

Language for understanding *clown, Yum! Please. Here you are. Thank you. Give me ...!*

Materials Poster 12, Fluency Book pp30–31, Fluency CD tracks 24–25, character flashcards 1–7, object flashcards 97, 101–105, word cards for *sweets, train, ball, ice creams, drinks* (for *After listening*)

Preparation Listen to the CD before the lesson. Make word cards.

Lesson 1 time division:

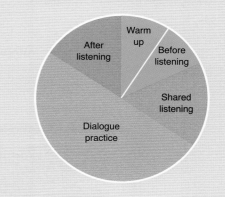

⬇ Lesson 1 Warm-up

1 Check with the class how many stars are missing. Say the *Star chant* (five stars are missing).

⬇ Before listening

2 Ask *Can you see the children on the ship? Where is Mobi?*
(point to boys in pool) *What are they doing?*
How many boys are in the water?
How many boys are swimming?
(point to woman eating) *What is she doing? What is she eating?*

⬇ Shared listening

2 Ask *Who is Mr Fun?*
Is there a swimming pool on the ship?
Is it big or small?
Is there a sweet shop?
Are there lots of sweets?
What shop is next to the sweet shop?
Is there a cafe?
What can you eat in the cafe?

3 Ask *What animal is the green balloon?*
Does Mobi want the green balloon?
What is Mobi doing?
What is in the green balloon?
How many stars have they got now?

⬇ After listening

1 Ask *What can you see on the umbrellas?*
How many?
How many balloons can you see?
What colours are they?
What toys are in the toy shop?

2 Do a matching shops and items activity. Stick up the flashcards 102–104 *(sweet shop, toy shop, cafe).*

Stick up these word cards in scrambled order below: *sweets, train, ball, ice creams, drinks.*

Children match the objects to the places. Elicit sentences, e.g. **There are sweets in the sweet shop. There is a train in the toy shop.**

Before reading

1. Lesson 2 warm-up. ⬇
2. 📖 Teach new words with flashcards 106–108.
3. Children open books (LB pp104–105). Ask questions. ⬇

Shared reading

1. 🎧 Play LCD2 track 69. Children follow text in book.
2. Read section by section. Ask questions. ⬇
3. Read with the class.

unit 12

We all love the mall

This is a great clothes shop. Girls' clothes are upstairs. Boys' clothes are downstairs.

There are lovely smells in the cake shop. There are buns and cakes and biscuits. Yum!

There are lots of restaurants at the mall. This restaurant is 'Gino's Place'. It's got delicious pizzas.

This toy shop is quite small. It's got lots of toy cars and trains and computer games. It's got a slide.

There are two bike shops. You can buy children's bikes at this shop. There are big bikes, small bikes and BMXs.

There is a computer shop. This shop has got great computers. You can buy a green computer or a purple computer or, of course, grey or black.

'Happy Books' is a children's bookshop. There's a very big book in the window.

There is a children's shoe shop. Look at all the shoes. There are trainers and boots and sandals.

This is a sweet shop. The chocolates are yummy. You can buy lovely presents here for mum or dad. It's also got ice creams!

There is one supermarket in the mall. It's enormous. You can buy food, clothes, toys, books and flowers.

Shopping Mall
Clothes · Girls' clothes · Boys' clothes · Cakes · Sweets · Toys · Computers · Bikes · Happy Books · Children's Shoes · Juices · Burger · Chinese Food · Hot Dog · Ice Cream · Gino's Place · Telephone · Toilets

104   *Parents   see extra material on page 166*   105

Reading practice

1. Give reading practice. Use some or all of the following:
   - Children read again as a class.
   - Groups read different sections.
   - Individuals read different sections.
2. 🎧 Class listens again to LCD2 track 69 and follows in LB.

After reading

Do the matching and speaking activity. ⬇

Lesson aim Reading

Lesson targets Children:

- follow a text read out to them
- listen for pronunciation and intonation
- read the text aloud with accurate pronunciation and intonation
- learn and understand new vocabulary items
- understand the sense of the text as a whole
- answer simple comprehension questions.

Key language (words) *book shop, bike shop, cake shop, clothes shop, mall, restaurant, shoe shop, supermarket* (structures) *There is ..., There are ..., You can buy ...*

Words for understanding *smells, BMX, quite, delicious, slide, enormous, great, of course, lovely, trainers, boots, sandals, buns, biscuits, shop* (v.)

Materials Language Book pages 104–105, Language CD2 track 69 flashcards 101–108, word cards for shop items, e.g. *trainers, boots, sandals, buns, biscuits, pizzas, books, clothes, chocolates, sweets*

Preparation Listen to the CD before the lesson. Make word cards as necessary.

Lesson 2 time division:

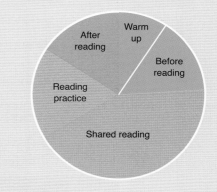

Lesson 2 Warm-up

1 Play *What's this?/What are these?* (TG p45) with new vocabulary and words from previous units.

Before reading

3 Ask *How many shops can you see?*
What shops can you see?
Can you buy things to eat? Where?
Can you buy toys? What toys can you see?

Let children come to the poster, point and name anything they can.

Shared reading

2 Ask *What can you eat in the restaurant?*
Is the toy shop big?
What can you buy there?
Is the supermarket small?
What colour computers can you buy?
What can you buy at the sweet shop?
Whose clothes are upstairs?
What shoes can you buy at the shoe shop?

After reading

Stick up flashcards of shops. Use word cards of items. Put them on your desk. Children take and put under the correct shop. Child makes statement **You can buy buns at the cake shop.** Class repeats. Afterwards ask questions of whole class or teams.

Where can you buy chocolates?
Who are the books for at the book shop?
What is in the window of 'Happy Books'?
How many bike shops are there in the mall?
What can you buy at the cake shop?

157

Reading and understanding

1. Session 1 warm-up.
2. Re-read *We all love the mall* (LB pp104–105).
3. Activity 1 (LB p106): Children read and circle.
4. Activity 2: Children read, look and circle.
5. Activity 3: Play the game around the class.
6. Play the *Get active!* game.
7. Prepare children for PB p82. Read the passage with them and check they understand the tasks. Children complete.

Working with words

1. Session 2 warm-up.
2. Activity 1 (LB p107): Children read the words in the box.
3. They write the words under the pictures.

Sentence building

1. Go through the information in the box (LB p107).
2. Activity 1: A child reads the first sentence. Write it on the board. Class reads. Ask a child to underline the preposition. Check with the class. Continue with the other sentences. Children underline in their books.
3. Prepare children for PB p83. Go through the box and check they understand the tasks. Children complete.

Extension activity

Children circle nouns and double underline verbs in the sentences on the board.

Reading and understanding

1. Read and circle answer A or B.

		A	B
1	There are lots of these in the mall.	restaurants	supermarkets
2	You can buy computer games here.	bookshop	toy shop
3	There are two of these shops.	bike shops	shoe shops
4	Girls can shop upstairs in this shop.	clothes shop	bookshop
5	There are lots of chocolates in this shop.	sweet shop	toy shop
6	You can buy flowers here.	supermarket	bookshop
7	You can buy delicious pizzas here.	sweet shop	Gino's place

2. Read, look and circle true (T) or false (F).

1. There is a clown. T F
2. There are four ice creams. T F
3. There are five people. T F
4. There are ten balloons. T F
5. There is a toy shop. T F
6. There is a supermarket. T F

3. Play a game: What can you buy at the mall?

At the mall I can buy toys.

At the mall I can buy toys and games.

At the mall I can buy toys, games and ...

Get active 12

106 Comprehension focus consolidation of new language in We all love the mall

---

Working with words

1. Look and write the words.

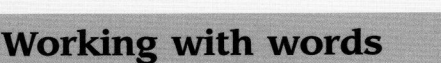

cake shop
bike shop
shoe shop
sweet shop
clothes shop
toy shop

Sentence building

A preposition can tell us **where** something is.

The ball is **on** the box.   It is **in** the box.   It is **under** the box.

The ball is **behind** the box.   It is **next to** the box.

1. Read the sentences. Underline the prepositions.

1 The doll is on the chair.   2 The cat is under the bed.
3 The dog is in the box.   4 The toys are behind the bed.
5 The teddy is next to the table.

Language focus shops, prepositions of place (in / on / under etc.)   107

Unit 12
Reading and understanding

1. Look and read.

In the mall there are lots of shops.
In the cake shop there are buns and cakes and biscuits.
You can get pizzas at 'Gino's Place'.
'Happy Books' is a children's book shop.
The toy shop is quite small.
You can get trainers and boots and party shoes at the shoe shop.
At the sweet shop you can get chocolates and ice cream.

2. Write the answers. Where can you get ...

1 cakes? at the cake shop   2 toys? _____
3 trainers? _____   4 ice cream? _____
5 pizzas? _____   6 books? _____

3. Write the answers. What can you buy at ...

1 the cake shop? _____
2 the shoe shop? _____
3 the sweet shop? _____

82

Unit 12
Sentence building

A *preposition* tells us where something is.

The drum is **on** the bed.

1. Complete the sentences.

| on | in | under | behind |

1 The dog is _____ the table.   2 The doll is _____ the bed.
3 The ball is _____ the chair.   4 The toys are _____ the box.

2. Where is it? Write.

1 Where is the doll?
_____
2 Where is the ball?
_____
3 Where is the dog?
_____

83

Lesson aim Comprehension, vocabulary and sentence building

Lesson targets Children:
- answer simple comprehension questions
- identify correct and incorrect statements about a picture
- practise naming items in shops
- match words for shops to pictures
- practise stating positions of objects.

Key language (words) *shops, in, on, under, behind, next to*
(structures) *You can buy flowers at the mall.*

Materials Language Book pp106–107, Practice Book pp82–83, flashcards of your choice for *Warm-up*, shop flashcards 103–104, 106–108, word cards of shop items (see *Get Active!*), a box and a ball (see *Sentence building*)

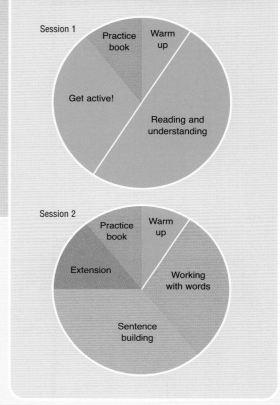

Lesson 3 time division:

Session 1

Session 2

Lesson 3 Session 1 Warm-up

1 Sing *Can you see the engines?* (LB p101, LCD2 track 67).

Reading and understanding

3 Individuals read each sentence. Class repeats. Individuals read the two words under A and B. Elicit the answer. If necessary, children look back to pages 104–5 to check.
Continue in the same way with the other sentences.

4 Explain that *true* means right and *false* means wrong. Children look at the picture for a few moments. Ask them what they can see before they read the sentences.
Individuals read and class repeats the first sentence. Ask *Is it true or false?* Elicit answers. Children circle. Continue in the same way with the other sentences.

6 **Get active!**
Put word cards of shop items (see list below) on the board. Class reads. Give out shop flashcards. Take word cards from the board and ask, e.g. *Where can I buy dolls?* Children with the toy shop stand up and say *You can buy dolls at the toy shop.*
toy shop: dolls, trains, computer games
shoe shop: trainers, boots, sandals
cake shop: buns, cakes, biscuits
sweet shop: chocolates, ice creams, sweets

Lesson 3 Session 2 Warm-up

Show flashcards of people and objects. Ask *He, She, It* or *They?*

Sentence building

1 Read the first sentence in the box. Children read each of the example sentences. Class repeats.
Use the box and ball you have brought in. Put the ball in different positions. Ask the class where it is. Bring children forward. Instruct them where to place the ball. Ask the class if it is correct.

159

Grammar

1 Lesson 4 warm-up. ⬇

2 Children read speech bubbles (LB p108). Class repeats.

3 Point out Mobi's box. Write the words on the board. Children read.

4 Activity 1: Children speak in pairs. ⬇

5 Activity 2: Children read and circle. ⬇

6 Prepare children for PB p84 by checking they understand the tasks. Children complete.

Listening

1 Read Nina's speech bubble (LB p109).

2 🎵 Activity 1: Ask what the shops are. Play LCD2 track 70. Children listen. Play it again. Children listen and answer. ⬇

3 🎵 Activity 2: Play LCD2 track 71. Children sing and do actions. ⬇

After listening

Practise the actions and say the words with the class several times. If you wish, teach the song in the usual way. Children sing the words and do actions without the CD.

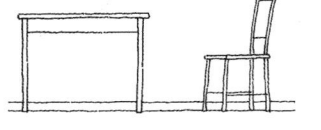

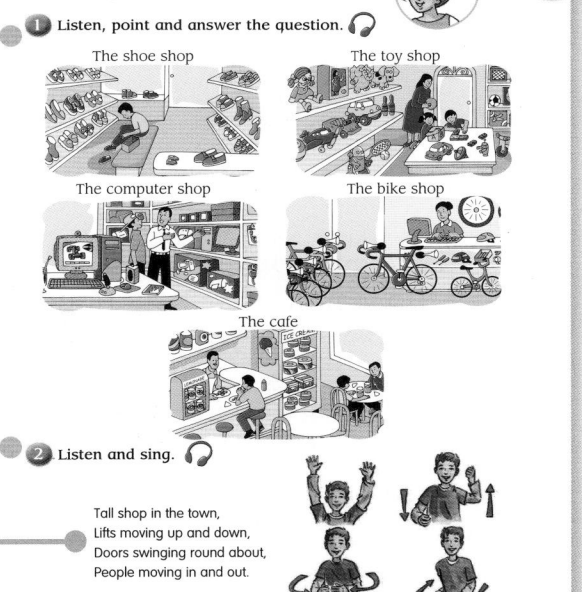

Lesson aim Grammar and listening

Lesson targets Children:

- practise *There is .../There are ...*
- recognise the long and short form *There is .../There's ...*
- listen to dialogue and recognise the context from the language
- sing and learn a short song.

Key language (words) from Lessons 1 and 2
(structures) *There is ..., There are ...*

Materials Language Book pp108–109, Practice Book p84, Language CD2 tracks 70–71, letters/phonemes for *Warm-up*

Preparation Listen to the CD before the lesson.

Lesson 4 time division:

⬇ Lesson 4 Warm-up

1 Play *Muddled letters* (TG p21).

⬇ Grammar

4 Children work in pairs. Listen to some of them. Check with the class all the things they have found.

5 Children try to read the first sentence alone. Ask a child to read it aloud with the correct form of the verb. Class repeats.

If children make mistakes, ask *Where is/are the ...?* Elicit **It is/They are ...** Child tries the sentence in the book again.

⬇ Listening

2 Children listen and point to the picture that matches what they hear. Play the CD again. Children answer in the pause.

3 Children look at the pictures. Play the song. Children listen. Demonstrate the actions. Children follow.

Play the song again. Do the actions and sing the song. Children do the same.

Audioscript

1
Girl	Wow! Look at that computer.
Boy	That game's fantastic.
Girl	Come on! Let's play it!
Voice	Where are they?

2
Mum	I'm hungry.
Girl	I'm thirsty.
Mum	Let's have an ice cream.
Girl	Can I have a lemonade?
Voice	Where are they?

3
Boy 1	Wow! Look at that plane. It's great!
Boy 2	And look at those cars.
Girl 1	I like the dolls.
Girl 2	I like the elephant.
Voice	Where are they?

4
Mum	These blue shoes are very nice.
Girl	Oh! They're too big.
Mum	Well, try the pink shoes.
Girl	Ow!! They're too small!
Voice	Where are they?

5
Boy 1	Look at this red bike. It's really fast.
Boy 2	And listen to this!
Voice	Where are they?

Activity 1

1. Lesson 5 warm-up. ⬇
2. (LB p110) Point out pictures and words with consonant + *l*.
3. 🎧 Play CD twice (LCD2 track 72). Children follow in books.
4. Read the text.
5. Read and ask questions. ⬇
6. Read with the class.

Activity 2

1. ⬇ Say the sounds.
2. Ask *What is it?*
3. Children say the word.
4. Children circle and write.
5. Write on board. Children check.

Activity 3

Children say the words and sentences. ⬇
Children write.

Activity 4

1. Write up words. Class/individuals read. ⬇
2. Children read in pairs. Listen to pairs.
3. Children check words and tick.

Practice Book

Children complete PB p85. ⬇

Phonics games and activities

1. Play *What's the word?* ⬇
2. Do *Look, write, check.* ⬇

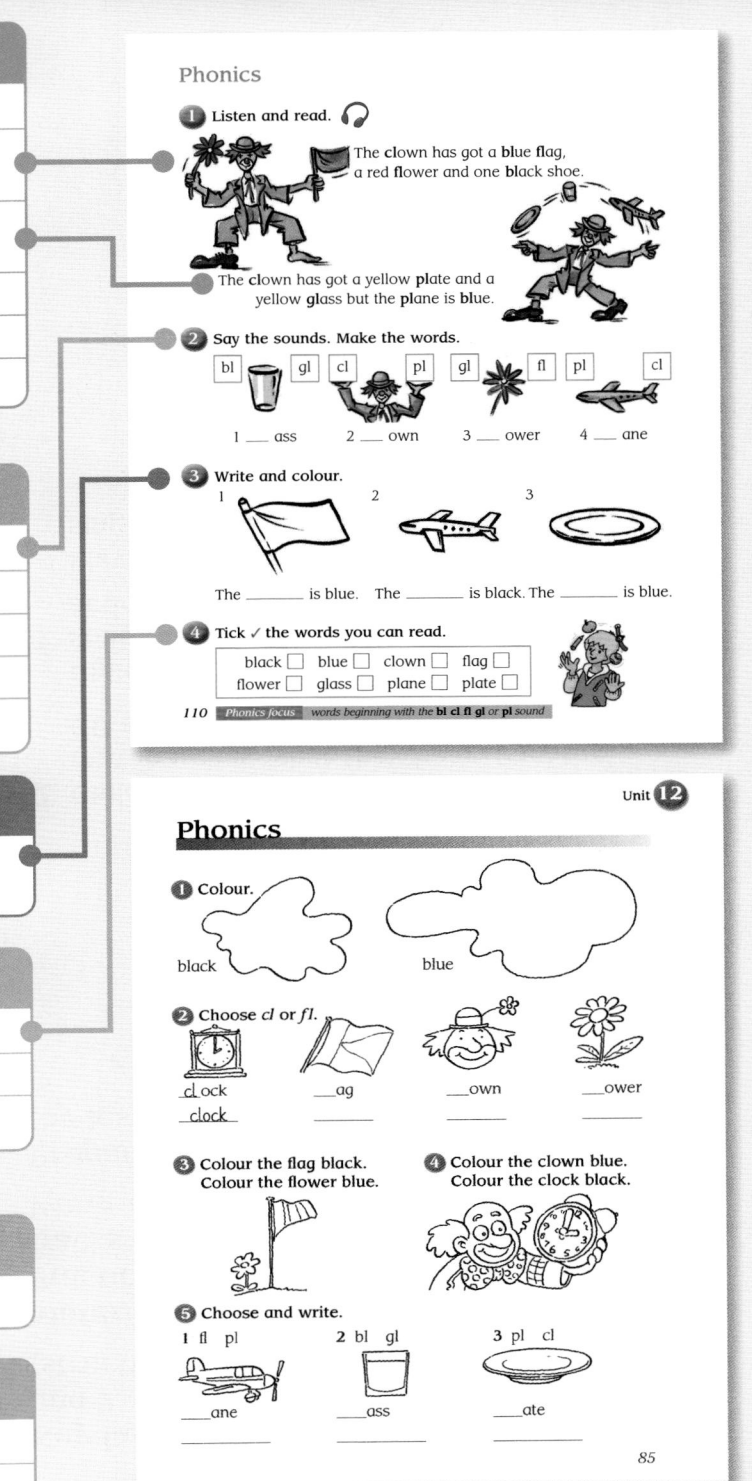

Lesson aim Phonic recognition

Lesson targets Children:

- read, pronounce and spell words with initial consonant blends: consonant + *l*
- recognise and sound out the different initial consonant blends (*bl, cl, fl, gl, pl*) in the target words
- write the target words from picture prompts.

Target words *black, blue, class, clock, clown, flag, flower, plane, plate*

Materials Language Book p110, Practice Book p85, Language CD2 track 72

Preparation Listen to the CD before the lesson.

Lesson 5 time division:

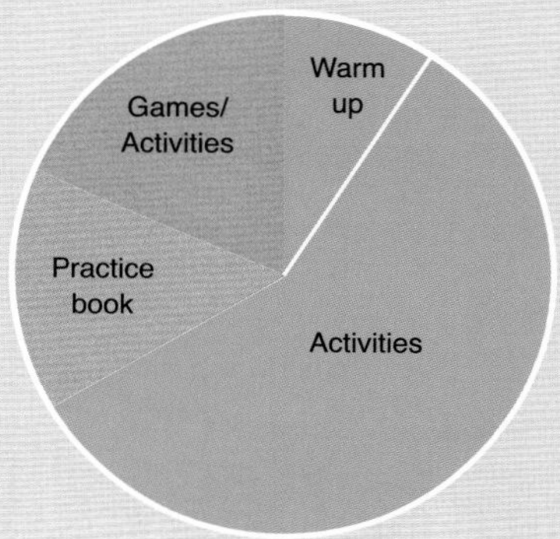

Lesson 5 Warm-up

1 Do the matching rhyming words activity (TG p25). Use, e.g. *brick, kick, brown, clown, clock, rock, duck, truck, king, ring.*

Activity 1

5 Ask *Who can you see? A clown. What has he got? A flower.*
What colour is the plane? Blue.
What colour is the flag? What is black?
Two things are yellow. What are they?
Two things are blue. What are they?

Make sure all the words in the text are understood.

Activity 2

Say the two choices of consonant blends for the first word. Class repeats each blend. Ask what the picture shows. Elicit *(a) glass.*
Children circle the correct blend for the beginning of the word. They write the word. Write it on the board. Children check.
Do the same with the other three words.

Activity 3

Children look at the picture and read the words. Ask/Help a child to say the whole sentence. Class repeats.

Children write the word.

Do the same with the other sentences. Children colour the pictures.

Activity 4

1 Write the eight words on the board. Point in random order. Individuals and/or the class reads them.

Practice Book

Children complete the five exercises. Check they can read all the words from Exercises 1 and 2 before they move on to Exercise 3.

Phonics games and activities

1 Play *What's the word?* (TG p75) Say the phonemes, e.g. *sh–o–p.* Children guess the word.

2 Do *Look, write, check* (TG p75).

163

Before writing

1. Lesson 6 warm-up.
2. Read Miss Plum's speech bubble (LB p111).
3. Activity 1: Children read the words. Children say what is in the picture. They draw and colour the small pictures in the large picture.

Shared writing

1. Activity 2 (LB p111): Children suggest sentences. Write them on the board. Class reads.
2. Rub off sentences. Children write their own short compositions.

Practice Book

Writing

(PB p86) Children match words and pictures. They write the words.

Your writing

(PB p87) Children write the shops there are. They write what can be got in them.

After writing

Children read their compositions *In the park* to the class. Hear as many as possible.

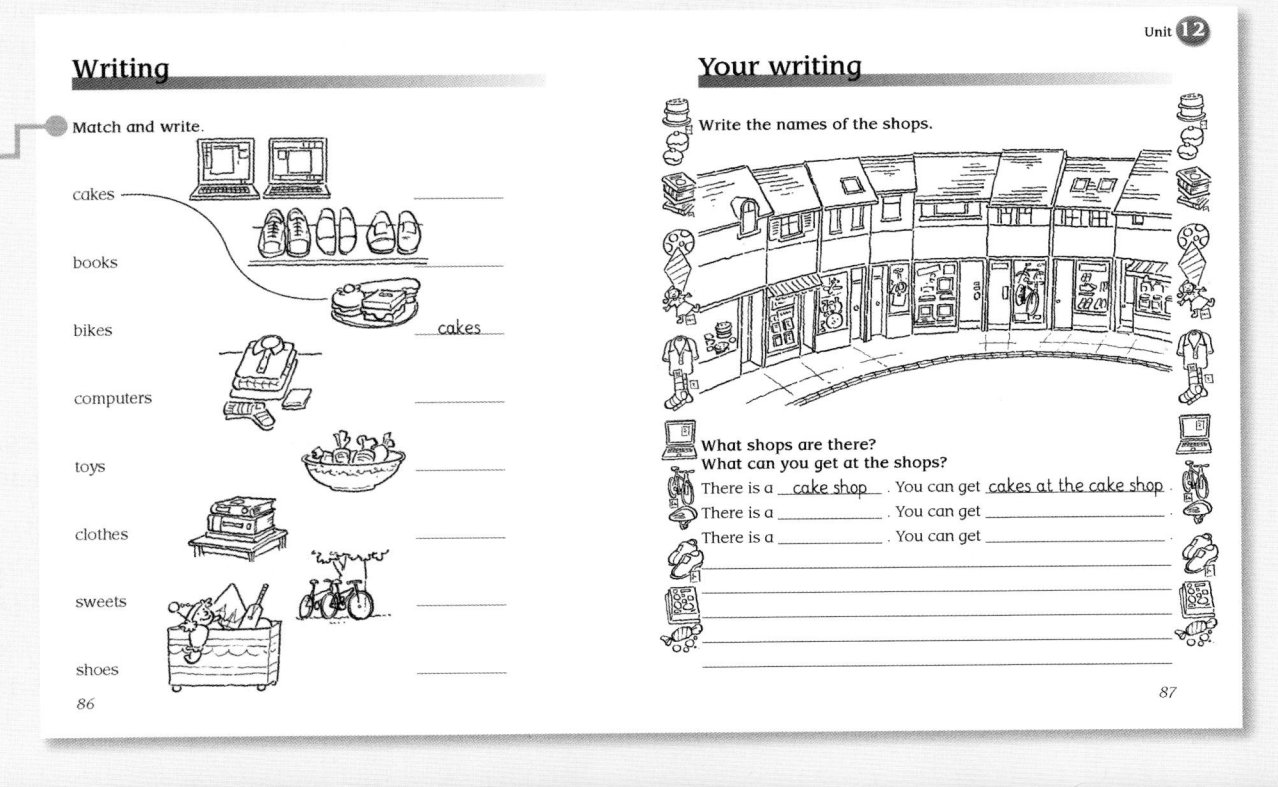

Lesson aim Writing

Lesson targets Children:

- describe a scene in a park
- match words to pictures
- write what shops are in a street and what people can buy in them.

Key language (words)
bees, birds, boy, girl, kites, owl, types of shop and shop goods
(structures) *There is ..., There are ..., You can get ...*

Materials Language Book p111, Practice Book pp86 and 87

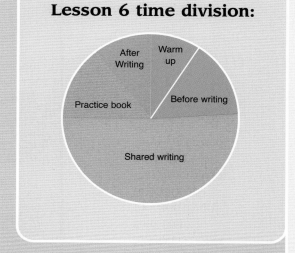

Lesson 6 time division:

After Writing

Warm up

Before writing

Practice book

Shared writing

⬇ Lesson 6 Warm-up

1 Sing *Tall shop in the town* from Lesson 4 (LB p109, LCD2 track 71). Play *Stand up colours* (TG p85, p248).

⬇ Before writing

3 Ask *What is in the park?*
Help them to remember any words they have forgotten. Elicit *a green frog on the slide; white ducks on the pond.*

Tell them to draw and colour the small pictures in the spaces in the big picture.

If you wish, prepare the class by asking, e.g. *Where can you draw the owl? the girl? the boy?* etc. They can colour the pictures as they wish.

⬇ Shared writing

1 Children read the three example sentences. Class repeats.

Ask what else there is in the park. Children suggest from what they have drawn, e.g. *There is an owl ...* Ask *What colour is it? Where is it?* if the child does not say the first time. Write the sentence on the board.

Ask different children to give you information about the other four things they drew. Class reads the whole composition.

2 Make sure children realise they must write according to what is in their own picture. Go around the class as they write, helping and monitoring their work.

165

Revision 4

You can do it!

1 Look at the pictures.
Is there a sports club near you? Do you like it? What can you do there, and when?

2 Listen and read. 🎧

3 Read and say.
Look at the football game.
What day and time is it? Who is playing? How many points has each team got?

Look at Nina and Tilly. What are they doing? What day and time is it?

Who is riding his bike? Where is he? What day and time is it?

Who is having a birthday party? How old is she?
How many children are there? What day and time is it?

What is happening this week:

Saturday Sunday Monday Tuesday Wednesday Thursday Friday

football   swimming   cycling   basketball   tennis   trampoline   birthday party

Look at Miss Plum. What is she doing? What day and time is it? Can you swim? Are you a good swimmer?

What is Mobi doing on Thursday? What time is it? Can you jump? Do you like it?

4 Listen and say the day and the time. 🎧

5 Choose a picture and act it out. Your friends guess.

6 Listen and say the chant. 🎧

Ha ha!
Look at the clowns.
Brrm! Brrm!
They're in a truck.
Quack! Quack!
They've got a duck.
Tick tock!
They've got a clock.
Ha ha!
Look at the clowns!

It is Saturday. It is 3 o'clock. There is a football match. Sam and Ben are in the red team. Who is winning?

It is Wednesday. It is 1 o'clock. Nina and Tilly are playing tennis. Where is the ball?

It is Monday. It is 4 o'clock. Ben is riding his bike. Is he going fast?

It is Friday. It is 6 o'clock. There are lots of children at a party. It is Lucy's birthday. How old is she?

It is Sunday. It is half past 9. Miss Plum is swimming. Is she a good swimmer?

It is Thursday. It is half past seven. Look at Mobi! He is jumping. Is he having fun?

Lesson aim Revision

Lesson targets Children:

• practise fluency and listening activities, including words ending in *ck* and blends consonant + *r*, consonant + *l*

• practise language and structures from Units 10–12 through a story, games and writing.

Key language *It is eleven o'clock. It is half past eleven. It is Saturday. What is/are he/she/they doing? There is … There are …*

Words for understanding *cycling, match, party, swimmer, tennis, trampoline, winning*

Materials Language Book pp112–113, Language CD2 tracks 73–75, Practice Book pp88–91

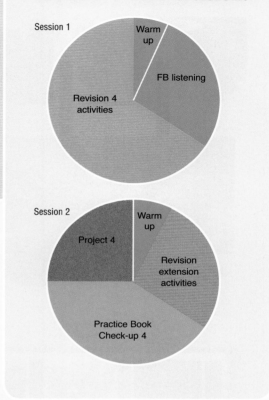

Revision 4 time division:

Sessions 1 and 2 Warm-ups

Sing favourite songs from Units 10–12.

Listening revision

Play Units 10–12 of the Fluency Book (FC tracks 20–25). Children look at their books and listen. Children close books and repeat during the pauses in the dialogue section.

Revision 4

1 (LB p112) Activity 1: Children name the sports they can see. Ask the questions.

2 🎧 Activity 2: Play LCD2 track 73. Children listen and follow the text silently.

3 Activity 3: Read or let children read out the questions. Elicit answers.

4 🎧 (LB p113) Activity 4: Play LCD2 track 74 twice. Children listen, find the picture and say the day and the time.

Audioscript

Presenter	Listen and say the day and the time.
Voice	Ben is riding his bike. Mobi is jumping. Lucy is having a birthday party. Miss Plum is swimming. Nina and Tilly are playing tennis.

5 Activity 5: Children take turns to mime the activity in the pictures. Others guess.

6 🎧 Activity 6: Play LCD2 track 75 twice. Children listen. The first time children listen. Then they join in.

Revision extension activities

1 Play flashcard games introduced in Units 10–12.

2 Use the text for reading practice, individually, in groups or with the whole class.

3 Use the phonic chant for reading practice. Teach it if you wish.

Practice Book

1 Children complete *Check-up 4* (PB pp88–89) covering vocabulary and language from Units 10–12 as a test, as preparation for a test or for homework.

2 Children complete *Move on with Mobi 4* (PB pp90–91). These pages give further general revision of Units 10–12 for homework or class work.

Project 4: Sports frieze

Children find or draw pictures of people doing sports. They stick them on a frieze or poster. They write sentences, e.g. *He is kicking. He/She is/They are running/jumping*, and stick them near the picture.

Class counts the number of different sports they have collected. Display the work.

Children read each other's sentences.

167

Before listening

1 Lesson 1 warm-up.

2 Show poster 13. Read the title. Ask questions.

3 Show number cards and name new numbers. Children come forward; find numbers in main picture.

4 Show number cards and name new numbers. Class repeats.

Shared listening

1 Play FCD track 26. Point to characters when they speak.

2 Ask about the main picture.

3 Ask about the small pictures.

4 Play FCD track 26 and point to characters again.

Dialogue practice

1 Say the new numbers. Children point in books (FB pp32–33). Point on poster for children to check.

2 Show number cards. Children name.

3 Children close books. Play FCD track 27 and show character flashcards. Class repeats lines in pauses.

4 Groups say lines by character.

5 Individuals act dialogue.

6 Play FCD track 26 again. Children follow text or point to main picture.

After listening

1 Show number cards. Children say numbers.

2 Do the number practice activity.

13 A hundred steps

10 ten 20 twenty 30 thirty 40 fourty 50 fifty 60 sixty 70 seventy 80 eighty 90 ninety 100 a hundred

13 A hundred steps

There is a big mountain on the island. It is Monday morning and the children are climbing up the mountain. They are going up and up and up. There is a white cloud at the top of the mountain. What is in the cloud?

At the top of the mountain, there is a castle.

In the middle of the castle, there is a garden.

In the garden, there is a tree. On the tree there are ...

Look! There are steps.
Come on, Tilly!
I'm tired.

I can see the top!
I'm thirsty.
Come on, Tilly!

How many steps are there?
Let's count them.
OK. Ten ... twenty ...
Thirty ... forty ...
Fifty ... sixty ...
Seventy ... eighty ...
Ninety ... ninety-nine ...
A hundred! Phew!

Wow! Stars!

There are lots of stars on the tree.
Is there a gold star? Who is sitting under the tree?

32 How many ... are there? Numbers 10 –100

33

Lesson aim Fluency

Lesson targets Children:

- listen for pronunciation and intonation
- repeat dialogue accurately
- act out dialogue with expression
- talk about numbers up to 100.

Key language (words) *ten, twenty, thirty, forty, fifty, sixty, seventy, eighty, ninety, a hundred*
(structures) *How many ... are there? Numbers 10–100.*

Language for understanding *castle, cloud, steps, in the middle, up, Phew!*

Materials Poster 13, Fluency Book pp32–33, Fluency CD tracks 26–27, character flashcards 2–5, number cards for *10, 20,* etc. to *100*

Preparation Listen to the CD before the lesson. Make number cards.

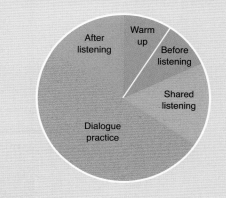

Lesson 1 time division:

⬇ Lesson 1 Warm-up

1 Sing *I've got two little hands* from Unit 9, (LB p83, LCD2 track 55).

⬇ Before listening

2 Ask *Where are the children?*
What are they doing?
Who is behind Sam?
Who is between Sam and Tilly?
Can you see Mobi?

⬇ Shared listening

2 Ask *Where are the steps?*
How many steps are there?
Who is tired?
Who is thirsty?
Who can see the top of the mountain?
Who can see the steps?

3 Ask *Where is the castle?*
What is in the middle of the castle?
What is in the garden?
What can the children see in the tree?
Is there a gold star?
Who is sitting under the tree?

⬇ After listening

2 If you wish, put number cards for 10, 20, etc. on the board for these activities. Practise counting up in tens (*10, 20,* etc.) with the whole class. Children each say a number around the class *10, 20 ...* to *100*, then start with *10* again.
Say a number. Class says the following number.

169

Before reading

1. Lesson 2 warm-up. ⬇
2. Children open books (LB pp114–115). Ask questions. ⬇
   Children point.

Shared reading

1. 🔊 Play LCD2 track 76. Children follow text in book.
2. Read line by line. Ask questions. ⬇
3. Read with the class.

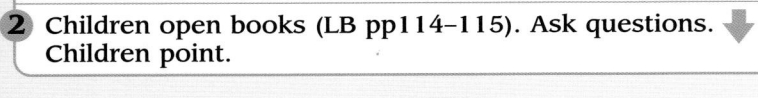

Dani can count!

This is Sami. These are his father's sheep.
Sami is looking after them on the hillside.
Today, his younger brother, Dani is here, too.
Sami is pointing to the sheep in front of them.
'Look at these sheep,' he says.
'How many are there?' asks Dani.
'I don't know,' says Sami.

Fourteen.

Thanks. Fourteen, fifteen, sixteen, seventeen …

… eighteen, nineteen …

… twenty! Twenty sheep!

And these sheep?

Oh! Twenty-one, twenty-two …

… thirty …

I can count all these sheep, Sami!

Can you?

Yes! One, two, three, four, five, six, seven … Hmmmm …

… forty …

…fifty …

… sixty …

Eight.

Oh, yes. Eight, nine, ten, eleven, twelve, thirteen …

So, how many sheep are there, Dani?

Shhhhhhh. Dani is sleeping.

zzzzzz

114   Parents: see extra material on page 166

115

Reading practice

1. Give reading practice. Use some or all of the following:
   - Children read again as a class.
   - Groups read different sections.
   - Individuals read different sections.
2. 🔊 Class listens again to LCD2 track 76 and follows in LB.

After reading

Do the numbers activities. ⬇

Lesson aim Reading

Lesson targets Children:

- follow a text read out to them
- listen for pronunciation and intonation
- read the text aloud with accurate pronunciation and intonation
- answer simple comprehension questions.

Words for understanding *in front of, younger, hillside, looking after*

Materials Language Book pp 114–115, Language CD2 track 76, number cards 10, 20, etc., number word cards for *Warm-up*, numbers 13–29 on small pieces of paper for *After reading*.

Preparation Listen to the CD before the lesson. Make number and word cards as necessary.

Lesson 2 time division:

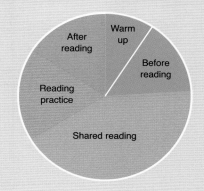

⬇ Lesson 2 Warm-up

1 Put up number words *ten, twenty*, etc. to *a hundred.* Children read. Put number cards below in any order. Children match.

⬇ Before reading

2 Ask *Are the boys inside or outside?*
What animals can you see?
Who is here today?
What does he want to do?

⬇ Shared reading

2 Ask *Are they Sami's sheep?*
Where are the sheep?
Who is looking after the sheep?
Who is Dani? Is he big or little?
Are the sheep behind Sami and Dani?
Can Dani count?
Can Dani count all the sheep?
How many sheep can he count?
Is Dani tired?
What is Dani doing at the end?

⬇ After reading

Count with the class 1–30.

If you wish, repeat in two teams. They say alternate numbers.

Play *Stand up numbers:* divide the class into five or more teams. Give each team three random numbers on small pieces of paper from 13–29. Teams stand up when a number they have is called. Teams change numbers every few turns.

171

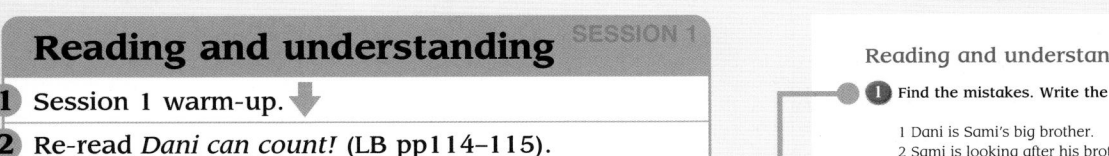

Reading and understanding

SESSION 1

1 Session 1 warm-up.

2 Re-read *Dani can count!* (LB pp114–115).

3 Activity 1 (LB p116): Children find incorrect statements. They write them correctly in their notebooks.

4 Activity 2: Individuals/Class reads the numbers, then match pictures to numbers.

5 Activity 3: Children read numbers. Play LCD2 track 77. Children circle the word they hear in each pair.

6 Play the *Get active!* game.

7 Prepare children for PB p92. Read the passage with them and check they understand the task. Children complete.

Working with words

SESSION 2

1 Session 2 warm-up.

2 Activity 1 (LB p117): Children read number words down and across. Ask individuals, groups and class.

Sentence building

1 Go through the information in the box (LB p117).

2 Activity 1: Children read the sentences alone. Children write.

3 Activity 2: Children read the sentences aloud. Class repeats.

4 Prepare children for PB p93. Read the verb in the box with them and check they understand the tasks. Children complete.

Extension activities

1 Class reads figures.

2 Match long/short forms of the verb *to have*.

Reading and understanding

1 Find the mistakes. Write the sentences.

1 Dani is Sami's big brother.
2 Sami is looking after his brother's sheep.
3 They are on a mountain.
4 Sami has got a cat.
5 'How many sheep are there?' asks Sami.
6 Dani can count to forty.

2 Read and match.

1 fifty ☐
2 twenty ☐
3 ten ☐
4 eighty ☐
5 thirty ☐
6 one hundred ☐

a b c d e f

We can also say **a** hundred.

3 Listen and circle.

| 1 | 13 30 | 2 | 16 60 | 3 | 18 80 |
| 4 | 14 40 | 5 | 17 70 | 6 | 19 90 |

Get active 13

116   *Comprehension focus*   *consolidation of new language in Dani can count!*

Working with words

1 Read the numbers down, then across.

one	eleven	ten
two	twelve	twenty
three	thirteen	thirty
four	fourteen	forty
five	fifteen	fifty
six	sixteen	sixty
seven	seventeen	seventy
eight	eighteen	eighty
nine	nineteen	ninety

Sentence building

This is the verb **to have**:

I have / I've   we have / we've
you have / you've you have / you've
he has / he's   they have / they've
she has / she's
it has / it's

I've got an apple.

1 Complete the sentences with *have* or *has*.

1 He _____ got a brother.   2 She _____ got a doll.
3 They _____ got ice creams. 4 Ben _____ got a dog.
5 The boys _____ got computer games.

2 Read the sentences.

Language focus   numbers 1-100; use of to have

117

Unit **13**
Reading and understanding

1 Look and read.

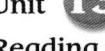

Dani is on the hillside with his dog.
He is looking after his father's sheep.
He is with his younger brother Sami.
There are lots of sheep on the hillside.
'How many are there?' asks Sami.
'I don't know,' says Dani.
'I can count all these sheep!' Sami says.
Sami can't count all the sheep.
He is tired and sleepy.

2 Circle the correct answer.

1 Dani is on the   train   (hillside)
2 Dani has got a   dog   cat
3 Dani is looking after his father's elephants sheep
4 Sami is Dani's younger   brother   sister
5 Sami says he can count the   dogs   sheep
6 Sami is   tired   hungry
7 Sami is   thirsty   sleepy
8 Sami can't   eat   count

92

Unit **13**

Sentence building

I **have**	we **have**
you **have**	you **have**
he **has**	they **have**
she **has**	
it **has**	

1 Complete the sentences with *have* or *has*.

1 He _____ got a brother.
2 I _____ got a dog.
3 You _____ got red socks.
4 She _____ got two sisters.
5 They _____ got bikes.
6 We _____ got big apples.

2 Complete the answers.

1 How many sheep has Dani got?

Dani _____ got three sheep.

2 How many dogs has Ben got?

Ben _____ got two dogs.

3 Have the girls got dolls?

Yes. The girls _____ got dolls.

93

172

Lesson aim Comprehension, vocabulary and sentence building

Lesson targets Children:

- identify incorrect statements and correct them
- read number words; match number words to figures
- identify spoken numbers
- practise long and short forms of the verb *to have*.

Key language (words) numbers and number words 1–100; verb *to have* (structures) *I have got ..., He/She/It has got ...*

Materials Language Book pp116–117, Practice Book pp92–93, number cards for *10, 20,* etc. to *100;* short form word cards of verb *to have*

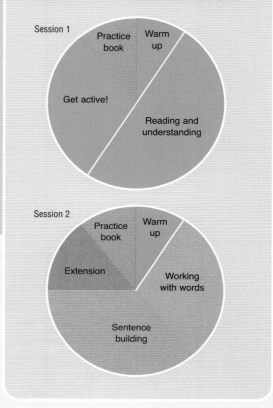

Lesson 3 time division:

Session 1
- Practice book
- Warm up
- Get active!
- Reading and understanding

Session 2
- Practice book
- Warm up
- Extension
- Working with words
- Sentence building

⬇ Lesson 3 Session 1 Warm-up

Children do a number chain around the class. Start from *1* or a higher number. See how far the class can count. If they find it difficult, keep practising 1–30.

⬇ Reading and understanding

3 A child reads the first sentence. Class repeats.
Ask *Is it true?* If necessary, ask: *Is Dani Sami's big brother?* Elicit **No (he isn't).** Children can check page 114 for answers.
Elicit **Dani is Sami's younger brother.** Write it on the board. Class reads. Continue with the other sentences. Rub sentences off the board before children write correct sentences in their notebooks.

6 **Get active!**
Give out number cards 10–50 in muddled order to five children.

Children put themselves in order. Repeat with 60–100.

If you have space indoors, or can go outside, give out 20–100 at one time. When they are in order, other children say the numbers.

Do the same with number words.

⬇ Lesson 3 Session 2 Warm-up

Class sings *Tall shop in the town* (LB p109, LCD2 track 71).

⬇ Sentence building

1 Read the sentence in the box. Read through the verb with the class. If you wish, go through the full form first. Make sure children understand that in speaking, the verb is usually shortened.

Ask a child to read Mobi's bubble. Class repeats. Read through the short forms with the class.

⬇ Extension activities

1 Write on the board a grid of numbers as in *Working with words.* Class reads numbers down and across.

2 Write up long forms of *to have.* Stick up word cards of short forms in muddled order. Children match short forms on cards. Class reads.

173

Grammar

1 Lesson 4 warm-up.

2 Children look at the picture (LB p118). Read the question. Elicit *Two*. Ask other questions.

3 Activity 1: Children find objects in the large picture, count and write the numbers. Check by asking *How many ... are there?*

4 Activity 2: Class reads the words in the box. Help children form questions. If possible, do the activity in pairs.

5 Activity 3: Children write the correct question for the given answer.

6 Prepare children for PB p94 by checking they understand the tasks. Children complete.

Listening

1 Read Nina's speech bubble (LB p119).

2 Explain the task.

3 Activity 1: Play LCD2 track 78. Children listen and look. Play it again. If necessary, help children to work out the answers. Children circle the number.

After listening

Do the team numbers activity.

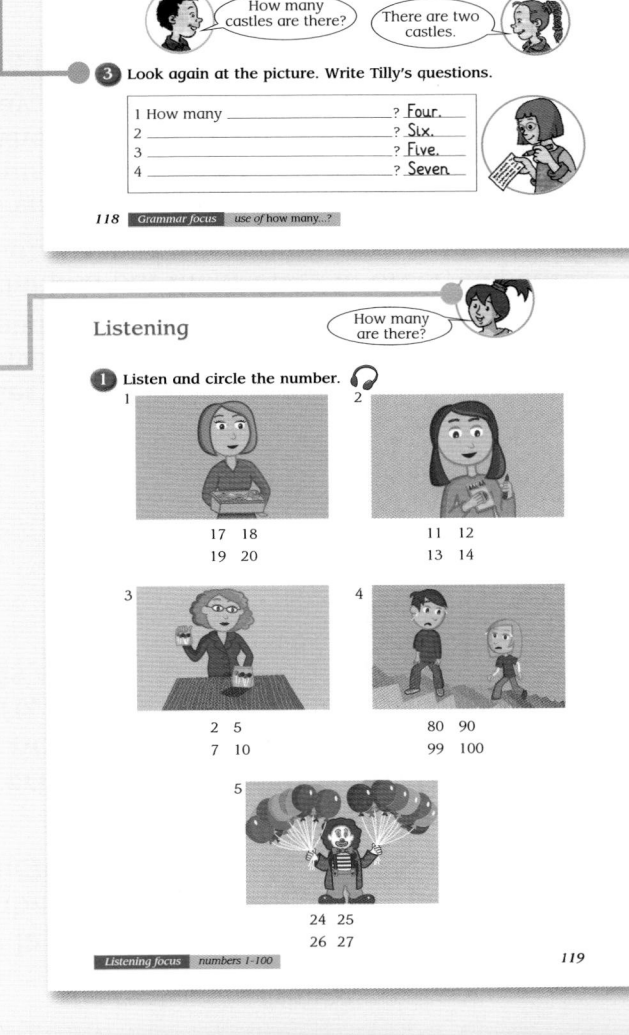

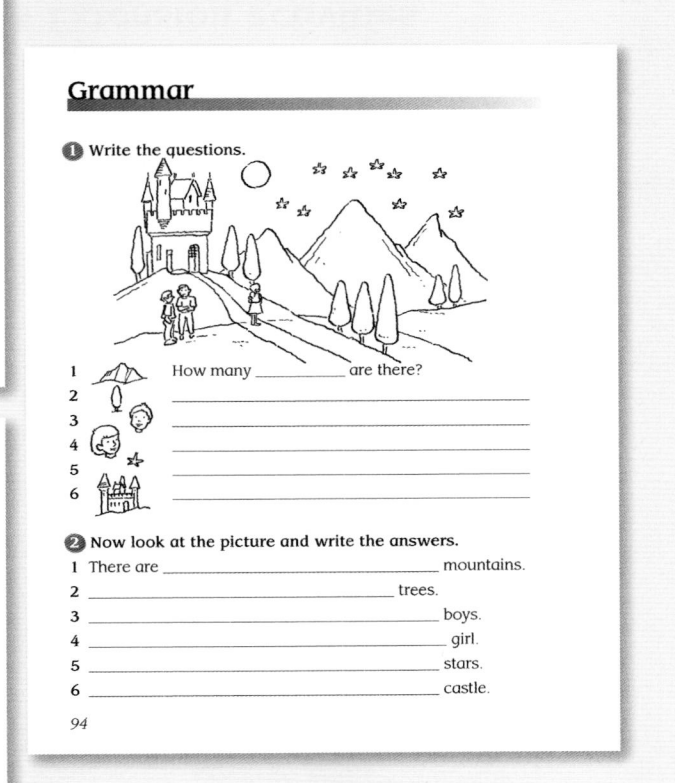

Lesson aim Grammar and listening

Lesson targets Children:

- count and state numbers of things in a picture
- ask and answer about numbers of items in pairs
- write questions from given answers
- listen to dialogue and work out answers to simple number tasks.

Key language (words and structures) as for Lessons 1–3

Materials Language Book pp118–119, Practice Book p94, Language CD2 track 78, number cards for *Warm-up* and *After listening*

Preparation Listen to the CD before the lesson.

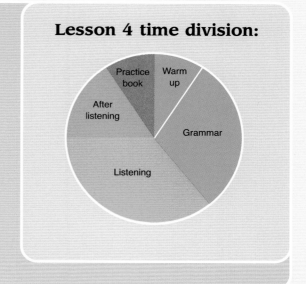

Lesson 4 time division:

(pie chart labels: Practice book, Warm up, After listening, Grammar, Listening)

⬇ Lesson 4 Warm-up

1 Play *Stand-up numbers* with 21–40 and the class in five or more teams.

⬇ Grammar

2 Ask children *What can you see?* Elicit **birds, trees, boys**, etc. Ask *How many ... are there?* Help children form answers, e.g. **There are five trees.**

5 Children look at the first answer. Say *There are four of these. What are they?* Elicit **Boys**. A child says the complete question. Class repeats.

Do the same with the other questions. Class writes.

⬇ Listening

3 **Audioscript**

Voice	1
Woman	I've got twenty sweets in this box. Here's one for you.
Girl	Thank you.
Woman	One for you.
Boy	Thank you.
Woman	And one for you.
Girl	Thank you.
Woman	How many sweets have I got now?
Voice	2
Girl	Two, four, six, eight, ten, twelve – and one red one. How many have I got?
Voice	3
Woman	Look! There are five lollipops in this bag.
Class	Mmm!
Woman	And look! I've got two bags.
Class	Oooh!
Woman	How many lollipops have I got?
Class	Um ...
Voice	4
Boy	Fifty ... sixty ...
Girl	Seventy ... eighty ...
Boy	Ninety ...
Girl	A hundred?
Boy	No. Ninety-nine.
Both	Phew!
Voice	5
Child	How many balloons have you got?
Clown	I've got 25. 25 beautiful balloons. [POP!] Oh!
Child	How many balloons have you got now?

⬇ After listening

Divide class into teams. Show number cards. The team that says the number first keeps the card.

175

Activity 1

1. Lesson 5 warm-up.
2. (LB p120) Point out pictures and words with *th*.
3. Play rhyme twice (LCD2 track 79). Children follow in books.
4. Read rhyme.
5. Read and ask questions.
6. Read with the class.

Activity 2

1. Children read words.
2. Children match and write words.
3. Children circle *th* in the words.

Activity 3

Children read and write. Children circle.

Activity 4

1. Write up words. Class/individuals read.
2. Children read in pairs. Listen to pairs.
3. Children check words and tick.

Practice Book

Children complete PB p95.

Phonics games and activities

Play *Start the word.*

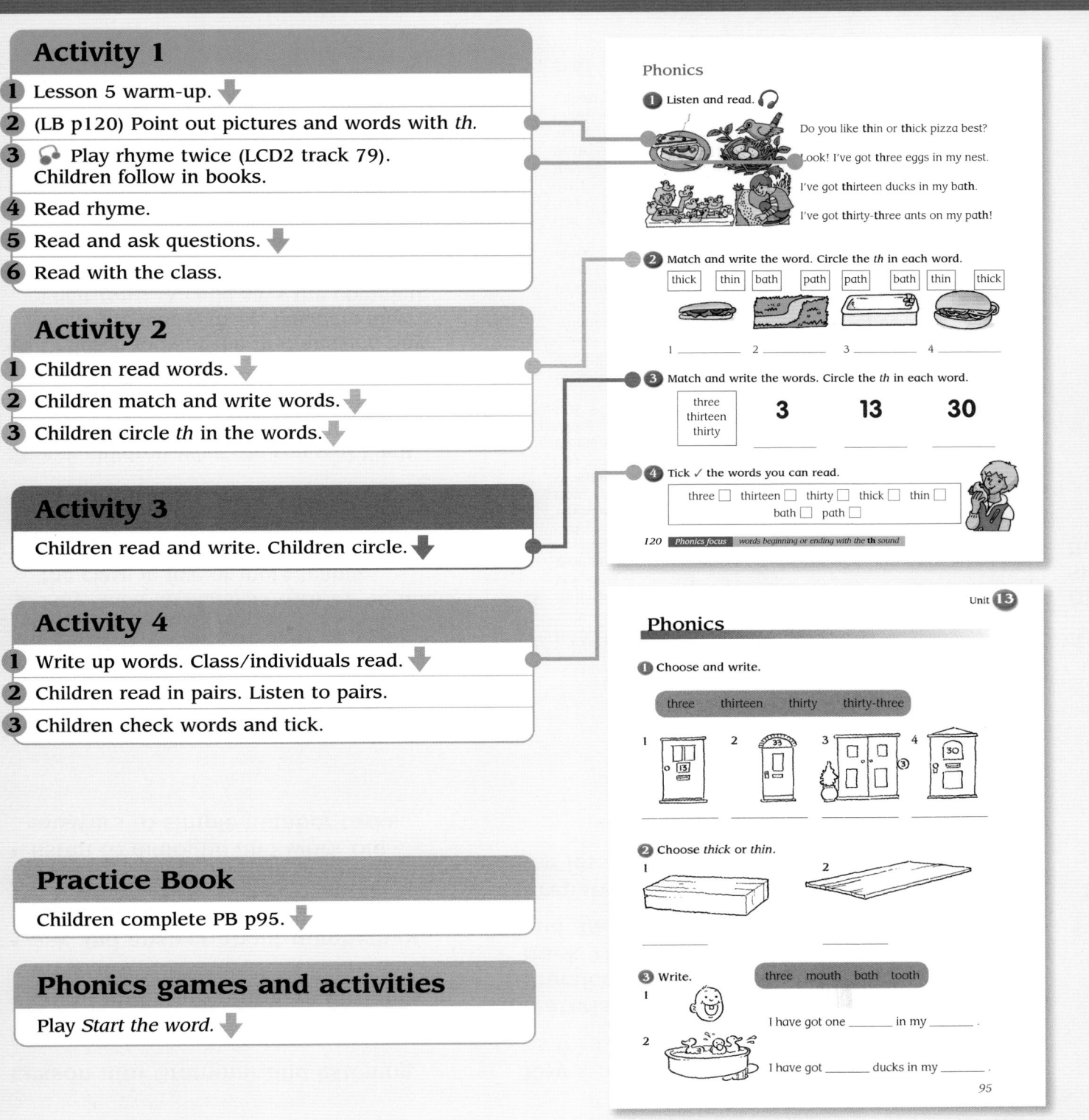

Lesson aim Phonic recognition

Lesson targets Children:

- read, pronounce and spell words beginning or ending with consonant digraph *th*
- identify and say consonant digraph *th* at beginning or end of word
- write the target words from picture prompts.

Target words *three, thirteen, thirty; thick, thin, bath, path*

Materials Language Book p120, Practice Book p95, Language CD2 track 79

Preparation Listen to the CD before the lesson.

Lesson 5 Warm-up

1 Play *What's the word?* (TG p75) with words from Lesson 5, Units 10–12. Say, e.g. *r–i–ng.* Class guesses *ring.*

Activity 1

5 Ask *Do you eat pizza?*
Do you like thin/thick pizza?
How many eggs are there? What colour are they?
Are the ducks swimming? Where are they?
How many ants are on the path?

Make sure all the words in the text are understood.

Activity 2

1 Children read the words above the first picture. Class repeats.

2 Ask *Is it thick or thin?* Elicit **It's thin.** Children write the word.

3 They circle *th* in the word.
Do the same with the other words and pictures.

Activity 3

Children read the words in the box. Class repeats.

Do the same with the numbers.

Children write the words. They circle *th* in the word they have written.

Activity 4

1 Write the seven words on the board. Point in random order. Individuals and/or the class reads them.

Practice Book

Children complete the three exercises. Check they can read all the target words when they have completed Exercise 3.

Phonics games and activities

Start the word
Write up endings, e.g. *_own, _ock, _ack, _ag.* Put letter cards in scrambled order below: *br, r, bl, b, fl, cl.* Children come forward and use the beginnings to make words. Class reads the words.

177

Before writing

1 Lesson 6 warm-up.

2 Read Miss Plum's speech bubble (LB p121).

3 Activity 1: Children count the pictured items in their classroom and write the numbers.

4 Activity 2: Children ask questions and answer. Point out the *Remember!* box.

Shared writing

1 Write up the sentence beginnings. Elicit the complete sentences.

2 Class reads all sentences. Rub them off. Children write.

Practice Book

Writing

1 Children read questions (PB p96).

2 Children complete/write answers.

Your writing

1 (PB p97) Children count animals.

2 Write up phrases, e.g. *eight sheep*.

3 Children write sentences.

After writing

Children colour and talk about their pictures.

Lesson aim Writing

Lesson targets Children:

- count items in the classroom
- write about the classroom from picture prompts
- complete and write sentences about numbers of animals
- write about numbers of animals on a farm.

Key language (words) numbers, animals
(structures) *There is a ..., There are*
(number + object)

Materials Language Book p121, Practice Book pp96 and 97, poster 4

Lesson 6 time division:

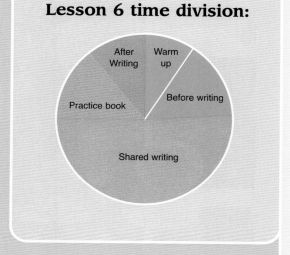

⬇ Lesson 6 Warm-up

1 Put up poster 4. Ask *How many ... are there?* Ask about *birds, butterflies, snakes, monkeys, trees, flowers, children, boys, girls.*

⬇ Before writing

3 Read the rubric. Individuals read the words. Help with new words. Class repeats.

Children count and write numbers. This can be done individually or in pairs. Alternatively the class can count together.

4 Children ask questions about things in the classroom. Other children answer. If possible, repeat this activity in pairs. Go around listening to some of them.

⬇ Shared writing

1 Write up the first words of the sentence. Ask children to think what there is one of, e.g. *one board, one teacher.* Ask/Help a child to complete the first sentence, e.g. *In my classroom there is a board and a teacher.* Class reads.

Write up the first words of the second part of the sentence. Ask/Help a child to make a sentence about windows and doors. Continue with desks/chairs; children; boys/girls.

2 Class reads all the sentences. Rub them off the board. Children write.

⬇ After writing

(PB p97) Children colour the animals as they choose. Hear as many children as possible talk about their pictures, e.g. **There is a black horse. There are two white cows.** Children write sentences in their notebooks. Let as many children as possible read their work to the class.

Before listening

1. Lesson 1 warm-up. ⬇
2. Show poster 13. Ask questions. ⬇
3. Show poster 14. Read the title. Ask questions. ⬇
4. Point and name weather words. Children come forward; find in main picture.
5. 🂠 Show weather flashcards (136–141) and name weather types. Class repeats.

Shared listening

1. 🎧 Play FCD track 28. Point to characters when they speak.
2. Ask about the sixth gold star. ⬇
3. Ask *Who? What?* questions. ⬇
4. 🎧 Play FCD track 28 and point to characters again.

Dialogue practice

1. Say the weather words. Children point in books (FB pp34–35). Point on poster for children to check.
2. 🂠 Show weather flashcards (136–141). Children name.
3. 🎧 🂠 Children close books. Play FCD track 29 and show character flashcards. Class repeats lines in pauses.
4. 🂠 Groups say lines by character.
5. 🂠 Individuals act dialogue.
6. 🎧 Play FCD track 28 again. Children follow text or point to main picture.

After listening

1. Do the weather match activity. ⬇
2. Say the *Star chant* (two stars are missing).
3. Children put the two sticker stars in the correct place on FB pp46–47.

Lesson aim Fluency

Lesson targets Children:

- listen for pronunciation and intonation
- repeat dialogue accurately
- act out dialogue with expression
- talk about weather types.

Key language (words) *cloudy, foggy, raining, snowing, sunny, windy* (structures) *What's the weather like? It's windy. It's raining.*

Language for understanding *snow, weather, take, beautiful, cold, old, silver, Good morning. Thank you very much. Come and see.*

Materials Posters 13 and 14, Fluency Book pp34–35, Fluency CD tracks 28–29, character flashcards 2–5, 8, weather flashcards 136–141, location flashcards 48–50

Preparation Listen to the CD before the lesson.

Lesson 1 time division:

⬇ Lesson 1 Warm-up

1 Check with the class how many stars are missing. Say the *Star chant*. Sing the *Rainbow song* (LB p7, LCD1 track 4).

⬇ Before listening

2 (poster 13) Ask *What are the children doing?*
What is at the top of the mountain?
What is in the middle of the castle?
What is in the garden?
What is on the tree?
Who is under the tree?

3 (poster 14) (small picture, left) Ask *Who is under the tree? Where does he live?*
(main picture) *Are the children inside the castle? What are they doing?*
Can you see Sam's tree house?/the ship?/the beach?/the jungle?/the castle?

⬇ Shared listening

2 Ask *Where is star number six?*
Who is holding it?
How many stars are missing?

3 Ask *What can the weather man see on his TVs?*
What is the weather like on the sea?/in the jungle?/at the beach?/at the tree house?/at the castle?
Who can see the weather on the sea?/in the jungle?/at the beach?/at the tree house?/at the castle?
(small pictures, right) *What are the children doing?*
What is the weather man looking at? What is falling?
What can the children see?

⬇ After listening

1 Child from team 1 chooses a weather flashcard and shows it to rest of team. Ask the team *What is the weather like?* They say full sentence, e.g. *It is raining.* Team 2 child chooses location flashcard; shows it to rest of team. They say the full sentence, e.g. *It is raining at the beach.*

181

Before reading

1 Lesson 2 warm-up. ⬇

2 Children open books (LB pp122–123). Ask questions. ⬇

Shared reading

1 🎧 Play LCD2 track 80. Children follow text in book.

2 Read section by section. Ask questions. ⬇

3 Read with the class.

unit 14

Splish, splash, splosh

boom-er-room-er-room!

kerash!

Clothes Clothes Cakes Supermarket

'It's Monday. We're going shopping,' says Mum.
'Oh! It's windy,' says Sue.
'Wooooooooooooooooooooo,' says Sally.

'Stop, Susan,' says Mum. 'Don't do that!'
Susan is splashing in the puddles.
'Splish, splash, splosh,' says Sally.

'Look at that black cloud,' says Mum.
'I can hear thunder,' says Sue.
'Boom-er-room-er-room,' says Sally.

'Let's hurry,' says Mum.
'Oh, no! It's raining,' says Sue.
'Pit, pat, pit, pat,' says Sally.

'Uh oh, there's lightning,' says Mum.
'Kerash,' says Sally.
'I'm scared,' says Sue.

'Here's the supermarket,' says Mum.
'Let's go inside,' says Sue.
'Awwwwww,' says Sally. 'I like the weather noises!'

122 *Parents: see extra material on page 166*

123

Reading practice

1 Give reading practice. Use some or all of the following:
  - Children read again as a class.
  - Groups read different sections.
  - Individuals read different sections.

2 🎧 Class listens again to LCD2 track 80 and follows in LB.

After reading

Talk about onomatopoeic words. ⬇

Lesson aim Reading

Lesson targets Children:

- follow a text read out to them
- listen for pronunciation and intonation
- read the text aloud with accurate pronunciation and intonation
- understand the sense of the text as a whole
- answer simple comprehension questions.

Words for understanding *thunder, lightning, scared, noises,* onomatopoeic words

Materials Language Book pp122–123, Language CD2 track 80

Preparation Listen to the CD before the lesson.

Lesson 2 time division:

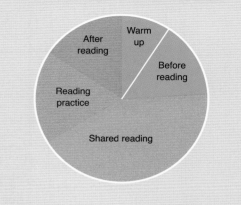

⬇ Lesson 2 Warm-up

1 Revise the days of the week. Write them up without the initial capital. Children write the capital letters.

⬇ Before reading

2 Ask *Is it sunny and warm?*
What's the weather like?
Can you see a shop? What is it?
Who has got an umbrella?
Are the children happy?

⬇ Shared reading

2 Ask (section 1) *What day is it?*
(section 2) *What is Susan doing?*
What does Sally say?
(section 3) *What colour is the cloud?*
What can Sue hear?
(section 4) *What noise does the rain make?*
(section 5) *What does Mum see?*
Is Sue happy?
(section 6) *Where are they going?*

⬇ After reading

Ask *What noises does the weather make? wind?/thunder?/rain?/lightning?*
Write the words on the board.

Ask *What sound does Sue make when she walks in the puddles?*

Explain to children that many English words sound like the noise they describe.

Ask children if they know any other words for sounds, e.g. *bang, pop.* List some words that describe sounds animals make, e.g. *buzz* (bee, fly), *hiss* (snake), *quack* (duck), *growl* (lion, bear).

Reading and understanding

SESSION 1

1. Session 1 warm-up.

2. Re-read *Splish, splash, splosh* (LB pp122–123).

3. Activity 1 (LB p124): Children read sentences. They circle *T* or *F*.

4. Activity 2: Children read sentences. Children match sentences and pictures.

5. Play *Get active!*

6. Prepare children for PB p98. Read the passage with them and check they understand the tasks. Children complete.

Working with words

SESSION 2

1. Session 2 warm-up.

2. Activity 1 (LB p125): Children read the words in the box and complete sentences orally. Class repeats. Children complete sentences with words from the box. To check, ask children to read sentences aloud.

3. Activity 2: Children look for weather words in the snake and circle them.

Sentence building

1. Go through the information in the box.

2. Activity 1 (LB p125): Children read and circle.

3. Activity 2: Children underline.

4. Prepare children for PB p99. Go through the box and check they understand the tasks. Children complete.

Extension activity

Do the adjective and noun activity.

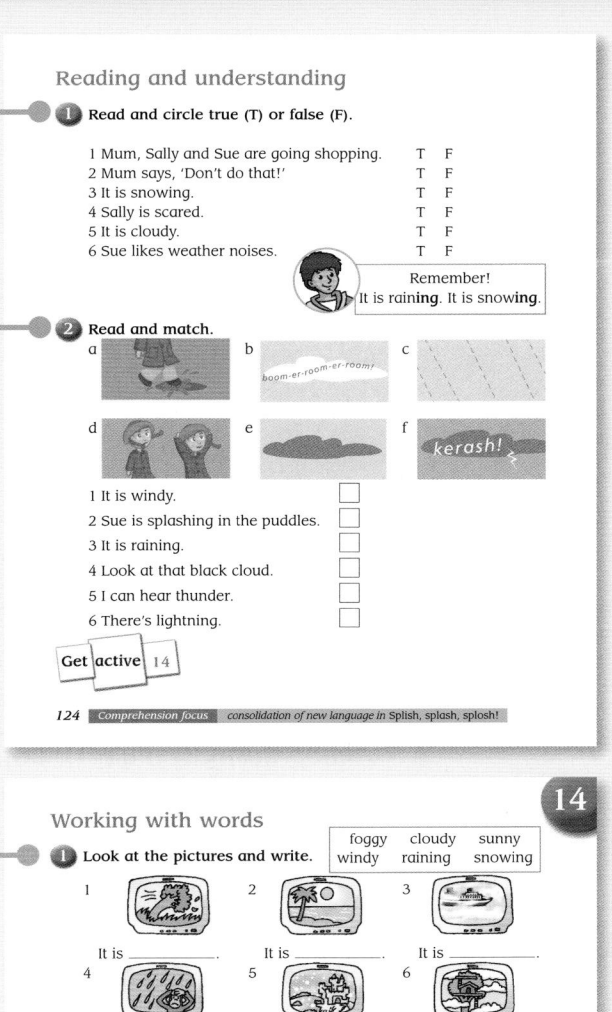

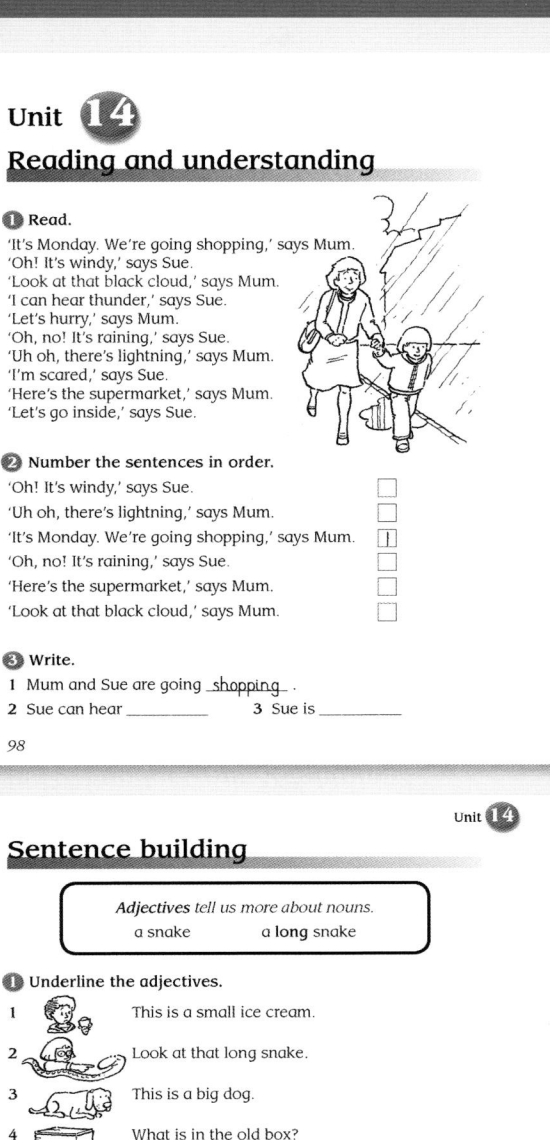

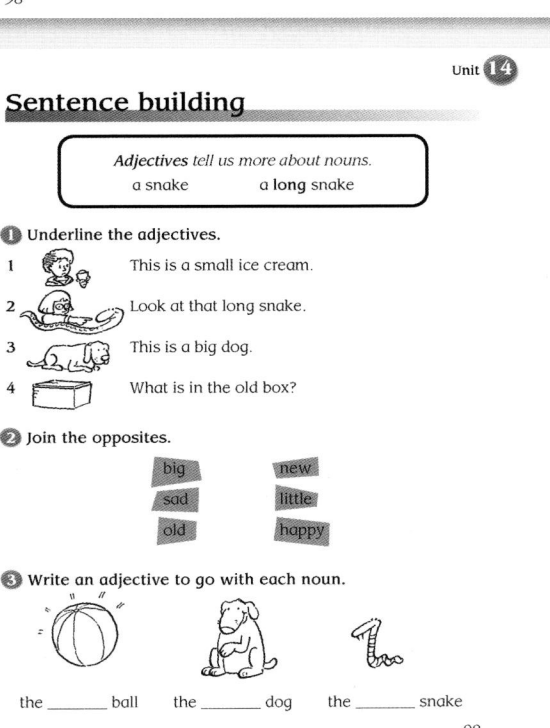

Lesson aim Comprehension, vocabulary and sentence building

Lesson targets Children:
- identify correct and incorrect statements
- match statements to pictures
- write about the weather using picture prompts
- find weather words in a word snake
- identify a variety of adjectives.

Key language (words) words for weather
(structures) *It is raining. It is a windy day.*

Materials Language Book pp124–125, Practice Book pp98–99, weather flashcards 136–141, days of the week word cards, word cards for *Get active!*, word cards of your choice for *Extension activity*

Preparation Make word cards as necessary.

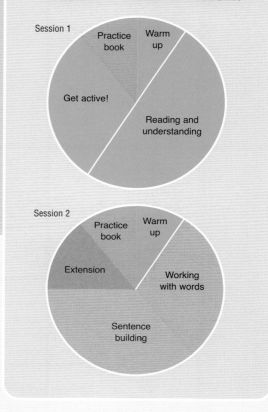

Lesson 3 time division:

Session 1: Practice book, Warm up, Get active!, Reading and understanding

Session 2: Practice book, Warm up, Extension, Working with words, Sentence building

⬇ Lesson 3 Session 1 Warm-up

1 Do sentence making with days word cards and weather flashcards. Children choose one of each card. Elicit, e.g. **Today is Sunday. It is sunny.**

⬇ Reading and understanding

3 Activity 1: Remind children that *true* means correct and *false* means incorrect.

Ask a child to read the first sentence. Class repeats. Ask if the sentence is true or false. Elicit the answer. Children circle *T*. Do the same with the other sentences. Children circle *T* or *F*.

4 Activity 2: Children read sentences. Class repeats. Children look at pictures and write the letter of the matching picture in the box. To check answers, ask different children to read a sentence and say the letter.

5 Get active!
Put up the weather flashcards 136–141. Children match word cards to the correct picture: *raining, snowing, sunny, windy, cloudy, foggy*. Elicit sentences using each word. Ask questions about each sentence you elicit, e.g. *Is it hot/cold? Can you hear/see the wind/rain/snow?* etc.

⬇ Lesson 3 Session 2 Warm-up

1 Write a selection of nouns, adjectives and verbs on the board. Children circle nouns, draw a box round adjectives and underline verbs.

⬇ Sentence building

1 Read the first sentence in the box. Read the second sentence and leave off *noun*. See if the class can tell you. If not, just say it yourself. Children read the phrases. Class repeats.

⬇ Extension activity

Put noun and adjective word cards on the board. Children put nouns and adjectives together and make phrases or full sentences, e.g. *(I can see) a small plane. (He is) a funny clown. (I have) a red ball.* If you wish, elicit phrases first. Write them on the board. Elicit sentence beginnings. Class reads whole sentence.

Teacher's note
A *puddle* is a small pool of water, usually left when it has rained. Children often enjoy splashing in puddles.

185

Grammar

1 Lesson 4 warm-up.

2 Children read sentences in box (LB p126). Class repeats.

3 Activity 1: Children read the speech bubbles. Children ask questions about the weather. Others answer.

4 Activity 2: Children read sentences. Children complete the sentences. Children write sentences.

5 Prepare children for PB p100 by checking they understand the tasks. Children complete.

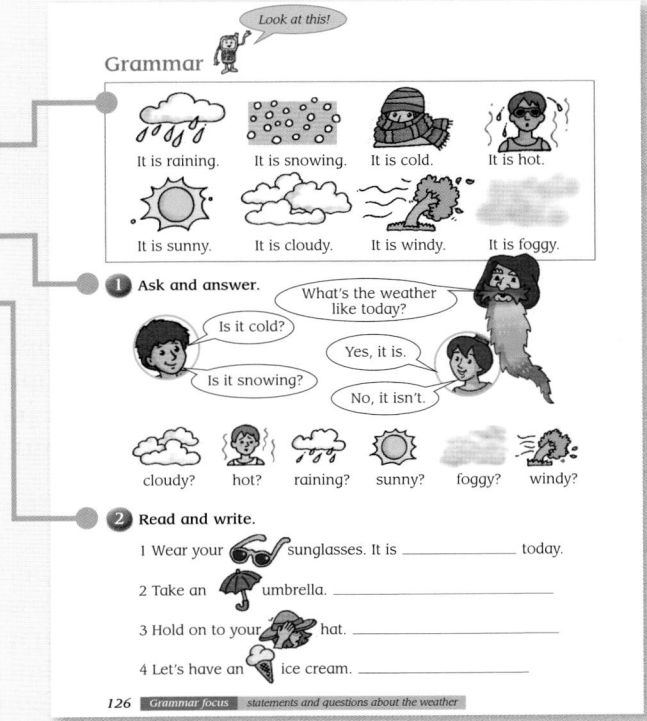

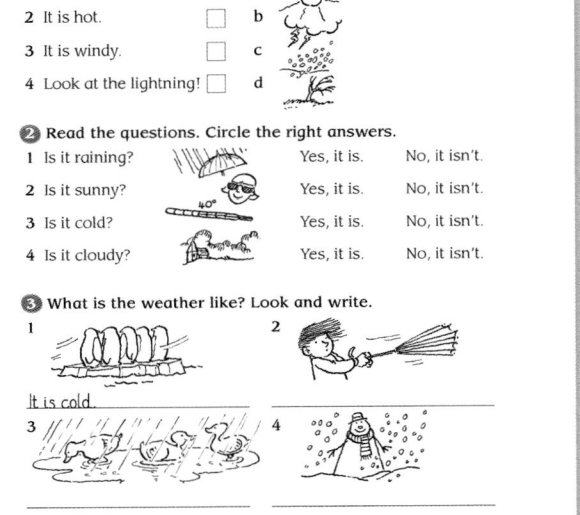

Listening

1 Read Nina's speech bubble (LB p127).

2 Explain the task.

3 🎧 Activity 1: Check children recognise the weather pictures. Play LCD2 track 81. Children listen and look. Play it again. Children draw the weather for each picture.

4 Activity 2: Children speak.

5 🎧 Activity 3: Play LCD2 track 82. Children listen and follow the words. Play the CD again and encourage children to join in.

After listening

Teach the first half of the song in the usual way.

Lesson aim Grammar and listening

Lesson targets Children:

- practise talking about the weather in pairs
- write sentences about the weather from word prompts
- listen for information
- sing and learn a short song.

Key language (words) weather words (structures) *Is it cold? Is it snowing?*

Materials Language Book pp126–127, Practice Book p100, Language CD2 tracks 81–82, rhyming word cards for *Warm-up*

Preparation Listen to the CD before the lesson. Make word cards as necessary.

Lesson 4 Time division:

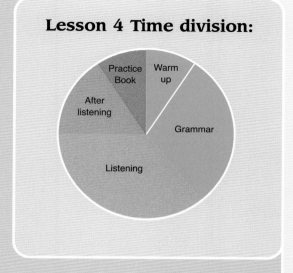

⬇ Lesson 4 Warm-up

1 Do the *Match rhyming words* activity p25), with e.g. *bath, path, thick, brick, thin, bin, three, tree, quack, black.*

⬇ Grammar

3 Ask a child to read the weatherman bubble. Pairs read the other bubbles. Children ask questions about the weather. Other children answer.

Repeat this activity in pairs. Listen to some of them.

4 A child reads the first sentence. Help with unfamiliar words. Class repeats. Ask for suggestions for the next sentence. Write it up. Class reads. Do the same with the other sentences.

⬇ Listening

3 Audioscript

1
Tilly	Oh, look, Nina!
Nina	It's snowing. We can play in the snow.

2
Sam [on radio]	Hello, Miss Plum.
Miss Plum	Hello, Sam. I'm afraid I can't land. It's too foggy.

3
Man	Uh oh, I can hear thunder.
Woman	I know. It's raining. [thunder/rain]

4
Miss Plum	What a nice day for a picnic! It's so warm and sunny.

5
Tilly	Oh dear, I can't see the sea. I can't see the jungle. I can't see anything.
Ben	No! It's too cloudy.

6
Sam	Wheeeeeeeee. This is fun.
Miss Plum	I know! But it's getting too windy. Let's go back.

4 Children read the speech bubbles. Class repeats. Children check their answer. Ask/Help a child to say the sentence about picture 2: *Miss Plum is in the helicopter.* The child adds the question. Elicit the answer. Children check their answers. Do the same with the other pictures.

187

Activity 1

1. Lesson 5 warm-up.
2. (LB p128) Point out pictures and words with *s* + consonant.
3. Play CD twice (LCD2 track 83). Children follow in books.
4. Read text.
5. Read and ask questions.
6. Read with the class.

Activity 2

1. Children hold sounds cards. Read the sounds.
2. Close up gradually.
3. Read the word.
4. Children look, say and write.

Activity 3

Children say the word and sentence.
Children write.

Activity 4

1. Write up words. Class/individuals read.
2. Children read in pairs. Listen to pairs.
3. Children check words and tick.

Practice Book

Children complete PB p101.

Phonics games and activities

1. Play *Start the word.*
2. Do *Look, write, check.*

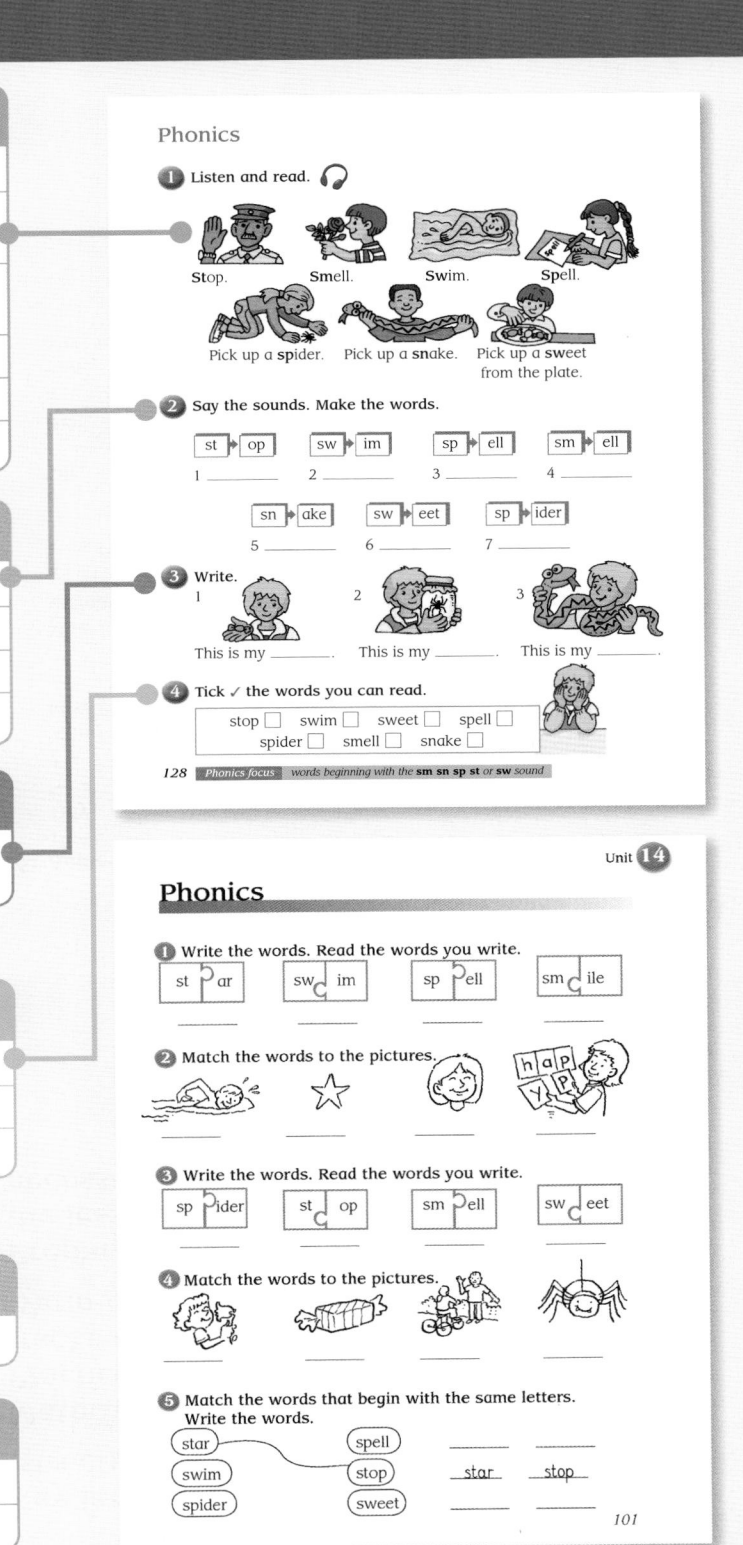

Lesson aim Phonic recognition

Lesson targets Children:

- read, pronounce and spell words with initial consonant blends *s* + consonant
- recognise and sound out different initial consonant blends (*st, sw, sp, sm, sn*) in target words
- write the target words from picture prompts.

Target words *smell, snake, spell, spider, stop, swim, sweet*

Materials Language Book p128, Practice Book p101, Language CD2 track 83, cards for sounds

Preparation Listen to the CD before the lesson. Make lists of words for *Warm-up*. Make large cards for the beginnings and endings of the words as shown in Activity 2 on LB p128.

Lesson 5 time division:

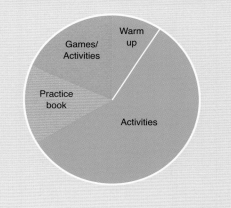

Lesson 5 Warm-up

1 Play *Odd one out* (p37). Use, e.g. *thick, brick, black, kick; thin, ten, bin, tin; bell, all, ball, mall.*

Activity 1

5 Ask *Can you swim? Can you spell? Who likes spiders?/snakes? Who says stop? What is she smelling? Is he running? Can she spell? Is the spider big? What colour is the snake? Who likes sweets?*
Make sure all the words are understood.

Activity 2

Follow the procedure for introducing the component parts of each word and reading each word which is given in detail in the Introduction (p10). Note: The words in this exercise are processed in two stages: initial consonant blend plus the rest of the word, rather than breaking each word down into individual phonemes.

Activity 3

Children look at the picture and read the words. Ask/Help a child to say the whole sentence. Class repeats.
Children write the word.
Do the same with the other sentences.

Activity 4

Write the seven words on the board.
Point in random order. Individuals and/or the class reads them.

Practice Book

Children complete the five exercises.
Check they can read all the words before they move on to Exercise 5.

Phonics games and activities

1 **Start the word**
Play *Start the word*. Put up endings, e.g. *_ll, _ng, _ck*.
Put beginnings below: *thi, spe, ba, ki*.
Class makes and reads as many words as possible: *thick, thing, spell, ball, king, kick*. Class may also make *bang* and *back*.

2 Do *Look, write, check* (TG p75) with some of these words.

189

Before writing

1 Lesson 6 warm-up.

2 Read Miss Plum's speech bubble (LB p129).

3 Two children read the speech bubbles. Class repeats.

4 Children look at the Monday picture. Say *It's Monday. What's the weather like?* Class answers. Continue with the other pictures. Children speak in pairs.

Shared writing

Activity 2 (LB p129): Child reads the first sentence. Elicit sentences for the other days. Children write.

Practice Book

Writing

1 Activity 1 (PB p102): Children read sentences. Class repeats.

2 Children write the correct sentence under each picture.

3 Continue in the same way with Activities 2 and 3.

Your writing

(PB p103) Children read the days of the week. They write sentences.

After writing

Children guess weather from clues.

Lesson aim Writing

Lesson targets Children:

- write sentences to match picture prompts
- match and write sentences to picture prompts
- write pairs of sentences about location and weather.

Key language (words) days of the week; weather words
(structures) *It is Monday. It is snowing.*

Materials Language Book p129, Practice Book pp102–103

Lesson 6 time division:

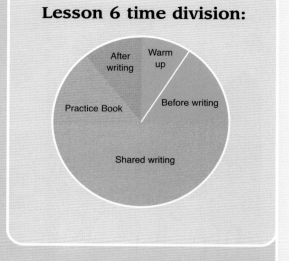

Lesson 6 Warm-up

1 Sing *Oh, Mr Sun, Sun* from Lesson 4 (LB p127, LCD2 track 82).

Before writing

4 If your class is confident, let children say the days and ask the questions. Otherwise continue asking the questions and eliciting answers.

To check understanding, ask individuals/class about days in random order.

Do the activity again in pairs. Children take turns to name a day and ask the question. Listen to some of them.

Shared writing

Elicit the next sentence. If necessary, tell children to look back at the picture above. Say *It's Tuesday. What's the weather like?*

Write the answer on the board. Class reads.

Elicit sentences for the other days. Class reads all the sentences. Rub them off before children write.

Practice Book

Your writing
Go through this exercise orally before children write. For each picture ask *What day is it? Where is Sam? What's the weather like?*

If children need further guidance, write the sentences on the board. Class reads before you rub off and they write.

After writing

Say sentences as clues. The class guesses what the weather is, e.g. *I am holding an umbrella.*
I am wearing sunglasses.
The cars are going slowly and we can't see anything.
It is cold and everything is white.
The men are holding onto their hats.
I can't see the sun now.

191

Lesson 1: Fluency

Before listening

1. Lesson 1 warm-up.
2. Show poster 15. Read the title. Ask questions.
3. Point and name new animal parts. Children come forward; find in main picture.
4. Show flashcards (43, 71–72, 142–145 and other animal flashcards as appropriate) and name animal parts. Class repeats.

Shared listening

1. Play FCD track 30. Point to characters when they speak.
2. Ask about the gold star.
3. Ask *Who? What?* questions.
4. Play FCD track 30 and point to characters again.

Dialogue practice

1. Say the new words. Children point in books (FB pp36–37). Point on poster for children to check.
2. Show flashcards (43, 71–72, 142–145). Children name animal parts.
3. Children close books. Play FCD track 31 and show character flashcards. Class repeats lines in pauses.
4. Groups say lines by character.
5. Individuals act dialogue.
6. Play FCD track 30 again. Children follow text or point to main picture.

After listening

1. Children guess the animal.
2. Do the animal talk activity.
3. Children put the next sticker star in the correct place on FB pp46–47.

Lesson aim Fluency

Lesson targets Children:

- listen for pronunciation and intonation
- repeat dialogue accurately
- act out dialogue with expression
- talk about animals.

Key language (words) *arms, ears, eyes, head, legs, mouth, neck, nose, trunk;* (structures) *They have got ..., We have got ..., How many ... have we got?*

Words for understanding *crocodiles, giraffes, grass, hippos, lions, rock, zebras, long, tall, through*

Materials Poster 15, Fluency Book pp36–37, Fluency CD tracks 30–31, character flashcards 2–5, flashcards 43, 71–72, 142–145, other animal flashcards as appropriate to demonstrate animal parts

Preparation Listen to the CD before the lesson.

Lesson 1 time division:

⬇ Lesson 1 Warm-up

1 Check with the class how many stars are missing. Say the *Star chant.*

⬇ Before listening

2 Ask *What animals can you see? Where are the monkeys? Where is the crocodile?/the hippo? What are the children doing?*

⬇ Shared listening

2 Ask *Have the children got another gold star? How many stars have they got now? How many stars are missing?*

3 Ask *What day is it? Is it cold? What are the children doing? (1st picture) Who is standing on the rock? Is it a rock? What is it? (2nd picture) Who is riding on the elephant? Where is Sam? (main picture) Where are the children? Are the lions running? What are they doing? Who is scared of the lions? What is the hippo doing? What animals have long necks? Where is the elephant drinking? What is in the water?*

⬇ After listening

1 Do a guess the animal activity.

Divide the class into two or more teams.

Make a statement about an animal, e.g. *It is big. It has big ears.* Children put up hands to guess **It's an elephant.** Continue with simple statements. *It can swim. It is big. It is grey.* (**hippo**)

Children can guess at any time, but if they are wrong the other team can listen to the full description before guessing.

2 When all animals have been guessed, show teams flashcards of animals. Teams take turns to make statements about animals. They get a point for every correct statement they can make about the animal. Continue until no teams can make any more statements.

193

Before reading

1 Lesson 2 warm-up.

2 📖 Teach new words (*soft*), (*fluffy*), any animal flashcard for body parts.

3 Children open books (LB pp130–131). Ask questions.

Shared reading

1 🎵 Play LCD2 track 84. Children follow text in book.

2 Read line by line. Ask questions.

3 Read with the class.

Reading practice

1 Give reading practice. Use some or all of the following:
- Children read again as a class.
- Groups read different sections.
- Individuals read different sections.

2 🎧 Class listens again to LCD2 track 84 and follows in LB.

After reading

Do the animal adjectives activity.

Lesson aim Reading

Lesson targets Children:

- follow a text read out to them
- listen for pronunciation and intonation
- read the text aloud with accurate pronunciation and intonation
- learn and understand new vocabulary items
- understand the sense of the text as a whole
- answer simple comprehension questions.

Key language (words) *duck, rabbit, tails, noses, soft, fluffy, feet* (structures) *I've got ..., We've got ..., I'm a ..., We're ...*

Words for understanding *leaves, dinner*

Materials Language Book pp130–131, Language CD2 track 84, animal flashcards 40, 71–72, 142–145, word cards for *After reading*

Preparation Listen to the CD before the lesson. Make word cards for *tall, big, fluffy, soft, small, long, short, little, grey, brown, green, white, orange.*

Lesson 2 time division:

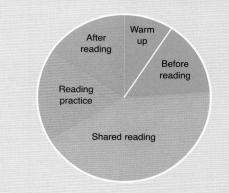

Lesson 2 Warm-up

1 Play *Simon says* (TG p95).

Before reading

3 Ask *What animals can you see?*
How many owls/rabbits are there?
What animal has orange feet?
Which animals can fly?

Shared reading

2 Ask *Where do owls live?*
What does a giraffe eat for its dinner?
Which animals have long noses?
Which animals have long tails?
Which animals love to swim?
Which animals have fluffy tails?
Which animal has a big mouth?
(*What have they got?* pictures):
Ask about each animal costume.
Whose head/tail/neck is it?
Whose arms/ears/legs/feet are they?

After reading

Divide the class into two or more teams. Put up the animals flashcards. Put up word card adjectives in any order: *tall, big, fluffy, soft, small, long, short, little, grey, brown, green, white, orange.*

Teams take turns to match adjectives to flashcards and make statements, e.g. (rabbit) **This is a rabbit. It is fluffy.**

195

Reading and understanding

1. Session 1 warm-up. ⬇
2. Re-read *Animal puzzles* (LB pp130–131).
3. Activity 1 (LB p132): A child reads first sentence. Class repeats. A child reads the question. Elicit the answer. Continue with the other sentences and questions.
4. Activity 2: Individuals read sentences. Class repeats. Children match pictures and number them.
5. 📖 Play the *Get active!* game. ⬇
6. Prepare children for PB p104. Read the text under the pictures with them. Check they understand the tasks. Children complete.

Working with words

1. Session 2 warm-up. ⬇
2. Activity 1 (LB p133): Children read the words. Children write words in the correct box. ⬇
3. Activity 2: Children read sentences. They write an animal that fits the description. ⬇

Sentence building

1. Read the sentence in the box (LB p133). Read the full form of the verb. Class repeats. Read the short form. Class repeats.
2. Activity 1: Children complete sentences. ⬇
3. Activity 2: Children read sentences. Check answers as they read.
4. Prepare children for PB p105. Read the verb in the box with them and check they understand the tasks. Children complete.

Extension activity

Do the animal descriptions activity. ⬇

Reading and understanding

1. **Answer the questions.**

   1 They are soft and they have got fluffy tails. What are they?
   2 It is very big and it has got big ears. What is it?
   3 They have got very long arms. What are they?
   4 It has got a long neck and it likes to eat leaves. What is it?
   5 They have got orange feet and they love to swim. What are they?
   6 It lives in a tree and it flies at night. What is it?
   7 It has got a big mouth and little ears. What is it?

2. **Read and number the pictures.**

   1 I'm a monkey!
   2 I'm a giraffe!
   3 We're rabbits!
   4 I'm a hippo!
   5 We're elephants!
   6 We're owls!
   7 We're ducks!

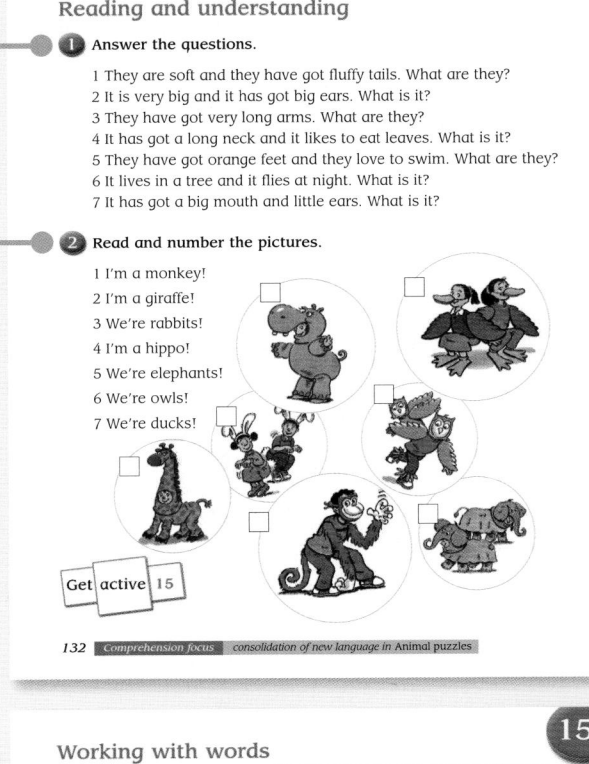

Get active 15

132 Comprehension focus consolidation of new language in Animal puzzles

---

Working with words

1. **Write about your body.**

   | eye foot ear nose head body |
   | hand arm leg knee shoulder |

I've got one …	I've got two …

2. **Write an animal.**

   1 It has got a tail. _____   2 It has got long ears. _____
   3 It has got a big mouth. _____   4 It has got big eyes. _____

Sentence building

This is the verb **to be**:

I am / I'm	we are / we're
you are / you're	you are / you're
he is / he's	they are / they're
she is / she's	
it is / it's	

I am Mobi!

1. **Complete the sentences with *am* or *is* or *are*.**

   1 I _____ a monkey.
   2 He _____ a giraffe.
   3 She _____ a hippo.
   4 They _____ rabbits.
   5 We _____ ducks.

2. **Read the sentences.**

Language focus body words; use of to be   *133*

Unit 15
Reading and understanding

1. **Read.**

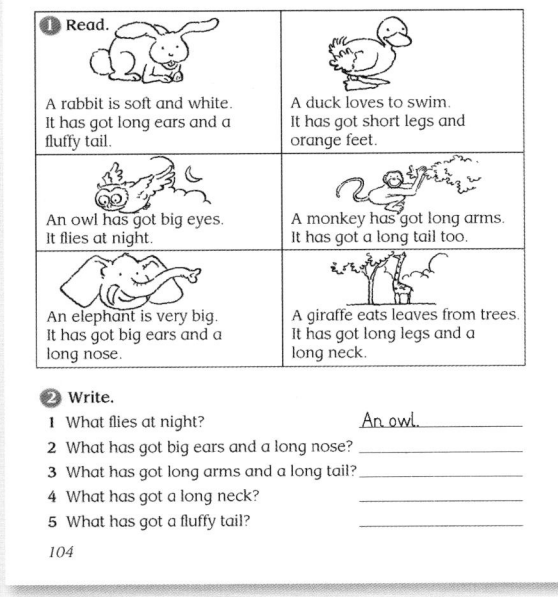

A rabbit is soft and white. It has got long ears and a fluffy tail.	A duck loves to swim. It has got short legs and orange feet.
An owl has got big eyes. It flies at night.	A monkey has got long arms. It has got a long tail too.
An elephant is very big. It has got big ears and a long nose.	A giraffe eats leaves from trees. It has got long legs and a long neck.

2. **Write.**

   1 What flies at night?   *An owl.*
   2 What has got big ears and a long nose? _____
   3 What has got long arms and a long tail? _____
   4 What has got a long neck? _____
   5 What has got a fluffy tail? _____

104

Unit 15
Sentence building

I am	we are
you are	you are
he is	they are
she is	
it is	

1. **Finish the sentences with *am* or *is* or *are*.**

   1 She _____ kind.   2 You _____ my sister.
   3 I _____ seven.   4 We _____ reading.
   5 He _____ my brother.

2. **Finish the answers.**

   1 Is Nina drawing?
     Yes, Nina _____ drawing.

   2 Is Ben sleeping?
     Yes, Ben _____ sleeping.

   3 Are the dogs running?
     Yes, The dogs _____ running.

105

Lesson aim Comprehension, vocabulary and sentence building

Lesson targets Children:
- understand and give simple descriptions and statements
- recognise body parts
- know the verb *to be* in long and short form and use it correctly.

Key language (words) *foot, head, body, hand, knee, shoulder*

(structures) verb *to be,* long and short forms

Words for understanding *flies, likes, lives*

Materials Language Book pp132–133, Practice Book pp104–105, animal flashcards 40, 71–72, 142–145 for *Get active!* and animal flashcards for *Extension activity*

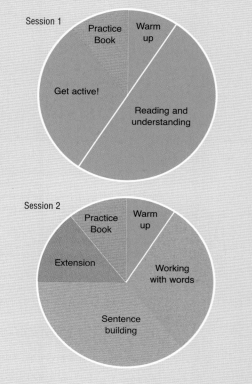

Lesson 3 time division:

Session 1
- Practice Book
- Warm up
- Get active!
- Reading and understanding

Session 2
- Practice Book
- Warm up
- Extension
- Working with words
- Sentence building

⬇ Lesson 3 Session 1 Warm-up

1 Play *Number chain game* (p248) around the class. Start from 1 or a higher number.

⬇ Reading and understanding

5 **Get active!**
Give pairs or groups of children a flashcard animal, e.g. *mouse, rabbit, duck, frog, owl, monkey, zebra, crocodile, lion, hippo, elephant, giraffe.*

Everybody starts standing up. Say statements. Children must sit down if the statement does not apply to their animal. E.g. *This animal has four legs.* (Duck, owl, monkey sit down.) *This animal has a long tail.* (Frog, hippo, elephant, giraffe sit down.) *This animal is small.* (Zebra, crocodile, lion sit down.) *This animal has long ears.* (Mouse sits down.) The rabbit is left.

⬇ Lesson 3 Session 2 Warm-up

1 Class sings *Oh, Mr Sun, Sun* (LB p127, LCD2 track 82).

⬇ Working with words

2 Read each word in the box. Class repeats. Explain new words by pointing.

If you wish, ask all the class to stand up. Point to each part as you say the word. Children point and repeat. Children sit down. Ask individuals around the class *How many ... have you got?* Explain *one foot/two feet.* Draw simple pictures on the board with the phrases.

3 Individuals read sentences. Children write an animal. Check answers by asking children to read sentences and their answers. Answers to number 1 can include any animal with a tail. Answer to number 3 can also include *crocodile.*

⬇ Sentence building

2 If your class is confident, let them complete the exercise without going through it orally first.

If children need guided practice, ask a child to complete each sentence. Class repeats. Children write.

⬇ Extension activity

Give pairs or groups of children animal flashcards of your choice. They write descriptions of the animal. They read them out to the rest of the class. Class guesses which animal it is.
Pairs win points for the number of correct sentences they say, and for guessing other pairs' animals.

197

Grammar

1. Lesson 4 warm-up.

2. Children look at the picture (LB p134). Two children read speech bubbles. Class reads speech bubbles. Point out the *Remember!* box.

3. Activity 1: Say new word *tusks*. Check understanding. Children read and tick.

4. Activities 2, 3: Children speak in pairs. Go around listening to some of them.

5. Prepare children for PB p106 by checking they understand the tasks. Children complete.

Listening

1. Read Nina's speech bubble (LB p135).

2. Activity 1: Play LCD2 track 85. Children listen and point. Children name animals.

3. Activity 2: Play the rhyme (LCD2 track 86). Children listen.

4. Play the rhyme again. Children join in.

After listening

Teach the actions for the rhyme. Children practise it.

Grammar

Look at the elephants! They've got long trunks.

We haven't got trunks. We've got little noses.

Remember!
they've = they have
we've = we have
haven't = have not

1 What have we got? What have elephants got? Tick ✓ the boxes.

tusks   ears   tails   trunks   four legs   two eyes

2 Ask and answer about elephants.

Have they got tusks?   Yes, they have.

3 Ask and answer about you and your friends.

Have we got trunks?   No, we haven't.

134   Grammar focus   statements and questions with have got

Listening

What are the animals?

1 Listen, point and say.

1 zebras   2 giraffes
3 monkeys   4 lions
5 elephants   6 crocodiles

2 Listen and say.

Take . . .
A head, some shoulders, knees and toes,
A mouth and eyes that see,
A pair of legs, two feet, one nose,
And what you've got is
ME!

Theresa Heine

Listening focus   physical features

135

Grammar

1 Read and circle.

A   B

1 They have got tusks. (A) B   2 They have got long noses. A B
3 They have got arms. A B   4 They have got little ears. A B
5 They have got trunks. A B   6 They have got hands. A B

2 Write *Yes, they have.* or *No, they haven't.*

1 Have they got two eyes? _____
2 Have they got little ears? _____
3 Have they got tusks? _____
4 Have they got long noses? _____

3 Write *Yes, we have.* or *No, we haven't.*

1 Have we got tails? _____
2 Have we got trunks? _____
3 Have we got two legs? _____
4 Have we got little ears? _____

106

Lesson aim Grammar and listening

Lesson targets Children:

- practise the spoken short form of *have*, affirmative and negative
- categorise physical characteristics as animal or human
- recognise animals from spoken descriptions
- sing and learn a short rhyme.

Key language (words) animal words, *tusks*
(structures) *They've got ..., We've got ..., No, they haven't. Yes, we have.*

Materials Language Book pp134–135, Practice Book p106, Language CD2 tracks 85–86, short form word cards for the verbs *to have* and *to be* for *Warm-up*

Preparation Listen to the CD before the lesson. Make word cards as necessary.

Lesson 4 time division:

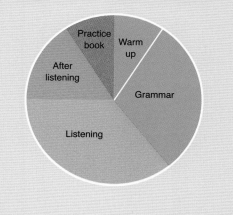

Lesson 4 Warm-up

1 Write up parts of the verbs *to have* and *to be* in muddled order. Stick the short form word cards at the bottom of the board. Children match.

Grammar

3 Ask *Have we got tusks?* **No, we haven't.** *Have elephants got tusks?* **Yes, they have.** Check that children tick only the lower box. If you wish, go through the whole activity orally. Alternatively, children read and tick.
Check answers by asking questions around the class *Have elephants/we got ...?*

Listening

2 Children look and read the words. Play the CD. Children listen and point to the animal they hear described. Play the CD again. Children answer in the pause.

Audioscript
These animals have got long arms. They can swing through the trees. What are they?
These animals have got four long legs and very long necks. What are they?
These animals have got four legs. They are not horses but they can run very fast. They are black and white. What are they?
These animals can swim. They have long bodies and short little legs. They are green or brown. Be careful! What are they?
These animals have got four legs. They have got trunks and tusks. They are very big. What are they?
Be careful of these animals! They can run very fast. They are big cats. Listen!
[lions roar] What are they?

After listening

Lead children in saying the rhyme and pointing to each body part as it is named. Children point to themselves on the last word.

199

Activity 1

1. Lesson 5 warm-up.
2. (LB p136) Point out pictures and words with *nd, nt, nk*.
3. Play rhyme twice (LCD2 track 87). Children follow in books.
4. Read rhyme.
5. Read and ask questions.
6. Read with the class.

Activity 2

1. Children hold sounds cards. Read the sounds.
2. Close up gradually.
3. Read the word.
4. Children look, say and write.

Activity 3

Children say the word and sentence.

Activity 4

1. Write up words. Class/Individuals read.
2. Children read in pairs. Listen to pairs.
3. Children check words and tick.

Practice Book

Children complete PB p107.

Phonics games and activities

1. Play *Muddled letters.*
2. Do some dictated spellings.

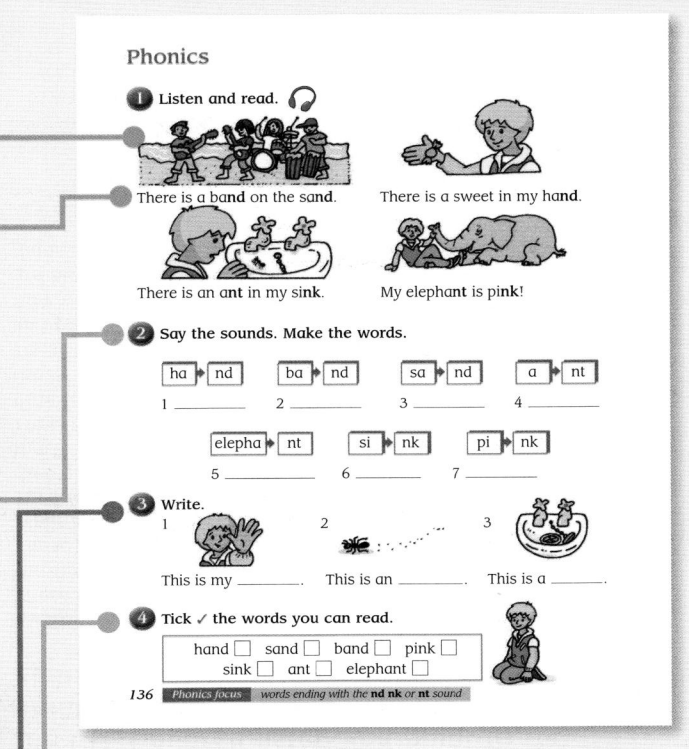

Phonics

1. Listen and read.

There is a band on the sand.   There is a sweet in my hand.

There is an ant in my sink.   My elephant is pink!

2. Say the sounds. Make the words.

| ha ▸ nd | ba ▸ nd | sa ▸ nd | a ▸ nt |
| 1 _____ | 2 _____ | 3 _____ | 4 _____ |

| elepha ▸ nt | si ▸ nk | pi ▸ nk |
| 5 _____ | 6 _____ | 7 _____ |

3. Write.

1 This is my _____.   2 This is an _____.   3 This is a _____.

4. Tick ✓ the words you can read.

hand ☐   sand ☐   band ☐   pink ☐
sink ☐   ant ☐   elephant ☐

136   *Phonics focus*   words ending with the **nd nk** or **nt** sound

Phonics

Unit 15

1. Choose and write.

hand   sand   hand   band   sand   band

_____   _____   _____

2. Circle the words.

qxebhandtyzbandcvbnksandhgf

3. Colour the sink pink.

4. Circle the ___ in the word.

elephant

107

200

Lesson aim Phonic recognition

Lesson targets Children:

- read, pronounce and spell words ending with final consonant blends *nd, nt, nk*
- recognise and sound out the different final consonant blends (*nd, nt, nk*) in the target words
- write the target words from picture prompts.

Target words *hand, band, sand, pink, sink, ant, elephant*

Materials Language Book p136, Practice Book p107, Language CD2 track 87, cards for sounds

Preparation Listen to the CD before the lesson. Make large cards for the beginnings and endings of the words as shown in Activity 2, LB p136

Lesson 5 time division:

[pie chart with segments labelled: Warm up, Games/Activities, Practice book, Activities]

⬇ Lesson 5 Warm-up

1 Say *Take ... a head* from Lesson 4 (LB p135, LCD2 track 86). Children join in and do the actions.

⬇ Activity 1

5 Ask *How many people are in the band?*
Is a man playing a drum?
What colour is the sweet?
Is there water in the sink?
Is it a toy elephant?

Make sure all the words in the text are understood.

⬇ Activity 2

Follow the procedure for introducing the component parts of each word and reading each word which is given in detail in the Introduction (p10).
Note: The words in this exercise are processed in two stages: word beginnings and final consonant blends, rather than breaking each word down into individual phonemes.

⬇ Activity 3

Children look at the picture and read the words. Ask/Help a child to say the whole sentence. Class repeats.

Children write the word.

Do the same with the other sentences.

⬇ Activity 4

1 Write the seven words on the board. Point in random order. Individuals and/or the class reads them.

⬇ Phonics games and activities

1 **Muddled letters**
Divide the class into groups. Give out small phoneme cards to make up words children have learned in Lesson 5 of any of Units 1–10.

Children make the word. Write it. Then change letters with another group. Check their lists of words.

2 Do dictated spellings with the same set of words.

Before writing

1. Lesson 6 warm-up.
2. Read Miss Plum's speech bubble (LB p137).
3. Children name the body parts.
4. Children complete and colour the four pictures.

Shared writing

1. Read Miss Plum's speech bubble again. (LB p137) Children read about the elephant.
2. Elicit sentences about the other animals. Write them on the board. Children read. Rub them off before children write.

Practice Book

Writing

1. Children read sentences (PB p108).
2. They label the cat.

Your writing

1. Children read the instructions (PB p109) and colour.
2. They label the dog.
3. They complete the sentences.

After writing

Teams read sentences.

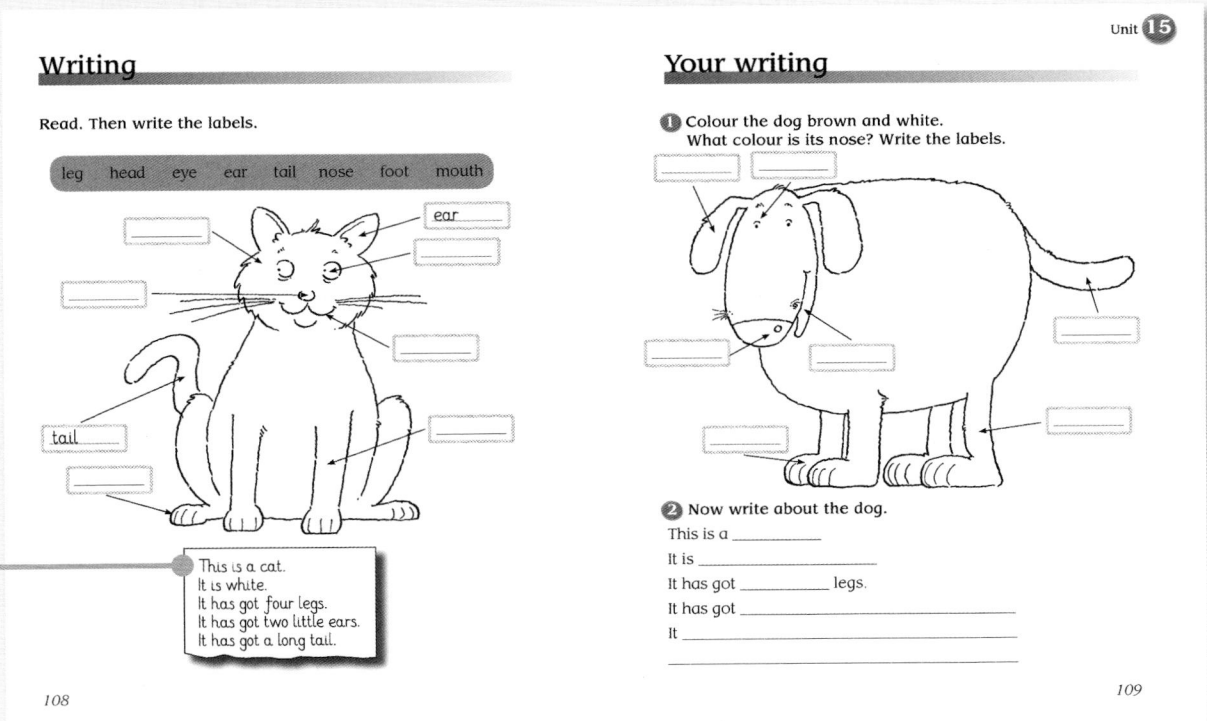

Lesson aim Writing

Lesson targets Children:

- write sentences describing animals
- complete sentences from picture prompts
- labels parts of an animal
- complete sentences describing an animal.

Key language (words) colours, parts of an animal's body
(structures) *This is a ..., It is ..., It has got ...*

Materials Language Book p137, Practice Book pp108–109, flashcards for *Warm-up*

Lesson 6 time division:

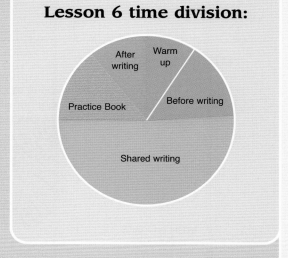

⬇ Lesson 6 Warm-up

1 Play *Flashcard/letter matching* (p35) with flashcards from Units 14 and 15.

⬇ Before writing

4 Make sure children understand they should copy the body parts onto the correct pictures below. If you wish, ask about each picture *What is missing?*

⬇ Shared writing

2 The first sentence should be *These are cats.* Children will probably also mention the colour. The other sentences can describe size and any body parts as well as legs and tail, e.g. *little ears, small eyes.* Write up statements the children suggest.

When children write they should produce three sentences about each picture.

⬇ After writing

Divide the class in two. Teams take turns to read out their sentences about the animals. If possible, write their sentences up in different colours. The teams go on reading out sentences so long as they have something different to say.

When they have finished reading, ask if either team can think of any other information to add. Add up the teams' sentences for each picture.

Teams can also add sentences about the elephant.

203

Revision 5

You can do it!

1 **Look at the pictures.** What and who can you see? Where are they?

2 **Listen and read.** 🎧

3 **Read and say.**
Look at picture 1: Where are Ben and Nina? What's the weather like? What has Nina got?

Look at picture 2: Who can you see? Where are they? What's the weather like?

Look at picture 3: Where are Ben and Sam? Is it raining? What are the boys doing?

Look at picture 4: What's the weather like? Who can you see? Where are they?

Look at picture 5: What's the weather like? Can Ben and Sam see all the island? What can they see?

In this photo it is hot and sunny. Ben and Nina are on the beach. They are very happy. Nina has got an ice cream.

Sam and Ben are on the mountain. It is snowing and it is very cold. The boys are playing in the snow. Ben has got a big snowball.

Ben and Sam are at the top of the tall tree. It is very foggy. They can't see the jungle. They can see the top of the mountain. They can see Miss Plum, too.

Miss Plum and the children are on the sea. They are in two little boats. It is very windy. Tilly is cold.

It is cloudy today. The sky is grey. Nina and Tilly are on the big ship. Mr Fun, the clown, has got lots of balloons. How many balloons are there?

The children are riding on an elephant. It is raining and it is very windy. They are under a big umbrella. Mobi has got a little umbrella.

Look at picture 6: Is it windy? Is it snowing? What are the children doing? What is Nina holding?

4 **Find and say the numbers.**

5 **Listen, point and say which picture.** 🎧

6 **Choose a photo and act it out. Your friends guess.**

7 **Listen and say the chant.** 🎧

A spider in the bath. Help!
A snake on the path. Help!
A big pink elephant swimming in the sea – with me! HELP!

Lesson aim Revision

Lesson targets Children:

- practise fluency and listening activities, including phonemes *ch, ll, ng*
- practise language and structures from Units 13–15 through a story, games and writing.

Key language *How many ... are there?* numbers 10–100; *What's the weather like? It's windy and it's raining. They have got ... We have got ... How many ... have we got?*

Words for understanding *snowball*

Materials Language Book pp138–139, Language CD2 tracks 88–90, Practice Book pp110–113

Revision 5 time division:

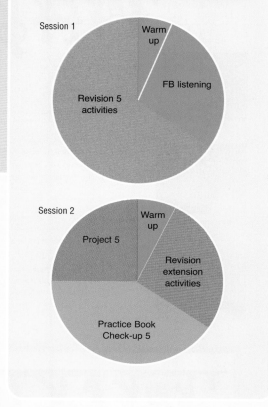

Sessions 1 and 2 Warm-ups

Sing favourite songs from Units 13–15.

Listening revision

Revise FCD tracks 26-31 as usual.

Revision 5

1 (LB p138) Activity 1: Children say as much as they can from observation.

2 🎧 Activity 2: Play LCD2 track 88. Children listen and follow.

3 Activity 3: Read questions. Elicit answers.

4 (LB p139) Activity 4: Children find numbers in the pictures.

5 🎧 Activity 5: Play LCD2 track 89 twice. Children listen and point then name the picture, e.g. ***It's picture 5.***

Audioscript

Presenter	Listen, point and say which picture.
Tilly	Brrr! I'm cold.
Ben	Hooray! It's snowing!
Nina	Mmm! This ice cream is fantastic.
Sam	I can't see the beach. It's too foggy.
Tilly	Look at the sky. It's cloudy today.
Ben	Come under our umbrella, Mobi!

6 Activity 6: In groups or pairs, children pose as one of the scenes.

7 🎧 Activity 7: Play the chant twice (LCD2 track 90). Children listen then join in.

Revision extension activities

1 Play flashcard games from Units 13–15.

2 Individuals, groups or the whole class read the story aloud.

3 Children read aloud the phonic chant. Teach it if you wish.

Practice Book

1 Children complete *Check-up 5* (PB pp110–111) as a test, as preparation for a test or for homework.

2 Children complete *Move on with Mobi 5* (PB pp112–113).

Project 5: Weather diary

Draw the symbols on the right on the board. Children name them. Write up

hot, cold and the days of the week.

Divide the class into groups. Give each child a piece of paper. Each child in the group chooses a different day of the week and different weather. They draw the weather and write sentences, e.g. ***Today is Saturday. It is raining on the island. It is cold.***

Groups read their diary to the class.

205

Before listening

1. Lesson 1 warm-up.
2. Show poster 16. Read the title. Ask questions.
3. Point and name new objects. Children come forward; find in main picture.
4. Show flashcards 96, 157–163 and name new objects. Class repeats.

Shared listening

1. Play FCD track 32. Point to characters when they speak.
2. Ask about the last gold star.
3. Ask *Who? What? Where?* questions.
4. Play FCD track 32 and point to characters again.

Dialogue practice

1. Say the new object words. Children point in books (FB pp28–29). Point on poster for children to check.
2. Show flashcards 96, 157–163. Children name.
3. Children close books. Play FCD track 33 and show character flashcards. Class repeats lines in pauses.
4. Groups say lines by character.
5. Individuals act dialogue.
6. Play FCD track 32 again. Children follow text or point to main picture.

After listening

Children write sentences.

Lesson aim Fluency

Lesson targets Children:

- listen for pronunciation and intonation
- repeat dialogue accurately
- act out dialogue with expression
- talk about picnics.

Key language (words) *apples, bananas, biscuits, cakes, chicken, grapes, orange juice, sandwiches*
(structures) *I like ..., He/She likes ...*

Words for understanding *box, picnic, waterfall, like, last, sad, behind, by, today*

Materials Poster 16, Fluency Book pp38–39, Fluency CD tracks 32–33, character flashcards 2–6, object flashcards 96, 157–163

Preparation Listen to the CD before the lesson.

Lesson 1 time division:

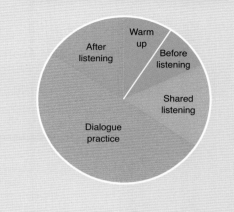

⬇ Lesson 1 Warm-up

1 Check with the class how many stars are missing. Say the *Star chant*. Use a ball and a box to revise prepositions.

⬇ Before listening

2 Ask *Where are the children?*
What are they doing?
Have they got some food?
What food can you see?
Do you have picnics?
Do you like picnics?

⬇ Shared listening

2 Ask *What do the children want to find by the river?*
Do they find it? Are they happy?
Where are they going now?

3 Ask *Who likes chicken?*
Who likes sandwiches?
Does Mobi like everything?
What have they got to drink?
The children look for the star. Where does Sam look? Where do Ben and Nina look? Where does Tilly look?

⬇ After listening

Children work in pairs. They each write a sentence about what they like, e.g. *I like grapes.* They show their sentence to their partner. Their partner writes, e.g. *(Name) likes grapes.*
Each child then has one sentence about him/herself and one about his/her partner. Hear some sentences.

Before reading

1 Lesson 2 warm-up. ⬇

2 Children open books (LB pp140–141). Ask questions. ⬇

Shared reading

1 🎧 Play LCD2 track 91. Children follow text in book.

2 Read line by line. Ask questions. ⬇

3 Read with the class.

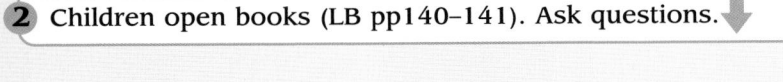

unit 16

Let's have a picnic!

Summertime, summertime,
We all love summertime.
When the sun is hot and the sky is blue,
This is what we like to do.
We find a cool place under a tree
And we have a picnic,
Mum and Dad
　　and Grandma and Grandpa
　　　　and Uncle Charlie and Auntie Betty
　　　　　　and Milly and Billy
　　　　　　　　and Polly and Molly
　　　　　　　　　　– and me!

Here's our basket!
What have we got?
Look at this!
There's such a lot!

Crunch on an apple,
Munch on a grape.
Here are the biscuits.
Yum! Have a cake.

Here are the sandwiches.
Have one of these.
Do you like orange juice?
Oh, yes, please!

Summertime, summertime,
We all love summertime.
When the sun is hot and the sky is blue,
This is what we like to do.
We find a cool place under a tree
And we have a picnic,
Mum and Dad
　　and Grandma and Grandpa
　　　　and Uncle Charlie and Auntie Betty
　　　　　　and Milly and Billy
　　　　　　　　and Polly and Molly
　　　　　　　　　　– and me!

140　Parents:　see extra material on page 166

141

Reading practice

1 Give reading practice. Use some or all of the following:
- Children read again as a class.
- Groups read different sections.
- Individuals read different sections.

2 🎧 Class listens again to LCD2 track 91 and follows in LB.

After reading

Do the chaining and matching activity with food flashcards. ⬇

Lesson aim Reading

Lesson targets Children:

- follow a text read out to them
- listen for pronunciation and intonation
- read the text aloud with accurate pronunciation and intonation
- understand the sense of the text as a whole
- answer simple comprehension questions.

Key language (structures) *I like ..., He/She likes ..., We like ..., They like ...*

Language for understanding *cool, Auntie, Uncle, a lot, crunch, munch, summertime*

Materials Language Book pp140–141, Language CD2 track 91, flashcards for food (96, 157–163) and word cards to match

Preparation Listen to the CD before the lesson. Make word cards for food items.

Lesson 2 time division:

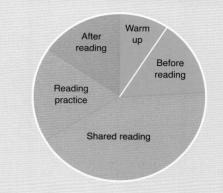

⬇ Lesson 2 Warm-up

1 Play *Alphabetical order* (p248).

⬇ Before reading

2 Ask *How many people are having a picnic?*
Where are they?
How many children are there?
How many girls/boys are there?
Can you see Grandma?/Grandpa?

⬇ Shared reading

2 Ask *What is the weather like?*
Is it hot under the tree?
Who is in the family?
What are the children's names?
What have they got to eat?
What have they got to drink?

⬇ After reading

Put flashcards 96, 157–163 on your desk. Put the word cards in any order at the bottom of the board.
Play the *I like ...* chain game with food flashcards: Children take a flashcard and stick it up, say *I like apples*. Next child sticks up another card and says *I like apples and bananas*, and so on until all cards are up.

Class looks at all the cards and says *I like apples, bananas, chicken*, etc.

Children take turns to match word cards to flashcards.

209

Reading and understanding
SESSION 1

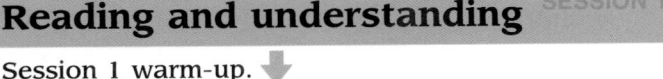

1. Session 1 warm-up.
2. Re-read *Let's have a picnic!* (LB pp140–141).
3. Activity 1 (LB p142): Children complete the sentences using words in the box. To check, children read out sentences.
4. Activity 2: Children read and circle. Ask questions and make up a class survey.
5. Play the *Get active!* game.
6. Prepare children for PB p114 by checking they understand the tasks. Children complete.

Working with words
SESSION 2

1. Session 2 warm-up.
2. Activity 1 (LB p143): Children circle the words and answer the questions. To check, ask children to read words.

Sentence building

1. Go through the information in the box (LB p143).
2. Activity 1: Children fill the blanks with singular or plural nouns.
3. Prepare children for PB p115. Go through the box and check they understand the tasks. Children complete.

Extension activity

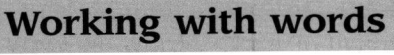

Ask children to draw a monster and label it, e.g. *one eye, six legs, four arms, one tail,* etc. Check for the plural *s* in the labels.

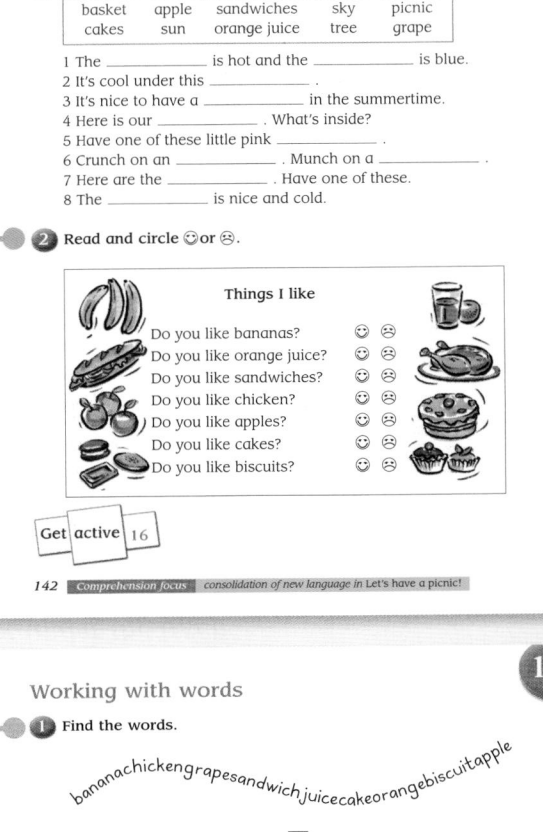

Reading and understanding

1. Complete the sentences.

basket	apple	sandwiches	sky	picnic
cakes	sun	orange juice	tree	grape

1 The _____ is hot and the _____ is blue.
2 It's cool under this _____ .
3 It's nice to have a _____ in the summertime.
4 Here is our _____ . What's inside?
5 Have one of these little pink _____ .
6 Crunch on an _____ . Munch on a _____ .
7 Here are the _____ . Have one of these.
8 The _____ is nice and cold.

2. Read and circle ☺ or ☹.

Things I like

Do you like bananas? ☺ ☹
Do you like orange juice? ☺ ☹
Do you like sandwiches? ☺ ☹
Do you like chicken? ☺ ☹
Do you like apples? ☺ ☹
Do you like cakes? ☺ ☹
Do you like biscuits? ☺ ☹

Get active 16

142   Comprehension focus   consolidation of new language in Let's have a picnic!

Working with words

16

1. Find the words.

bananachickengrapesandwichjuicecakeorangebiscuitapple

How many things can you eat? ☐
How many things can you drink? ☐

Sentence building

Remember, a noun is a naming word.

A **singular** noun is **one** thing.

book

A **plural** noun is **more than one** thing.

books

1. Complete the table.

singular noun	plural noun
one cup	two _____
one _____	three dogs
one orange	five _____
one _____	two baskets
one apple	four _____

Language focus   food; singular and plural nouns   143

Unit 16
Reading and understanding

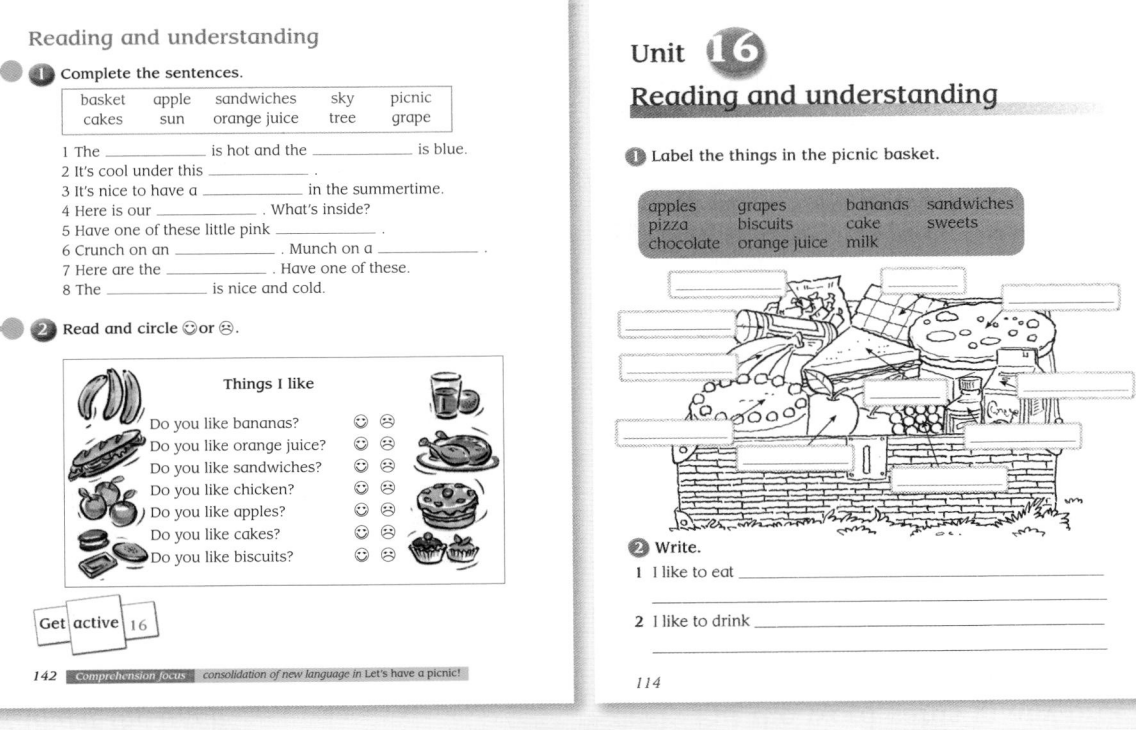

1. Label the things in the picnic basket.

apples	grapes	bananas	sandwiches
pizza	biscuits	cake	sweets
chocolate	orange juice	milk	

2. Write.
1 I like to eat _____
2 I like to drink _____

114

Unit 16
Sentence building

Singular means one.   one book
Plural means more than one.   books

1. Circle the plural nouns.

(dogs)	desk	apples	cats
	tables	lamp	train
oranges	snakes	rabbit	ducks

2. Finish the sentences.

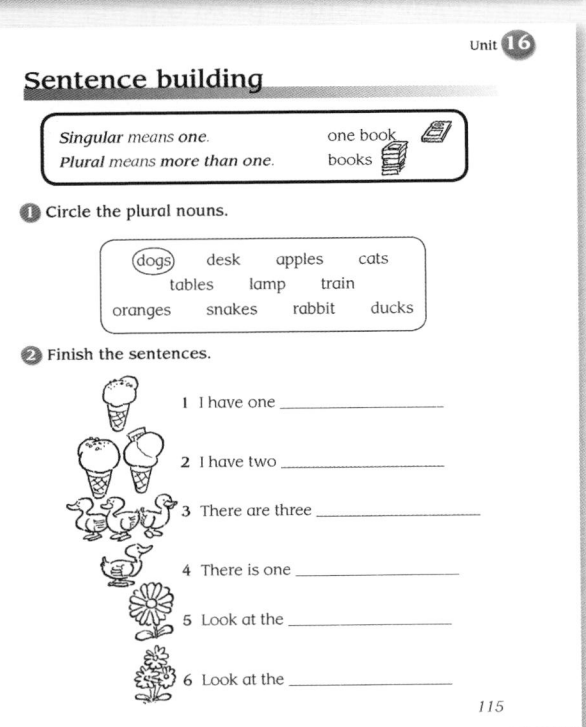

1 I have one _____
2 I have two _____
3 There are three _____
4 There is one _____
5 Look at the _____
6 Look at the _____

115

Lesson aim Comprehension, vocabulary and sentence building

Lesson targets Children:
- complete sentences using word prompts
- answer a short questionnaire
- ask questions about preferences and answer
- find words in a word snake
- understand the difference between the regular singular and plural forms.

Key language (words) food items

Materials Language Book pp142–143, Practice Book pp114–115, flashcards 96, 157–163

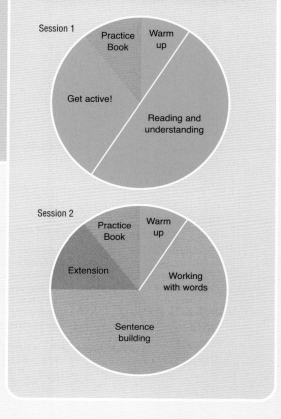

Lesson 3 time division:

Session 1
- Warm up
- Practice Book
- Get active!
- Reading and understanding

Session 2
- Warm up
- Practice Book
- Extension
- Working with words
- Sentence building

⬇ Lesson 3 Session 1 Warm-up

1 Play *What's missing?* (TG p109) with six or more food cards.

⬇ Reading and understanding

3 If your class benefits from guided tasks, follow this procedure: Children read the words in the box. Class repeats.

Children look at the first sentence. They find words in the box to fill the gaps. They can look back at the poem if they wish. Re-read the first verse if necessary. Elicit the complete sentence. Class repeats.

Continue in the same way with the other sentences. Children write the words.

4 Make a chart on the board:

	😊	🙁
bananas		
orange juice		
etc.		

Ask *Who likes bananas?* Count the hands. *Who doesn't like bananas?* Count again. If you wish, bring a child forward to count, or ask children to count each row. Do the same with the other items. When all the numbers are on the chart, ask, e.g. *How many children like apples? How many children don't like chicken?*

5 Get active!
Put all the food flashcards on the board. Children point and make statements about two things, e.g. *I like cakes and chicken. What do you like, ... (name)?* The named child comes forward, points and names two things and asks someone else.
Demonstrate the activity by making the first statements yourself. If you wish, play in teams. Each child names someone from the other team.

⬇ Lesson 3 Session 2 Warm-up

Play the chain game with food items: *I like grapes...*, etc

⬇ Sentence building

Read the sentences. Check understanding by holding up one item, e.g. a book. Ask *Singular or plural?* Hold up two books. Ask again.

Write up *book* and *books*. Underline the s. Ensure children understand that the regular plural form takes s.

Teacher's note
Chomp and *munch* are both words used for chewing food noisily and enthustiastically.

211

Grammar

1. Lesson 4 warm-up. ⬇

2. Children read the speech bubble and captions (LB p144). Class repeats.

3. Activity 1: Children talk about characters' likes. ⬇

4. Activity 2: Children complete the sentences according to the pictures.

5. Activity 3: Children write two sentences about their own likes.

6. Prepare children for PB p116 by checking they understand the tasks. Children complete.

Listening

1. Read Nina's speech bubble (LB p145).

2. Children look at the picture. Check understanding. ⬇

3. 🎧 Activity 1: Play LCD2 track 92. Children listen and tick the food each character likes. ⬇

4. Activity 2: Children point and say, e.g. *Mobi likes grapes.*

5. 🎧 Activity 3: Play the song (LCD2 track 93). Children listen. Play it again. Children join in.

After listening

Teach the song in the usual way. ⬇

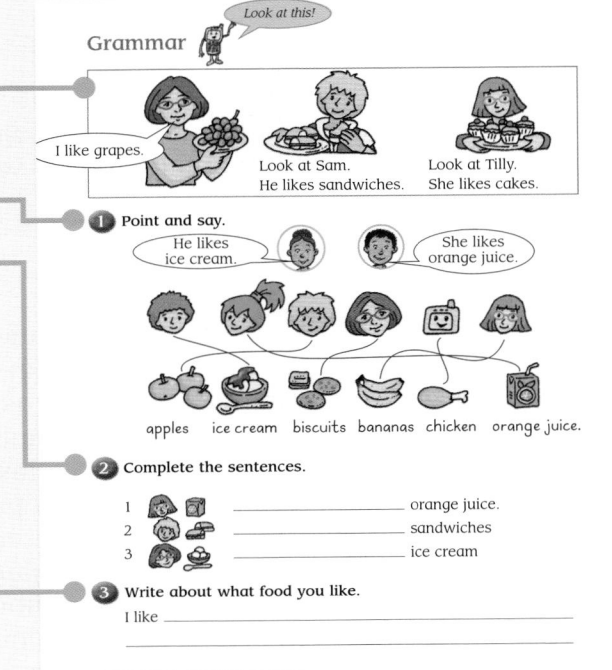

Lesson aim Grammar and listening

Lesson targets Children:

- practise talking and complete sentences about what book characters like
- write two sentences about their own likes
- listen for specific information
- sing and learn a short song.

Key language (words) words for food (structures) *I like ...*, *He/She likes ...*, *We like ...*

Materials Language Book pp144–145, Practice Book p116, Language CD2 tracks 92–93, flashcards of your choice for *Warm-up*

Preparation Listen to the CD before the lesson.

Lesson 4 time division:

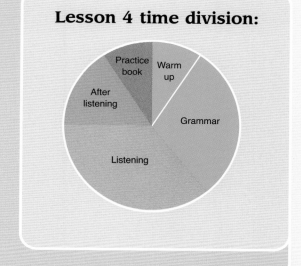

⬇ Lesson 4 Warm-up

1 Put eight flashcards of objects which start with different letters at the bottom of the board. Write the letters well-spaced above. A child shows the class a flashcard. Class says, e.g. **It's a frog.** Ask *What does it begin with?* Elicit the name of the letter: *f.* Child places the card next to the correct letter. Continue with the other cards.

⬇ Grammar

3 Children read speech bubbles. Class repeats.

Say *Look at Ben. What does he like?* Elicit **He likes apples.**

Continue with the other characters.

Children repeat the activity in pairs. Listen to some of them.

⬇ Listening

2 If necessary, explain that Miss Plum is writing a shopping list. They are all going on a picnic.

3 Play the CD. Children listen and point to the character they hear about.
Play the CD again. Children tick the item of food each character likes.

Audioscript

Miss Plum	Now, what can we have for our picnic, Tilly?
Tilly	Hmmmmmm. I know. Let's have apples! I like apples.
Miss Plum	Yes! And Mobi likes grapes. We can have grapes.
Tilly	Sam likes bananas ...
Miss Plum	Nina likes bananas, too. So, apples, grapes, bananas ... I like chicken. Let's have chicken.
Tilly	And sandwiches for Ben. He really likes sandwiches!
Miss Plum	So, apples, grapes, bananas, chicken, sandwiches ... Is that all?
Tilly	Well, Mobi likes orange juice.
Miss Plum	Mobi likes everything! So, orange juice and ... biscuits?
Tilly	Yes, biscuits. And cakes! We all like biscuits and cakes!

Teacher's note
A *daffodil* is a native UK flower, usually bright yellow. It grows wild and is also a popular garden flower for the spring. The *fireside* is a part of a living room which surrounds the fireplace. In the UK this is typically the sitting area of the room.

213

Activity 1

1. Lesson 5 warm-up.
2. (LB p146) Point out pictures and words with 'magic e'.
3. Play LCD2 track 94 twice. Children follow in books.
4. Read sentences.
5. Read and ask questions.
6. Read with the class.

Activity 2

1. Children hold sounds cards. Read the sounds.
2. Close up gradually.
3. Read the word.
4. Children look, say and write.
5. Children match rhymes.

Activity 3

1. Write up words. Class/individuals read.
2. Children read in pairs. Listen to pairs.
3. Children check words and tick.

Practice Book

Children complete PB p117.

Phonics games and activities

1. Play *What's the word?*
2. Play *Start the word.*

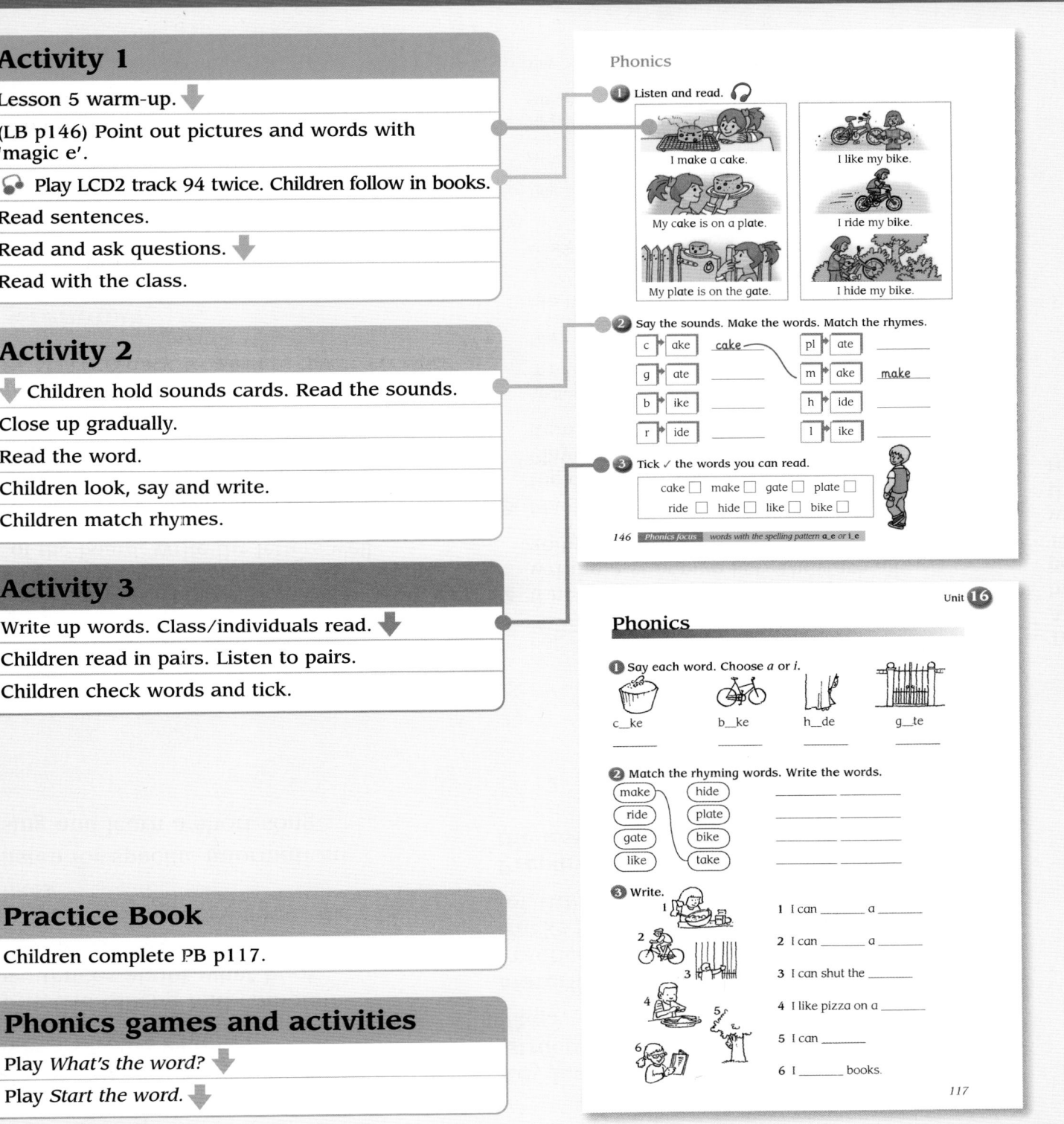

Lesson aim Phonic recognition

Lesson targets Children:

- read, pronounce and spell words ending with 'magic e'
- recognise and say the component parts of each word
- match rhyming words with 'magic e'.

Target words *cake, make, gate, plate, hide, ride, bike, like*

Materials Language Book p146, Practice Book p117, Language CD2 track 94, cards for sounds

Preparation Listen to the CD before the lesson. Make large cards for the beginnings and endings of the words as shown in Activity 2, LB p146.

Lesson 5 time division:

Lesson 5 Warm-up

1 Sing *I like the flowers* from Lesson 4 (LB p145, LCD2 track 93).

Activity 1

2 Ask (one question for each line)
Who can make a cake?
What colour is the plate?
Where is the plate?
What is Tilly standing next to?
Can she ride it?
Is she riding her bike now?

Make sure all the words in the text are understood.

Activity 2

3 Follow the procedure for introducing the component parts of each word and reading each word which is given in detail in the Introduction (p10).

Note: The words in this exercise are processed in two stages: word beginnings and word endings, rather than breaking each word down into individual phonemes.

If you wish, explain that 'magic e' at the end of a word makes the vowel in the middle of the word say its name instead of its sound: /a/ becomes /eɪ/; /ɪ/ becomes /ʌɪ/, etc.

Activity 3

1 Write the eight words on the board. Point in random order. Individuals and/or the class reads them.

Phonics games and activities

1 Play *What's the word?* (p75) with words from previous units.

2 **Start the word**
Put up endings *ate, ake, ide, ike.* Put up phonemes, e.g. *b, c, g, pl, m, r, t, sn.* Children make words and read.

215

Before writing

1. Lesson 6 warm-up.
2. Read Miss Plum's speech bubble (LB p147).
3. Children look at the picture.
4. A child reads the first sentence.
5. Another child reads *We like ...* and the list of food. If you wish, whole class reads again.

Shared writing

1. A child reads the first sentence (LB p147). Children say sentences for each character. Write them on the board.
2. Class reads. Rub them off before children write.

Practice Book

Writing

1. Children read the words (PB p118).
2. Children colour and write.

Your writing

1. (PB p119) Children match the characters and fruit.
2. Children write sentences.

After writing

Children practise finding parts of speech.

Class writing

Let's write about food we like!

Let's have a picnic! We like ...

pizza orange ice sandwiches
        juice cream

chicken cakes bananas grapes

1. Look and write.

The children love picnics. Tilly likes

Don't forget to draw and write what **you** like, too!

Writing focus   food; use of to like   147

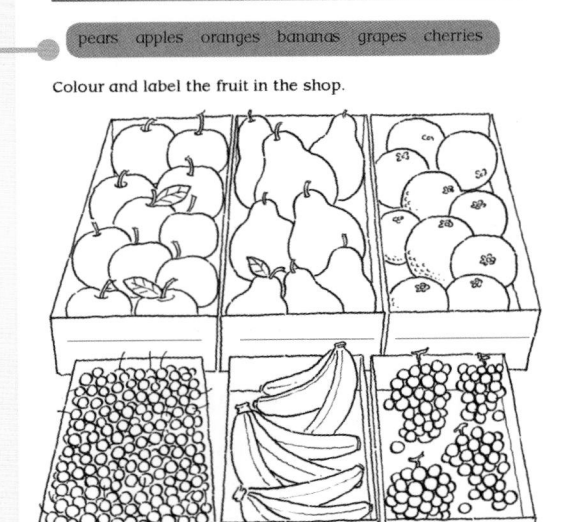

Writing

pears apples oranges bananas grapes cherries

Colour and label the fruit in the shop.

118

Your writing

Unit 16

Nina   Sam   Tilly   Ben   Meg   Scott

1. Write a sentence about each child.

Nina likes pears.

Sam likes _____

Tilly _____

_____

_____

2. Write about you.

I like _____

I _____

I _____

119

Lesson aim Writing

Lesson targets Children:

- write sentences using information in a picture
- label pictures from picture prompts
- write what other children like; write about personal likes.

Key language (words) *friend*, words for numbers

(structures) *He/She likes ..., I like ...*

Materials Language Book p147, Practice Book pp118 and 119

Lesson 6 time division:

After Writing / Warm up / Before writing / Practice book / Shared writing

⬇ Lesson 6 Warm-up

1 Play *Object chain* (p248) using foods.

Elicit all food/drink words children know. Write them on the board. Start the chain. When an item is mentioned rub it off. Continue the chain until all items are removed.

Variation: Ask about colours of items that vary, e.g. *apples, grapes, cakes, sweets.* List colours they suggest. Ask about the size of items. Elicit and write up *big, small.*

Start the chain again.
This time children add an adjective: ... *a red apple, a big pizza, a pink cake, a green apple, a small cake, etc.*

⬇ Before writing

3 Ask children to tell you everything they can about the picture and what is in it.

Ask *Who can you see?*
What is/are he/she/they doing?
What is on the board? etc.

⬇ Shared writing

1 Ask questions to prompt answers, e.g. *What does Tilly like?* Elicit the answer.

Write it on the board beginning with the proper noun. Ask about the other characters.

⬇ After writing

Write up sentences, e.g. *Sam likes yellow bananas. Nina likes green grapes. Tilly's cake is pink. Ben's pizza is thin.*

Ask different children to find the verb, the adjective, the noun and the proper noun. Children circle them in a different colour for each part of speech.

If colours are not available, children can underline, double underline and draw a circle and a box around the correct word.

Before listening

1. Lesson 1 warm-up.
2. Show poster 17. Read the title. Ask questions.
3. Point and name new clothes words. Children come forward; find in main picture.
4. Show flashcards 164–172 and name clothes. Class repeats.

Shared listening

1. Play FCD track 34. Point to characters when they speak.
2. Ask about the gold star.
3. Ask *Who? What? Whose?* questions.
4. Play the FCD track 34 and point to characters again.

Dialogue practice

1. Say the new words. Children point in books (FB pp40–41). Point on poster for children to check.
2. Show clothes flashcards 122–130. Children name.
3. Children close books. Play FCD track 35 and show character flashcards. Class repeats lines in pauses.
4. Groups say lines by character.
5. Individuals act dialogue.
6. Play FCD track 34 again. Children follow text or point to main picture.

After listening

1. Ask questions. Children find the answers in the book.
2. Do the flashcard and word card matching activity.
3. Children put the last sticker star in the correct place on FB pp46–47.

17 Time to go home

hat
shoes
T-shirt
jeans
dress
jumper
shorts
socks
skirt

17 Time to go home

The children are back in Sam's tree house. Today is their last day on the island. They are packing their bags. Tomorrow they are going home.

hat
skirt
dress
jumper
shorts
shoes
jeans
T-shirt
socks

What a mess! Look at all these clothes!
Come on. Let's pack our bags.
OK.

Whose T-shirt is this?
It's Ben's T-shirt.

Whose hat is this?
It's Tilly's.

Whose jeans are these?
They're Nina's, I think.

And whose socks are these?
They're Sam's.

Here you are, Sam. Catch!

Hey! Careful!

What's this? What's in my sock?

Look! It's a star!

Wow!

Fantastic! The children are very happy. They have got the nine gold stars.
How can they put the stars back in the sky?

Star light, star bright,
No stars are missing tonight.

40 Whose ... is this? It is ... 's ... Whose ... are these? They are ... 's

41

218

Lesson aim Fluency

Lesson targets Children:

- listen for pronunciation and intonation
- repeat dialogue accurately
- act out dialogue with expression
- talk about clothes.

Key language (words) *dress, hat, jeans, jumper, shoes, shorts, skirt, socks, T-shirt* (structures) *Whose ... is this? It's ...'s ... . Whose ... are these? They are ...'s.*

Language for understanding *bags, clothes, pack, What a mess! Catch!*

Materials Poster 17, Fluency Book pp40–41, Fluency CD tracks 34–35, character flashcards 1–5, flashcards 164–172 and word cards for clothes

Preparation Listen to the CD before the lesson. Make word cards for clothes (see key words).

Lesson 1 time division:

Lesson 1 Warm-up

1 Check with the class how many stars are missing. Say the *Star chant*. Play *Action mime* (see p99, 248).

Before listening

2 Ask *Where are the children?*
Are they playing?
Are they watching TV?
What are they doing?
What is Miss Plum doing?
Look at the children.
Who likes blue?/green?/pink and purple?/red and brown?

Shared listening

2 Ask *What is in Sam's sock?*
How many stars have they got now?
How many stars are missing?
Are the children happy?

3 Ask *Whose hat is Ben holding?*
What is Sam holding?
Whose jeans is Tilly holding?
Who is holding Sam's socks?

After listening

1 Ask *Can you find Ben's hat? Where is it?*
Can you find Tilly's jumper? Where is it?
Can you find Nina's skirt? Where is it?
Can you find Sam's jumper? Where is it?
Can you find Mobi? Where is he?

2 Put up flashcards of clothes items. Children take turns to match word cards to pictures. Class reads all the words. This could be done in two teams.

Ask questions, e.g. *What colour is the dress? What colour are the shorts?*

219

Before reading

1. Lesson 2 warm-up. ⬇

2. 📖 Revise clothes words with flashcards 164–172.

3. Children open books (LB pp148–149). Ask questions. ⬇

Shared reading

1. 🎧 Play LCD2 track 95. Children follow text in book.

2. Read line by line. Ask questions. ⬇

3. Read with the class.

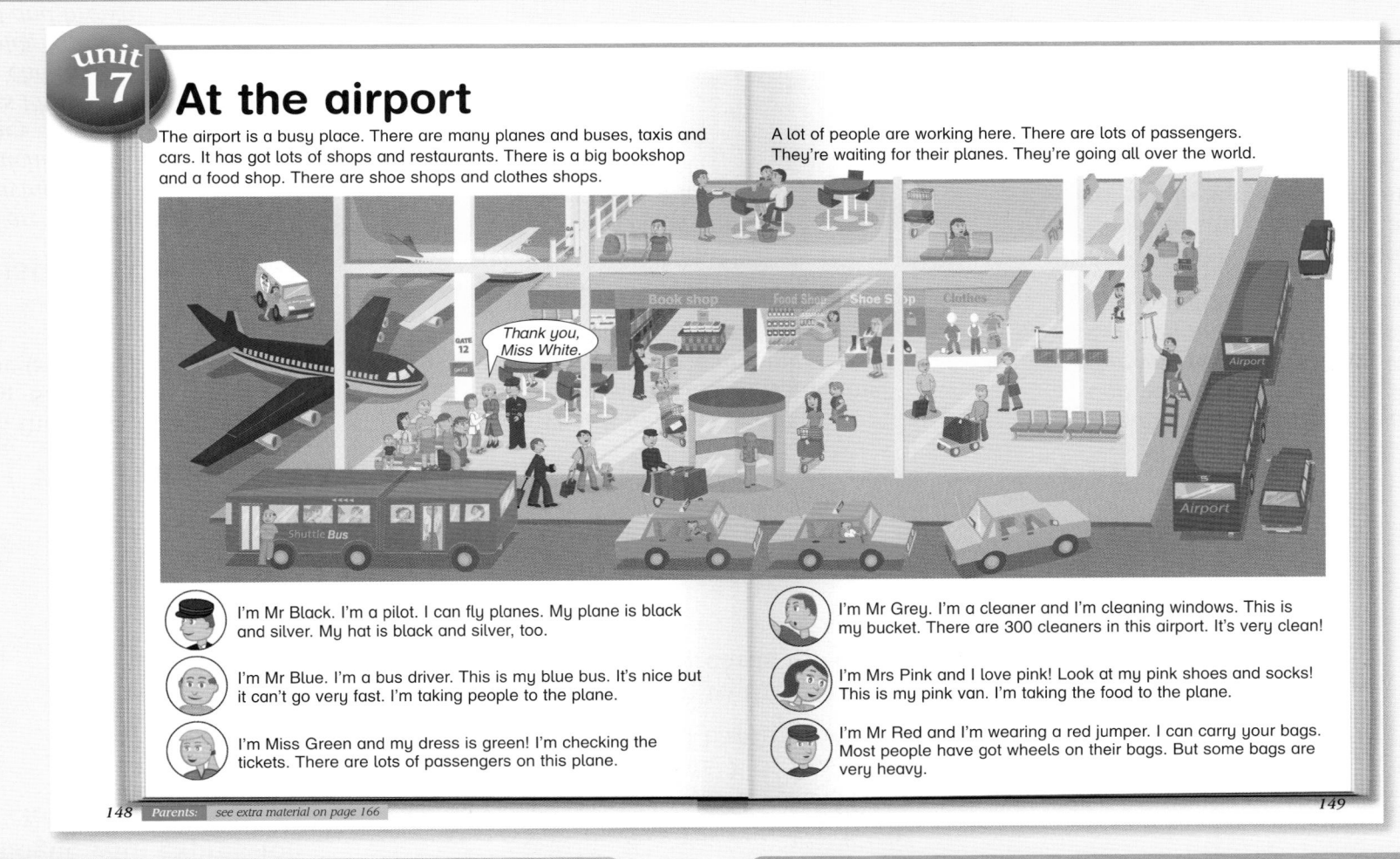

unit 17

At the airport

The airport is a busy place. There are many planes and buses, taxis and cars. It has got lots of shops and restaurants. There is a big bookshop and a food shop. There are shoe shops and clothes shops.

A lot of people are working here. There are lots of passengers. They're waiting for their planes. They're going all over the world.

Thank you, Miss White.

I'm Mr Black. I'm a pilot. I can fly planes. My plane is black and silver. My hat is black and silver, too.

I'm Mr Blue. I'm a bus driver. This is my blue bus. It's nice but it can't go very fast. I'm taking people to the plane.

I'm Miss Green and my dress is green! I'm checking the tickets. There are lots of passengers on this plane.

I'm Mr Grey. I'm a cleaner and I'm cleaning windows. This is my bucket. There are 300 cleaners in this airport. It's very clean!

I'm Mrs Pink and I love pink! Look at my pink shoes and socks! This is my pink van. I'm taking the food to the plane.

I'm Mr Red and I'm wearing a red jumper. I can carry your bags. Most people have got wheels on their bags. But some bags are very heavy.

148 Parents: see extra material on page 166

149

Reading practice

1. Give reading practice. Use some or all of the following:
   - Children read again as a class.
   - Groups read different sections.
   - Individuals read different sections.

2. 🎧 Class listens again to LCD2 track 95 and follows in LB.

After reading

Play *Guess the person*. ⬇

Lesson aim Reading

Lesson targets Children:

- follow a text read out to them
- listen for pronunciation and intonation
- read the text aloud with accurate pronunciation and intonation
- learn and understand new vocabulary items
- understand the sense of the text as a whole
- answer simple comprehension questions.

Key language (words) *dress, hat, jeans, jumper, shoes, shorts, skirt, socks, T-shirt* **(structures)** *Whose is this/are these? It's/They're ... 's.*

Words for understanding *airport, busy, taxi, pilot, driver, passengers, cleaner (n.), cleaning, wheels, bags, heavy, bucket, carry*

Materials Language Book pp148–149, Language CD2 track 95, flashcards 164–172

Preparation Listen to the CD before the lesson.

Lesson 2 time division:

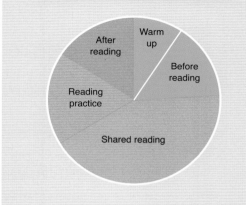

⬇ Lesson 2 Warm-up

1 Say *Take ... a head, some shoulders* (LB p135).

⬇ Before reading

3 Ask *How many taxis are there? Where's the shoe shop? Where's the book shop? What colour is the bus? Where is Mrs Pink? Where is Mr Blue?*

⬇ Shared reading

2 Ask *What can Mr Black do? What colour is his plane? Where is it? Can Mr Blue's bus go fast? Does he take people to the shops? What is Miss Green doing? What is Mr Grey doing? How many cleaners are there at the airport? What does Mrs Pink like? Is she taking bags to the plane? What is she taking? What can Mr Red do? Are the bags small?*

⬇ After reading

Guess the person
Say, e.g.
He drives a bus.
He wears a black and silver hat.
She drives a van.
He has a grey bucket.
She is standing at the gate.

Class must guess who the person is.

Lesson 3: Comprehension and sentence building

UNIT 17

Reading and understanding
SESSION 1

1. Session 1 warm-up.
2. Re-read *At the airport* (LB pp148–149).
3. Activity 1 (LB p150): Children read the words in the box. Ask what the first picture shows. Ask a child to say the whole sentence. Children write the word. Class reads the sentence. Continue with the other sentences.
4. Activity 2: Children read and circle.
5. Activity 3: Two children read the bubbles. Class repeats. Children talk about the pictures in pairs.
6. Play the *Get active!* game.
7. Prepare children for PB p120. Read the text under the pictures with them and check they understand the task. Children complete.

Working with words
SESSION 2

1. Session 2 warm-up.
2. Activity 1 (LB p151): Children look in the wordsearch for the pictured items. They write the words.

Sentence building

1. Go through the information in the box (LB p151).
2. Activity 1: Children order the words and write.
3. Prepare children for PB p121. Read the sentence in the box and check they understand the task. Children complete.

Extension activity

Do the word order activity.

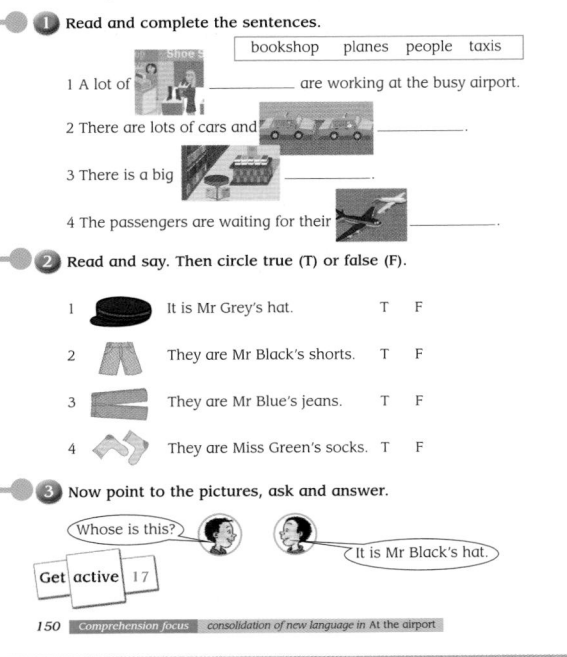

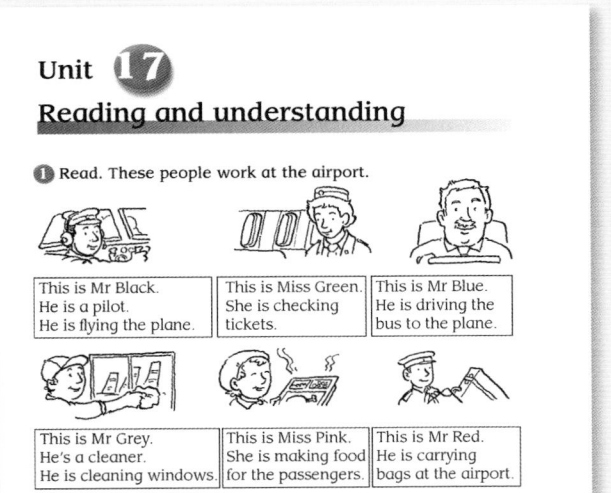

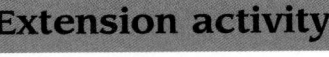

222

Lesson aim Comprehension, vocabulary and sentence building

Lesson targets Children:
- complete sentences using picture clues and given words
- identify correct/incorrect statements
- talk about possession
- recognise and write vocabulary items
- order words in a sentence correctly.

Key language (words) words for clothing (structures) *Whose is this?*

Materials Language Book pp150–151, Practice Book pp120–121, words on separate cards for *I have got, pink, socks,* flashcards 164–172 for *Get active!*, word cards for your choice for *Extension.*

Preparation Make word cards for *Sentence building* and *Extension.*

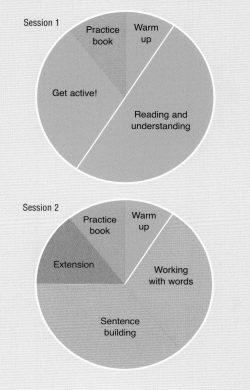

Lesson 3 time division:

Session 1 — Warm up, Practice book, Get active!, Reading and understanding

Session 2 — Warm up, Practice book, Extension, Working with words, Sentence building

⬇ Lesson 3 Session 1 Warm-up

1 Play *It begins with …* Use three items for up to five different letters, e.g. *bed, books, balloons, crab, clock, cake, snake, stars, sky, radio, rock, rabbit, lamp, lions, legs.*

When the cards are placed under each letter, say *I can see something that begins with* (e.g.) *r.* Children guess the item.

⬇ Reading and understanding

4 A child reads the sentence. Class repeats. Check that children remember: *true* means correct; *false* means incorrect. Children circle *T* or *F.*

To check answers ask *Is it Mr Grey's hat? Whose hat is it?*

6 Get active!
Put up flashcards of *hat, jeans, jumper, shoes, shorts, socks.*

Below in scrambled order on the left write the initial phoneme for each word. Write the rest of each word on the right, again in scrambled order.
Children find initial sounds for each item then the rest of the word. Then draw a line between the two halves and put the correct flashcard next to it. Class reads.

⬇ Lesson 3 Session 2 Warm-up

Play *Simon says* (TG p95).

⬇ Working with words

2 Explain that jeans and shorts are treated as plural items because they have two legs. Put up the hat flashcard. Ask *How many?* **One.** Write *This is a hat.* Put up the jeans/shorts flashcards and write the words underneath. Underline the *s.* Count the legs on the jeans. Write *These are jeans.* Do the same with shorts.

⬇ Sentence building

1 Read the first sentence in the box. Ask children to read the example sentences. Put the word cards on the board for the first example. Ask children to name the noun/adjective.
Explain that in English the adjective goes in front of the noun. Let a child order the sentence correctly.

⬇ Extension activity

Put up scrambled sentences. Children take turns to order the words.

223

Grammar

1. Lesson 4 warm-up.

2. Pairs of children read the speech bubbles (LB p152). Class repeats.

3. Point out the *Remember!* box.

4. Activity 1: Two pairs read the speech bubbles. Class repeats. Ask/Help individuals to form questions about the other items of clothing. Other children answer.

5. Activity 2: Children read the sentences. Class repeats. Elicit the next two sentences. Class repeats. Children write.

6. Prepare children for PB p122 by checking they understand the tasks. Children complete.

Listening

1. Read Nina's speech bubble (LB p153).

2. Explain they will hear the people in the pictures.

3. Activity 1: Play LCD2 track 96. Children listen and look. Play it again. Children write the numbers.

4. Activity 2: Play the song (LCD2 track 97). Children listen. Play it again. Encourage children to join in.

After listening

Teach the song in the usual way.

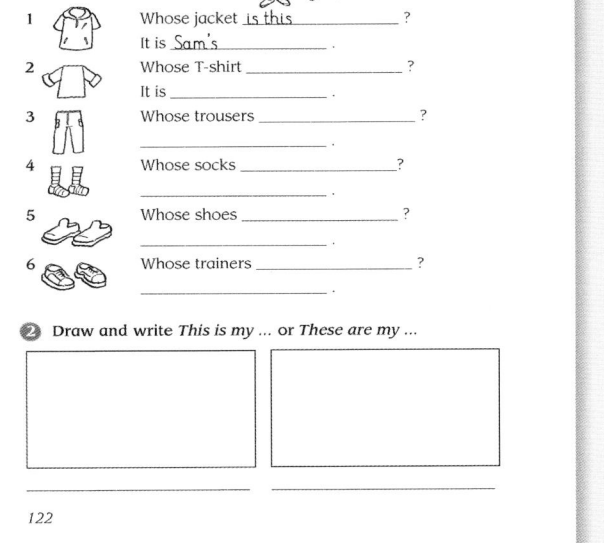

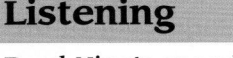

Lesson aim Grammar and listening

Lesson targets Children:

- practise questions and statements about possessions
- write statements about possessions
- listen for gist
- sing and learn a short song.

Key language (words) words for clothing
(structures) *Whose is this?/are these? It's ..., They're ...*

Materials Language Book pp152–153, Practice Book p122, Language CD2 tracks 96–97

Preparation Listen to the CD before the lesson.

Lesson 4 time division:

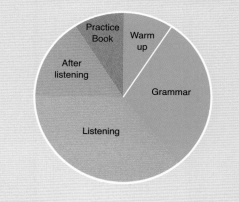

⬇ Lesson 4 Warm-up

1 Play *Object chain* (TG p248) with clothes and colours: *In my bag I've got a green hat, a yellow T-shirt and blue jeans.*

⬇ Grammar

3 Write *It's* = *It is* on the board. Read each phrase. Class repeats.

Do the same with *They're* = *They are*.

⬇ Listening

2 Children look at the pictures. Ask who the people are. Ask what they do. If you wish, children can look back at pp148–9 and find the people working at the airport.

3 Audioscript

Voice	1	
Mr Blue		Get on the bus, please. The bus is leaving now.
Voice	2	
Miss Pink		We've got sandwiches, orange juice and cakes today.
Voice	3	
Miss Green		Can I see your ticket, please?
Voice	4	
Mr Black		Welcome aboard flight number S24. Have a good flight.
Voice	5	
Mr Grey		Where's my bucket? Oh, there it is.
Voice	6	
Mr Red		Oh, this bag is so big.

225

Activity 1

1. Lesson 5 warm-up.
2. (LB p154) Name the objects on the right of the box.
3. Play LCD2 track 98 twice. Children follow in books.
4. Read text.
5. Read and ask questions.
6. Read with the class.
7. Demonstrate changing the beginnings of the words.

Activities 2 and 3

1. Children hold sounds cards. Read the sounds.
2. Close up gradually.
3. Read the word. Class reads.
4. Children match and write.

Activity 4

1. Write up words. Class/individuals read.
2. Children read in pairs. Listen to pairs.
3. Children check words and tick.

Practice Book

Make sure children understand the activities on PB p123. Children complete.

Phonics games and activities

1. Play *Odd one out.*
2. Play *Look, write, check.*

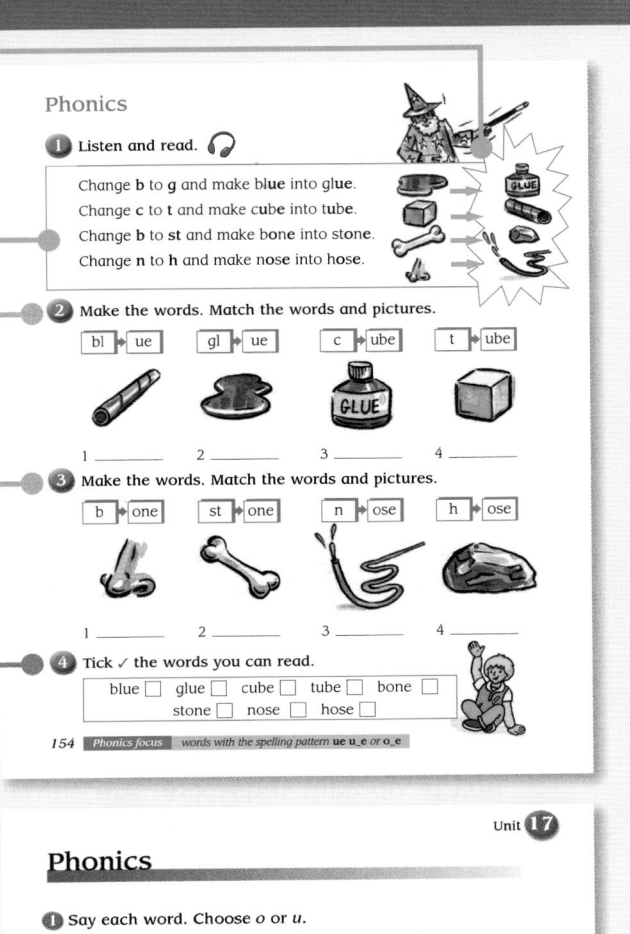

Lesson aim Phonic recognition

Lesson targets Children:

- read, pronounce and spell words ending with 'magic e'
- recognise and say the component parts of each word
- match rhyming words with 'magic e'.

Target words *blue, glue, cube, tube, bone, stone, nose, hose*

Materials Language Book p154, Practice Book p123, Language CD2 track 98, cards for sounds

Preparation Listen to the CD before the lesson. Make large cards for the beginnings and endings of the words as shown in Activities 2 and 3 on LB p154

Lesson 5 time division:

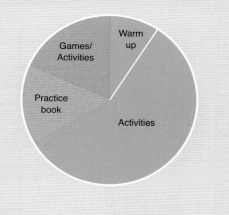

Warm up
Games/ Activities
Practice book
Activities

⬇ Lesson 5 Warm-up

1 Sing *Little silver aeroplane* from Lesson 4 (LB p153, LCD2 track 97).

⬇ Activity 1

5 Ask *It is long and thin. What is it?*
Nina likes this colour.
It's in the middle of your face.
It has six sides the same.
You can stick paper with it.
You have lots of these in your body.
You can use this to put water on plants.

Make sure all the words in the text are understood.

7 Write up *ue*. Put *bl* in front. Children read. Change to *gl*. Children read. Do the same with the other word endings and beginnings.

⬇ Activities 2 and 3

1 Follow the procedure for introducing the component parts of each word and reading each word which is given in detail in the Introduction (p10).

Note: The words in this exercise are processed in two stages: word beginnings and word endings, rather than breaking each word down into individual phonemes.

Children look at the picture and find the matching word. Ask *What is number 1?* etc. Elicit answers. Children write.

⬇ Activity 4

1 Write the eight words on the board. Point in random order. Individuals and/or the class reads them.

⬇ Phonics games and activities

1 Play *Odd one out* (p37). Use, e.g. *spell, ball, smell, bell, wind, hand, sand, band, cake, make, gate, take, stop, star, stone, shoe.*

2 Do *Look, write, check* (TG p75) with these words or any others you wish the class to practise.

227

Before writing

1. Lesson 6 warm-up.
2. Read Miss Plum's speech bubble (LB p155).
3. Children read the words under the pictures.
4. Children draw and colour two or more items in each bag.

Shared writing

1. Ask a child to read the first sentence (LB p155).
2. Elicit two sentences for each character. Write them on the board. Class reads.
3. Rub them off before class writes. Point out the *Remember!* box.

Practice Book

Writing

1. Children read the words (PB p124).
2. Children complete the dot-to-dot and label the clothing.

Your writing

1. (PB p125) Talk about the places.
2. Children choose a place.
3. They choose and colour four items.
4. Children write.

After writing

Children read their sentences. Hear as many as possible.

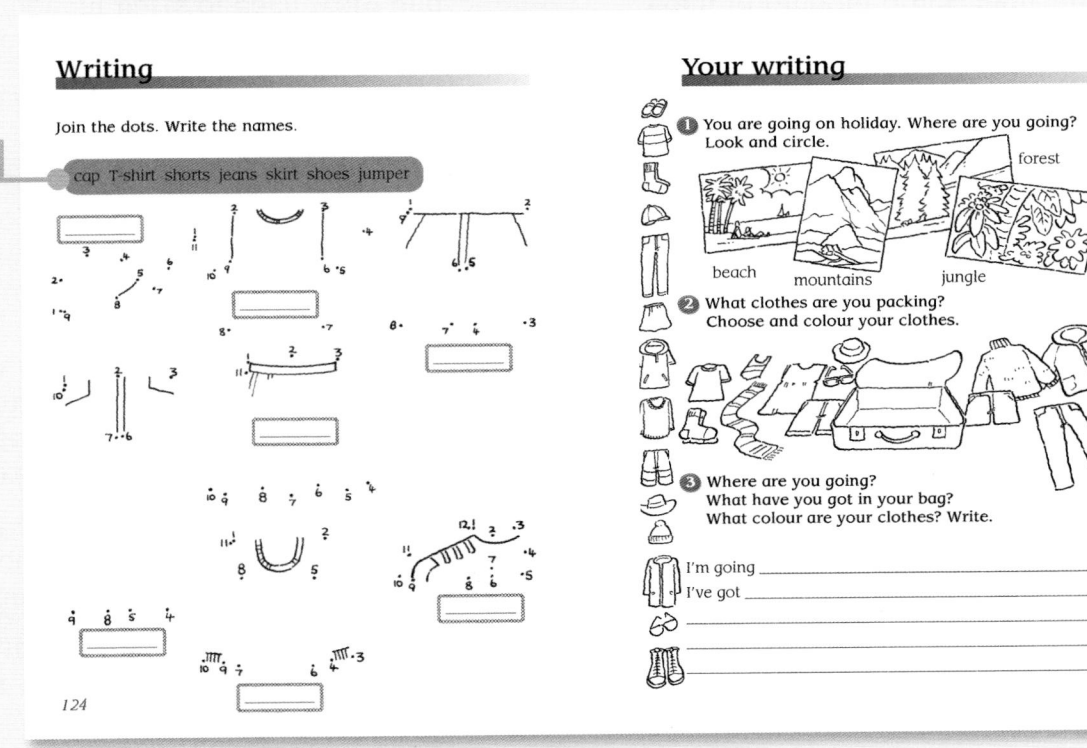

Lesson aim Writing

Lesson targets Children:

- draw pictures and write sentences describing them
- draw and label clothing items
- colour items of clothing and write about them.

Key language (words) words for clothing
(structures) *Sam has got ..., I have got ...*

Materials Language Book p155, Practice Book pp124–125

Lesson 6 time division:

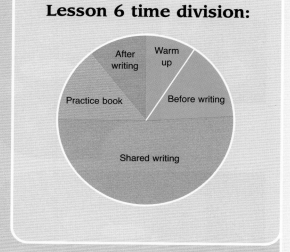

After writing | Warm up
Practice book | Before writing
Shared writing

⬇ Lesson 6 Warm-up

1 Do a numbers game, e.g. *Number chain, Stand up numbers , Line up numbers* (TG p43, p248).

⬇ Shared writing

2 Ask a child to tell you one thing that Nina has got. Write it on the board, e.g. **Nina has got a blue T-shirt.** Ask for a second sentence, e.g. **She has got blue jeans.**

Continue in the same way with the other characters.

3 When children begin writing, make sure they understand that they must write their own sentences according to what they have drawn and coloured.

Go around helping them as they work.

⬇ Practice Book

1 **Your writing**
Ask what the places are: **beach, mountains, forest, jungle**. Write them on the board.
Ask what the weather is like in each place. *Is it hot? Is it raining?* etc.
Ask what clothes children would take for the different places. Write two or three items under each place.

4 Children complete the first two sentences and write three more.

Before listening

1. Lesson 1 warm-up.
2. Show poster 18. Read the title.
3. Ask questions about the first four pictures.
4. Ask if the children like fireworks.

Shared listening

1. 🎵 Play FCD track 36. Point to characters when they speak.
2. Ask about the stars.
3. Ask *What? Where? How?* questions.
4. Make sure children understand *round, over, into, towards*. Use pictures on poster. Demonstrate movements using classroom objects if you wish.
5. 🎵 Play FCD track 36 and point to characters again.

Dialogue practice

1. Say phrases from speech bubbles. Children point in books (FB p43). Point on poster for children to check.
2. 🎵 📇 Children close books. Play FCD track 37 and show character flashcards. Class repeats lines in pauses.
3. 📇 Groups say lines by character.
4. 📇 Individuals act dialogue.
5. 🎵 Play FCD track 36 again. Children follow text or point to main picture.

After listening

1. Children close books. Ask children if they can remember where each of the stars was found.
2. Review

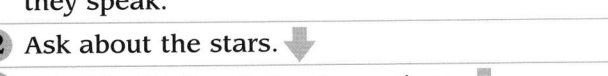

18 Fireworks!

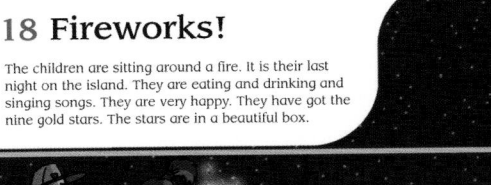

18 Fireworks!

The children are sitting around a fire. It is their last night on the island. They are eating and drinking and singing songs. They are very happy. They have got the nine gold stars. The stars are in a beautiful box.

Look! Fireworks!

Oh! They're beautiful!

Wow!

Fantastic!

Well done, children. You've got all the stars.
Yes, we have. But how can we put the stars in the sky?
Like this. Open the box, Sam.
OK.

Take two or three stars each.
Be careful, Ben! Don't drop them.
Walk round the fire in a circle.

Like this?
Yes. That's right. Count to three and throw your stars into the fire.
One, two, three!

Fireworks are flying over the children's heads.
They are flying up into the sky.
They are flying towards the moon.

Look at the sky!

The stars are in the sky.

There isn't a big hole.

Hooray!

Well done!

42 round   into   over   towards

43

230

Lesson aim Fluency

Lesson targets Children:

- listen for pronunciation and intonation
- repeat dialogue accurately
- act out dialogue with expression
- talk about events in the story.

Key language (words) *round, into, over, towards*

Language for understanding *box, circle, fire, fireworks, songs, drop, throw, flying, Well done! That's right. Count to three.*

Materials Poster 18, Fluency Book pp42–45, Fluency CD tracks 36–38, character flashcards 1–5

Preparation Listen to the CD before the lesson. If you have a star poster in the classroom which shows where the stars were found, you may wish to take it down.

Lesson 1 time division:

Warm up
Before listening
Shared listening
Dialogue practice
After listening

⬇ Lesson 1 Warm-up

1 Sing *Twinkle, twinkle little star* from LB p31, LCD1 track 22.

⬇ Before listening

3 Ask (1st picture) *Is it day or night?*
What is Sam holding?
What is in the box? Can you guess?

(2nd picture) *What are the children doing?*
What are they holding?

(3rd picture) *What can you see in the sky?*
What colours are they?

(4th picture) *Where are the gold stars now?*
Is the moon sad?

⬇ Shared listening

2 Ask *Where are the nine stars now?*
Is there a hole in the sky?
What does Mobi say?

3 Ask *What are the children doing?*
Where are the nine gold stars?
How can they put the stars back in the sky?
Where are the fireworks flying?

⬇ Review

Children look at FB pp44 and 45. Play FCD track 38. Children listen and follow. Ask *What is your favourite part of the story? Why? What is your favourite place on the island? Why?*

Encourage children to tell you about things they like on the pages.

Before reading

1 Lesson 2 warm-up. ⬇

2 Teach *quickly*. Demonstrate by walking quickly. Say *I am walking quickly*. Do the same for *slowly*.

3 Children open books (LB pp156–157). Ask questions. ⬇

Shared reading

1 🎧 Play LCD2 track 99. Children follow text in book.

2 Read line by line. Ask questions. ⬇

3 Read with the class.

Reading practice

1 Give reading practice. Use some or all of the following:
- Children read again as a class.
- Groups read different sections.
- Individuals read different sections.

2 🎧 Class listens again to LCD2 track 99 and follows in LB.

After reading

Talk about words for sounds and noises. ⬇

Lesson aim Reading

Lesson targets Children:

- follow a text read out to them
- listen for pronunciation and intonation
- read the text aloud with accurate pronunciation and intonation
- learn and understand new vocabulary items
- understand the sense of the text as a whole
- answer simple comprehension questions.

Key language (words) *quickly, slowly*

Words for understanding *faster, roman candle, rose, flow, glow, sparkler, silver, onomatopoeic words*

Materials Language Book pp156–157, Language CD2 track 99, flashcards 32–33 for *Warm-up*

Preparation Listen to the CD before the lesson.

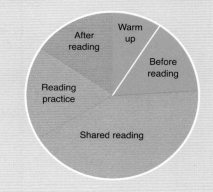

Lesson 2 time division:

After reading · Warm up · Before reading · Reading practice · Shared reading

---

⬇ Lesson 2 Warm-up

1 Play *Action mime* (TG p99, p248). Use all the flashcards for actions from Units 8–11.

⬇ Before reading

3

Ask *What can you see in the sky?*
What colours can you see?
Can you see a firework like a wheel?/like a flower?/like a waterfall?

⬇ Shared reading

2 Ask *What colour does Mum like?*
What colour does Dad like?
What sound does the wheel make?
What colour is the rose?
Where does it go?
Does the waterfall start fast?
Is it bright?
Does it flow slowly now?
Is this firework like a road?/the sea? What is it like?
What sound does it make?
What colours is the roman candle? What sounds does it make?
Look at the firework at the bottom. What sounds does it make?

⬇ After reading

Elicit words for the sounds of fireworks. Ask what other words for sounds the class can think of. Write all words for sounds on the board.

Remind the class of Unit 14. Children can look back and find the weather noises. What other things make these noises?
Draw these items:
fire, drum, insect, clock, car, can of cola.
Ask the class what sound on the board best matches the object, e.g.
fire – crackle; drum – bang; insect – whizz; clock, car, - whirr; can of cola – fizz.

Reading and understanding

1. Session 1 warm-up.

2. Re-read *Fireworks!* (LB pp156–157).

3. Activity 1 (LB p158): Children read the sentences. They find the matching picture and write the letter.

4. Activity 2: Children read the words in the box. They read the words below and write the rhyming word from the box.

5. Play the *Get active!* game.

6. Prepare children for PB p126. Read the poem with them and check they understand the tasks. Children complete.

Working with words

1. Session 2 warm-up.

2. Demonstrate the *I spy* game (LB p159).

3. Children play the game in pairs.

Sentence building

1. Write up the verb (LB p159). Underline the 3rd person singular *s*. Read it with the class. Read Mobi's bubble. Elicit sentences using the verb.

2. Activity 1: Children complete sentences. Go through the sentences orally before children write.

3. Prepare children for PB p127. Read the verb in the box and check they understand the tasks. Children complete.

Extension activity

Groups sort muddled sentences.

Reading and understanding

1 Read and match the pictures.

1 This firework goes round and round. ☐
2 You can write your name with this. ☐
3 It falls slowly, then faster. ☐
4 Way up high. There it goes. It's a firework rose. ☐
5 The candle glows and goes Ffffffffft! ☐
6 You can see silver and gold stars. ☐

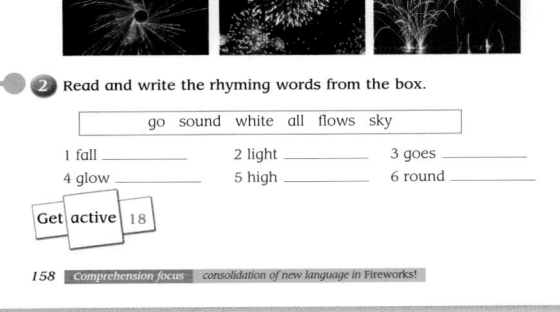

2 Read and write the rhyming words from the box.

go sound white all flows sky

1 fall _____   2 light _____   3 goes _____
4 glow _____   5 high _____   6 round _____

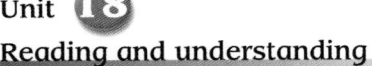 Get active 18

158   *Comprehension focus*   *consolidation of new language in Fireworks!*

Unit 18
Reading and understanding

1 Read.

The catherine wheel goes round and round.
It makes a whizzing, whirring sound.

You can write your name in a sparkler's light
You can write it in blue and yellow, pink and white.

The waterfall is a river of light.
It fizzes and falls and lights up the night.

Look at the roman candle and see it glow
Watch the lights as they go
Ffffffffffffffffffffffffft. Ploof!

2 Write.

1 What goes round and round?
   The catherine wheel goes round and round.

2 What fizzes and falls and lights up the night?
   _____

3 What goes Ffffffffffffffffffffffffft. Ploof!
   _____

3 What word rhymes with:

1 round? __sound__   2 light? _____
3 night? _____   4 glow? _____

126

Working with words

18

1 Play a game.

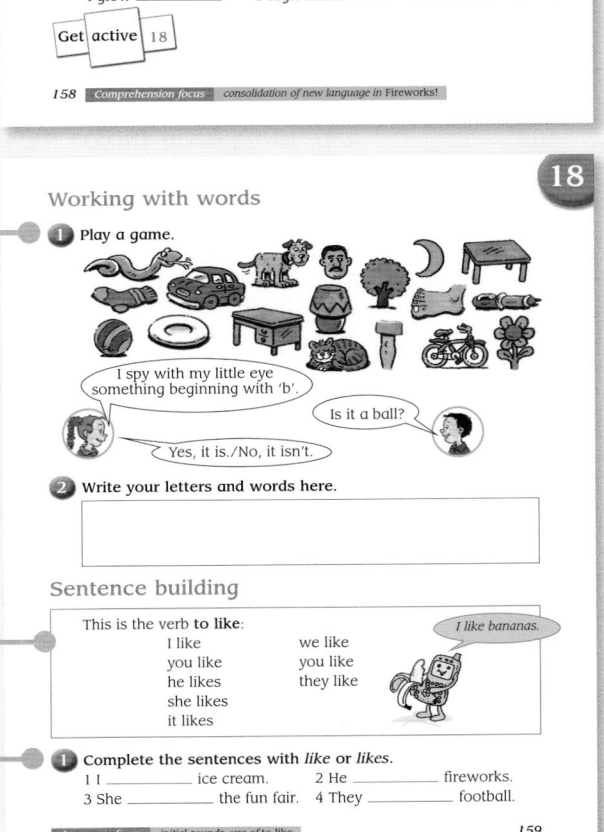

I spy with my little eye something beginning with 'b'.

Is it a ball?

Yes, it is./No, it isn't.

2 Write your letters and words here.

Sentence building

This is the verb **to like**:

I like   we like
you like   you like
he likes   they like
she likes
it likes

I like bananas.

1 Complete the sentences with *like* or *likes*.

1 I _____ ice cream.   2 He _____ fireworks.
3 She _____ the fun fair.   4 They _____ football.

Language focus   *initial sounds; use of to like*

159

Sentence building
Unit 18

I like	we like
you like	you like
he **likes**	they like
she **likes**	
it **likes**	

1 Complete the sentences with *like* or *likes*.

1 She _____ red apples.
2 I _____ you.
3 He _____ computer games.
4 We _____ bees.
5 You _____ playing football.

2 Complete the answers.

1   Does Nina like oranges?
    Yes. Nina _____ oranges.

2   Does Ben like the dog?
    Yes. Ben _____ the dog.

3   Do the girls like flowers?
    Yes. The girls _____ flowers.

127

Lesson aim Comprehension, vocabulary and sentence building

Lesson targets Children:
- match sentences to pictures
- match and write rhyming words
- play a game using initial letters
- practise the verb *to like*.

Key language (words) words from Lessons 1 and 2
(structures) *I like ..., He/She likes ...*

Materials Language Book pp158–159, Practice Book pp126–127, flashcards 28, 56, 61, 168 and word cards for *Get active!*, flashcards of your choice for *I spy* (see *Working with words*); cut-up sentences for *Extension*

Preparation Make word cards as necessary. Make cut-up sentences (see *Extension*)

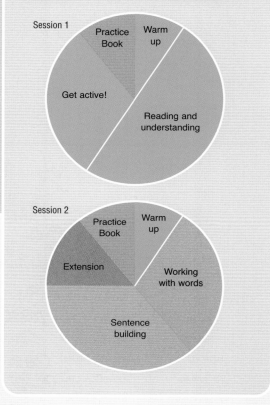

Lesson 3 time division:

Session 1
- Warm up
- Practice Book
- Get active!
- Reading and understanding

Session 2
- Warm up
- Practice Book
- Extension
- Working with words
- Sentence building

⬇ Lesson 3 Session 1 Warm-up

1 Use flashcards to practise telling the time and describing the weather. These can be team games.

⬇ Reading and understanding

3 Ask a child to read sentence 1. Class reads. Check they understand *round and round*. Children suggest the matching picture. Continue with the other sentences.

4 Children read words in the box. Class repeats. Ask a child to read the first word. Class repeats. Write it on the board. Say *Find the rhyming word in the box*. Elicit *all*. Write it beside *fall*.

Continue with the other words. Class reads all the pairs of rhyming words on the board. Rub them off. Children write.

5 **Get active!**
Put up flashcards of, e.g. *ball, fall, cat, hat, rock, sock, bed, red* (colour card), in

muddled order. Children look at the pictures, think of the word. Children take turns to match the words that rhyme.

Put up word cards. Children match them to flashcards. Class reads the rhyming pairs.

⬇ Lesson 3 Session 2 Warm-up

Play *What is it?* (TG p248) with animal flashcards.

⬇ Working with words

2 Put up sets of flashcards of objects with the same initial letter, e.g. *egg, elephant, ear, orange, owl, polar bear, pond, plane*. Say, e.g. *I spy (touch your eye) ... something beginning with p*. Children name an object beginning with *p*. Answer *Yes, it is.* or *No, it isn't.* Continue until they guess correctly. Do this once or twice more.
Invite one or two children to choose an object, say the sentence and let the class guess.

3 Children play in pairs using their books. They write the initial letters and the objects that begin with those letters in the box.

⬇ Extension activity

Write simple sentences on pieces of paper, e.g. *Sam likes ... I can see/hear ... Whose ... is this?* etc. Cut them up. Give them to groups to sort out. Groups change over sentences.

235

Grammar

1. Lesson 4 warm-up.

2. Children look at the picture (LB p160). Ask what the characters are doing.

3. Activity 1: Children read sentences. Class repeats and points.

4. Activity 2: Children read words in the box. Children complete the sentences orally, then write.

5. Prepare children for PB p128 by checking they understand the tasks. Children complete.

Listening

1. Read Nina's speech bubble (LB p161).

2. Explain the task.

3. 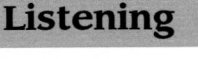 Activity 1: Play LCD2 track 100. Children point to the firework they hear mentioned.

4. Activity 2: Play the song (LCD2 track 101). Children listen. Say it, demonstrate the actions, children repeat and follow. Play the song again. Children do the actions and join in.

After listening

Teach the song in the usual way. Practise the words with the actions.

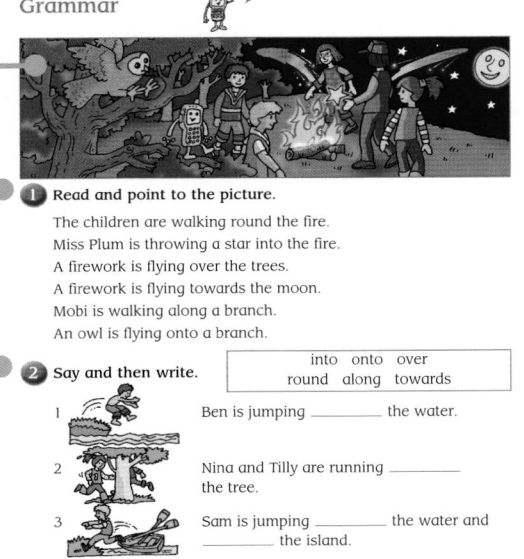

Grammar

Look at this!

1. Read and point to the picture.

The children are walking round the fire.
Miss Plum is throwing a star into the fire.
A firework is flying over the trees.
A firework is flying towards the moon.
Mobi is walking along a branch.
An owl is flying onto a branch.

2. Say and then write.

| into | onto | over |
| round | along | towards |

1. Ben is jumping _____ the water.

2. Nina and Tilly are running _____ the tree.

3. Sam is jumping _____ the water and _____ the island.

4. Mobi is sailing _____ the river _____ the waterfall.

160   Grammar focus   prepositions of movement

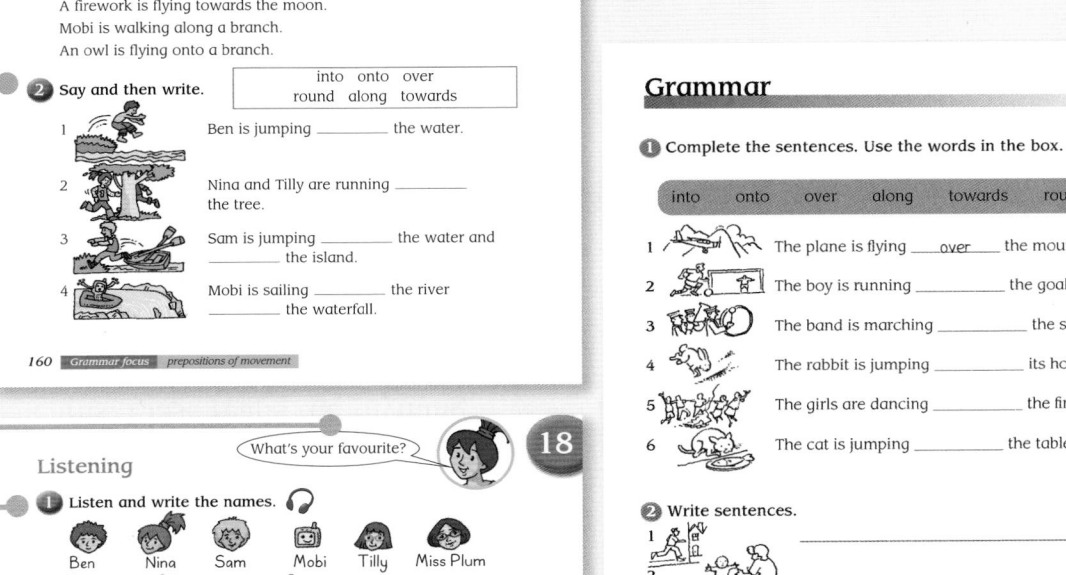

What's your favourite?

18

Listening

1. Listen and write the names.

Ben   Nina   Sam   Mobi   Tilly   Miss Plum

1

2

3

4

5   BANG   CRACKLE   BANG

6

2. Listen and sing.

Up goes a rocket!
Whooooosh! Bang!
Look at all the stars shining in the sky!
Up goes a rocket!
Whooooosh! Bang!
And all the stars fall down.

Listening focus   descriptions with colour and movement   161

Grammar

1. Complete the sentences. Use the words in the box.

| into | onto | over | along | towards | round |

1. The plane is flying __over__ the mountains.

2. The boy is running _____ the goal.

3. The band is marching _____ the street.

4. The rabbit is jumping _____ its hole.

5. The girls are dancing _____ the fire.

6. The cat is jumping _____ the table.

2. Write sentences.

1.
2.
3.
4.

128

Lesson aim Grammar and listening

Lesson targets Children:

- match statements to a picture
- use prepositions of movement correctly
- listen for specific information
- sing and learn a short song.

Key language (words) *into, onto, over, round, along, towards,* names of fireworks

Words for understanding *branch, favourite*

Materials Language Book pp160–161, Practice Book p128, Language CD2 tracks 100–101, a doll and a box for *Warm-up*

Preparation Listen to the CD before the lesson.

Lesson 4 time division:

Lesson 4 Warm-up

1 Use any kind of doll and a box to teach and practise prepositions of movement, e.g. going *along* the table and *into, over, towards, round* the box. Move the doll and ask *Where is she/he going?*

Listening

2 Children must listen and write the name of the character who likes each firework underneath the picture of it.

3 If they find this difficult, go through what each picture is before they listen again.

Children write the names.

Audioscript

Miss Plum	What's your favourite firework, Sam?
Sam	I like rockets. They go high in the sky. Wow! Look at that one! Look at the green and silver stars! It's fantastic!
Miss Plum	What about you, Tilly? What's your favourite?
Tilly	I like the waterfall, the golden waterfall. It's like a golden river falling down over the rocks. It's beautiful.
Miss Plum	And you, Ben? What's your favourite?
Tilly	Ben likes sparklers.
Ben	Yes, sparklers are great. I can write my name with them. And I can draw pictures, too. Look!
Miss Plum	What's your favourite firework, Nina?
Nina	I like the roman candle. It's beautiful and it isn't noisy. Look at that one! Look at those pink and purple stars!
Sam	What's your favourite, Miss Plum?
Miss Plum	My favourite? Hmmm. I think my favourite is the catherine wheel. It goes round and round so fast and the colours are beautiful.
Nina	What about Mobi? What's his favourite?
Ben	That's easy. Mobi likes bangers. Look out! Here he comes!

237

Activity 1

1. Lesson 5 warm-up. ▼
2. (LB p162) Point out pictures and words with the final consonant blends. ▼
3. 🎧 Play rhyme twice (LCD2 track 102). Children follow in books.
4. Read rhyme.
5. Read and ask questions. ▼
6. Read with the class.

Activity 2

1. Children look for the target words in the bricks.
2. They circle them.

Activity 3

Children complete sentences using target words. ▼

Activity 4

1. Write up words. Class/individuals read. ▼
2. Children read in pairs. Listen to pairs.
3. Children check words and tick.

Practice Book

Children complete PB p129. ▼

Phonics games and activities

1. Play *What's the word?* ▼
2. Children read word cards. ▼

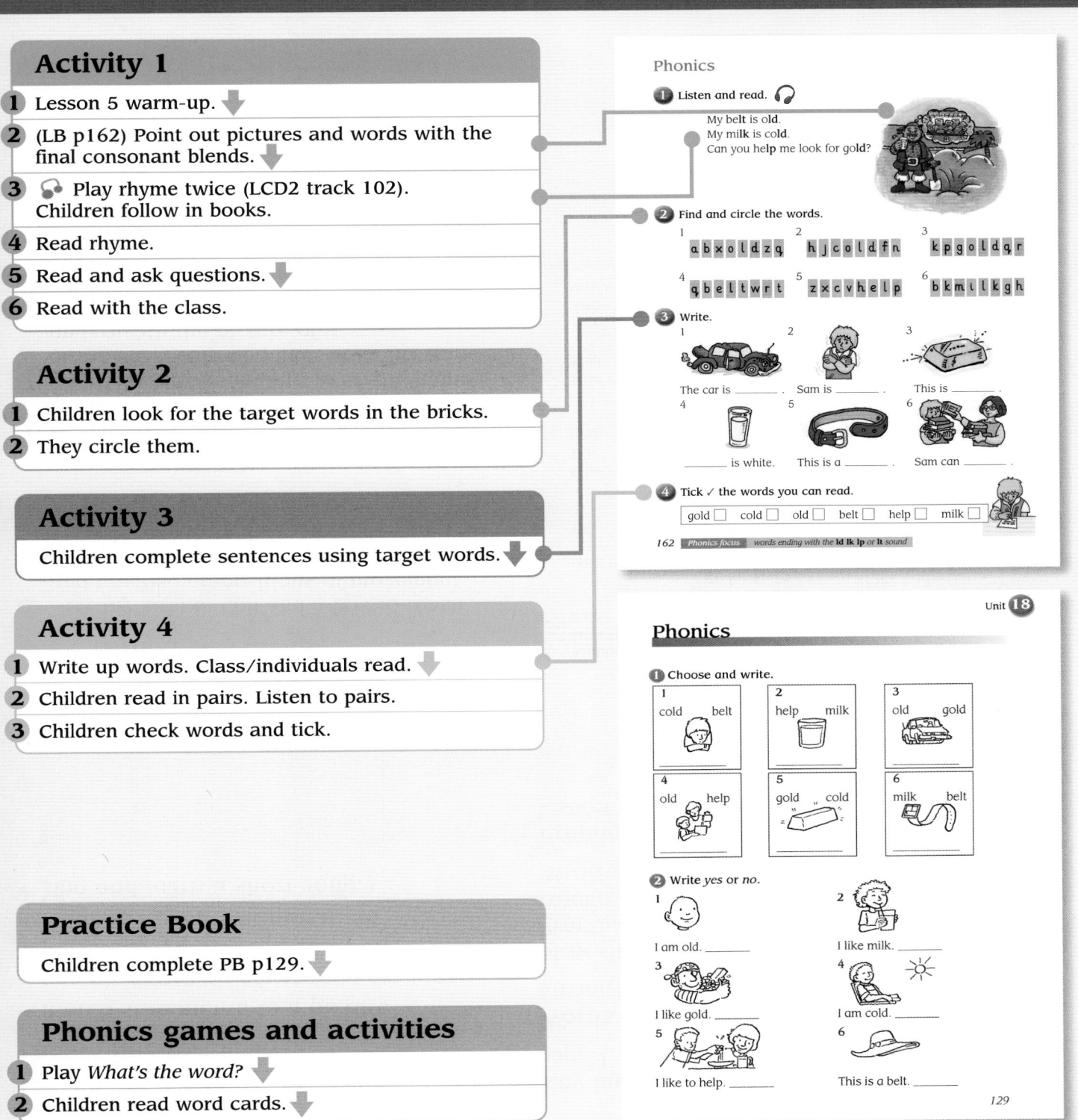

Lesson aim Phonic recognition

Lesson targets Children:

- read, pronounce and spell words with consonant blends *ld, lt, lp, lk*
- recognise and say the component parts of each word
- write the words from picture prompts.

Target words *belt, cold, gold, help, milk, old*

Materials Language Book p162, Practice Book p129, Language CD2 track 102, word cards for *Phonics games and activities*

Preparation Listen to the CD before the lesson.

Lesson 5 time division:

Lesson 5 Warm-up

1 Children sing *Up goes a rocket* from Lesson 4 (LB p161, LCD2 track 101) and do the actions.

Activity 1

2 Explain *belt*. Tell children to point to it. Ask *What is the pirate drinking?*

5 Ask *Is the belt new?*
Is the milk hot?
What is the pirate looking for?
Does he want some help?

Make sure all the words in the text are understood.

Activity 3

If you wish, ask a child to read and complete the first sentence. Class repeats. Children write. Continue with the other sentences.

Activity 4

1 Write the six words on the board. Point in random order. Individuals and/or the class reads them.

Practice Book

Children complete the two exercises. Check they can read all the words in Exercise 1 before they move on to Exercise 2.

Phonics games and activities

1 Play *What's the word?* (TG p75) with a variety of words they have learned, e.g. *sw–i–ng, sp–e–ll, bl–a–ck, pl–ane, c–ake, ch–i–ps.*

2 Show a variety of word cards used in the course. Children volunteer to read them. If they read correctly, they keep the card. This could be done as a team game.

239

Before writing

1 Lesson 6 warm-up.

2 Read Miss Plum's speech bubble (LB p163).

3 Children read the speech bubbles.

4 Class repeats.

5 Children look at the picture. Elicit/Prompt sentences.

Shared writing

1 A child reads the first sentence (LB p163). Class reads.

2 Children say complete sentences. Point out Miss Plum's box. Class reads the sentences.

3 Ask questions. Elicit sentences. Write them on the board. Class reads.

4 Rub sentences off. Children write.

Practice Book

Writing

1 Class reads the words in the box. (PB p130)

2 A child reads the example. Class repeats.

3 Elicit prepositions for the pictures.

4 Elicit full sentences. Children write.

Your writing

(PB p131) Children look at the pictures. Children write sentences.

After writing

Hold a class discussion about the fun fair.

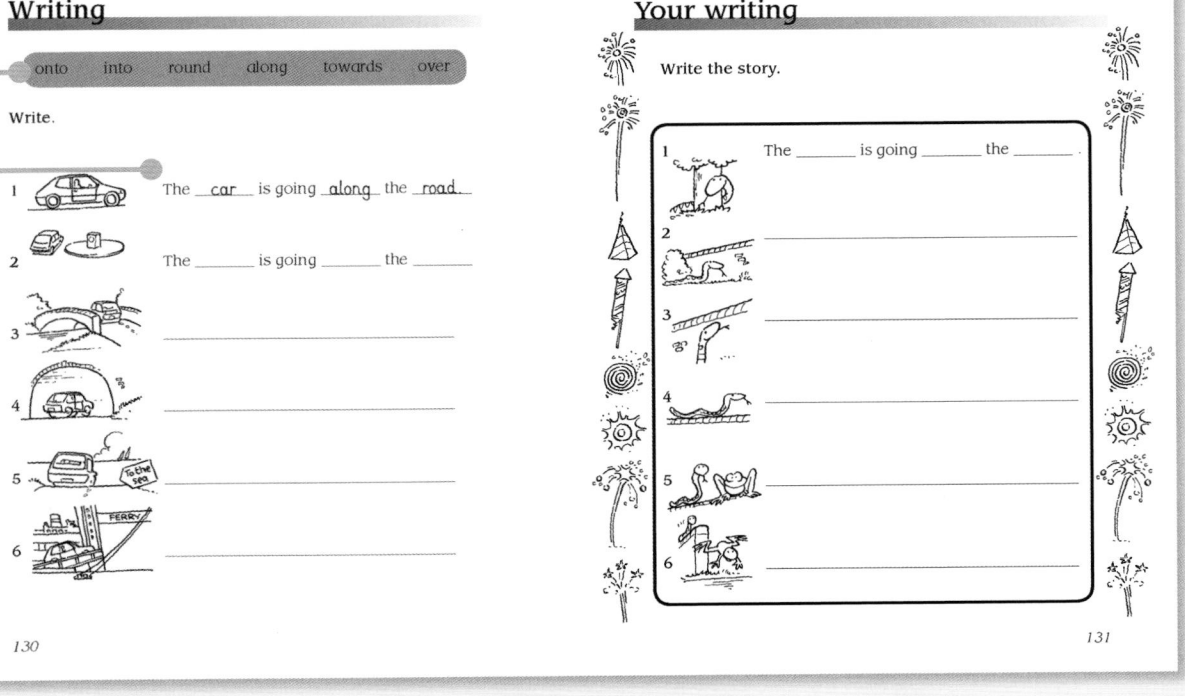

Lesson aim Writing

Lesson targets Children:

- talk about a picture then write sentences about it
- complete sentences and write sentences from picture prompts
- write a short story from picture prompts.

Key language (words) prepositions of movement
(structures) *I can see a ..., He/She/It is going ..., They are going ...*

Materials Language Book p163, Practice Book pp130 and 131

Lesson 6 time division:

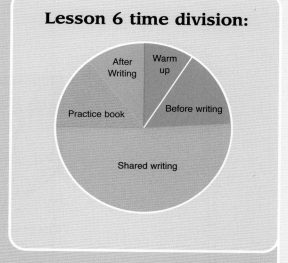

Lesson 6 Warm-up

1 Sing *Stand up! Sit down!* from Unit 7 (LB p67, LCD1 track 45) or play *Simon says* (TG p248) or choose another song or game that the class has enjoyed.

Before writing

5 Ask, e.g. *Can you see a girl? Where is she? Is she going up?*
Can you see a boy? Where is he? Is he going down?
Can you see a firework? What is it doing?

Continue to ask questions about objects in the picture.

Shared writing

2 A child begins the second sentence. Help the child to complete it, if necessary. Write it on the board. Class reads. Do the same with the third sentence.

3 Ask, e.g. *Can you see a girl? What is she doing?*

4 Continue asking similar questions as necessary. Elicit sentences.

Alternatively, leave a framework on the board if the class needs guided support. Go round helping children and monitoring their work.

Practice Book

Your writing
Go through the exercise orally. If necessary, elicit the preposition for each picture before eliciting the whole sentence.

Write sentences on the board if children need guidance. Class reads. Rub sentences off or leave a framework. Children write.

After writing

Ask children to look at the picture on LB p163 again. Ask questions, e.g. *What do you like at the fun fair? Why? Is it noisy? What can you hear at the fun fair? What do you want to ride on? What do you want to do at the fun fair?*

Help children to form answers.

Revision 6

You can do it!

1 **Look at the pictures.**
Do you like picnics?
What can you eat on a
picnic? What can you
drink?

2 **Listen and read.** 🎧

3 **Read and say.**
Look at picture 1.
Who can you see? Who
has got blue shoes?
What have they got on
their backs? What is
Ben holding?

Look at picture 2.
Look at the map.
Where are they going?
Are they going into the
trees? Are they going
under the bridge?

Look at picture 3.
Who wants to swim?
Or play ball? Or eat?

Look at picture 4.
Look at the blue bag.
Whose bag is it? What
has she got in her bag?

Look at picture 5.
Look at the green bag.
Whose bag is it? What
has he got in his bag?

1 The children are going on a picnic.
Sam is wearing green shorts and a brown
jumper. Tilly has got a pink dress and a
white hat. All the children have got bags.

3

Let's swim!

Let's play ball!

*I'm hungry.
Let's eat!*

5 Whose bag is this?
It is Sam's. He has
got chicken and
orange juice.

What is in this bag?
Grapes and biscuits.

2 They are going along the path, around the
trees, over the river, towards a waterfall.

This is a good
place for a picnic.

4 Whose bag is this?
It is Nina's. She has
got cakes and a banana.

What is in this bag?
Sandwiches and an apple.

6 Look at Mobi! What has he got? Whose
cake is this? It is Nina's. Whose sandwiches
are these? They are Ben's. Mobi likes picnics.

*Mmmm!
I like picnics!*

Look at picture 6.
What has Mobi got?
Whose biscuits are
they? Whose orange
juice is it? Is Mobi
happy?

4 **Listen and say which
picture.** 🎧

5 **Act out the story.**

6 **Listen and say the
chant.** 🎧

Take a cake from the plate.
Have a glass of cold milk.
Cake and milk. Mmm!
Milk and cake. Mmm!
I like cake and milk. Mmm!

Lesson aim Revision

Lesson targets Children:

- practise fluency and listening activities, including spelling patterns *a_e, i_e, ue, u_e, o_e*; word ending blends *ld, lk, lp, lt*
- practise language and structures from Units 16–18 through a story, games and writing.

Key language *I like … He/She likes … Whose … is this? It is …'s. Whose … are these? They are …'s. round, into, over, towards*

Materials Language Book pp164–165, Language CD2 tracks 103–105, Practice Book pp132–135, flashcards for actions

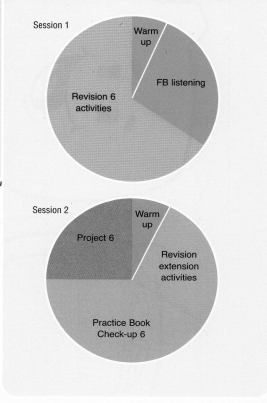

Revision 6 time division:

Session 1

- Warm up
- FB listening
- Revision 6 activities

Session 2

- Warm up
- Revision extension activities
- Practice Book Check-up 6
- Project 6

Sessions 1 and 2 Warm-ups

Sing favourite songs from Units 16–18.

Listening revision

Play FCD tracks 32–38. Children look at the poster and listen. Children close books and repeat during the pauses in the dialogue section.

⬇ Revision 6

1 (LB p164) Activity 1: Ask how many children like picnics. Write up ideas for picnic food and drink.

2 🎧 Activity 2: Play LCD2 track 103. Children listen and follow.

3 Activity 3: Read out the questions. Elicit answers.

4 🎧 (LB p165) Activity 4: Play LCD2 track 104 twice. Children listen and point then name the picture, e.g. *It's picture 5.*

Audioscript

Presenter	**Listen and say which picture.**
Sam	Come on, Ben! The river looks great!
Mobi	Nina has got cakes.
Sam/Ben/ Tilly/Nina	We're going on a picnic. We're going on a picnic.
Mobi	Sam has got orange juice.
Mobi	Mmm! Biscuits, chicken, cakes, orange juice. I like picnics!
Sam	Look! We go around the trees and over the river. Then we can see the waterfall.

5 Activity 5: Individuals, groups or the whole class read narrative and speech bubbles. Individuals come forward and read and act the story.

6 🎧 Activity 6: Play LCD2 track 105 twice. Children listen, then join in.

Revision extension activities

1 Play flashcard games introduced in Units 16–18.

2 Play action games from TG p248.

3 Individuals, groups or the whole class read the story aloud.

4 Children read aloud the phonic chant. Teach it if you wish.

Practice Book

1 Children complete *Check-up 6* (PB pp132–133) as a test, as preparation for a test or for homework.

2 Children complete *Move on with Mobi 6* (PB pp134–135) for homework or class work.

Project 6

1 Cut-out figures and clothes. See page 247.

2 Fireworks frieze. See page 246.

243

Project instructions

Mobi puppet

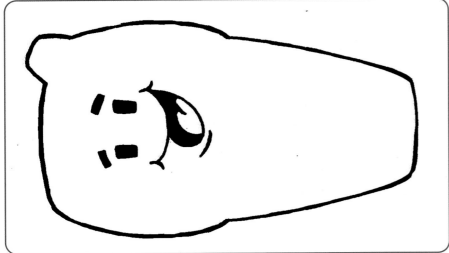

A sentence begins with a capital letter.

Mobi puppet instructions

Photocopy a Mobi phone for each child. Children make the phone.

Colour and cut out.

Cut out the screen.

Spread the glue.

Stick together.

Children write each *Sentence building* rule on a small piece of paper and slip it into the phone as a reminder when they do the *Sentence building* exercises in LB and PB.

When the rule has been practised, children stick it in their copy books and write an example sentence beside it. Alternatively, children make a Mobi sentence building *book* containing all the rules.

Class puppet: Make a large Mobi puppet. Stick it on an empty box. Put messages onto the screen, e.g. *Nine stars are missing tonight. A sentence ends with a full stop.* Mobi could also tell the class what the homework is. If you wish, add paper or card arms and legs. Keep *Sentence building* rules in the box for quick revision sessions.

Island of adventure model (Revision 2)

Children write vocabulary from each unit. Add new places as they appear in the story. Make stand-up animals and trees.

green paper

blue paper

brown paper

stand-up animals and trees

Garden and beach friezes (Revision 2)

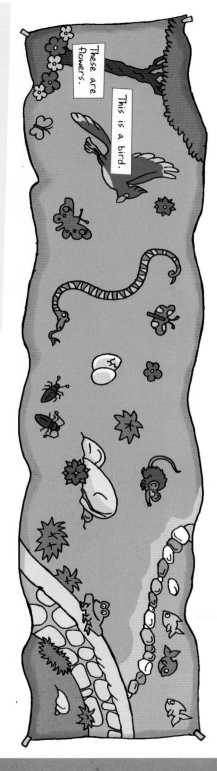

These are flowers.

This is a bird.

Children make frieze using different coloured paper.
Children draw and stick on pictures.
Children write sentences to label the frieze.

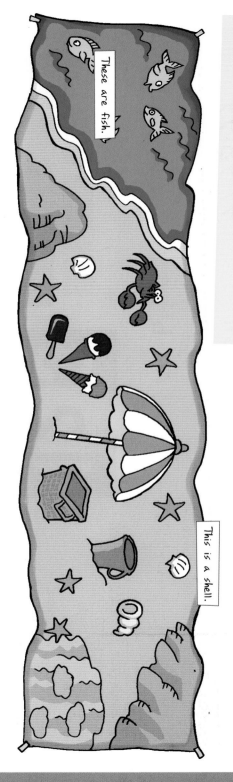

These are fish.

This is a shell.

Monkey (Revision 3)

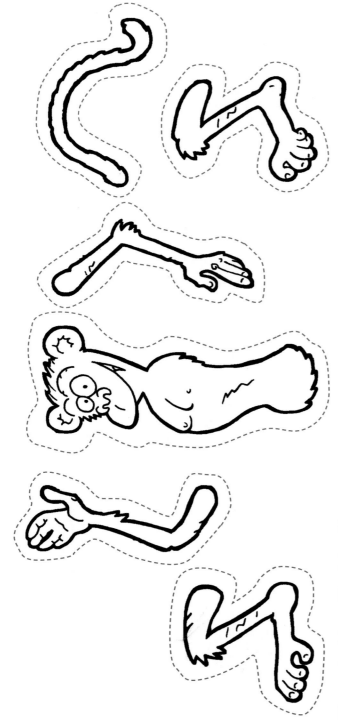

Fireworks frieze (Revision 6)

Children draw and colour fireworks to stick on the frieze.
Children write colours to label, e.g. **gold, silver, red, yellow, orange, purple.**
Children write words for sounds to label, e.g. **whizz, whirr, bang, crackle, whoosh, ploof.**
Children write sentences to label, e.g. **The rocket goes up. The wheel goes round. The stars fall down,** etc.

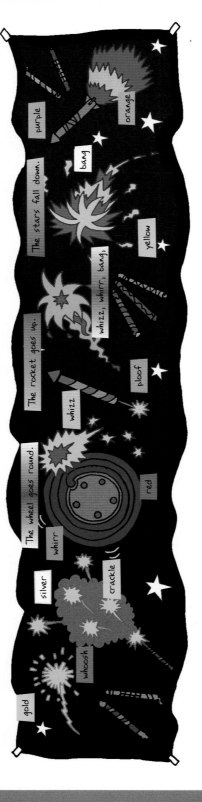

Additional resources

Teachers may wish to make these resources for a variety of games and activities in the course:

flashcard size:
- number cards 1–20
- colour cards

small cards (7cm x 7cm approximately):
- number cards 1–100
- letters/phonemes cards
- the alphabet, capitals
- the alphabet, small letters

246

Cut-out figures (Revision 6)

Children show and talk about their people, e.g. She is wearing a blue skirt and a yellow T-shirt, etc. Children can also stick them on paper and write sentences.

If you wish, give children questions to answer about their person: *What is his/her name? How old is he/she? What can he/she do? What does he/she like?* etc.

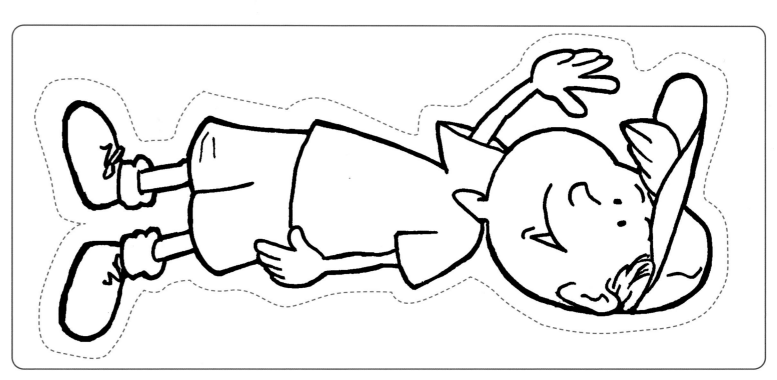

Games

Action mime
Children mime an action. Others guess.

Alphabetical order
Put all letters of the alphabet (or a–m or n–z) in muddled order on the board. Children take turns to find the first, second, etc. letter in the sequence.

Flashcard/letter match
See *Word/Letter match*, but children place flashcards under initial letters.

Guess the animal
Make statements about animals, e.g. *It is small. It is green. It lives in a pond.* Children guess *It's a frog.*

Guess the object
Make statements about objects e.g. *They are blue. They are in the nest.* Children guess. *They are eggs.*

I spy ...
Children guess an object in the room or in a picture, beginning with a named letter given by the leader of the game: *I spy with my little eye, something beginning with ...* Alternative: **Look at the picture. Find something beginning with ...**

Line-up letters
Give out sequences of five letters e.g. *a–e, f–j* in muddled order. Children line up in order and show letters.

Line-up numbers
Give out sequences of five number cards in muddled order. Children line up in order while the rest of the class says the numbers.

Number chain
Children number around the class. Start from 1 or a higher number.

Object chain
Teacher: *In my bag I have got a ball.* Child 1: *In my bag I have got a ball and a doll.* Child 2: *In my bag I have got a ball, a doll and a book*, etc.

Easier version: put flashcards of objects around the classroom. Point to the first one as you say it.

Object chain + colours
As above, but add a colour, e.g. *In my bag I have got a green ball*, etc.

Simon says
Children only follow commands preceded by *Simon says ...*(for a more detailed description, see p95).

Stand up colours
Give teams two or three colour cards. When their colour is called, children stand up or put their hands up. Change colours after a few turns.

Team letters
Give teams three or four letters on cards. Say a cvc word. Teams stand up or put their hands up if they have a letter in the word.

Team numbers
Class in four or six teams: give each team three or four mixed numbers. Say numbers in any order. When a team's number is called they put their hands up.

What is it?
Show flashcards of objects. Children name them *It's a ... They're ...*

What's missing?
Put up six to eight flashcards. Children look. Take them down. Remove one. Put the rest up again in any order. Children remember what is missing.

Word/letter match
Put initial letters at the top of the board. Put words with the initial letters in any order below. Children place words under initial letters.

Phonics games and activities
Letter-changing game (p25)
Look, write, check (p75)
Muddled letters (p201)
Odd one out (p37)
Start the word (p37)
What's the word? (p75)

Language Book 1 – Answer Key

Unit 1

Reading and understanding (p12)
1 1 tall 2 helpful 3 kind 4 funny
2 1 brother 2 father
3 teacher

Working with words (p13)
1 1 brother 2 grandma 3 grandpa
4 sister 5 dad 6 mum

Grammar (p14)
2 1 He is eight. 2 She is six.
3 She is seven.

Listening (p15)
1 1 dad 2 sister 3 grandpa 4 brother
5 grandma 6 mum

Phonics (p16)
2 1 cat 2 mat 3 hat
3 1 Sam/hat. 2 cat/mat.

Class writing (p17)
1 1 I am Nina. 2 I am seven.
3 Sam is my friend. 4 He is eight.

Unit 2

Reading and understanding (p20)
1 1 A 2 A 3 B 4 B 5 A
2 1 A doll and a train,
2 A plane and a ball.
3 These are my toys,
4 And I love them all.

Working with words (p21)
1 1 table 2 ball 3 chair 4 desk
5 doll 6 plane
2 toy box – ball, doll, plane
bedroom – desk, chair, table

Sentence building (p 21)
1 1 c 2 a 3 e 4 b 5 d

Grammar (p22)
1 1 a ball 2 chairs 3 books
4 a computer
2 1 These are 2 This is
3 1 This is a doll. 2 This is a ball.
3 This is a train. 4 This is a house.
5 These are elephants.
6 These are planes.
7 These are cars.
8 These are books.

Listening (p23)
1 1 a 2 d 3 c 4 f 5 e 6 b

Phonics (p24)
2 1 Ben 2 pen 3 hen
3 1 Ben/red/bed 2 Ben/red/pen

Unit 3

Reading and understanding (p28)
2 light/bright/tonight/might

Sentence building (p28)
1 1 a 2 an 3 an 4 a 5 a 6 a

Grammar (p30)
2 1 I can see the sun. I can't see the moon.
2 I can see a tree. I can't see a star.
3 I can see a bird. I can't see a butterfly.

Listening (p31)
3 1 I can hear an owl.
I can hear a train.
I can hear a cat.
I can hear a dog.
I can hear a boy.
I can hear a car.

Phonics (p32)
2 1 bin 2 tin 3 wig
3 1 tin 2 wig 3 big

Unit 4

Reading and understanding (p38)
1 1 an orange goldfish in the pond
2 a green frog on a rock
3 red apples on a tree
4 a long brown snake in the tall grass
5 three small blue eggs in a nest
6 purple flowers on the wall
2 1 tall 2 beautiful 3 small 4 long

Working with words (p39)
1 colours: brown, purple, green, orange; animals: butterfly, goldfish, beetle
2 blue eggs/red apples/orange goldfish/brown snake

Grammar (p40)
1 1 frog 2 wall 3 butterfly
4 goldfish
2 1 butterflies 2 apples 3 flowers
4 beetles
3 1 What is this? It is a flower.
2 What are these? They are frogs.
3 What are these? These are apples.
4 What is this? It is a tree.

Listening (p41)
1 1 an elephant 2 monkeys 3 cats
4 a frog
2 1 It is an elephant.
2 They are frogs.
3 It is a monkey.
4 They are birds.
5 It is a mouse.
6 They are cats.
3 1 run/sun 2 jug/mug

Phonics (p42)
2 1 sun 2 bun 3 run 4 mug 5 jug

Class writing (p43)

Unit 5

Reading and understanding (p46)
1 1 2, 2 5, 3 6, 4 10, 5 7, 6 11
2 1 is 2 is not 3 is 4 is not 5 is not

Working with words (p47)
2 one two five six nine ten

Sentence building (p47)
1 1 red 2 grey 3 green 4 brown
2 plane/mouse/bird/eggs

Grammar (p48)
1 1 Yes 2 No 3 Yes 4 Yes 5 No 6 No
3 1 It is between the books.
2 It is under the table.
3 It is next to the parrot.
4 It is in the car.

Phonics (p50)
2 1 log 2 dog 3 fog 4 fox 5 box
3 1 log 2 fox/box

Unit 6

Reading and understanding (p54)
1 1 The sky is blue.
2 Dad has got a hat.
3 It is very hot.

Language Book 1 – Answer key

4 Mikey's crab is red.
5 Mikey is in the water.
6 It is a baby starfish.
7 Grandma has got some shells.
8 Pat can see a starfish.

2 1 no 2 no 3 yes 4 no 6 yes

Working with words (p55)
1 1 crab 2 fish 3 shell 4 rock
2 1 a shell 2 a fish 3 a rock 4 a crab

Sentence building (p55)
1 1 Mikey 2 Tilly 3 Ben 4 Nina
5 Sam 6 Pat

Grammar (p56)
3 1 He has got a dog.
2 She has got a cat.

Listening (p57)
1 a, c, d, f, g, h

Phonics (p58)
2 1 shop 2 ship 3 dish 4 fish
3 1 shop 2 ship 3 fish/dish

Unit 7

Reading and understanding (p64)
1 1 G 2 H 3 A 4 D
5 C 6 F 7 B 8 E

2 1 Get up! 2 Don't stand up!
3 Don't run! 4 Shut the window.

Working with words (p65)
1 climb/look/jump/open/run/sit
2 1 run 2 look 3 climb 4 jump
5 sit 6 open

Sentence building (p65)
1 1 open 2 climb 3 look 4 jump

Grammar (p66)
1 1 b 2 d 3 e 4 a 5 c

2 1 Listen 2 fall 3 sit 4 Look

Phonics (p68)
2 1 lunch 2 munch
3 1 children 2 chips
3 chicken 4 chocolate

Class writing (p69)
1 1 Stop! 2 Look all around!
3 Listen! 4 Wait!
5 Look and listen! 6 Walk! Don't run!

Class writing (p85)

2 1 Is Sam swimming? No, is not.
2 Is Nina dancing? Yes, she is.
3 Is Mobi singing? Yes, he is.
4 Is Ben riding? Yes, he is.
5 Is Miss Plum running? No, she is not.
6 Is Tilly climbing? No, she is not.

Unit 10

Reading and understanding (p90)
1 1 hungry 2 tired 3 happy
4 thirsty 5 sad

2 1 c 2 e 3 a 4 b 5 d 6 f
3 early/thing/head/bed/sing

Working with words (p91)
1 1 thirsty 2 happy 3 tired
4 hungry 5 sad

2 1 He is hungry. 2 She is thirsty.
3 He is tired.

Sentence building (p91)
1 S/S/M/T/W/T/F

Grammar (p92)
2 1 one o'clock 2 five o'clock
3 eleven o'clock 4 half past three
5 half past ten 6 half past two

Listening (p93)
1 Monday c/Tuesday d/Wednesday
b/Thursday f/Friday g/Saturday
a/Sunday e

Phonics (p94)
2 1 sock 2 rock 3 clock 4 tick
5 duck 6 quack

3 1 clock/tock 2 sock/rock
3 duck/sack

Unit 11

Reading and understanding (p98)
1 1 pic 4 2 pic 2 3 pic 3
4 pic 1 5 pic 5

2 1 c 2 b 3 d 4 a

Working with words (p99)
1 eat: crisps/cake drink: juice/water
get off: bike/train

Sentence building (p99)
1 1 It 2 They 3 He 4 She

Unit 8

Reading and understanding (p72)
1 2/3/4/6

2 1 ice/snow 2 foxes/bears
3 hippos/elephants 4 elephants

3 1 bear 2 butterflies 3 snake 4 frog

Working with words (p73)
1 1 elephant 2 polar bear
3 fox 4 crocodile 5 tiger

Sentence building (p73)
1 1 Is the elephant red?
2 Are the boys happy?
3 Is she nine? 4 Is the dog black?

Grammar (p74)
1 1 yes 2 no 3 no 4 yes
2 1 It is 2 They are 3 She is 4 He is

Listening (p75)
1 1 He is swimming. 2 They are
playing in the playground. 3 She is
holding a bird. 4 It is sleeping.

Phonics (p76)
2 1 hill 2 bell 3 doll
4 wall 5 mall 6 ball

3 1 mall 2 bell/ball

Unit 9

Reading and understanding (p80)
1 1 yes 2 no 3 yes 4 no

2 1 pic 5 2 pic 3 3 pic 1 4 pic 6
5 pic 4 6 pic 2

Working with words (p81)
1 ride: horse/bike climb:
tree/mountain play: football/game

Sentence building (p81)
1 1 is 2 are 3 is 4 are

Grammar (p82)
2 1 pic 2 2 pic 1 3 pic 1 4 pic 2

3 1 is not 2 are not
3 are not 4 is not

Phonics (p84)
2 1 ring 2 king 3 sing
4 wing 5 swing

3 1 king/sing 2 king/swing
3 ring 4 wing

Grammar (p100)
1 1 What is he doing? He is reading.
2 What is she doing? She is singing.
3 What are they doing? They are fishing.
4 What is she doing? She is eating.
5 What are they doing? They are running.
6 What is he doing? He is climbing.

Phonics (p102)
2 1 brick 2 crab 3 grass 4 truck
3 1 dress/blue 2 drink/green

Unit 12

Reading and understanding (p106)
1 1 A 2 B 3 A 4 A 5 A 6 A 7 B
2 1 T 2 F 3 T 4 F 5 F 6 T

Working with words (p107)
1 1 cake shop 2 sweet shop 3 toy shop 4 shoe shop 5 clothes shop 6 bike shop

Sentence building (p107)
1 on 2 under 3 in 4 behind 5 next to

Phonics (p110)
2 1 glass 2 clown 3 flower 4 plane
3 1 flag 2 plane 3 plate

Unit 13

Reading and understanding (p116)
1 1 Dani is Sami's younger brother.
2 Sami is looking after his father's sheep.
3 They are on the hillside.
4 Sami has got a dog.
5 'How many sheep are there?' asks Dani.
6 Dani can't count to forty.
2 1 c 2 d 3 f 4 e 5 a 6 b
3 1 30 2 16 3 18 4 40 5 17 6 90

Sentence building (p117)
1 1 has 2 has 3 have 4 has 5 have

Grammar (p118)
1 1 2, 2 4, 3 3, 4 6, 5 5, 6 7
3 1 How many boys are there?
2 How many birds are there?
3 How many trees are there?
4 How many stars are there?

Listening (p119)
1 1 17, 2 13, 3 10, 4 99, 5 24

Phonics (p120)
2 1 thin 2 path 3 bath 4 thick
3 three/thirteen/thirty

Unit 14

Reading and understanding (p124)
1 1 T 2 T 3 F 4 F 5 T 6 F
2 1 d 2 a 3 c 4 e 5 b 6 f

Working with words (p125)
1 1 windy 2 sunny 3 foggy 4 raining 5 snowing 6 cloudy
2 rain/snow/cloud/wind/thunder/sun/lightning

Sentence building (p125)
1 1 new 2 big 3 pink 4 windy
2 bed/desk/doll/day

Phonics (p128)
2 1 stop 2 swim 3 spell 4 smell 5 snake 6 sweet 7 spider
3 1 sweet 2 spider 3 snake

Unit 15

Reading and understanding (p132)
1 1 rabbits 2 elephant 3 monkeys 4 giraffe 5 ducks 6 owl 7 hippo
2 1 F 2 F 3 T 4 F

Sentence building (p133)
1 1 am 2 is 3 is 4 are 5 are

Grammar (p134)
1 We have got: ears/two eyes. Elephants have got: tusks/ears/tails/trunks/four legs/two eyes.

Phonics (p136)
2 1 hand 2 band 3 sand 4 ant 5 elephant 6 sink 7 pink
3 1 hand 2 ant 3 sink

Unit 16

Reading and understanding (p142)
1 1 sun/sky 2 tree 3 picnic 4 basket 5 cakes 6 apple/grape 7 sandwiches 8 orange juice

Working with words (p143)
1 banana/chicken/grape/sandwich/juice/cake/orange/biscuit/apple
2 You can eat eight things. You can drink one thing.

Sentence building (p143)
1 one cup/one dog/one orange/one basket/one apple/two cups/three dogs/five oranges/two baskets/four apples

Grammar (p144)
2 1 She likes orange juice.
2 He likes sandwiches.
3 She likes ice cream.

Listening (p145)
1 apples – Tilly/grapes – Mobi/bananas – Sam and Nina/chicken – Miss Plum/sandwiches – Ben/orange juice – Mobi/cakes and biscuits – all

Phonics (p146)
2 cake/make gate/plate bike/like ride/hide

Unit 17

Reading and understanding (p150)
1 1 people 2 taxis 3 bookshop 4 planes
2 1 F 2 F 3 T 4 F

Working with words (p151)
1 It is a: hat/jumper/skirt/dress/T-shirt. They are: socks/shoes/jeans/shorts

Language/Practice Books 1 – Answer keys

Language Book 1 (continued)

Sentence building (p151)

1 1 I like ice cream.
2 I can fly planes.
3 There are lots of cars.

Listening (p153)

1 4 1 3 6 5 2

Phonics (p154)

2 1 tube 2 blue 3 glue 4 cube
3 1 nose 2 bone 3 hose 4 stone

Unit 18

Reading and understanding (p158)

1 1 d 2 c 3 b 4 a 5 f 6 e
2 1 all 2 white 3 flows 4 go
5 sky 6 sound

Sentence building (p159)

1 1 like 2 likes 3 likes 4 like

Grammar (p160)

2 1 into 2 round 3 over/onto
4 along/towards

Listening (p161)

1 1 Miss Plum 2 Sam 3 Tilly
4 Ben 5 Mobi 6 Nina

Phonics (p162)

2 1 old 2 cold 3 gold 4 belt 5 help
6 milk
3 1 old 2 cold 3 gold 4 milk 4 belt
5 help

Class writing (p163)

2 (suggested answer) I can see a
catherine wheel. It is going round.
I can see a big wheel. It is going
round. I can see fireworks. They are
going up. I can see a boy. He is
going up the slide. I can see a girl.
She is going down the slide. I can
see balloons. They are going up.

Practice Book 1

Review (p2–3)

1 1 ball 2 cat 3 nut 4 queen 5 jug
6 van
2 1 doll 2 ball 3 box 4 tree
5 book 6 chair
3 1 six 2 three 3 two 4 one 5 five
6 four
4 1 cat 2 balls 3 dog 4 frogs 5 van
6 pens

5 1 big 2 little 3 little 4 big 5 little
6 1 on 2 under 3 in 4 under

Unit 1

Reading and understanding (p4)

1 1 Ben 2 big brother 3 sister
4 baby brother
2 1 father 2 mother
3 grandfather/grandmother

Sentence building (p5)

2 1 The boy has a dog.
2 He is nine.
3 My brother is three.
4 She is my friend.
5 This is my mum and dad.

Grammar (p6)

2 1 He is three. 2 She is ten.
3 He is two. 4 She is five.
5 He is six. 6 He is eight.
7 She is nine. 8 He is one.

Phonics (p7)

1 cat/bat/mat
2 1 bat 2 mat 3 cat
3 1 cap 2 map 3 tap
4 1 cat/cap 2 cat/bat
3 bat/map/mat 4 cap/tap/mat

Writing (p8)

1 This is Emma. She is nine. 2 This is
Tom. He is six. 3 This is Anna. She is
eight. 4 This is Dan. He is five. 5 This
is Meg. She is ten. 6 This is Scott. He
is seven.

Unit 2

Reading and understanding (p10)

2 1 Yes, it is. 2 No, it isn't.
3 No, it isn't. 4 Yes, they are.
5 No, they aren't. 6 No, they aren't.

Sentence building (p11)

1 1 plane 2 house 3 bed 4 boy
5 mum 6 radio

Grammar (p12)

1 1 c 2 d 3 e 4 a 5 b
2 1 These are 2 This is
3 This is 4 These are

3 1 This is a bed. 2 These are toys.
3 This is a ball. 4 These are books.
5 This is a plane. 6 This is a desk.

Phonics (p13)

1 1 hen/men/ten/pen
2 hen/men/ten/pen
3 1 a hen with a pen 2 ten men
3 ten men with a hen
4 bed/red
6 1 c 2 b 3 a

Writing (p14)

1 This is my desk. 2 These are my
books. 3 This is my computer.
4 This is my bed. 5 These are my
toys. 6 These are my chairs.

Unit 3

Reading and understanding (p16)

1 1 ✓ 2 ✓ 3 ✗ 4 ✓ 5 ✓ 6 ✗ 7 ✗ 8 ✓
9 ✗ 10 ✗ 11 ✗ 12 ✓
2 1 ✗ 2 ✗ 3 ✓ 4 ✗ 5 ✗ 6 ✗ 7 ✓ 8 ✓

Sentence building (p17)

1 1 an 2 a 3 an 4 a
5 an 6 a 7 an 8 a
2 1 an 2 a 3 an 4 a

Grammar (p18)

1 1 Yes, I can.
2 No, I can't.
3 Yes, I can.
4 No, I can't.
5 No, I can't.
2 1 I can't see 2 I can see
3 I can see 4 I can't see
5 I can see
3 1 I can see the sun.
2 I can't see the moon.
3 I can't see a car.
4 I can see a plane.
5 I can't see an elephant.

Phonics (p19)

1 bin/pin/tin
2 tin/bin/pin
3 tin/bin/pin
4 1 tin/bin 2 pin/bin 3 pin/tin
5 dig/wig/big

Writing (p20)
1 the moon 2 a star 3 a bird 4 a tree
5 a cat 6 a dog

Check-up 1

Grammar (p22)
1 1 is 2 are 3 is
2 1 This is 2 These are
3 These are 4 This is
3 1 can 2 Can 3 can't 4 can

Sentence Building (p23)
1 1 Nina is my friend. 2 She is seven.
3 This is Ben's brother.
2 1 computer 2 books 3 boy

Phonics (p23)
1 1 a 2 an 3 a 4 an 5 a
bat/pen/bin

Move on with Mobi (pages 24/25)
1 1 This is a butterfly. 2 This is a
balloon. 3 This is a mouse. 4 This is
a plane. 5 This is a star. 6 This is a
doll. 7 This is a cat. 8 This is an egg.
2 bed/toys/chairs/table/book/
desk/pens/door

Unit 4

Reading and understanding (p26)
2 1 This is a blue egg. 2 This is a
yellow butterfly. 3 These are black
beetles. 4 This is a red apple.
5 These are green frogs.

Sentence building (p27)
3 1 Is this your house?
2 Is this an elephant?
3 Can you see the frog?

Grammar (p28)
1 1 this 2 these 3 these 4 this

Phonics (p29)
1 1 bun 2 run 3 sun
3 1 jug 2 bun 3 mug 4 rug
5 sun 6 run

Writing (p30)
1 This is a flower. 2 These are eggs
3 These are apples. 4 This is a butterfly.

Writing (p36)
1 on the table 2 under the chair 3 in
the box 4 between the book and the
lamp 5 next to the computer 6 under
the chair 7 on the box 8 in the bed
9 next to the lamp 10 between the
chair and the bed

Unit 5

Reading and understanding (p32)
1 1 Ben 2 Sam 3 Tilly 4 Meg 5 Nina
6 Ben

Sentence building (p33)
1 a red ball/a blue flower/a green
snake/a purple chair
2 1 blue 2 green 3 yellow 4 grey

Grammar (p34)
1 1 e 2 d 3 a 4 c 5 b
2 1 on 2 under 3 next to 4 between

Phonics (p35)
1 dog/log/box/fox
2 1 yes 2 no 3 no 4 yes
3 1 dog/log 2 fox/box 3 dog/box
4 fox/log
5 dog and log/fox and box/hot and
not

Unit 6

Reading and understanding (p38)
2 1 beach 2 blue 3 chairs 4 hat
5 umbrella 6 water 7 red
8 starfish

Sentence building (p39)
1 1 Ben 2 Mobi 3 Sam 4 Nina
5 Tilly

Phonics (p45)
1 The dog can run. 2 The fish is on
the dish. 3 The sun is hot.

5 This is a fish. 6 These are snakes.

Your writing (p31)
1 They are snakes. 2 It is a flower.
3 It is a fish. 4 They are eggs. 5 They
are apples. 6 It is a butterfly.

Grammar (p40)
1 1 has got 2 have got 3 has got
4 have got
2 1 No, he hasn't. 2 Yes, she has.
3 No, she hasn't. 4 Yes, he has.
3 1 Has she got a cat?
2 Has he got a dog?
3 Has she got a parrot?
4 Has he got a fish?

Phonics (p41)
1 shell/shop/ship/fish/dish
2 shell/shop/ship/fish/dish

Writing (p42)
1 starfish 2 crab 3 shell 4 hat
5 book 6 ice cream

Your writing (p43)
2 1 Nina has got a shell. It is pink.
2 Tilly has got a book. It is red.
3 Sam has got a crab. It is brown.
4 Meg has got a starfish. It is
orange. 5 Ben has got an ice
cream. It is yellow. 6 Scott has got
a hat. It is blue.

Check-up 2

Grammar (p44)
1 1 What are these? They are stars.
2 What is this? It is the moon.
3 What is this? It is an owl.
4 What are these? They are trees.
2 1 on 2 under 3 next to 4 between
3 1 has got 2 have got
3 Have/got 4 Has/got

Sentence Building (p45)
1 1 What is this?
2 What are these?
3 Can you see the mouse?
2 1 red 2 blue

Move on with Mobi (pages 46/47)
1 1 shell 2 fish 3 flower 4 snake
5 jug 6 crab 7 umbrella 8 box
3 1 on 2 under 3 between
4 next to 5 in

2 1 Ben 2 Tilly 3 Nina 4 Sam
5 Mobi

Practice Book 1 – Answer key

Unit 7

Reading and understanding (p48)
1 Good morning! Get up! 2 Don't stand up! 3 Shut the window! 4 Run! Run! 5 Don't run! 6 Please sit down.

Sentence building (p49)
1 1 look 2 sit 3 run 4 write

2 1 Listen 2 Read 3 Open 4 Shut

Grammar (p50)
1 1 Don't run! 2 Climb the tree! 3 Don't open the door!

2 1 fall 2 write 3 sit

3 1 sit 2 open 3 run

Phonics (p51)
1 1 cheese 2 shop 3 fish 4 shell 5 chips 6 watch 7 children 8 dish 9 chicken

Writing (p52)
1 1 Sit down, please! 2 Listen, please! 3 Please read! 4 Please open the door! 5 Sing! 6 Don't run!

Unit 8

Reading and understanding (p54)
1 1 The tiger is black and yellow. 2 The bear is white. 3 The crocodile is green. 4 The owl is brown and white.

2 tiger/crocodile/owl/bear

Sentence building (p55)
1 1 Ben is holding a ball. 2 Is Tilly cold? 3 Is the elephant grey? 4 Nina is sleeping.

2 1 Is he swimming? 2 Are they playing football?

3 1 The boys are fishing. 2 They are singing.

Grammar (p56)
1 1 b 2 a 3 c

2 1 She is 2 They are 3 It is 4 He is

3 1 He is jumping. 2 They are sleeping. 3 It is swimming.

Phonics (p57)
1 1 ill 2 hill 3 till 4 fill

2 1 hill 2 till 3 ill 4 fill

---

3 1 wall 2 bell 3 doll

Writing (p58)
1 playing 2 swimming 3 sitting 4 climbing 5 writing 6 sleeping 7 jumping 8 running

Unit 9

Reading and understanding (p60)
1 playground 2 marching 3 skipping 4 football 5 girls 6 climbing

Sentence building (p61)
1 She is swimming. 2 They are sleeping. 3 He is sitting. 4 They are drawing. 5 It is climbing. 6 They are playing.

Grammar (p62)
1 1 Yes, they are. 2 Yes, he is. 3 No, she isn't. 4 Yes, she is. 5 No, they aren't. 6 No, he isn't.

2 1 She is not 2 He is not 3 They are not 4 It is not

Phonics (p63)
1 king/ring/sing/wing

2 king/ring/sing/wing

3 1 ring 2 sing 3 king 4 wing

Writing (p64)
1 Nina is dancing. 2 Sam is swimming. 3 Tilly is marching. 4 Ben is clapping. 5 Scott is jumping. 6 Meg is fishing.

Check-up 3

Grammar (page 66)
1
1 The baby is sleeping. 2 The boys are jumping into the water. 3 I am reading a book.

2 1 The girl is not riding an elephant. 2 Is the girl holding a cat? 3 The children are not playing the drums.

3 1 open/shut 2 climb 3 dance/sing

Sentence Building (p67)
1 1 shut 2 stand 3 jump

2 1 Is 2 are 3 are

Phonics
1 sing/chips/hill/king/children/wall

Move on with Mobi (pages 68/69)
1 elephant/tiger/crocodile/monkey/snake

4 1 sitting 2 kicking 3 jumping 4 reading 5 eating 6 drinking 7 climbing 8 running

Unit 10

Reading and understanding (p70)
2, 3, 1, 4, 6, 5

Sentence building (p71)
1 1 Saturday 2 Sunday 3 Monday 4 Tuesday 5 Wednesday 6 Thursday 7 Friday

2 1 Sunday 2 Monday 3 Tuesday 4 Wednesday

Grammar (p72)
1 1 e 2 f 3 d 4 a 5 b 6 c

2 1 It is seven o'clock. 2 It is half past nine. 3 It is two o'clock.

3 1 Tuesday 2 Thursday 3 Saturday 4 Wednesday 5 Friday 6 Monday 7 Sunday

Phonics (p72)
1 1 sock 2 rock 3 clock

2 1 a sock on a clock 2 a sock on a rock 3 a clock on a rock 4 a clock on a sock

3 1 sack 2 truck 3 duck

Writing (page 74)
1 This is a bus. 2 This is a boat. 3 This is a horse. 4 This is an elephant. 5 This is a train. 6 This is a bike.

Unit 11

Reading and understanding (p76)
1 fast 2 reading 3 looking 4 listening 5 talking 6 drinking

Sentence building (p77)
1 1 He 2 they 3 It 4 he 5 She

2 1 She 2 They 3 It 4 He 5 He 6 They 7 He

Grammar (p78)
1 1 She's 2 He's 3 They're 4 I'm

2 1 What are they doing?
They are running.
2 What is it doing?
It is sleeping.
3 What is she doing? She is riding.

3 The grass is green.
The brick is brown.

Phonics (p79)
1 drum/dress/brick/brown/
green/grass

Writing (p80)
1 walking 2 eating 3 I can see a girl.
She is swimming. 4 I can see a dog. It
is drinking. 5 I can see a woman. She
is running. 6 I can see a boy. He is
reading.

Check-up 4
Grammar (p88)
1 1 It is nine o'clock. 2 It is eleven
o'clock. 3 It is one o'clock. 4 It is
half past seven.

Phonics (p85)
2 clock/flag/clown/flower
5 plane/glass/plate

Grammar (p84)
2 1 There are dolls 2 There is a bear
3 There are planes 4 There are
cakes 5 There is a clown 6 There
is a bike

Phonics (p85)
1 1 thirteen 2 thirty-three
3 three 4 thirty

2 1 thick 2 thin

3 1 I have got one tooth in my mouth.
2 I have got three ducks in my bath.

Writing (p96)
1 There are ten sheep. 2 There is one
dog. 3 There are six cows. 4 There
are three horses. 5 There are twenty
chickens. 6 There are three ducks.
7 There is one cat.

Unit 12
Reading and understanding (p82)
2 1 at the cake shop 2 at the toy
shop 3 at the shoe shop
4 at the sweet shop
5 at 'Gino's Place'
6 at the book shop

3 1 At the cake shop you can buy
buns and cakes and biscuits.
2 At the shoe shop you can buy
trainers and boots and party shoes.
3 At the sweet shop you can buy
chocolates and ice cream.

Sentence building (p83)
1 1 under 2 on 3 behind 4 in

2 1 The doll is on the table.
2 The ball is under the table.
3 The dog is on the chair.

Grammar (p84)
2 1 There are three mountains.
2 There are eight trees.
3 There are two boys.
4 There is one girl. 5 There are
nine stars. 6 There is one castle.

Phonics (p95)
1 1 thirteen 2 thirty-three
3 three 4 thirty

Writing (p96)
2 1 What is he doing? 2 What are
they doing? 3 What is she doing?

3 1 There is 2 There are
3 There are 4 There is

Unit 13
Reading and understanding (p92)
2 1 hillside 2 dog 3 sheep 4 brother
5 sheep 6 tired 7 sleepy 8 count

Sentence building (p93)
1 1 has 2 have 3 have 4 has 5 have
6 have

2 1 has 2 has 3 have

Grammar (p94)
1 1 How many mountains are there?
2 How many trees are there?
3 How many boys are there?
4 How many girls are there?
5 How many stars are there?
6 How many castles are there?

Phonics (p95)
1 1 is 2 is 3 are

Grammar (p100)
1 1 c 2 a 3 d 4 b

2 1 Yes, it is. 2 Yes, it is.
3 No, it isn't. 4 Yes, it is.

3 1 It is cold. 2 It is windy.
3 It is raining. 4 It is snowing.

Sentence Building (p89)
1 1 Thursday 2 Saturday 3 Friday

2 1 She 2 They 3 He

3 1 on 2 in 3 on

Move on with Mobi (pp90/91)
1 1 e 2 f 3 g 4 a 5 d 6 b 7 c

3 1 toy/toys/toy shop
2 bike/bikes/bike shop
3 sweet/sweets/sweet shop
4 clothes/clothes/clothes shop
5 book/books/book shop

Unit 14
Reading and understanding (p98)
2 2, 5, 1, 4, 6, 3

3 1 shopping 2 thunder 3 scared

Sentence building (p99)
1 small 2 long 3 big 4 old

2 big – little/sad – happy/old – new

3 Example answers: 1 the new ball
2 the happy dog 3 the thin snake

Grammar (p100)
1 1 c 2 a 3 d 4 b

2 1 Yes, it is. 2 Yes, it is.
3 No, it isn't. 4 Yes, it is.

3 1 It is cold. 2 It is windy.
3 It is raining. 4 It is snowing.

Phonics (p101)
1 star/swim/spell/smile

2 swim/star/smile/spell

3 spider/stop/smell/sweet

4 smell/sweet/stop/spider

5 spider – spell/star – stop/swim –
sweet

Writing (p102)
1 1 It is cold. 2 It is hot.

2 1 It is snowing. 2 It is raining.
3 The sun is shining.

3 1 It is foggy. 2 It is cloudy.
3 It is windy.

Unit 15
Reading and understanding (p104)
2 1 An owl. 2 An elephant.
3 A monkey. 4 A giraffe.
5 A rabbit.

Sentence building (p105)
1 1 is 2 are 3 am 4 are 5 is

2 1 is 2 is 3 are

Grammar (p106)
1 1 A 2 A 3 B 4 B 5 A 6 B

2 1 Yes, they have. 2 Yes, they have.
3 No, they haven't. 4 No, they
haven't.

3 1 No, we haven't. 2 No, we haven't.
3 Yes, we have. 4 Yes, we have.

255

Phonics (p107)

1 1 hand 2 band 3 sand

2 hand/band/sand

4 'ant' should be circled

Check-up 5

Grammar (p110)

1 1 It is raining. 2 The sun is shining./It is sunny. 3 It is foggy. 4 It is snowing.

2 1 How many trees are there?
2 How many owls are there?
3 How many stars are there?

3 1 Have you got a brother?
2 We have got a nice teacher.
3 The children have not got mobile phones.

Sentence Building (p111)

1 1 has 2 have 3 have

2 1 cloudy 2 green 3 big

3 1 is 2 is 3 are

Phonics (p111)

1 three 2 mouth 3 smell 4 star 5 hand 6 elephant

Move on with Mobi (p112/113)

2 1 monkey 2 crocodile 3 zebra 4 elephant 5 rabbit 6 giraffe

Unit 16

Sentence building (p115)

1 dogs/apples/cats/tables/oranges/snakes/ducks

2 1 ice cream 2 ice creams 3 ducks 4 duck 5 flower 6 flowers

Grammar (p116)

1 1 I don't know. 2 Yes
3 I don't know. 4 I don't know.
5 Yes 6 I don't know.

Phonics (p117)

1 cake/bike/hide/gate

2 ride – hide/gate – plate/like – bike/make – take

3 1 make/cake 2 ride/bike 3 gate 4 plate 5 hide 6 like

Your writing (page 119)

1 Nina likes pears. Sam likes apples. Tilly likes oranges. Ben likes grapes. Meg likes bananas. Scott likes cherries.

Unit 17

Reading and understanding (p120)

2 1 Mr Grey 2 Mr Red 3 Mr Blue 4 Miss Green 5 Miss Pink 6 Mr Black

Sentence building (p121)

1 Mr Grey is a cleaner. 2 My dress is green. 3 These socks are Ben's. 4 This hat is Tilly's. 5 The dog is big. 6 What is your name?

Grammar (p122)

1 Whose jacket is this? It is Sam's.
2 Whose T-shirt is this? It is Tilly's.
3 Whose trousers are these? They are Sam's. 4 Whose socks are these? They are Tilly's. 5 Whose shoes are these? They are Tilly's. 6 Whose trainers are these? They are Sam's.

Phonics (p123)

1 1 bone 2 cube 3 nose 4 stone 5 glue 6 hose 7 tube

2 nose – hose/blue – glue/bone – stone/tube – cube

Unit 18

Reading and understanding (p126)

2 1 The catherine wheel goes round and round. 2 The waterfall fizzes and falls and lights up the night. 3 The roman candle goes Fffffffffffffffffffft. Ploof!

3 1 sound 2 white 3 light 4 go

Sentence building (p127)

1 1 likes 2 like 3 likes 4 like 5 like

2 1 likes 2 likes 3 like

Grammar (p128)

1 1 over 2 towards 3 along 4 into 5 round 6 onto

Phonics (p129)

1 1 cold 2 milk 3 old 4 help 5 gold 6 belt

2 1 no 2 yes 3 yes 4 no 5 yes 6 no

Writing (p130)

1 The car is going along the road. 2 The car is going round the roundabout. 3 The car is going over the bridge. 4 The car is going into the tunnel. 5 The car is going towards the sea. 6 The car is going onto the boat.

Check-up 6

Grammar (p132)

1 1 I like elephants.
2 He likes hippos.

2 1 Whose hat is this? It is Nina's hat.
2 Whose socks are these? They are Sam's socks.

3 1 along 2 over/into 3 round

Sentence Building (p133)

1 apples/cakes/oranges

2 1 He has blue shoes.
2 Look at the pink socks!
3 Whose jumper is this?

3 likes/likes/like

Phonics (p 133)

bone – stone/cake – take/cube – tube/ride – hide

Move on with Mobi (p134/135)

2 Anna likes apples. Ben likes bananas. Carl likes cakes. Edward likes eggs. Fred likes fish. Gary likes grapes. Ian likes ice cream.

4 1 It is Pam's. 2 They are Sam's.
3 It is Sam's. 4 It is Sam's.
5 They are Sam's. 6 They are Pam's.
7 They are Pam's. 8 It is Pam's.